UNMAKING
THE
JAPANESE
MIRACLE

UNMAKING THE JAPANESE MIRACLE

MACROECONOMIC POLITICS, 1985–2000

William W. Grimes

Cornell University Press

ITHACA AND LONDON

First published 2001 by Cornell University Press

Printed in the United States of America

Library of Congress Cataloging-in-Publication Data

Grimes, William W.
    Unmaking the Japanese miracle : macroeconomic politics, 1985–2000 / William W. Grimes.
        p.   cm.
    Includes bibliographical references and index.
    ISBN 0-8014-3849-7
        1. Japan—Economic policy—1989– . 2. Structural adjustment (Economic policy)—Japan. I. Title.
HC462.9 .G74 2001
339.5'0952—dc21   00-012396

Cornell University Press strives to use environmentally responsible suppliers and materials to the fullest extent possible in the publishing of its books. Such materials include vegetable-based, low-VOC inks and acid-free papers that are recycled, totally chlorine-free, or partly composed of nonwood fibers. Books that bear the logo of the FSC (Forest Stewardship Council) use paper taken from forests that have been inspected and certified as meeting the highest standards for environmental and social responsibility. For further information, visit our website at www.cornellpress.cornell.edu.

Cloth printing   10 9 8 7 6 5 4 3 2 1

To my parents

Contents

Acknowledgments

It has taken me many years to complete this book. It has expanded far beyond my initial plans in terms of both time period and conception. I could not have written it without the help of many individuals and institutions. I wish to express my gratitude to all of them.

I carried out my initial research in 1992–93 with the help of a Fulbright-IIE Fellowship, funded by the generosity of Japanese Fulbright alumni. At Princeton University, I was able to concentrate on my research thanks to the Woodrow Wilson Foundation Society of Fellows, of which I was a member in 1991–92 and 1993–94. My living expenses in summer 1994 and spring 1995 were covered by an A. W. Mellon Dissertation Writing Fellowship.

After leaving Princeton, I was fortunate to spend a year as an Advanced Research Fellow at Harvard University's Program on U.S.–Japan Relations in 1995–96. In summer 1997, I returned to Tokyo for additional research thanks to a Japan–U.S. Friendship Commission summer travel grant from the Association for Asian Studies. Finally, Harvard University's Reischauer Institute of Japanese Studies granted me a semester of leave in fall 1999 during a year spent there as a visiting assistant professor. I am grateful to all these organizations for their generosity. Brooke and Craig Jack and Yumiko Mikanagi and Jeff Young generously offered their homes to me in Tokyo, allowing me to extend research stays in 1997, 1999, and 2000, for which I am also grateful.

I have also received research support from a number of institutions. In Tokyo, these include the Ministry of Finance's Institute of Fiscal and Monetary Policy (now renamed the Policy Research Institute), at which I spent six months in 1993 and one month each in 1999 and 2000; the Foundation for Advanced Information and Research, where I spent nine months in 1992–93; the University of Tokyo, where I was a visiting research student in the Faculty of Law in 1992–93 and a visiting scholar at the Institute of Social Science for a month in 1999; and the Bank of Japan's Institute of Monetary and Economic Studies, which allowed me access to its library in 1993. In the United States, both Boston University and Harvard University have provided supportive environments and material assistance.

Many individuals have contributed to this project as well. I wish particularly to thank Kent Calder, Robert Gilpin, Keisuke Iida, and Joanne Gowa for their constant and continuing support, and for their many helpful suggestions and criticisms. Kent Calder was and still is the best adviser and mentor that I can imagine. Inoguchi Takashi and Sasaki Takeshi were kind enough to serve as my advisers at the University of Tokyo in 1992–93. Susan Pharr and Andrew Gordon were especially gracious hosts at Harvard. I appreciate the willingness of the Department of International Relations and the College of Arts and Sciences at Boston University to allow me to take a leave of absence for the 1999–2000 academic year.

In 1990–92, I was privileged to work as a research assistant to Toyoo Gyohten and Paul Volcker on their book *Changing Fortunes*. Listening to their recollections and interpretations of important international monetary events was a unique and valuable experience, and their integrity and expertise have given me a deep appreciation of what true public service can be. Mr. Gyohten has given unstintingly of his time in the years since, and has helpfully provided a variety of introductions in Tokyo.

Interview research was central to this study, and I have consistently been impressed at the willingness of officials and experts to devote time to educating a relatively unknown scholar. I am grateful to all of them, named and unnamed, for their generosity in sharing their time and knowledge with me. Most asked not to be quoted directly, and a few requested full anonymity. I have respected all such requests. Among current and former Ministry of Finance officials: Ezawa Yūichi, Hatanaka Sugio, Hirasawa Sadaaki, Hosomi Takashi, Iwasaki Fumiya, Kaneko Yoshiaki, Kanzaki Yasushi, Kashiwagi Shigeo, Katō Takatoshi, Kawakami Nobuhiko, Kishimoto Shūhei, Kogayu Masami, Kondō Takehiko, Kubota Isao, Kuroda Haruhiko, Mizoguchi Zenbei, Murao Nobuaki, Nagatomi Yūichirō, Nishigaki Akira, Ōba Tomomitsu, Tamaki Rintarō, Takeuchi Yō, Utsumi Makoto, Yamaguchi Mitsuhide, and Yoshino Yoshihiko. Among current and former Bank of Japan officials: Matsuda Keiji, Mieno Yasushi, Nakayama Yasuo, Ogata Shijūrō, Ohta Takeshi, Onishi Yoshihisa, Dr. Suzuki Yoshio, Tanabe Masanori, Dr. Ueda Kazuo, Yoshikuni Shin'ichi, and Wakatsuki Mikio. Also: Takemura Masayoshi, Kaneda Katsutoshi, Yanagisawa Hakuo, Isobe Asahiko, Shinohara Hajime, Robert Feldman, Richard Hanson, Horiuchi Akiyoshi, Itō Shunzō, and Shiota Ushio.

I also thank the many colleagues who read and commented on all or part of this manuscript at one stage or another. They include Nobuhiro

Hiwatari, Yumiko Mikanagi, Frank Schwartz, Kurt Tong, Ezra Vogel, Steven Vogel, Ming Wan, and Jeffrey Young, as well as several anonymous readers for Cornell University Press. Shinju Fujihira and my father deserve special thanks for having read in full a draft of this book. Roger Haydon, my editor at Cornell, has also read multiple drafts. True to his reputation, he has been a joy to work with, providing both good-natured support and the occasional whip crack when needed. This book is much improved for the input of all of these people.

My wife, Melinda Stanford, has known me for our entire courtship, engagement, and marriage as the author of this book. Without her support and patience, I could not have completed it. More important, she has unfailingly provided the happiness that this project usually could not.

Finally, I thank my parents, who are responsible for my having gone to Japan in the first place. They got me through the first twenty-two years of my life intact and curious and have supported me in a variety of ways ever since. If it is ultimately my fault that I have chosen this path, any success I have found is due to them.

I am grateful for all the help I have received from so many quarters; any errors that remain are solely my own responsibility. I am sure that many of the individuals I have quoted or interviewed will disagree with my interpretations of the structures and events described. However, I hope that none are offended by my interpretations. Although this book is critical of decisions associated with certain individuals, I wish to make clear that I am not attacking those people, many of whom I admire enormously—indeed, one of the main points of this book is that in many cases they had tragically few choices. In the end, however, I stand by my research, reasoning, and analysis.

W. W. G.

A Note on Japanese Names and Terms

Japanese names are written in the Japanese order, with family name followed by personal name. The only exceptions to this rule are Japanese authors who publish in English; in citing these authors, I have followed Western convention. All long vowels in Japanese words and names are denoted by a macron, except in the case of place names such as Tokyo.

Introduction: A Miracle Unmade

"The years since 1989 have been Japan's lost decade."

Nobuyuki Idei, president of Sony

The major puzzle facing observers of the Japanese economy in the 1990s has been a straightforward one: "What went wrong?" Perhaps the better question, however, is "*Why* did it go wrong?" For while there is at least some consensus that mistaken economic policies were primarily to blame, there is less agreement as to why Japanese macroeconomic authorities formulated and implemented those policies. To understand the "why" question, we must turn to politics. In this book, I argue that the structure of power in macroeconomic policy making was largely responsible for the policy failures we have seen since the mid-1980s.

The basic story is well known. In the late 1980s, Japan experienced a period of prosperity and growth—real GDP growth averaged 4.6 percent per year between 1985 and 1990, the Nikkei stock index tripled in value, and land prices ballooned. By 1991, however, asset prices had fallen sharply and economic growth had flattened. It soon became apparent that the prosperity of the late 1980s had been fueled by a speculative bubble. The bursting of that bubble, beginning in 1989, led to the worst recession Japan has experienced since the 1940s, replete with anxiety over employment and fears of financial collapse. Since 1992, government policies have focused with increasing urgency—and even desperation—on restoring economic growth, largely through macroeconomic means. At least nominally, the Japanese government has thrown over ¥120 trillion (nearly twice as much as the central government's average annual budget in the 1990s) into the struggle.[1] In spite of the apparently strenuous efforts of the political leadership, however, these policies have been largely unsuccessful.

1. This is a simple sum of the declared value of the various fiscal stimulus packages between 1992 and 1999. (Another plan was passed in autumn 2000.) This figure also does not include the approximately ¥43 trillion in funds committed in 1998 for shoring up deposit insurance

It has been hard for observers of the Japanese political economy in the go-go 1980s to accept the vision of Japan in recession. It is perhaps even harder to accept that the same policy pathologies that led to the bubble could have been responsible for the years of failed attempts at economic stimulation in the 1990s. That, however, is precisely what I argue. Japan's macroeconomic pathologies have included an excessive reliance on monetary policy to solve large-scale macroeconomic problems and an extreme aversion to loosening fiscal policy. These pathologies were not the result of incompetence or corruption on the part of policy makers (many of them among Japan's "best and brightest"); rather, they were structural in nature, the products of a policy-making process in which political leaders, the Ministry of Finance, and the Bank of Japan competed to advance their own versions of the national interest. Like the French army dutifully fortifying the Maginot Line in 1939, Japan's macroeconomic policy institutions had developed to address problems that no longer existed, and were incapable of effectively handling a new strategic situation. Only with profound changes in policy-making structure in 1998 did profound policy changes become possible. Through an in-depth examination of institutional power and interests, I lay bare the roots of the problem, and show how macroeconomic policy-making structures have shaped actual policies since 1985.

The years from 1985 to 2000 are important for three reasons. First, this period represents an unprecedented era of macroeconomic policy mistakes in Japan. Second, by starting after the international upheaval that followed the breakdown of fixed exchange rates and the two oil shocks, we can look more directly at the dynamics of Japan's domestic policy-making system. Finally, 1985 was the year of the Plaza Agreement, which in many ways set in motion the chain of events on which I focus.

The story begins with the Plaza Agreement in September 1985, which marked the beginning of international economic policy coordination among the (then) G-5 countries to increase the value of the yen and other currencies relative to the dollar. From just before the agreement was signed to December 1987, the yen rose from ¥238 to the dollar to the ¥120s. Meanwhile, coordination, which originally focused on exchange market intervention, soon expanded to include macroeconomic policy, with a particular focus on expanding Japanese domestic demand. (Expanded domestic demand in Japan was meant to make up for the expected slowdown in U.S. economic growth.) External pressures on Japanese macroeconomic policy continued until "Black Monday," the U.S. stock market crash of October 19, 1987.

---

and recapitalizing banks. As such, it is not an accurate estimate of the actual fiscal impact: on the one hand, other measures such as increased spending or decreased taxes in the regular budget do not appear in it; on the other, the numbers attached to fiscal stimulus packages are invariably overstated, as I make clear in later chapters.

Following the international macroeconomic tumult of 1985–87, the years from 1988 to 1990 were relatively calm. Exchange rates were relatively stable, and world current account imbalances saw significant reduction. In Japan, however, an asset bubble had already begun, and would grow unchecked until May 31, 1989, when the Bank of Japan began a series of interest rate hikes to cut off the economy's supply of easy money. These actions began to have visible effects by early 1990, as stock prices began to drop rapidly after having tripled in only five years. The sixth and last of the interest rate hikes was enacted on August 30, 1990; in a little more than a year, the official discount rate had risen from 2.5 percent to 6 percent.

The results of restrictive monetary policy were striking. Stock prices dropped dramatically, land speculation cooled, and businesses began to complain of lack of access to credit. Although economic growth rates in 1990 and 1991 remained strong, it was clear that the economy was slowing down, and in July 1991 the BOJ began relaxing monetary policy again. Despite considerable loosening, however, by 1992 economic growth was slipping rapidly. Crisis enveloped the financial system, as borrowers became unable to pay back loans collateralized with land and securities whose value was plummeting. Fiscal stimulation did not begin to play even a nominal role in the efforts to rejuvenate the Japanese economy until August 1992, signaling the end of benign neglect by the central government.

Despite public efforts by the government, in late 1992 the economy fell into stagnation. Since 1993, we have seen a series of ever more strenuous attempts to put an end to the recession and financial crises. As of 2000, they had not been successful in restoring a pattern of stable growth; instead, the Japanese government has suffered a series of severe policy challenges, including the collapse of the real-estate lending corporations (*jūsen*), several major banks, and other financial institutions; dangerous drops in stock prices; the end in 1993 of thirty-eight years of one-party rule followed by radical changes in the electoral system; a 1995 bout with an "ultra-high yen" (peaking at over ¥80 to the dollar); a variety of scandals surrounding policy makers and financial institutions; and full-fledged recessions in 1997 and 1998 and again in 1999. Fiscal policy took a leading role in 1992–96, with the introduction of six fiscal stimulus packages in addition to increasingly expansionary budgets through FY 1996.[2] The FY 1997 budget and tax legislation changed the direction yet again, with a fiscal austerity program that led to economic downturn, including a disastrous annualized drop in GDP of 11.2 percent in the second quarter of 1997 and the failures that November of Hokkaido Takushoku Bank and Yamaichi Securities. Starting in late FY 1997, the pendulum again swung back toward expansionary fiscal policy, with the introduction of two major stimulus plans and two bank bailout

---

2. The Japanese fiscal year begins April 1.

plans in 1998, further stimulus plans in November 1999 and October 2000, and unusually expansionary regular budgets for FY 1999 and 2000.

While policy makers have continued for years to struggle with the consequences of the FY 1997 budget, other legislation passed in 1997 and 1998 laid the groundwork for much more effective fiscal stimulation in the economy. In 1998, a major revision to the Bank of Japan Law (effective in April) and the removal of the Ministry of Finance's powers of financial supervision (effective in June) changed the institutional structure of macroeconomic policy making fundamentally. The new structure weakened the hand of fiscal conservatives, and strengthened the hand of monetary authorities. It also created the possibility for a real assertion of political authority over Japan's financial and macroeconomic policy making and implementation.

While the structure of the policy-making game and the resulting policy outputs changed, however, the relevance of political structure in explaining economic mismanagement did not. The processes I describe in this book remain essential to understanding Japan's struggle for effective policy.

In this book I address Japan's macroeconomic policy making in a logical progression. Chapter 1 lays out the structure of macroeconomic politics. Chapters 2–3 offer more detailed analyses of each of the relevant institutions, elucidating and making more concrete the basic story told in chapter 1.

Some readers may want to jump directly from chapter 1 to chapters 4–7, in which I show the impact of the macroeconomic policy-making structure on Japanese behavior in each of four periods. The 1985–87 period is the subject of chapter 4. In chapter 5 I consider 1988–92, a period in which the economic bubble first expanded rapidly, and then burst. In chapter 6 I examine the years from 1993 to 1997, during which time Japan's economic authorities struggled with the aftermath of the bubble economy. In chapter 7 I analyze the structural changes of 1997–98 and their impacts on subsequent macroeconomic policy.

In chapter 8 I draw out the implications of this study both for the Japanese political economy and for the study of comparative political economy, focusing in particular on how structures persist or change. I also make predictions concerning the long-term effects on Japanese macroeconomic policy and political economy in general of the Bank of Japan Law revision and of other key changes in the macroeconomic policy-making structure.

A Note on Methodology

My central premise in this book is that the way policies are made has an important effect on the shape of the policies themselves. Due to the difficulties of measuring such variables, I rely primarily on case studies of major policy actions over a decade and a half.[3] In chapters 4–7 I compare the predictions generated by my analysis with the actual historical record, following George's dictum that "the plausibility of an explanation is enhanced to the extent that alternative explanations are considered and found to be less consistent with the data and/or less supportable by available generalizations."[4] In each of the four broad chronological chapters, I address the major issues that confronted policy makers at the time, detail the ways in which they responded, and demonstrate why my explanation is consistently more useful than alternatives.

3. A number of studies have been written concerning the case study method. King, Keohane, and Verba (1994) argue that "one of the fundamental goals of inference is to distinguish the systematic component from the nonsystematic component of the phenomena we study" (56). In order to do so, they write, it is important to have variation across both dependent and independent variables. The case studies in this book clearly have both. Nonetheless, the main method of argumentation will follow George's (1979) "structured-focused comparison"— demonstrating that my own explanation is more consistent with the facts than are other explanations. In the end, the careful use of case studies is the only way of making reliable statements about structure, behavior, and interaction of phenomena, as Eckstein argues (1975, 87–90). See also Lijphart 1975, Skocpol and Somers 1980.
4. George 1979, 57–58.

Abbreviations

BOJ	Bank of Japan
DIC	Deposit Insurance Corporation
DY	*Daily Yomiuri*
EPA	Economic Planning Agency
FEFSA	Foreign Exchange Fund Special Account
FILP	Fiscal Investment and Loan Program
FRC	Financial Reconstruction Commission
FSA	Financial Supervision Agency (renamed Financial Services Agency as of July 2000)
FT	*Financial Times*
FY	Fiscal Year
JC	*Journal of Commerce*
Jiji	*Jiji Press Ticker Service*
Kyodo	*Kyodo News Service*
LDP	Liberal Democratic Party
MOF	Ministry of Finance
Nikkei	*Nihon Keizai Shimbun*
NYT	*New York Times*
OB	"Old Boy" (retiree)
PARC	Policy Affairs Research Council
PKO	"Price-Keeping Operation"
PR	Proportional Representation
SDPJ	Social Democratic Party of Japan
SII	Structural Impediments Initiative
SMD	Single-Member District
WP	*Washington Post*
YS	*Yomiuri Shimbun*

UNMAKING
THE
JAPANESE
MIRACLE

1

Organizational Conflict

Men make their own history, but they do not make it just as they please;
they do not make it under circumstances chosen by themselves, but under
circumstances directly found, given and transmitted from the past.

Karl Marx, *The Eighteenth Brumaire of Louis Bonaparte*

Since 1985, Japanese macroeconomic policy makers have confronted a series of economic challenges, of both international and domestic origins. Japan's macroeconomic policy-making structure provides the key to understanding the state's responses to both international and domestic stimuli. In this chapter I describe that structure; in subsequent chapters I elaborate on it, demonstrate how it contributed to the expansion and eventual bursting of the bubble and to the recession of the 1990s, and show how changes in structure have finally altered the menu of available policy choices.

Approaches to Understanding Japanese Macroeconomic Policy

A variety of explanations have appeared in recent years to account for both specific Japanese macroeconomic policies and the larger sweep of policy since the mid-1980s. Some have been rather *ad hoc* (or perhaps more fairly, concerned primarily with their own contemporary situations), while more systemic explanations have focused variously on the problem of exchange rates, on international power, on failures of the bureaucracy, or recently (and in parallel with this study) on policy-making structures.

While it is difficult to generalize about *ad hoc* explanations, the key ones seem to emphasize either structural rigidities in the economy or misjudgments on the part of policy makers. Structural rigidities arguments were particularly popular around the time of the bubble. A key structural rigidity noted in such explanations was the outdated land tax system, which was seen as distorting incentives and leading to higher land prices.[1] High stock

1. See, for example, Calder 1988a, chap. 9; Takenaka 1991, chap. 9; Ramseyer and Nakazato 1999, 37–42.

1

price-earnings ratios could be explained partly as the result of cross-share-holding and the increase in the value of capital and land held by the firm.[2] But while these factors were surely important in understanding why *asset* price inflation occurred rather than normal price inflation, it is difficult not to accept that the actual cause of the inflation was the rapid increase in money supply that began in 1986 and continued most of the way through 1989.[3]

In the aftermath of the bubble, the structural rigidities argument has focused on the incentives facing various types of financial institutions, and the so-called convoy system (the implicit guarantee that no bank would be allowed to fail).[4] Policies such as the convoy system and different lending rules for banks and housing loan corporations certainly had the effect of increasing the risk that financial institutions were willing to assume, but again the risks taken and their consequences depended on the macroeconomic policies that first fueled and then burst the bubble. Thus, the key puzzles to explain are why policy makers allowed the money supply to expand so rapidly and then stopped its expansion so abruptly.

One explanation—the difficulty of controlling money supply in the 1980s—has often been advanced by officials of the Bank of Japan.[5] There are two nonexclusive versions of this argument, which seeks to explain why the bank did not act decisively against asset price inflation from mid-1987 (by which time Japan's recovery was abundantly clear) until May 1989, a full year and a half later. The first is that the volatility of various money supply indicators increased sharply in the 1980s, due to financial liberalization and the resulting large-scale changes in financial portfolios held by corporations and, to a lesser extent, by individuals. The second is that asset inflation is inherently difficult to judge and that therefore the authorities sensibly focused on the nearly nonexistent price inflation.[6] Both of these arguments are plausible to an extent. But both ignore the fact that top policy makers in the Bank of Japan were increasingly worried about the monetary situation from late 1986, while interest rate hikes did not occur until 1989.[7] Given the sentiment against monetary laxness in the top offices of the central bank, we

2. Ito 1992, chap. 14; Taniguchi 1993.
3. Noguchi (1992) shows how easy money worked through structural rigidities to produce asset price inflation. Cargill, Hutchison, and Ito (1997, chaps. 4–5) provide econometric corroboration for the central role of money. Ohta (1991) and Ogata (1996), among others, also base their analyses on this assumption.
4. See, for example, Nakakita 1999.
5. Mieno 2000, chaps. 5, 6, 11, 12; interviews.
6. Cargill, Hutchison, and Ito (1997, 57–59) reject the first of these arguments, but are sympathetic to the second.
7. Then–deputy governor Mieno Yasushi asserts that he and other top officials were pushing for more restrictive interest rate policy by fall 1986. Indeed, he even voiced his fears about asset price inflation in Diet testimony on October 3, 1986, only weeks before the fourth of the five interest rate *cuts* that stoked the bubble (NHK 1996, 127). Former

must instead turn our gaze to the question of why the BOJ acted against its own better judgment for nearly three years.

Several systemic arguments have been advanced as explanations. One focuses on the exchange rate and U.S.–Japan relations. In a nutshell, the threat to the Japanese economy of an overvalued yen meant both that monetary policy was the instrument of choice for domestic demand expansion and that raising interest rates, especially after Black Monday in October 1987, would have been destabilizing in the extreme for both Japan and the world economies.[8] A stabilized yen-dollar relationship in 1989 and 1990 allowed higher interest rates; finally, a highly volatile yen in the years of the 1990s recession prevented fiscal expansion efforts from having their desired effects.[9] This interpretation again holds a degree of truth, as Japanese policy makers have noted,[10] but it too is exaggerated. For one thing, bubble-era yen-dollar rates had clearly stabilized by mid-1988, at which point Japan could have followed Germany's example and raised domestic interest rates at least marginally.[11] Also, given the massive domestic demand that had appeared, the Japanese economy was by late 1987 in a position to handle a further reduction in exports.[12] Finally, concerning the issue of U.S.–Japan relations, it is difficult to argue that Japan alone should have had the responsibility of preventing the U.S. currency from going into free fall. As for the 1990s, the yen situation seems to have had an effect on policy only in the extreme situations of 1995 when the exchange rate shot past ¥80 to the dollar and 1998 when the yen dropped to the ¥140s.

In the academic literature, the exchange rate explanation is most forcefully espoused by McKinnon and Ohno.[13] In their formulation, Japan was constrained in its monetary policies by what they call the "Syndrome of the Ever-Higher Yen," in which the yen-dollar exchange rate is a "forcing variable" for monetary policy. They argue that in trying to use the exchange rate to solve what are essentially savings-investment imbalances between Japan and the United States, Japan has become trapped in a deflationary spiral. This dynamic was most apparent in the years after 1989, but they argue that it has held since the waning days of Bretton Woods, albeit with an anomalous high dollar in the early and mid-1980s.

---

deputy governors for international affairs Ohta Takeshi and Ogata Shijūrō agree with that analysis (NHK 1996, 115–116). I have also confirmed this analysis in interviews with numerous BOJ and MOF officials with direct knowledge of monetary policy making at the time.

8. Mieno 2000, chaps. 11–12.

9. The argument of McKinnon and Ohno (1997) fits well with the second half of this sentence, albeit only uncomfortably with the first half.

10. For example, Ohta 1991, 98.

11. This point is made as well by Nakakita (1999, 30).

12. Kojo (1993) demonstrates that from a longer-term perspective, domestic coalitions in favor of a strong yen had strengthened considerably by the mid-1980s.

13. McKinnon and Ohno 1997.

I find the McKinnon-Ohno model unconvincing. It is at its best in explaining the dynamic of high yen and domestic deflation for the period after the bubble. However, using their analysis to explain the growth of the bubble requires substantial logical gymnastics, since that growth was the result of *over*-provision of liquidity in the face of international currency pressures. Moreover, even in addressing the post-bubble recession McKinnon and Ohno's explanation is not totally satisfactory, because they completely ignore the crumbling financial system through which monetary policies had to pass. In the end, therefore, the various forms of the exchange rate approach are informative, but not sufficient.[14]

McKinnon and Ohno actually occupy a middle ground between international economic and international political explanations. International realists have focused on power differentials between Japan and its economic partners, especially the United States. In this set of explanations, the more powerful United States has sought to shift economic adjustment costs onto Japan, whether through exchange rate policy, trade policy, or calls for Japanese macroeconomic stimulus. In turn, Japan's ability to resist such attempts should increase as its economic power increases.[15] As we shall see, international pressures have been sporadically important, but the international story alone is far too simplistic to explain the macroeconomic policies of the world's second largest economy.

The third type of argument looks at domestic Japanese politics. One version considers patterns of state-society relations.[16] A second version, which mirrors my own approach, looks at domestic institutional structure. It has become common wisdom among many Japanese that irresponsible monetary policy in the bubble period was forced by the Ministry of Finance, either because of its recalcitrance in fiscal expansion[17] or because it was able to pressure the BOJ to promote the domestic economy through easy money policies.[18] The institutional arrangements held responsible for this state of affairs are either the lack of independence of the Bank of Japan vis-à-vis the

14. Cargill, Hutchison, and Ito (1997, chap. 5) make a different exchange rate argument—that imperfect sterilization of foreign exchange market intervention was the cause of the bubble. That is functionally equivalent to the loose money argument that underlies this book.
15. Suzuki 2000, 5–10; Funabashi 1989; Iida 1990. All of these authors recognize, and in some cases emphasize, the importance of domestic as well as international politics.
16. Suzuki 2000, Henning 1994.
17. Tachi, et al. 1993 is considered MOF's *mea culpa* in this regard. Ogata Shijūrō, the former BOJ deputy governor for international affairs, also makes the case quite strongly: "As for Japan, given the situation after the Plaza, I think we should have used more timely and appropriate fiscal policy. Had a fiscal stimulus plan been carried out early and appropriately, in the end wouldn't economic recovery have been faster, the bubble smaller, and the scale of the fiscal deficit smaller?" Ogata 1996, 26–27.
18. This interpretation appears often in journalistic accounts, such as Shiota (1995) and Asahi Shimbun (1997), as well as in some scholarly works such as Mabuchi (1997) and Nakakita (1999).

Ministry of Finance, or the (often unexplained) power of the Ministry of Finance to deny politicians access to budget-making. In this book I offer a comprehensive and rational argument as to how and why such institutional arrangements persisted in Japan, providing a logical basis to support many of the often intuitive impressions concerning institutional power.

One final explanation considers the problem of the recession from a non-financial point of view. In a more systematic version of the structural rigidities view already described, Richard Katz focuses on how political patronage since at least the early 1970s had created large pockets of protected industries with declining productivity, leading to overinvestment in the least productive sectors.[19] Lending to such unproductive enterprises was inherently dangerous, but the risks were camouflaged by protective policies and the healthy growth of other sectors. The bubble, in this point of view, was important mainly for having hastened a long-term slump that was waiting to happen.

Katz's argument contributes to our understanding of the difficulty of recovery in the 1990s, but it does not address the pattern of monetary and fiscal policies that first produced and then responded to the bubble. More broadly, this "structural fatigue" approach looks at how certain aspects of Japan's developmental system that had contributed to postwar economic success were unable to respond successfully to a changing international economic environment or to shifting power bases within the domestic political economy. This has been particularly obvious in regulation of banking and cartels. Over the long run, structural rigidities can have profound negative effects on economic growth. In the shorter term, however, it is fiscal and monetary policies that must respond to internal and external shocks. Indeed, policies that promote structural adjustment generally cause pain and dislocation in the short run, creating political dilemmas for policy makers. From a different angle, though, systemic fatigue can in fact be seen in macroeconomic policy making itself, where the failure to change long-established institutional patterns of behavior led to policy failure. I return to these broader points in the concluding chapter.

Domestic Institutions

In examining policy outcomes, it is important to consider how policies are actually made. State institutions can act to channel interests, systematically including or excluding various interests or viewpoints. The argument that domestic policy-making structures and processes have a major effect on foreign policy or macroeconomic outcomes is not a new one.[20] Ikenberry and

19. Katz 1998.
20. See Allison 1971; Halperin 1974; Katzenstein 1978a and b; Krasner, ed. 1983; Hall 1986; Ikenberry, Lake, and Mastanduno, eds. 1988; and Bendor and Hammond 1992, among others.

his collaborators, for example, find that "the state serves as an important independent or intervening variable between social and international forces on the one hand, and foreign economic policy on the other."[21] Moreover, bureaucracies and bureaucrats have incentives of their own. And the "national interest" is defined in the end by bureaucracies or the political leadership.[22]

The central focus of this approach has been to understand the role of the state (or policy-making structure), with a particular emphasis on the meaning and role of state autonomy. For example, Skocpol's key variable in explaining the role of the state in a given issue area is insulation from societal interests, which is largely a function of organization, financial resources, and the skill level of bureaucrats.[23] Similarly, my analysis emphasizes the importance of appropriating information and the role of networks in doing so.

Looking at "policy networks" can help us to understand the role of the state in forming economic policies: "It is the character of the *policy network* spanning both the public and the private sector which conditions [policy instruments]. The number and range of policy instruments emerge from the differentiation of state from society and the centralization within each."[24] This is a theoretically and practically useful way of looking at the resources and incentives that face bureaucracies, and it provides us with a meaningful concept of a "state" separate from pluralist policy preferences.[25] Considering the formation of interests within relevant institutions and the structural relationships among those institutions enables us to delineate the limits and possibilities facing decision makers.

Central Bank Independence

A more specific issue regarding domestic institutions in the macroeconomic realm is central bank independence, which is often held to correlate with lower inflation.[26] The degree of autonomy and patterns of control over the Bank of Japan are a major theme of this book. And the increased autonomy granted under the 1997 BOJ Law revision is the most important of all the changes that have occurred in Japan's macroeconomic policy-making structure in the years considered in this study, and probably in the entire postwar period. Rather than dwelling here on the specifics of the Bank of Japan's re-

21. Ikenberry, Lake, and Mastanduno 1988, 2.
22. Krasner 1978.
23. See Skocpol 1985.
24. Katzenstein 1978a, 306–308.
25. In counterpoint to the state autonomy view, many American principal-agent theorists have argued strongly in favor of control by politicians. Niskanen, for example, explicitly rejects the idea of an "organic" state (1971, 4).
26. Eijffinger and de Haan 1996; Cukierman 1992; Drazen 2000; Mayer, ed. 1990; Goodman 1991, 1992.

lationship to the government, I offer a brief overview of the burgeoning literature on central bank independence (so ubiquitous that many writers simply abbreviate it as "CBI") and comment on how that literature is relevant to Japan. In chapter 8 I will return to this issue by addressing the ways in which Japan's experience might affect our understanding of central bank independence.

CBI is commonly broken down into two components: "goal" and "instrument" independence. Goals are at least broadly defined by central bank establishment laws, and emphasize to varying degrees price stability, economic growth, and financial sector stability; in practice, they must be interpreted. To the extent that the interpretation is done within the central bank itself rather than by the central government, we can speak of a degree of goal independence. Instrument independence, commonly considered the more important of the two components, is a measure of the degree to which the central bank controls the instruments of monetary policy implementation (for example, decision-making authority over the discount rate and reserve requirements, freedom from responsibility to fund government budget deficits, and the right to intervene freely in financial and/or currency markets).[27]

Economists argue that central bank independence is important primarily because of the potential for "time inconsistency" and the problem of "credibility."[28] The time inconsistency argument assumes that inflation has short-term stimulative effects, but in the long run only creates costs. Thus, the optimal long-term policy aims at low or nonexistent inflation. However, policy makers with a desire for short-term stimulation (such as politicians facing an upcoming election) will likely prefer inflationary policies and will create long-term costs. Increasing central bank independence from electoral cycles can encourage a more long-term focus for monetary policy.

Monetary policy is only part of the inflation story, though, since markets and individuals alter their behavior based on their *expectations* of the likely course of monetary policy. This dynamic points up the need for credibility of the central bank's commitment to monetary policy conservatism—without credibility, such conservative policies are likely to create much higher short-term costs than if the bank's commitment were accepted fully and immediately by markets.[29]

The actual verification of the relationship between independence and inflation has been problematic, for several reasons. In the optimistic reading, "high CBI (however measured) is correlated with low-inflation performance" and lower variability of inflation, with no cost in real economic growth or unemployment.[30] However, the statistical correlations are not

27. Drazen 2000 142; Blinder 1998, 53–59.
28. Cukierman 1992, chaps. 11–12, 18; Blinder 1998, chap. 3; Drazen 2000, 143–149.
29. Cukierman 1992, chap. 11. Blinder (1998) rejects this notion of credibility on empirical grounds.
30. Drazen 2000, 148.

very high. One reason for this may be the difficulty of measuring independence. From a different angle, Adam Posen argues that socioeconomic variables for whether a society is willing to accept higher or lower inflation are a better predictor than institutional arrangements.[31] Another view is that credibility must be earned by past actions, and not just by institutional arrangements.[32]

Writers on CBI have traditionally had trouble dealing with Japan. By all legal measures, the Bank of Japan had (until 1998) extremely low levels of independence, yet Japan had one of the best inflation records in the world.[33] While some authors tried to point to informal mechanisms that gave the BOJ more independence than its legal status suggested,[34] others argued that the Ministry of Finance itself had a strong (if unexplained) anti-inflationary bias.[35] Alternatively, it may be that the long-term ruling party did not fear loss of support as a result of anti-inflationary policy. A final economic explanation is that monetary stimulus may not have been as effective in Japan as in other countries (in other words, a steep short-run Phillips curve) due to structural factors in the economy such as labor market rigidities.[36]

The lack of an obvious relationship between BOJ independence and low Japanese inflation may be beside the point, however. In Japan's bubble economy, normal price inflation was not even an issue. But the BOJ's inability to act on its own to head off what it saw as inflationary pressures was a key element contributing to Japan's long-term financial and economic malaise. While the system worked admirably in normal times in postwar Japan, the years from 1985 to 2000 were no ordinary time. In practice, the institutional arrangements of BOJ dependence had tragic consequences, but not in the usual sense predicted in the CBI literature.

Politics and Policy Making in Japan

Stepping beyond the specific question of BOJ autonomy, we must look broadly at Japan's overall institutional setting. Unfortunately, there is little agreement on how Japanese state institutions work. Studies of Japanese politics and policy making can generally be divided into two (highly dichoto-

---

31. See Cukierman, Webb, and Neyapti (1993) on measurement, and Eijffinger and de Hann (1996, chap. 4) on the sensitivity of the inflation-independence relationship to the measure of independence used. The Posen argument is cited in Drazen 2000, 149.
32. Blinder 1999.
33. Hutchison 1986; Cargill 1989.
34. Cargill 1989, chap. 5. This is not actually a very convincing argument. For example, using Cukierman, Webb, and Neyapti's (1993) questionnaire component of independence, I calculate the independence of the BOJ before 1998 as roughly equal to the central bank of Belgium, which is exactly where it ranks in the legal components. The rest of this book (especially chapter 3) demonstrates this assertion more concretely.
35. Cukierman, Webb, and Neyapti 1993, 28.
36. Cargill, Hutchison, and Ito 1997, 157.

mous) points of view: the bureaucratic-led interpretation and the pluralist interpretation. Pluralists argue that while benefits are not actually distributed equitably across the society, distributive policies are formed through a democratic process. In general, such authors argue, the weight of the pluralistic political arena, once loosed, has been dominant even in previously bureaucratic-led policy areas.[37] Two challenges that tend to weaken bureaucracies are transparency and the development of standard operating procedures, both of which offer politicians useful points of intervention in the policy-making process.[38]

One potentially troubling point for pluralists has been the apparent unresponsiveness of the Japanese government to demands for large-scale policy change. An ingenious solution to that problem comes from Calder's observation that major policies were initially formed as equilibrium political solutions that had to satisfy the unusually broad range of interests that support the long-dominant Liberal Democratic Party (LDP). Because of the difficulty of coming to agreement, the original solutions could remain virtually unchanged even in the face of major changes in societal preferences. Calder argues that only when such changes spark actual electoral crises has the (essentially non-ideological) LDP been able to respond in more than an incremental way.[39] That tendency is presumably amplified in coalition governments such as we have seen since 1993.

A more controversial application of pluralist assumptions has been the use of principal-agent models of legislative and bureaucratic behavior. Ramseyer and Rosenbluth, for example, argue that the Japanese Diet maintains effective control over the processes of policy making and implementation by forcing bureaucrats to "write the bills that will best promote LDP electoral odds, and administer them in ways that will best lead to the same end. [Bureaucrats] do so because they have no choice. Should they try anything else, LDP leaders will not pass the statutes they write, will legislate against the regulations they promulgate, and may do what they can to see that their careers go nowhere."[40]

Critics of the principal-agent approach (and indeed of strong pluralist arguments in general) retort that the "tension between a powerful bureaucracy and a weak party system is one of the main features of Japanese politics at the present time. It is what political science needs to explain, rather than asserting that all power flows from the voters to their elected representatives, and

---

37. Yamaguchi 1987; Inoguchi and Iwai 1987; Inoguchi 1983; Satō and Matsuzaki 1986; Curtis 1988; Muramatsu and Krauss 1984.
38. Yamaguchi 1987, 98–99. Compare this to Crozier (1964, 153–154), and to Kane's (1990) examination of the U.S. Federal Reserve Board's insistence on discretion. Kato (1994) also explores the last of these points.
39. Calder 1988a.
40. Ramseyer and Rosenbluth 1993, 122. See also Cowhey and McCubbins, eds. 1995; Woodall 1996.

that these representatives in turn control the bureaucrats."[41] This critique comes from a traditionally more important school of thought concerning Japanese policy making: the "economic bureaucrat" model, best exemplified by Chalmers Johnson's various works. Leaving aside his argument about Japanese economic development, Johnson makes clear his belief that actual policy making in Japan has been the province of the bureauracy rather than the politicians. As Johnson puts it, "Politicians reign but do not rule; the actual decision makers are an elite bureaucracy of economic technocrats."[42] A number of Japanese scholars have also used a bureaucratic leadership approach to analyze administrative guidance and the "bureaucratic-dominant state."[43] Many of these authors are concerned with reducing the power of the bureaucracy and have advocated various proposals for serious administrative reform. The approach has also been quite popular outside of academe, although popular analyses have not necessarily been theoretically or empirically convincing.[44]

Clearly, something is going on that deserves careful study. Even prominent pluralist writers condition their arguments by pointing to some of the advantages enjoyed by bureaucrats.[45] Thus, for an increasing number of analysts, the key to understanding the relative power of bureaucrats and politicians in a given area is to look at the actual power resources available to each. The essential question is the degree to which specific actors can shape policies to their own agendas.

In this regard, Rosenbluth argues that "the apportionment of costs and benefits [of a policy] must mirror the distribution of political resources, or the settlement will be challenged until it does."[46] Nonetheless, many decisions about policy formulation and implementation are made outside the political realm. In other words, political control is a question of *ratification*. There may be significant room for bureaucratic influence through agenda-setting and other means, but while politicians cannot easily micromanage, they can use their veto power when they consider it expedient.[47] Since they are most likely to do so when support groups push strongly, we can predict a quasi-pluralist solution to hotly contested issues.

---

41. Johnson and Keehn 1994, 17.
42. Johnson 1982, 87.
43. Shindō 1992, 1997; Katō 1997; Sasaki 1994.
44. See, for example, Fingleton (1995a and b) and Murphy (1996), both of which depend crucially on the unexplained power of a profoundly powerful Ministry of Finance.
45. Inoguchi 1983; Satō and Matsuzaki 1986; Muramatsu and Krauss 1987; Yamaguchi 1987; Calder 1988a.
46. Rosenbluth 1989, 209–210. Unfortunately, despite a rich case history, her analysis does not really address the question of how political resources are amassed or in what ways they can be used. For such an analysis, a good source is Ōtake 1996, especially chap. 1.
47. This is essentially what McCubbins and Schwartz (1987) call "fire-alarm oversight."

Where ambiguity exists concerning how a solution will ultimately affect groups, however, this dynamic may be blunted. Perhaps more importantly, if there are more than two groups involved in an issue with multiple facets, potential bargaining solutions multiply, and the final outcome may be unpredictable. Thus, even if politicians have veto power and perfect information, there are considerable opportunities for a bureaucracy, in the role of mediator or agenda-setter, to put its own stamp on the issue.

Building on that point, Kato argues that bureaucratic influence in the Japanese policy-making process is not structurally or historically given, but is rather contingent both on the situation and on the strategies chosen by the ministries concerned. It is therefore important "to identify specific conditions that give an advantage to bureaucratic influence."[48] Bureaucrats may best be able to achieve advantage in policy making by actively involving themselves in politics—influencing political agendas and policy discourses—rather than by insulating themselves from the political world.[49] Finally, institutional setting is important in both the pluralist and the bureaucratic dominance stories. As Vogel demonstrates, deeply entrenched organizational norms and ways of dealing with the world can lead to characteristic policy solutions—in Japan, bureaucracies have largely focused on continued state control even in the face of considerable pressure for change.[50]

Broadly speaking, organizations (both bureaucratic and explicitly political) and the individuals who make them up have incentives to maximize or at least maintain their power and advance their policy preferences. These actors will attempt to use their political, technical, and organizational resources to do so. Thus, a certain degree of conflict is inevitable among major actors in any political system. These actors include not only elected politicians and their constituents, but also the bureaucrats who carry out actual policy making and implementation. To understand actors' behavior, we must consider the practical incentives that drive them.

The Structure of Japanese Macroeconomic Policy Making

Japanese macroeconomic and exchange rate policy making is essentially a game among the three official actors—the Ministry of Finance, the Bank of Japan, and the leadership of the Diet. This game becomes most visible in times of crisis, when there is no widespread agreement on policy directions. The years from 1985 to 2000 were largely made up of such crises.

While only the official actors are directly involved in policy making, both private-sector actors and foreign governments often make efforts to get in-

48. Kato 1994, 12.
49. The logic, which is based on bounded rationality, is laid out in Kato 1994, chap. 1.
50. Vogel 1996.

volved, especially when their interests are suffering under the status quo. Even then, however, they are unable to involve themselves directly, so their influence is on one or another official actor, following established networks. Because such networks are formed by cooperation over time, it is fairly easy to predict both how a given private-sector actor will attempt to shape policy and how each official actor will respond. Thus, for the sake of simplicity, I concentrate on the official actors in this model, although when we come to the actual events of the period other actors will reappear.

Power in the domestic policy game is based on information and structure—or, to be more exact, the incomplete and asymmetric nature of information provides the environment in which actors behave rationally in the pursuit of internally generated goals.[51] The ability of a given institutional actor to appropriate crucial policy information or expertise is a key source of power in the game, since it reduces other actors' ability to monitor or subvert the original actor's purposes. Similarly, if an actor can substantially conceal or stall its actions, it gains important advantages in the time-bound game of macroeconomic policy. Thus, networks and regimes of information management are central features of the structure; to understand these, we must look at individual-level incentives and asymmetrical information.

Several structural factors are of particular importance in shaping policy outcomes: the actors involved, how they relate to one another, and their "social permeability" (the extent to which a state actor is subject to the demands of social actors, whether from a specific constituency or a variety of actors).[52] The recruitment and career patterns of bureaucrats, and the legal framework and social organization within which the agency functions, are of primary importance in determining permeability.

Legal jurisdictions offer a useful first cut, although they are often vague in Japan. While informal mechanisms can also be crucial, they are usually constrained by issues of jurisdiction. Moreover, they often have legal bases— in Japan, many apparently informal powers of agencies are justified (at least by the agencies themselves) by broad mandates. Japanese government agencies often interpret their laws of establishment (*setchi hō*) and other vague mandates as giving them broad informal powers.[53] Other laws tend to be written rather broadly as well, necessitating Cabinet or Ministerial Orders to make them more specific. Even then, considerable latitude is granted to divisions in interpreting laws and orders, through directives known as *tsūtatsu*. As policy moves down from the level of law to *tsūtatsu*, politicians naturally have less input.

---

51. This formulation is similar to Kato's (1994). See also Pfeffer and Salancik 1978; Harsanyi 1986.
52. Henning (1994) applies a similar concept to international macroeconomic policy coordination.
53. Shindō 1992; Haley 1991.

A second issue, which gets to the heart of the concept of social permeability, is career patterns. For example, what is the extent of personnel flows in and out of relevant institutions? Are these two-way or one-way paths, and if the latter, in which direction? The permeability of an agency is minimized to the extent that decision-making posts are occupied by career bureaucrats rather than by outsiders from other agencies, the political world, or the general public. Moreover, if an agency is able to "colonize" other associated agencies or societal actors by placing its own career bureaucrats in decision-making roles, it should have even more control over its environment, and thus be less socially permeable.

Third, how is information managed?[54] In any political economy, the management of information is an essential source of power, both for the individual and for the agency; in Japan it is perhaps even more so, due to the general non-transparency of the policy process. Control over information can be used to constrain the choices of other actors; it is also important for each actor in attempting to make correct judgments about the needs for and constraints on policy. Just as individuals seek to obtain and then dispense information to their own advantage by means of personal networks, organizations also seek to manage information to their advantage. The ability of an institutional actor to obtain, process, and retain pertinent information is a key element in the policy making power structure. Given that an organization gathers great quantities of information, there are two conditions for using that information to its advantage: that it be efficiently disseminated and analyzed within the organization; and that information, including information on the process of making specific internal decisions, not be easily available outside the organization. In other words, members must not leak sensitive information, or at least must do so only selectively. Thus, information management is about networks and about leverage within specific networked relations.

A final consideration specific to the case of macroeconomic policy coordination is that fiscal policy will tend to have more inertia than monetary policy due to both implementation lags and the necessity of legislative approval. In Japan, the opacity of fiscal policy increases that inertia.

The Individual Level

Policy making is a game played on two levels: the individual and the institutional. In the case of macroeconomic policy in Japan, we must first ask ourselves what incentives face individuals in the Ministry of Finance, the Bank of Japan, and the political parties. These are primarily a function of career paths—the patterns of hiring (or election), advancement within an organi-

54. Pfeffer and Salancik (1978) provide a general framework. Aoki (1988) relates it to career patterns. For an analysis of MOF-politician relations, see Kato 1994.

zation, and opportunities outside of it. The games on the level of the individual are an important factor in the games on the institutional level. The idea of institutions working with or against each other is not new; however, without an explanation of why individuals within an institution may be expected to act in a given way, it lacks bite.[55]

To make sense of collective action, we must begin at the level of the individual. In other words, what incentives does the individual member of the organization face? The individual will pursue his goals subject to the constraints and incentives defined by his environment. (I use the masculine pronoun advisedly—the overwhelming majority of Japanese bureaucrats and politicians are male.) While the constraints and incentives vary by institution and by time frame, I assume the main goals to be power and prestige.

Why power and prestige? I begin with bureaucrats.[56] The bureaucrat does not join his agency with the intent of amassing wealth, given the relatively low pay offered in the public sector. Nor is leisure (the labor economist's usual substitute for income) likely to be the goal of a college senior who has set his sights on a government ministry—late nights and weekends at the office are the lot of any Japanese bureaucrat. I personally believe that many bureaucrats enter their careers through a sense of duty, or commitment to ideals they believe they can further through government service. Even if that is true, however, the best way to advance those ideals is to advance one's own personal position in an agency whose mission is consonant with one's own—in other words, by seeking power and prestige.

For politicians, the central goal is election and reelection; whatever other goals a politician may have—whether ideological or pecuniary—entry and participation in the political process is essential. (There is an apt saying in Japanese politics: "A politician who loses is just a man." Presumably, the point is not lost on politicians.) While some conservative politicians have become rather wealthy during their time in office, that wealth reflects fund-raising prowess, which in turn tends to be identical with increasing power. Thus, we are left with the simplifying assumption that politicians too pursue power and prestige.

MOF Bureaucrats

The next question is how the individual goes about attaining these goals. To begin with the MOF bureaucrat,[57] the most important point to bear in mind is the

55. See Allison 1971; and Bendor and Hammond's (1992) critique.
56. Here I include both MOF and BOJ officials, although the Bank of Japan is technically not a bureau of the government. I do so because the BOJ is de facto part of the government due to its official responsibilities in the Japanese economy, and because the career paths of individual bank employees closely parallel those of their MOF counterparts.
57. This discussion concentrates on elite-track bureaucrats (known in the ministry as "career"), who have passed the highest-level civil service examinations. Non-elite-track bureaucrats (known as "veterans") do not reach key management and policy positions; therefore I do not deal with them here. A similar division exists within the Bank of Japan.

bureaucratic career pattern, in particular the difficulty of moving between employers in the Japanese system. Having chosen the ministry as his calling, a MOF bureaucrat is generally constrained to stay there until he reaches a senior level. The major exception is to enter electoral politics. This is not unusual (there were twenty-three former MOF officials in the Diet as of May 2000,[58] and there are more in prefectural offices), but it is not the normal career path. Being essentially constrained to stay in the ministry, the typical bureaucrat must seek advancement within it, by conforming to its norms. Moreover, in order to increase his own power and prestige within the ministry, he must support actions that extend the power of the ministry as a whole.

The incentive to maximize the power of the ministry exists for both lower-level and senior bureaucrats, despite the latter's very real need to secure post-retirement (so-called *amakudari,* or "descent from heaven") jobs and their increased contact with politicians. One reason is that jobs for retiring bureaucrats are secured by officials in the secretariat, who do not reward behavior that hurts the ministry. Moreover, MOF has a vast array of secure jobs in government financial institutions and public corporations, which means that top-level officials seldom need to depend on the kindness of strangers, or even non-MOF acquaintances. And since the quality of *amakudari* jobs is largely a function of rank at the time of retirement, competition for those jobs does not come at the expense of tending to internal politics.

BOJ Officials

The employee of the Bank of Japan faces a similar incentive structure. The average new employee of the Bank of Japan is very similar to his MOF counterpart—a top graduate of the law or economics faculty of one of the top universities. He expects to stay in the bank for the bulk of his working life, after which he will move to an *amakudari* job, generally with either a private-sector client of the BOJ (typically a bank or banking federation) or a public financial institution.[59] As in most elite Japanese organizations, horizontal mobility is highly restricted, and relatively few BOJ personnel leave the bank in mid-career for other opportunities. The rational strategy for the individual is thus to seek to advance the power and prestige of his organization while avoiding risky confrontations with banks and the Ministry of Finance.

Two differences in career path between the BOJ and MOF should be noted. First, entry into electoral politics is extremely rare: as of May 2000 there were only two BOJ alumni in the Diet, one first elected in 1993 and

---

58. *Seikai Jinjiroku* 1997. *Seikan Yōran* 1999, Insert 7–10.

59. BOJ retirees tend to be placed at slightly lower positions than their MOF counterparts, particularly in public financial institutions. Thus, they once again have to heed the directives of their erstwhile bureaucratic rivals. See Tsutsumi 1997; Calder 1989; and van Rixtel 1994 for figures.

the other in 1996.[60] The historical scarcity of BOJ alumni in elected positions appears to reflect the low level of direct day-to-day contact between the bank and the Diet and the fact that the bank has relatively few resources with which to bargain. Since elected office is not generally a realistic alternative to advancement within the BOJ, there is little incentive for individual, informal communication with the political world. While this reduces permeability, it also leaves the BOJ without political allies when it takes an unpopular position.

Another difference from the ministry is the comparatively greater concentration of *amakudari* jobs in private-sector financial institutions, particularly small ones. The Bank of Japan has not gained widespread control over organizations that can provide its bureaucrats with comfortable post-retirement jobs. Retiring BOJ employees are thus more dependent on the good will of the bank's clients, the private-sector financial institutions.[61] This tends to increase social permeability.

Party Politicians

At first glance, the incentive structure facing Diet members should be quite different from those facing individuals in MOF and the BOJ. After all, the central requirement of the job is to satisfy one's constituency sufficiently to get reelected every few years. But while the basic requirement for achieving power through electoral politics is election (and reelection), that is only a necessary condition. Japanese electoral politics by the 1980s had become highly bureaucratized. The main factor was the system of effective one-party dominance on the part of the Liberal Democratic Party: from 1955 to summer 1993, power in the Diet was essentially a function of power within the LDP.[62] By the 1980s, the attainment of power within the party followed rather specific patterns.

Three factors tended to account for success within the LDP: longevity, prominence in factional politics (largely a function of fund-raising skills), and expertise in a given policy area. Measuring success by frequency of ap-

60. One BOJ alumnus in the Diet, Shiozaki Yasuhisa, inherited his Lower House seat in 1993 from his father, a former MOF Tax Bureau chief. He moved to the Upper House in July 1995, and returned to the Lower House in June 2000. The other BOJ alumnus serving in the Diet as of 2000, Suzuki Yoshio, is well known as an author and economic analyst. (See various issues of *Seikai Jinjiroku* and *Seikan Yōran* as well as www.seiji-koho.co.jp/GIIN/index.html).
61. Calder (1989) finds that BOJ *amakudari* positions are concentrated in institutions that could most benefit from having an inside pipeline to the bank, such as regional banks. Van Rixtel (1994) and Schaede (1995) generally confirm Calder's findings. Tsutsumi (1997, 38) finds that about 60 percent of BOJ OBs are employed by financial institutions and federations.
62. The LDP's long-term one-party dominance has been a major subject of investigation among students of Japanese politics. Some of the better examinations include Satō and Matsuzaki 1986; Inoguchi 1983, Inoguchi and Iwai 1987; Calder 1988a; Curtis 1988; and Kohno 1997. For a comparative perspective, see the essays in Pempel, ed. (1990).

pointment to Cabinet and top party posts, those who were more successful became so either by tending to the financial affairs of their factions or by gaining policy expertise (the so-called *zoku,* or "policy tribe," approach).[63]

Like MOF and BOJ bureaucrats, politicians try to maximize their control over specific areas of jurisdiction—in the LDP politician's case, these would be areas of electoral advantage or areas through which he could improve his credentials with his faction or key interest groups. The interests of an individual LDP Diet member during the period of one-party dominance were thus skewed in the direction of policies that served the interests of specific constituencies that could deliver either votes or money. The easiest such targets have been pork-barrel projects in agriculture and public works, with a smattering of financial regulation. In general, politicians tend to avoid areas in which public opinion is sharply divided.[64] In the post-1993 period, securing votes within districts tended to require similar behavior of any realistic candidate.

Areas such as macroeconomic policy and international currency affairs are certainly more palatable than debates over teaching ethics in public schools, but they remain relatively unenticing because they affect the economy broadly and are quite technical. Thus, politicians have often been content to leave them to the experts in the Ministry of Finance and the Bank of Japan. Politicians with direct jurisdiction, such as the prime minister and the minister of finance, have the strongest incentive for close personal involvement, since such matters reflect personally on them. Even here, however, they tend toward "fire-alarm oversight,"[65] only stepping in when private actors (or the media) complain—in other words, they are more results-oriented than process-oriented. In addition, Japanese political leaders tend not to be expert in the field of macroeconomics, and the lags involved in macroeconomic policy making (reinforced by the rigidity of the budget calendar) often make oversight ineffective.[66] The costs of obtaining unbiased information from an often recalcitrant Ministry of Finance also reduce the effectiveness of such oversight. The result is that leadership by politicians in macroeconomic policy has often been of only the bluntest and most generalized sort.

Since 1993, the pattern of incentives that existed under the system of medium-sized electoral districts has undergone significant changes both at the district level and in parties, although the basic goals of election and re-election remain unchanged. As I demonstrate in chapter 2, the changes in the Lower House electoral system tend to increase politicians' interest in

63. Satō and Matsuzaki 1986, esp. 49, fig.
64. As Inoguchi and Iwai demonstrate, *zoku* in the controversial areas of defense and education have been minute in comparison to agriculture, public works, and telecommunications *zoku.* See particularly 1987, 132–147.
65. McCubbins and Schwartz 1987; Calvert, Moran, and Weingast 1987.
66. Lags are particularly important in that the average tenure for a Cabinet minister is only a little over a year.

macroeconomic policy. Moreover, to the extent that party politics remain unsettled, there is more room for "political entrepreneurs" who can leverage their knowledge of important issues or their contacts with members of other parties to gain personal power. Macroeconomic policy has been one target of such individuals.

The Institutional Level

Building from the incentive structure for the individual, we may speak of institutions as players in a strategic game among institutions. The Ministry of Finance, for example, attempts to increase its power and prestige relative to other institutional actors through the means at its disposal, while ensuring that it does not run afoul of the ruling party or coalition, the only institution that can severely curtail its powers. It has done so primarily through its monopoly on information and expertise—as well as its legal jurisdiction— over a huge range of functions.

The Ministry of Finance

The Ministry of Finance has had a truly extraordinary range of functions and jurisdictions; in none of these has it had serious bureaucratic competitors. Until FY 1998, the Ministry of Finance was responsible for all budget making and examination, tax policy formation and tax collection, management of postal savings and national property, formulation and enforcement of tariffs and quotas, and formulation and enforcement of regulations governing every aspect of the financial markets.[67] It also has regulatory authority over all government-approved monopolies and the alcoholic beverage industry and effective control over a variety of public corporations.

For the most part, and like most government ministries, the Ministry of Finance does not produce anything tangible, other than vast quantities of printed and written material.[68] It is, perhaps, most accurate to think of the ministry as a huge data processing mechanism. It absorbs information and pressures relevant to its missions, processes them, and produces outputs in the form of analysis, guidance, and policies. Management of information is central to MOF's mission, as it is to governing in general.

67. The year 1998 brought establishment of the Financial Supervision Agency and the Financial Reconstruction Commission, thus separating some of the implementation of financial regulation from policy making. In July 2000, all domestic financial system policy making and implementation was removed from MOF's jurisdiction. In January 2001, its Japanese name was changed from Ōkurashō (Ministry of Finance) to Zaimushō (Ministry of the Treasury). However, the English name remains unchanged.
68. The Mint Bureau and the Printing Bureau, of course, are in the business of producing— their main products are coinage, paper money, and government publications. MOF also has Treasury functions like overseeing and disbursing public funds.

One of MOF's greatest strengths is its ability to gather huge amounts of information. Sources of economically and politically important information have included bank inspections (eliminated from MOF's toolbox with the establishment of the Financial Supervision Agency in June 1998), budget making, tax collection, and temporary transfers of its members to various agencies and institutions including (until 1998) the Bank of Japan.

The Ministry of Finance is also extremely effective in its internal dissemination of information.[69] Frequent movement of personnel among bureaus and sections and frequent social interaction among "classmates" and between *sempai* and *kōhai* (seniors and juniors) lead to the formation of networks of communication. Moreover, organizational tendencies toward consultative decision making and incrementalism ensure that both sufficient time and the necessary channels exist to circulate needed information.[70]

Since officials have an interest in adhering to the norms of the ministry and in working to advance its power and prestige, individuals find it difficult to advance their own interests by excessive leaking of information. This is the more true due to the threat of detection, a possibility that certainly increases over the course of a thirty-year bureaucratic career. The Ministry of Finance is not some kind of informational black hole—there is in fact a considerable and constant flow of information among all the relevant policy actors. However, the incentive structure facing the career bureaucrat makes leaking of critical information or analysis a generally unattractive option. Indeed, even in the banking inspection scandals of 1997–98, very few elite-track MOF bureaucrats were directly implicated.

One effect of MOF's vast legal jurisdiction and the career patterns of its members has been that it has considerable and appropriable information resources, which in turn can translate into power in the policy-making process. This power has been increased by the lack of credible alternative sources of data and analysis in the Diet and the political parties, or through nonprofit or academic organizations.

The broad range of MOF responsibilities—in particular, its responsibility for budget and tax policy—also means that the ministry has a broad range of tradable political resources. Since individual politicians and other ministries must often make requests for specific line items, they must also be willing to compromise. The ability to manage political trades gives immense power to the Ministry of Finance, particularly to the career budget specialists who tend to occupy the top administrative positions.

The combination of political power and the need to place retiring officials in *amakudari* jobs has led to considerable "bureaucratic imperialism." The ministry has acted to secure post-retirement job slots in the public and

69. For more detail, see chapters 2–3. On management of information within Japanese organizations, see Aoki 1988, chap. 2.
70. These tendencies are highlighted in Campbell 1977.

quasi-public sector, thus ensuring that its retiring top officials virtually always find well-paid and prestigious employment without having to depend on ministry clients in the private sector for favors. This network of secure positions (known informally as *shitei seki,* or "reserved seats") reduces MOF's social permeability considerably, and increases the latitude of top officials to resist often vociferous demands from politicians and financiers, secure in the knowledge that they will not be blackballed from future employment.

Finally, while power is important, we need to look at institutional motivations and objectives to understand how it will be used. Building up from the individual level, I have argued that institutional power and autonomy are a major objective and have shown how breadth of jurisdiction and bureaucratic imperialism constitute both power resources and organizational objectives. We can also make some conclusions about policy stance. For example, the jurisdiction objective long contributed to unwillingness to support financial liberalization.[71] In terms of macroeconomic policy objectives, the overriding one is fiscal consolidation.[72] If it is unable to maintain scarcity of budget resources, MOF loses one of its primary bases for political trades. The autonomy objective also implies minimal deficits for another reason: when deficits become large, other political actors may be motivated to fix the problem. Austerity is also generally attractive because it is very difficult to cut spending once it has been approved—thus, a preemptive strategy toward new or expanded programs is typical of budget bureaucrats.

The Bank of Japan

The Bank of Japan is essentially another bureaucratic actor, and thus faces incentives that parallel those of the Ministry of Finance (even though its policy goals may often differ). The environment within which it must act, however, is strikingly different.[73] That difference has two primary dimensions—the bank's positions in the political world and in the market.

The BOJ is not a Cabinet ministry. Since the BOJ neither generates nor enforces laws, it has little regular input into the lawmaking process, and its dealings with politicians have traditionally been limited. Before 1998, the Cabinet technically became involved with personnel only at the levels of governor and deputy governor, and that only occurred once every five years. (The BOJ Law revision that took effect in FY 1998 requires the BOJ governor to give semiannual reports to the Diet.) Thus, personal advancement

71. Vogel 1996; Norville 1998.
72. See Yamaguchi 1987; Kato 1994; Campbell 1977; Shiota 1995; Kishi 1996; and Ishizawa 1995, among others.
73. For a pessimistic account of the BOJ's ability to chart its own course, see Suzuki 1992. An excellent theoretical treatment of the role of the external environment is Pfeffer and Salancik 1978.

within the BOJ does not depend heavily on closeness with politicians. The dearth of former bank officials in the Diet only reinforces the division.

Perhaps a more obvious constraint on the BOJ has been its institutional relationship with the Ministry of Finance. Until it was comprehensively revised in 1997, the Bank of Japan Law, written during World War II and patterned on the German Reichsbank Law, gave the minister of finance authority to constrain and in some cases even prevent or counteract actions by the BOJ. As chapter 3 demonstrates, the ministry had formal or informal veto power over nearly all major policy decisions by the Bank of Japan.

Unfortunately for the Bank of Japan, its power resources in terms of information have been limited. In particular, it is difficult for the BOJ to monopolize information relevant to monetary policy. This is not because BOJ officials have loose lips,[74] but because much relevant information—including interest rates, exchange rates, and asset prices, among others—is easily and often immediately available to anyone who is interested. Also, a whole series of personnel practices and other procedures has long guaranteed MOF access to BOJ decision making.

None of this would be an issue if the BOJ and MOF always had identical objectives. That is not always the case, however. The bank's overriding objective since at least the early 1970s has been price stability. In practical terms, central banks are most severely blamed after the fact for inflationary mistakes, and as the central bank autonomy literature shows, central banks left to their own devices are more likely to choose price stability over growth stimulation. BOJ officials explicitly reject the possibility of a trade-off between growth and inflation, a view that has been institutionalized in the revised BOJ Law.[75] While the Ministry of Finance does not advocate inflationary policies as a general rule, it has a host of other institutional concerns that can affect its macroeconomic stance, including the need for a growing tax base, the financing of public debt, and its own political position. These concerns can affect MOF objectives with regard to exchange rates as well. There are also likely to be differences of opinion between the Ministry of Finance and the Bank of Japan over prudential regulation and financial innovations, but these are not directly relevant to my discussion.[76]

Until the recent revision of the BOJ Law, the enormous political resources at the disposal of the Ministry of Finance limited the Bank of Japan's potential level of autonomy considerably. The BOJ's main strategy for maintaining or increasing autonomy was to improve its hold over information resources; however, its ability to do so was constrained by the factors discussed above. Moreover, the bank has not had obvious recourse in dis-

74. This has never been the case, but the 1997 BOJ Law revision (Article 29) legally prohibits leaking.
75. Personal interviews; revised BOJ Law, Article 2.
76. See Horiuchi 1998 for a general criticism of such regulation in Japan.

putes—it has few political connections (and few political "horses" to trade) and cannot easily appeal to "the market" on a case-by-case basis. Thus, the BOJ has picked its battles carefully, while generally going along with MOF. Only since 1998 has the bank been able to steer an autonomous route in the face of MOF opposition.

Political Parties

The incentive structures of the LDP and its offshoots as institutions have been shaped by the overwhelming logic of individual members' need for reelection. In the medium-sized electoral districts that existed in the Lower House (the more powerful house of the Diet) until 1994, election turned on a politician's ability to mobilize a committed group of niche voters and to gain name recognition among the general public. This situation called for pork-barrel benefits and lots of money for campaigning.[77] That was particularly true in the 1980s, when ideology appeared to be a declining force in Japanese electoral politics—the smaller centrist parties had taken on more and more of the LDP's platform and even elements of the Socialist Party had begun to accept major tenets of the conservative agenda.[78]

Organizations of politicians (i.e., parties and factions) survive on the basis of their ability to influence government policy and to raise funds for members' campaigns. This has been particularly true in the LDP and its factions, which lack captive constituencies such as the labor unions and religious organizations upon which traditional opposition parties relied. Driven by competition among factions, the party for much of its existence concentrated on fighting only those battles that affected the public's approval of it, while leaving plenty of room at the margins for pork barrel for individual districts. Administration, and even substantial legislation, could for the most part be left to the bureaucracy. This has been even more true given the fragmented nature of LDP ideology—although by the 1980s the party had become quite bureaucratic in organization, the trend toward uniformity has not extended to the policy preferences of its members.[79] Even greater fragmentation characterizes the eclectic and *ad hoc* opposition parties of the post-1993 period.

77. It also strongly encouraged intraparty factions among those parties big enough to have to run more than one candidate in an election district. Kohno 1997 chap. 6.
78. In the late 1970s, even the Japan Communist Party supported Cabinet bills upwards of 60 percent of the time. In the 1980s, opposition party support for Cabinet bills declined, but the Democratic Socialist Party and Kōmeitō stayed over 80 percent, and even the Socialists were above 50 percent. Satō and Matsuzaki 1986, 139.
79. Even factions have very little to do with ideology; Ramseyer and Rosenbluth (1993, 59) pithily describe the LDP faction as a "nonideological conduit of particularism." Krauss (1989, 48) also observes that factions "are based on personal loyalty and political self-interest" and show few policy differences across factional lines.

The political shake-ups of the mid- to late 1990s changed some of the incentives and resources for political parties. First, the emergence of a viable opposition overturned a key assumption of the old one-party dominant system. In a situation of potentially alternating administration, the ruling party or coalition must be more concerned with its short-term hold on power than with the longer term. Thus, post-1993 governments became more willing to intervene in macroeconomic policies to create a political business cycle.[80]

Second, single-member electoral districts require broader appeal than the previous medium-sized districts, thus prompting politicians to campaign based on issues of general interest, including macroeconomic policies. The need for coalitions may also increase macroeconomic activism if coalition partners with very different goals use spending hikes or tax cuts as lubrication for compromises on controversial policies.

One real factor working against greater political involvement in macroeconomic policy making (at least early in the coalition period that began in 1993) was the general lack of governing experience of many non-LDP politicians. Moreover, nascent party organizations have been unable to generate reliable independent analyses of macroeconomic trends or the effects of various policies, putting them at the mercy of the better informed.

The Macroeconomic Policy Game

Until the BOJ Law revision took effect in April 1998, the Ministry of Finance was the central actor in Japanese macroeconomic policy making, due to its broad legal jurisdictions, low social permeability, and effective management of information. In terms of jurisdiction, it is responsible for fiscal policy and exchange rate management, although it is legally answerable to the Diet (in other words, to the LDP until 1993, and to various formal and informal coalition governments since).[81] Outside MOF's direct supervision, the minister of finance also has had formal and informal veto rights over various monetary policy actions, and MOF has both recommended and supplied candidates for the top posts of the Bank of Japan. Its main objective in macroeconomic management has been to maximize its autonomy in fiscal policy. It has also sought to maintain leverage over monetary policy, at least partly in order to protect its fiscal prerogatives.[82]

80. The same was true under the one-party dominant system when the LDP sensed an electoral crisis. Calder 1988a.
81. Actually (as shown in Calder 1988a and Krauss 1984), Japan's parliamentary process gave rather more leverage to the opposition than might be supposed in a system that experienced one-party dominance for nearly forty years. Nevertheless, opposition leverage prior to 1993 and again after 1996 had to work *through* the Liberal Democratic Party, which remained the only major political actor in the area of macroeconomic policy.
82. Mabuchi 1997, 25–28.

The Bank of Japan's role has been to make monetary policy and to act as the agent for the Ministry of Finance in exchange rate intervention. The BOJ has had fewer resources than MOF in terms of institutional power; as a result its role in macroeconomic policy has been secondary. It is responsible for day-to-day monetary management, where it has pursued two objectives: low inflation, and improved autonomy in the conduct of monetary policy. Until recently, it had no choice but to ultimately accede to pressure from the Ministry of Finance and the political world on major policy decisions.

The third actor is the Diet, which has the authority (if not always the ability) to direct the Ministry of Finance to serve the nation as it sees fit. More specifically, the relevant relationships are with the finance minister and prime minister, the LDP's Policy Affairs Research Council before 1993, and the ruling coalitions' policy affairs councils since. The objectives of the Diet leadership have been focused on electoral success. This has generally made for a rather hands-off approach to macroeconomic and exchange rate management, policy areas of less-than-obvious appeal to local voters unless recession or large-scale yen appreciation force them onto the agenda (as they often did between 1985 and 2000). Moreover, the policy experts in the Ministry of Finance and Bank of Japan have effectively argued that macroeconomic policy is a highly technical area that can be jeopardized by extensive political interference. In general, when politicians apply pressure on the BOJ and MOF in these areas, they do so bluntly, leaving specific questions of implementation to the bureaucrats.

Strategies

This brief description begs a broader question concerning the dynamics of delegation. Although delegation does not imply a complete cession of power, it does change the shape of policy networks and their accompanying patterns of information flows and reciprocal exchange. As these patterns become more and more institutionalized over time, breaking them requires more and more effort—even if the effort is made by the delegating authority. Thus, while politicians are generally able to threaten bureaucratic control, actually regaining control often costs more than it is worth in terms of both political resources and time. Moreover, history and public opinion can have profound effects on the legitimacy of various actors' behavior; in Japan both have tended to support the claim of the bureaucracies to considerable autonomy.[83] What strategies, then, were available to the political leadership, the Ministry of Finance, and the Bank of Japan in pre-1998 macroeconomic policy making, short of actually altering the policy-making structure?

---

83. The recessions and bureaucratic scandals of the 1990s seem to have reduced respect for bureaucrats considerably. See, for example, Mabuchi 1997, especially the "Introduction."

Politicians' best means of ensuring real fiscal policy change is often to use indirect tactics. These include public exhortations and threats to change the parameters within which MOF operates. For example, they might threaten to strip the ministry of some of its functions (not necessarily even functions connected to the battle at hand). These types of threats can lead to a costly political battle, but when credible, MOF must pay serious heed. Indeed, politicians used such tactics, with various results, in the years covered in this study.

Politicians also have the ability to alter fiscal policy directly, by changing tax policy or the official budget framework. There are considerable difficulties involved here, however. For one, actually carrying out a contentious policy is much more difficult than presenting a threat, even a credible one. Leaders would have to be able to convince backbenchers who might be swayed by the arguments of bureaucrats or who might have close, long-term, reciprocal connections with them. Also, even in fiscal policy, MOF has had the ability to circumvent formal policy, at least over the short term.

The Ministry of Finance has several ways to resist political dictates. For one thing, its broad jurisdictions and its control over microbudgeting provide considerable resources with which it can enlist allies even within the ruling party or coalition. This ability has for many years been further bolstered by the presence in the LDP of a large and influential group of former MOF officials who are wary of cutting the ministry down to size. Thus, political leaders are seldom able to garner enough support to carry through on really drastic threats.

Another point, which is perhaps particularly pertinent in the case of fiscal policy, but which often gives bureaucrats an advantage in political battles, is bureaucracies' ability to stall. To the extent that drafting of policies requires bureaucratic input—which it certainly does in Japan, where neither party research organizations nor independent think tanks are necessarily well-developed—foot-dragging can be a very effective tactic. Budgets in particular, due to their typically rigid calendars, have automatic inertia.

Where agencies seek to follow an independent path, another logical strategy is to manipulate information in such a way that politicians are not aware of what is being done. In other words, bureaucrats who wish to avoid accommodation or outright resistance may choose subterfuge—purporting to accommodate demands while actually not making effective changes. Obviously, this is easier to do in policy areas that hold little electoral advantage for individual politicians and are relatively technical. Subterfuge often appears less costly in terms of short-term political resources and control over a given function, but there is always the danger of detection and the resulting damage to reputation. The Ministry of Finance is uniquely equipped to make fiscal choices whose consequences are not what they appear, particularly through the use of trust funds and nontransparent accounting techniques, and through manipulation of official economic forecasts. Over time, however, subterfuge is a dangerous strategy, since long-term misinformation cannot work; it is thus primarily useful for short-term purposes. When short term turns into long term, as occurred in the 1990s, the bureaucracy may find itself in trouble.

A different way to think about the use of information is presented by Kato. She argues that in many cases ministries will only be able to gain the support of politicians by *sharing* information: "Utilizing their unique position as policy experts in the government, bureaucrats achieve an advantage through active involvement in politics—especially by exercising their influence on policy discourse and political agendas."[84] Between the mid-1970s and 2000 MOF bureaucrats consistently made great efforts to convince both LDP and non-LDP administrations that Japan's fiscal situation made further fiscal stimulation of the economy dangerous. In the end, however, even Kato's interpretation of bureaucratic information management hinges on selective, and thus strategic, presentation of evidence and analysis.

Finally, as I suggested earlier in this chapter, the Bank of Japan was less well-suited to carry out independent actions. It was thus limited to presenting technical arguments for its favored policies or waiting until political opportunity presented itself to carry out major policy changes, unless the leadership was willing to take on enormous, and perhaps permanently injurious, political pressure. While the BOJ leadership occasionally stood its ground, its ability to do so over a period of more than a few months was generally limited. The expanded autonomy granted by the 1997 BOJ Law revision released it to some extent from the game of macroeconomic politics.

Results

The result of this three-way interaction was that in general the fiscal goals of the Ministry of Finance would not be compromised in response to shocks in the short to medium term such as falling asset prices, weak growth, or foreign calls for policy coordination. The Ministry of Finance has been uniquely well-positioned as budgetmaker, gatekeeper of foreign input, and key influence on official macroeconomic projections; while it cannot block pressure, it can act as a filter by distributing information selectively, thus shaping political actors' perceptions of a given situation. Moreover, the essential immobility of fiscal policy, embodied in the budget calendar, gave MOF basic advantages in maintaining fiscal policy.

In the short term, politicians are generally not interested in macroeconomic policy, and are not sufficiently confident of their judgment in that area to override their putative agents in the ministry. They may well have more direct interest in exchange rates (especially if they are from export-dependent areas); again, however, they lack either the knowledge or the

84. Kato 1994, 7.

means to intervene directly.[85] The best they can do is make their feelings known to the bureaucrats; if the heat is turned up high enough, the bureaucrats will do what they feel is necessary to alter the situation or to appease the politicians. Over time, the temperature can become uncomfortably hot and can force more and more concessions on the fiscal front. However, because macroeconomic and many related matters have been delegated to the Ministry of Finance, even the LDP leadership was in general unable to affect them in the absence of some crisis and of the willingness to expend considerable political capital.[86]

In other words, the policy-making structure implied a preference ordering for state action. If international adjustment was necessary, the preferred first response was exchange rate intervention.[87] This is an easy guess, since most actors have an overall preference for stability in the exchange market anyway, and intervention need not have an appreciable impact on actual macroeconomic policies in any event.

When domestic adjustment was needed, or if exchange market intervention was insufficient to satisfy the situation, monetary rather than fiscal policy was the preferred first response. Again, this statement seems unremarkable on its face; monetary policy is by its nature more flexible than fiscal policy—for response to short-term conditions, a change in monetary policy is the economically rational measure. Also, economic theory makes clear that monetary policy has the most direct influence on exchange rates, and that for open economies monetary policy has greater transmission effects to other countries, which is useful in instances of international coordination.[88] My point here is slightly different. The game I have laid out suggests that *long-term, unbalanced reliance on monetary policy will occur before any alteration in fiscal policy.* Moreover, if intervention signaled changes in macroeconomic policy, it would be expected to signal *monetary* policy change, even though intervention is controlled by the Ministry of Finance. (Almost all intervention in practice has been against yen revaluation, so the policy change in question is invariably expansionary.) One caveat to the general picture

85. Kojo (1993) argues that political parties have been hypersensitive to the desires of small export-oriented businesses for an undervalued yen. She does not provide a mechanism through which politicians directly affect exchange rate intervention; instead, she argues that (except in 1985–86) they have sought to use fiscal policy rather than yen revaluation to rectify external payments imbalances.

86. For a full analysis of the crisis dynamic in Japanese policy making, see Calder 1988a, esp. chaps. 1–4, 11.

87. Some readers may object that exchange rate intervention by governments and central banks is bound to have little or no effect, citing theoretical, empirical, and even anecdotal evidence. This point is largely true (though for a somewhat contrary view, see Dominguez and Frankel 1993). Nonetheless, finance ministry and central banks officials throughout the world clearly believe that intervention does *something*, otherwise they would not waste money and effort on it. Since my interest is policy making and not policy effectiveness, theirs is the judgment that matters most.

88. Based on the standard Mundell-Fleming model.

of expansionary pressure is that the nature of monetary policy makes it much more flexible than fiscal policy in responding to economic overheating—thus, when inflationary pressures are clear, monetary tightening will always precede fiscal austerity.

The final step down in the preference ladder was fiscal policy. While MOF would make every attempt to avoid that circumstance, if other measures were ineffective for long enough to produce significant political pressure, fiscal policy was not sacred. The ministry was thus left with damage control—trying to minimize the effect on its central objective of control over the budget by resisting either overtly or covertly. We see examples of both in the period covered in this study. Over time, however, obfuscation and intransigence lose their effectiveness. If the crisis passes in a couple of years, then things settle down to normal again. But if the crisis continues, as it did from the early 1990s until at least 2000, overoptimistic forecasts of the effects of fiscal stimulus packages or of general prospects for the economy are in time shown to be incorrect. The resulting heightened political interest leads to heightened political involvement, and politicians begin to be able to use some methods that are not credible threats over the short term, including their right to veto top-level promotions. In such circumstances, outcomes shift toward greater fiscal expansion. As for monetary policy over such a period, the overall weakness of the BOJ's political position before 1998 meant that it would be heavily constrained for the duration.

The Post-1998 Era

In 1998 a number of key structural variables changed, leading to a major change in the game of macroeconomic politics. Chapters 2, 3, 7, and 8 contain much more detail on the changes and their effects, but a quick summary at this point should be useful.

There were two major structural-legal changes in 1998: the implementation of a revised Bank of Japan Law and the establishment of the Financial Supervision Agency (since renamed the Financial Services Agency). In addition, from 1993 onward evolutionary structural change is evident in the types of networks developed by policy makers in the field of macroeconomic policy. All of these factors were important in reducing the power and networks of the Ministry of Finance.

By legally affirming the monetary policy autonomy of the BOJ and explicitly taking away many of MOF's former privileges, the Bank of Japan Law revision freed the bank from MOF control. The bank's autonomy was further increased by the removal of MOF "old boys" (OBs) from its top ranks. The establishment of the FSA was the first step toward completely removing domestic financial regulation and oversight from MOF, a process that was completed in July 2000. With the loss of its monetary policy and financial regulatory functions, the ministry lost its comprehensiveness, and thus its control over important sources of information and political power. Meanwhile, politicians from all the major parties gained access to more information and expertise in the area of macroeconomic policy than they had ever had before.

The effects on macroeconomic politics are profound. Most obviously, monetary policy has largely been taken out of the political arena. The Bank of Japan must still address the needs of society, and it is officially answerable to the Diet, but for the most part it has near total independence in making decisions in the short term. Fiscal policy, by contrast, is back in the political arena. The weakened Ministry of Finance now faces politicians who are bolder than at any time since the 1970s, and better informed than at any point in probably the entire postwar period.

Institutional strategies are likely to remain roughly similar, but their effectiveness has changed. Thus, we see a new preference ordering for macroeconomic policy. While monetary policy is still most capable of addressing problems rapidly, fiscal policy has become much more flexible and responsive to economic fluctuations, and it is likely to stay that way. In the old game, fiscal policy was relatively fixed, and monetary policy had to accommodate any major shocks. In the new game, it is fiscal policy that is expected to deal with shocks whose effects extend beyond the short term.

Finally, to add two nonpolitical variables to the pot, Japan's aging society and the immensity of its public debt mean that long-run fiscal consolidation will again be necessary. This is likely to reduce politicians' leeway in responding to economic downturns, but for the structural reasons given, it is not likely to return effective power over the path of consolidation to the Ministry of Finance.

2

Institutional Actors

> No agency head can ever achieve complete autonomy for his or her organization.... The best a government executive can do is to minimize the number of rivals and constraints.
>
> James Q. Wilson, *Bureaucracy*

In this chapter I flesh out the previous schematic description of the institutional actors, and examine the resources and constraints under which the Ministry of Finance, the Bank of Japan, and politicians must operate—their relevant legal jurisdictions, individual career paths, and management of information.

Career paths and information management patterns are central to understanding an organization's power. The macroeconomic policy game is played in an environment of asymmetric information, which means that the ability to appropriate and assimilate relevant information is key to an institutional actor's ability to realize its goals. Thus, it is important to show clearly the information capabilities and networks of the major actors, and to demonstrate how they affect the macroeconomic policy-making process.

MOF Resources and Constraints

The Ministry of Finance has had a degree of authority over macroeconomic policy making and implementation, as well as regulation of financial institutions and markets, that is unusual among advanced industrial countries.[1] Tax policy and collection, budget making, and legal (and to some extent prudential) regulation of financial institutions and insurance companies have all been centralized in the ministry. It also administers the very substantial trust funds and assets of the government. Finally, it has considerable authority over international economic policy, including sole authority over exchange market intervention. (The last of MOF's authority over the domestic financial system was transferred to the Financial Services Agency in

1. Cargill (1989, 48) calls it an "encompassing government entity."

July 2000, while the governmental reorganization in January 2001 bestows on MOF a new Japanese name [*Zaimushō,* or Treasury Ministry], although the English name remains unchanged.[2])

Organization

Until 1998, the Ministry of Finance was divided into seven internal bureaus, the Minister's Secretariat, two external bureaus, and the National Tax Administration. (In June 1998, the supervisory functions of the Securities and Banking Bureaus were stripped from the ministry, and the Financial System Planning Bureau formed from what remained. In July 2000, MOF also lost its role as drafter of financial regulation when that bureau was eliminated and its functions were shifted to the new Financial Services Agency.) In addition, MOF controls ten regional finance bureaus, twelve regional taxation bureaus and their subordinate offices, and the nation's customs houses. For macroeconomic policy, the most important organs are the Budget, Financial, and International (until 1998, International Finance) Bureaus, and the Minister's Secretariat.[3] All of these remained in the ministry following the reorganization of January 2001.

The Budget Bureau is by tradition the most powerful in the ministry. One indication of this power is that from 1960 to 2000, twenty out of thirty administrative vice-ministers (the top civil servant position) were former Budget Bureau chiefs (officially, directors-general).[4] Also, the chief of the Budget Bureau is a salary grade above the chiefs of other bureaus, and invariably has already been the chief of another bureau. The power of the Budget Bureau, which derives from the political importance of the budget, makes budgeting the central concern of all MOF decision making. The bureau is broken down into functional (for example, the Coordination, Research, and Legal Divisions) and funding areas. For each broad funding area, there is a budget examiner, who with his staff evaluates budget requests from the various ministries and then drafts a proposed budget.

The Financial Bureau is a step down from the Budget Bureau in the hierarchy. Its function is to manage the assets and liabilities of the Japanese government. As treasurer, the bureau manages the current inflows and outflows of the government and structures its debt. From the perspective of macroeconomic policy, its most important function is its stewardship of na-

2. This reorganization has been in the works since the early days of the Hashimoto administration, stretching back to 1996. It entails a large-scale restructuring of virtually all ministries and agencies, as well as a strengthening of the Cabinet Office (*naikakufu*), formerly the Prime Minister's Office. Management and Coordination Agency, "Supplementary Data on Administrative Reform in Japan," mimeo, February 28, 2000.

3. The other internal bureaus are the Tax Bureau and Customs and Tariffs. The external bureaus, which are of no interest in terms of policy, are the Mint and Printing Bureaus.

4. *Ōkurashō Meikan* 2000, 348–351.

tional trust funds (including postal savings, government shares of privatized industries, and national pension funds) through short-term financial investments and through the Fiscal Investment and Loan Program (FILP, or *zaiseitōyūshi*). It also manages government-owned property and businesses.

The International Bureau (formerly the International Finance Bureau) has several functions, including regulation of international financial transactions by Japanese financial institutions and businesses and foreign aid policy. It also oversees Japan's international monetary commitments, including exchange market intervention and liaison with international economic organizations such as the World Bank, the International Monetary Fund, and the Organization for Economic Cooperation and Development.

The top official in international finance, the *zaimukan* (a position created in 1968, and officially translated as vice-minister of finance for international affairs), is not technically a part of the International Bureau, but since the early 1970s the position has invariably been assigned to an outgoing chief of that bureau (although not all International Bureau chiefs become *zaimukan*). The *zaimukan*'s job is essentially to act as representative of the Ministry of Finance in all deputy-level international conferences, meetings, and negotiations. The *zaimukan* is also responsible for setting the international strategy of the ministry.

The Minister's Secretariat is the center of information management within the ministry. It is responsible for internal coordination of policies, personnel policies, internal management, internal research and planning, and coordination with other agencies, including the Bank of Japan. Its head (the *kanbōchō*, or deputy vice-minister), while technically equivalent in rank to a bureau chief, is usually promoted from the ranks of run-of-the-mill bureau chiefs, and often moves on to become chief of the Budget Bureau, and then administrative vice-minister.[5] The secretariat itself is not large and has no specific policy jurisdiction, but it plays a role in policy making and in formulating the incentives MOF bureaucrats face in their careers. Perhaps its most important role is in personnel, where it helps to place retiring officials in *amakudari* jobs and to manage personnel within the ministry. The secretariat, as the locus of all personnel information and decision making, has a significant role in the socialization of bureaucrats and in enforcing ministry norms. It is nonetheless important not to overstate the role of the secretariat: MOF has maintained its reputation as being "all bureaus, no ministry" for good reason. Even the relatively small size of the secretariat is inflated by the listing of a number of officials who are only nominally attached to it, and who actually work full-time in one of the bureaus.[6] In other words, cen-

---

5. From 1970 to 2000, thirteen out of nineteen *kanbōchō* had gone on to become administrative vice-minister before leaving the ministry. *Ōkurashō Meikan* 2000, 350–351.
6. For example, of the twelve *shingikan* ("councillor of the Minister's Secretariat"), only three are actually assigned to the secretariat; the rest are more accurately described by the official

tral coordination is not the norm for MOF policy making, thus making informal, or horizontal, management of information all the more crucial.

Career Paths

Like other Japanese government ministries, MOF is an archetypal professional bureaucracy. Elite-class bureaucrats join directly out of university and staff virtually all positions of responsibility below the minister.[7] The maximum length of career in the ministry runs slightly over thirty years, but even those who never reach the level of bureau chief tend to stay in the ministry for more than twenty years. MOF elite change jobs every one to two years, both within and among bureaus. Career advancement generally depends on broad experience in a number of different functional areas, although the highest fliers tend to have a particularly deep expertise in the all-important budget function.

Recruitment

The stereotype of the Japanese bureaucracy is of a cadre of highly capable and motivated, if overworked and underpaid, male graduates of the Law Faculty of the University of Tokyo (Tōdai). They are expected to spend their careers in the bureaucracy, eventually to retire into comfortable *amakudari* sinecures. Of all the government bureaucracies, the Ministry of Finance is perhaps truest to these stereotypes. To begin with, elite MOF bureaucrats belong to a small and select group, the size of an entering "class" ranging from the low- to mid-twenties (dropping under twenty with the removal of domestic finance from MOF's jurisdiction). The concentration of Tōdai graduates has seldom slipped below 75 percent.[8] Hiring is done through the demanding higher civil service examination. According to a late 1980s analysis, a candidate had to score among the top fifty exam-takers to have a realistic shot at one of the approximately twenty-five spots at the Ministry of Finance.[9]

English translation of their titles, "deputy director-general of the _____ Bureau." The same is true to a lesser extent of the lower-ranking *sanjikan* ("counselor of the Minister's Secretariat") and *kikakukan* ("special officer"). See *Ōkurashō Meikan* (any year) for titles and translations. On the small size of the secretariat in MOF, see Calder 1993, 96–98.

7. Until January 2001, there were also two parliamentary vice ministers, one each from the Lower and Upper Houses. However, they are usually excluded from discussions of the bureaucracy for the simple reason that they had no real role in policy making. Since January 2001, a more elaborate system of political oversight, including the appointment of Diet members as deputy ministers (*fuku daijin*), has been in effect in all ministries.

8. Koh 1989, 92; Kawakita 1989, 123; *Kanryō kyokuhi jinjiroku* 1996, 16–17. Again, "elite" refers not to those bureaucrats who hold the top ranks in a given ministry, but to all bureaucrats who have passed the higher civil service examination. There are many other employees of each ministry, but they are essentially support staff, and are unable to rise to the top levels in the hierarchy.

9. Koh 1989, 78.

Socialization

Once hired, recruits undergo a brief period of training, and then receive their first assignments. From then on, they will change jobs every year or two and will gain experience in a broad range of policy areas. Through the subsequent series of one- or two-year positions in various offices, they will gain a breadth, and eventually depth, of experience that will serve them and the ministry well as they move up the career ladder. As Aoki notes in a corporate context, "the job rotation system facilitates *knowledge sharing* among workers in the following sense: The knowledge possessed by a single worker extends beyond a particular job jurisdiction."[10]

Perhaps even more than marriage, the decision to enter the Ministry of Finance implies a lifetime commitment. The ministry will occupy the bulk of the bureaucrat's time and energy until he retires, and will have profound implications for his employment after he leaves. In most cases, he will stay with the ministry until the relentless "up or out" system eases him out. At that point, personnel managers in the secretariat will help him to find a new job, either with a public corporation or financial institution or in the private sector.[11]

The process of socialization of a MOF bureaucrat is essentially carried out on the job, although a number of important informal means come into play as well.[12] I will not attempt to provide a comprehensive description of this socialization, but the incentive structure for the typical bureaucrat is clear: buying into the organizational ethos will promote his career.[13] Such socialization is self-reinforcing from an evolutionary standpoint, insofar as those bureaucrats who buy into the ethos are also the most likely to rise high in the ranks. The result has been the elevation of the MOF ideal almost into a religion.

The "MOF Religion"

The fundamental values a bureaucrat is expected to hold are those that maximize the autonomy and influence of his ministry, with which his own

10. Aoki 1988, 15, emphasis in original. Aoki argues that a strong and centralized personnel system is necessary for the efficient operation of any organization with long-term careers and job rotation.

11. Actually, private-sector jobs involve an additional approval stage through the National Personnel Authority (*Jinji-in*). Nevertheless, the real contact between the OB and his new employer is through the secretariat. For specifics, see Schaede 1995.

12. Prominent among these are the experience of living with other bureaucrats in ministry dormitories and apartments, and informal drinking sessions with bosses and colleagues. In keeping with the marriage analogy from the preceding paragraph, mentors are often responsible for arranging marriages, extending the relationship with the ministry even further into the personal sphere. Indeed, the secretariat's Secretarial Division offers help in arranging marriages to officials in their late twenties who have not had luck on their own. Personal interviews.

13. As March and Olsen point out, traditional institutionalists will often describe individual action in terms of duty rather than choice—"political actors associate certain actions with certain

fortunes are so closely entwined. The "MOF religion" can be summed up in two words: discipline and control. These are not surprising tenets for a career bureaucrat's ethos,[14] but MOF officials often carry them to extremes. The discipline on which the ministry most prides itself is fiscal discipline, particularly on the spending side. MOF bureaucrats are socialized to see their ministry as a ruthless agent of efficiency, set on balancing national budgets and cutting unnecessary spending. The ideal of discipline extends also to the individual, who is expected to be willing to dedicate himself to long hours at modest pay, in a relentless display of self-sacrifice seldom seen in other wealthy nations outside of wartime conditions.

The other part of the MOF ethos is control. MOF bureaucrats have seen the ministry as the central figure in the financial sector, maintaining the sector's health and stability only through vigilance and strict regulation.[15] (It was MOF's failures in this regard that led to the loss of its financial system oversight and planning functions.) In order to maintain discipline in the budget and (in the past) control in the markets, the ministry must defend its autonomy against actors that may constrain it. Bureaucrats are thus expected to defend vigorously the prerogatives and missions of the ministry against all comers, particularly politicians and competing agencies.[16] In this way, the integrity of the ministry becomes bound up in the minds of its cadres with the very stability and health of the Japanese economy.

Amakudari

The effects of socialization reach beyond an official's career as a bureaucrat, into post-retirement jobs. *Amakudari* presents an important and interesting case of the effects of socialization into the ministerial ethos. While some good studies of *amakudari* are available, they tend to be only suggestive about how the former bureaucrat actually behaves. Within some of the literature there is an assumption that he is an instrument of ministry control over his new place of work.[17] Other analysts, focusing on the demand side, point out that corporations are most interested in maximizing their influence with their regulatory agency, which suggests that the former bureau-

---

situations by rules of appropriateness. What is appropriate for a particular person in a particular situation is defined by the political and social system and transmitted through socialization" (1984, 741). I argue that people keep to their duties because of the consequences associated with carrying or not carrying them out.

14. See, for example, Niskanen 1971; Wilson 1989.

15. Rosenbluth (1989) discusses why this urge is so strong. Johnson (1989) also describes bureaucratic turf-consciousness, while Vogel (1996) shows that MOF's desire for strict vigilance comes through even in the process of financial liberalization.

16. See, for example, Shiota 1995; Kishi 1996; Asahi Shimbun Economics Bureau 1997.

17. Johnson 1982, 70–73.

crat is co-opted by his association with his new employer.[18] A more cynical view is that *amakudari* constitutes a "spoils" system for bureaucrats that yields neither more efficient bureaucratic control nor benefits to firms.[19] Certainly the most complex case is that of bureaucrats-turned-politicians, whose incentives are particularly convoluted. I consider them after considering the general case.

One determinant of a bureaucrat's post-retirement activities is surely socialization—having spent half of one's life adhering to a given set of ideals, anyone who is not extremely cynical or disaffected is likely to accept those ideals as a filter for understanding related issues. To the extent that a given analysis leads generally to a limited set of responses, and to the extent that the former bureaucrat's new goals do not differ too markedly from those of the ministry, his thinking should not diverge strongly from that of active MOF bureaucrats.

Moreover, he faces incentives to maintain his allegiance to the ideals and goals of the ministry. His value to his new organization depends very much on his continued close relations with his erstwhile colleagues at the ministry.[20] Continuing these relations, cemented during his active years by mutual efforts in the interest of the ministry, hinges on a continued sharing of the values that once held them together. From a more personal standpoint, the ministry has in a very real sense been the retired bureaucrat's social life, and even extended family. Rare is the man who cavalierly rejects some of the closest personal ties he has ever experienced.[21] The fact that the ministry also tends to arrange subsequent *amakudari* jobs makes that decision even less palatable.

Bureaucrats-Turned-Politicians

Bureaucrats-turned-politicians constitute a special case within the overall category of *amakudari,* for two reasons. First, they are the only OBs ("Old Boys," as retired bureaucrats are popularly known) who are in a position to affect MOF policy directly, rather than be affected by it. Their relationships

18. Both Calder (1989) and van Rixtel (1994) offer evidence that regional banks have higher concentrations of *amakudari* than city banks. Since regional banks have less natural political influence, the implication is that they attempt to purchase it by hiring MOF retirees. Schaede (1995) argues that bureaucratic OBs are in greatest demand at those firms that are subject to regulation or "external constraints" (trade) managed through administrative guidance by their regulating agency.

19. Nakano 1998a.

20. For the basis of this argument, see Calder 1989. The former bureaucrat in this model is seen as a mediator, ensuring a sort of bureaucratic "gains from trade": he may be expected by each side to understand and represent its interests to the other when a conflict arises.

21. Evidence for this statement may be found in the undisguised nostalgia ex-bureaucrats exhibit for their former organizations. Ministries reciprocate the affection, providing retirees with both comprehensive directories of the positions of all active and retired bureaucrats and regular opportunities to socialize with former colleagues and subordinates. Personal interviews and direct observation.

with their former colleagues are thus at least potentially shaped by the structure of power that results. Second, MOF OB politicians tend to leave the ministry much earlier in their careers than the average retiring bureaucrat. While their MOF socialization may remain an important factor in their political judgments, it is by no means a foregone conclusion that it will be decisive. Identification with the MOF ethos should be expected to increase with seniority and position within the ministry. Moreover, those who are successful as politicians may well not be those who would be successful remaining within the bureaucracy.[22] Since intrabureaucratic survival of the fittest will tend to favor those who adopt the credo, at least some of those who make a rational decision to opt out of the Ministry probably have a lower degree of enthusiasm for that credo.

Unfortunately, there is little solid evidence that addresses the question of whether MOF OBs in the Diet tend to work with or against their former colleagues. It is thus also impossible to determine whether such factors as length of service in the ministry or Diet have any effect on how these OBs act. We are left with only public declarations, and journalistic and scholarly analyses of specific politicians. And there is clearly variation among individual OBs.

One study argues that the Ministry of Finance has been able to remain far more autonomous than any other government bureaucracy in the face of considerable political pressure because of "the existence of a corps of Finance Ministry bureaucrats-turned-politicians." The authors attribute this to the importance of *zoku* policy making, in which groups of Diet members with special expertise and interests tend to dominate policy making in a given area. Because financial issues are so complex, the finance *zoku* in the LDP has been dominated by MOF OBs, making it a kind of "MOF OB Club."[23]

Nonetheless, it is clear that these OBs face a real dilemma. It is always tempting for politicians to try to shape budget and tax policy to the advantage of their constituents. Members of the finance *zoku*, like other politicians, find it necessary to make promises to their constituents and to make deals with other politicians at the expense of fiscal stringency.[24] Moreover, the finance group is relatively small. In the end, even if MOF OBs are generally loyal to their former organization, the ministry must still depend on the patronage of top LDP officials in order to keep control over core functions.

This is best seen in two areas. The first is financial regulation, where competition between banks and securities firms, and among different types of

22. There is at least some anecdotal evidence for this statement. For example, I was told by an LDP staffer that a particular MOF man with strong political connections would probably not go into electoral politics for a while because his career was going so well within the ministry. If his bureaucratic career were to plateau, however, he would be expected to run for the Diet. As it turned out, the man was elected as an LDP Diet member while still successful in his MOF career.

23. Inoguchi and Iwai 1987, 206, 208, and see 205–209 on MOF OB politicians.

24. Inoguchi and Iwai 1987, 208.

banks, has been fought out in the political arena to a considerable degree.[25] The second is the budget, where in the late 1960s the ministry lost a great deal of control over budgeting;[26] one of its great victories in the 1980s was regaining control over fiscal outcomes, although the 1990s have seen yet another reversal of fortune.

Implications

These personnel practices have a variety of implications, at both personal and organizational levels.[27] The absence of outsiders from decision-making positions suggests that the views of the elite bureaucrats, rather than those of each new administration, will be reflected in ministry policy drafts, and especially in implementation of regulations. Not surprisingly, MOF tends toward conservatism and toward broadening its jurisdiction.

A second important implication is for the management of information. Communications are maintained within the Ministry informally as well as formally. Informal methods include both horizontal and vertical means, ensuring that when necessary, communication will be both swift and based on a considerable degree of common knowledge.

Third, this career pattern maximizes the likelihood of effective internal coordination, without resorting to outside actors such as politicians (as is occasionally necessary between ministries).[28] This is an extremely important function given the fragmented nature of power in the Japanese political economy. The principle of internal coordination holds true in spite of the reputation of the ministry as "all bureaus, no ministry." Retired and current senior officials almost invariably describe interbureau coordination as occurring "between friends."[29] While it is undoubtedly not the case that such negotiations are entirely noncompetitive, or that all top MOF bureaucrats are actually friends, this sort of statement is indicative of a very important facet of intra-ministry relations. By the time officials reach the level of bureau chief, they have known each other for nearly thirty years (and often longer, given the concentration of University of Tokyo Law Faculty graduates among entering classes), and can reasonably expect their performances to have an impact on their imminent post-ministry careers. Thus, they have a good idea of what to expect from each other, as well as a strong incentive to behave cooperatively for the benefit of future encounters.

25. Rosenbluth 1989; Horne 1985, 1988; Vogel 1996.
26. This was the result of slowing growth, rising demands from citizens for policies that required large-scale spending, and declining LDP advantage over opposition parties. See Mabuchi 1994; Yamaguchi 1987; Noguchi 1993; Campbell 1977.
27. This phase of the argument applies to any agency, Japanese or otherwise, where these basic conditions apply, as Aoki (1988) suggests.
28. Johnson 1989; Horne 1985.
29. Personal interviews.

Finally, retirement after thirty years or less raises the necessity of *amaku-dari* jobs. Public sector *amakudari* jobs (sometimes called *yoko-suberi*, or "side-slipping") include board and management positions on various government financial institutions, commissions, and public corporations. The OBs in such positions serve to extend both the control and the information-gathering capabilities of the ministry, acting essentially as much better paid, slightly more independent representatives of the ministry. In private-sector jobs the roles are somewhat more complex, because organizations must benefit from hiring the OB. This means that flows of information and considerations of the other party's interests must be more mutual. Thus, research on *amakudari* among financial institutions suggests that those banks with the greatest need of consideration from MOF and the BOJ have been the most likely to take on OBs from each bureaucracy.[30] In both public and private cases, however, regular communication between current and former MOF bureaucrats ensures that the ministry has ample, privileged information on which to base its policies.

BOJ Resources and Constraints

The main counterpart to the Ministry of Finance in macroeconomic and exchange rate policy is the Bank of Japan. As Japan's central bank, the BOJ's official goals are "price stability" and the "maintenance of an orderly financial system."[31] Operationally, it is responsible for monetary policy and prudential oversight of banks, and is the lender of last resort to financial institutions in need of additional funds. While these are its technical functions, however, the BOJ also exists within a separate political world that revolves not around the minutiae of financial data or even around dealings with its financial sector clients, but around the Bank's relationships with the Ministry of Finance and elected politicians. In this world the BOJ long found itself at a distinct disadvantage, forcing it to struggle to increase its autonomy. In a comparative sense as well, the BOJ was considered one of the world's least independent central banks—Cukierman rated it nineteenth out of twenty-one developed country central banks, while Grilli, Masciandaro, and Tabellini gave it only one point out of six on their scale of political independence.[32] Only when the revised BOJ Law came into effect in 1998 did that struggle change qualitatively.

30. Calder 1989; van Rixtel 1994; Schaede 1995.
31. Bank of Japan Law (revised, 1998), Articles 1–2.
32. Eijffinger and de Haan 1996, 23. Other measures rank the BOJ as somewhat more independent, but on average, observers acknowledged its high level of dependence.

Career Patterns

Elite career patterns at the Bank of Japan resemble those at the Ministry of Finance (or, for that matter, at any Japanese ministry or large corporation), although the bank tends to select more economics graduates than law graduates. As in the ministry, officials rotate through domestically and internationally oriented jobs, changing positions every one to three years. Like the Ministry of Finance, the Bank of Japan encourages continuing education, and sends its young employees abroad to study subjects such as economics, finance, and international relations. Finally, officials tend to stay with the Bank for most of their working lives, after which they retire to *amakudari* jobs, largely in private-sector financial institutions.

In general, however, BOJ networks are not as extensive as MOF's. In particular, they do not span the political divide—BOJ officials-turned-politicians remain a rarity, secondment to government ministries is limited, and even OBs in government financial institutions tend not to be directly in charge of key policy decisions. This isolation limits the flexibility of the bank in virtually any area that brings it into conflict with official government actors.

The Shadow of the Ministry of Finance

One interesting feature of BOJ personnel practices is the cultivation of so-called "princes"—individuals among the elite-track bank employees who are identified early (in their thirties) as being of BOJ Governor caliber. There are only one or two "princes" in a given set of five entering classes, and they are moved through the most important slots in the bank and watched carefully. The reason for this assiduous nurturing is that the "princes" are expected to serve an exceedingly important function—to stand up to the hegemonic Ministry of Finance on behalf of career BOJ officials. It is therefore not surprising to find that two common attributes among BOJ "princes" are having graduated from the University of Tokyo's Faculty of Law and having turned down an employment offer from the Ministry of Finance.[33]

Of more direct importance is the nature of personnel exchanges between the BOJ and MOF: they have been almost entirely one-way, from ministry to bank.[34] From 1969 to 1998, the top two posts (governor and deputy governor) alternated between MOF OBs and BOJ "princes." (In 1998, after MOF OB Matsushita Yasuo was forced to step down in order to take responsibility for a series of scandals, the pattern was broken; the new governor, Hayami

33. Personal interviews. This was the case with at least two of the most prominent career BOJ officials of the last two decades—Maekawa Haruo and Mieno Yasushi (Fujiwara 1991).
34. At lower levels (deputy division chief and below), exchanges are more reciprocal, but there are very few—for example, there is generally one MOF junior official in the BOJ Market Operations Division, and there generally used to be a single BOJ official working in the ministry in bank oversight. Personal interviews.

Masaru, was a former high-ranking BOJ official.) This is an enormously important fact, given the high internal centralization of authority vested in the governor.[35] Even when the governor was a career BOJ official, the deputy governor was a MOF OB who had access to the same information as the governor. In addition, of the seven executive directors, one was traditionally a retiring MOF Banking Bureau official, with responsibility for bank oversight. The final upper-echelon MOF official, a non-voting member of the BOJ's formerly somnolent Policy Board, may have been superfluous in function, but also symbolized the continuing watchfulness of the ministry. (That position was eliminated by the revised BOJ Law, but MOF still has the right to send a representative to Policy Board meetings.)

Partially in response, the operational departments of the BOJ embrace secrecy as their basic *modus operandi*. The bank is generally successful in maintaining technocratic confidentiality; however, there are significant limits to its ability to do so in monetary policy.

Amakudari

It is in the post-retirement careers of BOJ officials that differences between their career paths as individuals and those of MOF bureaucrats become most apparent. The fifty or so elite-track officials who retire each year tend to move into regional banks and financial institutions, or financial industry associations, rather than into government financial institutions or other public-sector jobs.[36] Since the BOJ does not have the substantial cushion of public-sector *amakudari* jobs that MOF has, high-ranking bank officials are largely dependent on private-sector financial institutions for their continuing employment. Several implications follow from this pattern. First, the Bank of Japan must take financial sector interests very seriously. Second, it cannot have the kind of broad hegemony over public agencies and institutions that MOF and other powerful ministries have. While bank OBs can be found on the boards of various public financial institutions, their concentration among all BOJ retirees is much lower than among MOF OBs. Where they find themselves in the same organizations as ministry retirees, they are usually subordinate to the latter. Thus, even to the extent that bank OBs pursue the interests of the BOJ as an organization, their ability to shape the financial sphere to their liking is quite limited, given their typical positions in regional banks and as subordinates to ministry OBs in public-sector financial institutions.

A second characteristic that distinguishes BOJ retirees from their MOF counterparts is involvement in electoral politics. As of May 2000 only two

---

35. The 1997 BOJ Law revision was meant to reduce some of that authority in favor of a revitalized Policy Board.

36. Calder 1989; van Rixtel 1994; Schaede 1995; Tsutsumi 1997.

former BOJ officials were members of the Diet, both rather new, in contrast
to twenty-one former MOF bureaucrats in the Lower House.[37] This is not a
historical anomaly—the one major example of a BOJ OB who had a prominent political career was former Governor Ichimada Naoto, who was finance
minister from 1954 to 1956 and from 1957 to 1958.[38]

Political involvement has proved problematic for the Bank of Japan for
several reasons.[39] Most importantly, it lacks the political advantages of a Cabinet ministry—it is not headed even nominally by a powerful politician, it is
not directly involved in lawmaking, and it is generally not in a position to
grant subsidies or favors to important political interests. Bank officials have
relatively little to make them attractive to potential political mentors other
than their expertise. The one area where bank jurisdictions would seem to
have major political implications for specific constituencies is financial institution oversight, which politicians could more easily affect through the
Ministry of Finance before 1998, and through the Financial Supervision
Agency (since July 2000, the Financial Services Agency) and Financial Reconstruction Commission (subsumed under the FSA as of January 2001) after 1998. Thus, politicians have not gone out of their way to cultivate BOJ
bureaucrats, and BOJ officials' contacts with the political world are quite cir-
cumscribed. The result is that there simply is not a pool of BOJ bureaucrats
with sufficient political connections to be electorally viable. This effect is
only heightened by the need for the central bank to be seen as a technocratic, nonpolitical agency.

While the lack of political connections certainly reduces day-do-day political involvement in bank policy making and implementation, it actually
increases the vulnerability of the BOJ to political pressures when they are
brought to bear. Because of its lack of contact, and particularly its lack of
OBs in the Diet, the BOJ has relatively little influence over the formation
of policies (laws and Cabinet Orders) that affect it directly. Ironically, this
was true to a surprising degree even of the 1997 BOJ Law revision that so
increased its autonomy. Instead the bank has had to go through its financial sector constituency or the Ministry of Finance to affect the political process. This route had obvious dangers if the bank happened to
be in disagreement with the ministry over a given issue, but the BOJ's political precariousness generally left it little choice but to embrace its some-
time rival.

---

37. *Seikan Yōran* 1999, Insert, 7–10.
38. For basic data, see Satō and Matsuzaki 1986, esp. pt. III. In the late 1950s, he tried to form
his own faction in order to become a major power in the LDP, a venture that lasted less than
two years (1986, 241).
39. The following draws on a number of personal interviews.

MOF Management of Information

Each element of information management is closely linked to the management of personnel. Indeed, Aoki describes Japanese personnel practices as working to solve the problem of "providing the employee ... with the incentive to develop the skills, knowledge, expertise, and cooperative attitude needed to effectively operate the horizontal informational structure."[40] Management of information falls into two categories: internal and external. The external side must be further divided into inflow (acquisition) and outflow (outputs and secrecy). While the preceding analysis of career paths has particular relevance to the internal management of information and to managing the outflow of information, I will begin with acquisition, and then progress to processing and transmission.

Information Gathering

The ministry's main asset in the acquisition of useful information has been its vast jurisdiction—its powers in budget making and taxation, its treasury functions, its erstwhile authority to investigate the financial institutions it regulated, the process of making regulatory policy, and its network of OBs placed in various important positions in the financial sector and the world of politics. Here I confine myself to techniques that are of direct relevance to macroeconomic policy.

Budgeting and taxation provide MOF with key data on macroeconomic trends while also supplying important political information. Besides the overall size of the budget, which is clearly important, MOF budget examiners receive detailed sectoral and regional data to justify budget requests. Perhaps more important is the political information conveyed during the budget-making process—Diet members get closely involved in budget items that are near and dear to constituents and support groups.[41] By watching out for the interests of well-placed Diet members in microbudgeting, the ministry can expect cooperation on matters more central to its missions.

The ministry's tax role is similarly important. In the policy-making stages, the ministry gains the same sort of political information provided by budgeting. Tax collection also provides useful data. Through monthly and quarterly tax receipts, MOF learns almost immediately about changes in the nation's fiscal position and in the economy at large.[42] According to rumor, the ministry is also able to use knowledge of tax code violations by politicians to ensure that

40. Aoki 1988, 49.
41. See Campbell (1977, passim) for a detailed picture.
42. The office of the deputy vice minister for policy coordination prepares monthly reports and forecasts of economic activity that are not released to outsiders (including the minister), and officially do not exist. Personal interviews. Opinion varies as to the sophistication and accuracy of these internal analyses.

its autonomy is not threatened by its ostensible parliamentary overseers. Meanwhile, MOF's Financial Bureau disburses budgeted (and FILP and special account) funds and keeps track of government spending as it occurs.

The regulatory activities of the Ministry of Finance similarly provided a window on the Japanese economy and financial system. Until June 1998, the ministry's main tool for obtaining information on the banking system was its right of inspection of all financial institutions. MOF bank inspections were comprehensive matters, allowing ministry officials to examine any and all records they considered relevant, including lending practices and credit evaluations.[43] Such examinations gave MOF insight into the condition of the financial system, and also allowed the ministry to ensure that banks were following ministry directives, whether formal or informal. (Unfortunately, they did not always guarantee sound banking practice, as the 1990s demonstrated.)

The making of regulatory policy and ministry approval procedures also afforded MOF extensive opportunities to find out about financial institutions, at least until 1998 (approvals) or 2000 (regulatory policy). More important than formal hearings was the constant and extensive dialogue with interesting parties. During drafting of laws concerning financial institutions, for example, it was not unusual for several dozen industry representatives to visit relevant divisions each day.[44] Corporate activities that required ministry approval or licensing provided another opening for regulators to gaze into the inner workings of the financial institutions making the applications. For example, until well into the 1990s, bond underwriting by securities companies required MOF approval. Since this effectively gave the ministry approval over domestic bond issuance by any Japanese corporate actor, its impact extended well beyond the financial sector.[45]

Externally, officials often meet with relevant politicians and employees of companies under their jurisdiction. Groups also invite officials to speak at industry gatherings; after-hours meetings expand the scope of contact even more. However, while considerable information is exchanged, the incentive remains not to transmit information that would be harmful to the ministry—slips are simply too likely to be detected and to work to the detriment of one's career. (One the other hand, events in 1997 and 1998 made clear that one piece of information that did pass from MOF to some banks was the timing of "surprise inspections"—a very useful fact for banks to know.

43. Personal interviews. Carrying out an extremely comprehensive inspection can also constitute a sort of informal punishment, because of the way it cuts into the normal functioning of the bank.
44. Personal interviews. While *shingikai* (advisory councils) are prevalent in Japanese policy making, their most important work often happens inside the agencies to which they are attached or through more informal discussions. The most complete account of *shingikai* policy making is Schwartz (1997); on MOF *shingikai* and their role, see Vogel (1996, chap. 8).
45. The cumbersome approval process is one more reason many firms moved to bond issuance in the Euromarkets in the 1980s and 1990s (Oka 1996, chap. 2).

Interestingly, most of the MOF bureaucrats who were directly implicated were not elite-track.) Finally, there is the network of MOF OBs in the financial sector, public financial institutions, and politics. Through regular contacts between current and retired MOF officials, all sorts of political and economic information and gossip filters into the ministry.

Internal Management of Information

Internal management of information is closely linked to personnel patterns, from the perspective of the individual as well as the organization. Effective internal transmission is a function of the formal vertical structure of decision making, informal means of communication, and institutional memory.

Although informally the information structure of the Ministry of Finance has a strong horizontal component, the formal structure is actually vertical. Information gathering and policy making are largely decentralized to the division level, but actual responsibility lies above the division chief. His bureaucratic superiors have the right to veto or change any proposals he makes, and he must pass along information relevant to the proposal. Higher officials might change such proposals for any of several reasons, including personal judgment, political pressure, or a need to coordinate with other policies. Political pressure may be exerted through informal communications or through formal questioning in the Diet (until 1999, when ministers and parliamentary vice-ministers were no longer allowed to have bureaucrats give testimony on their behalf) or in the political parties' policy councils. In any event, such pressure must be weighed carefully by the bureau chief, who is ultimately responsible for ensuring that a given policy measure is satisfactory to both the ministry and the Diet.

The vertical arrangement of the ministry affects internal coordination of policies. Horne's description of intra-MOF policy making concerning financial market reform is particularly instructive.[46] He shows the increasing difficulty of coordinating policies as the locus of coordination moves up the hierarchy. Within a given bureau, mechanisms exist to make coordination of policies relatively easy; these include the coordination division and three or more deputy directors-general. In accordance with the common characterization that MOF is "all bureaus, no ministry," the bureau chief has final say within his fiefdom. Coordination across bureaus is more difficult, although here too there are coordination mechanisms, preeminently the Minister's Secretariat (in particular, the deputy vice-minister and the Overall Coordination Division). While Calder points out the relative weakness of the MOF secretariat in imposing solutions to interbureau conflicts, it is useful as a mediator.[47] When its efforts fail, the final decision falls to the ad-

46. Horne 1985.
47. Calder 1993, 96–98.

ministrative vice-minister. Inter-bureau battles can be quite difficult to quell, particularly when different sets of clients are being affected; nevertheless, internal resolution is such an important goal of the ministry that a settlement acceptable to all MOF actors is almost guaranteed.[48] Disputes with other ministries are the most difficult to mediate and often require the intervention of powerful politicians.[49]

In addition to these formal arrangements, information follows informal pathways as well. Some of these are horizontal and some are vertical, but in all cases information is transmitted through human networks. The structure of the ministry encourages the formation of such networks—indeed, having strong personal connections throughout and outside the ministry is of critical importance in gaining promotion to the highest ranks. A good example of a semi-institutionalized horizontal network is the *dōkyūkai* ("classmates association"), composed of all bureaucrats who entered in the same year; *tate no kai* ("vertical associations"), composed of all current and retired bureaucrats who have held a particular job, are a kind of semi-institutionalized vertical network. In addition to formal meetings, *dōkyūkai* and *tate no kai* offer opportunities for members to form personal connections with other members. *Gakubatsu,* or old school ties, often prove useful not only in vertical and horizontal networking within ministries, but also in dealing with other agencies or with the private sector. Finally, the ministry provides funds for regular office gatherings, particularly after the completion of some large task, in order to encourage strong feelings of loyalty within the group.[50]

Putting these semi-institutionalized arrangements together with informal interactions among colleagues and mentor relations, we get a picture of extensive human interaction across boundaries of section or bureau. These interactions are strongly supported by the ministry, and for good reason. They reinforce the informational benefits of frequent job rotation while also facilitating compromise and consensus on potentially divisive issues. And they provide for institutional memory, which is important in an organization characterized by so much job rotation.

Managing Outflows

The final component of information management is external insulation. In other words, to what extent is the Ministry able to keep information in-

48. By "acceptable," I mean a decision that will not be appealed by bureaucrats within the ministry. It is quite possible, however, that such a decision will not be acceptable to a bureau's clienteles, which can then independently plead their cases to supportive politicians (Horne 1985; Rosenbluth 1989).
49. See Okimoto 1989, Calder 1988b; Johnson 1989; and Prestowitz 1988 for some examples.
50. Information on these channels of communication comes from personal interviews. Ironically, *gakubatsu* relationships are considered to be rather weak inside MOF, due to the extraordinary concentration of University of Tokyo Law graduates. The more active school networks are among those who went to the same high school or overseas graduate program.

ternal and to have its own interpretation of reality accepted by other actors?

Perhaps the most succinct statement of Japanese bureaucratic standards regarding secrecy comes from Dr. Miyamoto Masao, a former Ministry of Health and Welfare bureaucrat: "As much as possible, you simply don't give out information to the public; that is the first principle.... When I entered the government, one of the most important things I was told was: 'We control the information. When you give information to anybody, you are doing them a favor. They have no right to this information.' "[51] Even though the Ministry of Finance puts out reams of information and analyses for political and public consumption, it also makes great efforts to keep secrets and to shape the information that is made public to fit its own needs.

While strict laws concerning classified information have been emphasized in the United States, in Japan the preference has been for *structural* disincentives to such behavior. The key is the pattern of long-term employment within an agency followed by *amakudari* sinecure jobs, along with the relative lack of exit options outside the agency. Because the career bureaucrat is so dependent on his agency throughout his working years, it strongly behooves him to play by its rules, particularly if the probability of detection is relatively high. Given the breadth and depth of MOF networks throughout the political and financial worlds, and the relatively small number of elite bureaucrats, a habitual leaker cannot depend on the safety of anonymity. The implicit threat to the career of a loose-lipped bureaucrat constitutes a powerful deterrent to discussing sensitive ministry business too closely with outsiders. Those who do not play the game properly are not awarded sensitive positions, thus promoting a generally high standard of informational integrity throughout the ministry. As one American observer puts it, "MOF leaks like a sieve as an institution (not individuals), but in ways that it hopes will further its group interests."[52]

The degree of openness depends on the policy area for both supply and demand reasons. First, some types of information are more appropriable than others. For example, other actors do not have access to proprietary information concerning banks and other financial institutions, such as lending policies and operating strategies. Therefore, such information has been highly appropriable by MOF. On the other hand, budget line-items (once published) are public knowledge.[53] Second, actors outside the ministry have differing degrees of desire for information. For example, politicians are likely to have little interest in the specifics of currency intervention even if

---

51. Quoted in "Japanese Begin to Crack the Wall of Secrecy around Official Acts," *NYT,* May 15, 1994, 20.
52. Personal communication.
53. Until MOF submits its draft budget to the Diet (after which it is relatively difficult to change line items), however, the Budget Bureau takes great pains to keep its spending plans under wraps. Campbell 1977; Kawakita 1989; personal interviews.

they are interested in the results, while foreign exchange banks will be interested in both. On the other hand, politicians are likely to be very interested in drafts of budget line-items that concern their constituencies or financial backers.

Institutional Advantages

At the institutional level, MOF has several effective methods of insulating itself from the curious eyes and ears of external actors besides the internal disincentives to leaking sensitive information already described. These include its monopoly over budget-making expertise, the complexity of the budget, the discretionary nature and complexity of the Fiscal Investment and Loan Program (FILP), asymmetrical power relationships with clients, and control over EPA forecasts.

MOF's position as preparer of the budget and the FILP (see chapter 3) puts it in a position to manipulate information on fiscal policy to a degree that is quite surprising from a comparative perspective. The main reason is that the Japanese general budget is enormously complicated, confounding international norms of public accounting practices and containing many accounts that can serve as hiding places for budget savings or public-sector borrowing.[54] A major example is the treatment of local government finance, which is largely controlled by MOF—the ministry has been known to stretch out payments or to call its loans to local government bodies in order to manipulate revenue and spending figures.[55] The FILP is, if anything, even less transparent, and the Ministry of Finance has consistently proven itself able to get away with simply adding together spending and lending increases and presenting them to the public as aggregated fiscal stimulus plans.

The asymmetry of power relations with clients stems from both history and structure. The main clients of the Ministry of Finance have been Japan's financial institutions. Starting with wartime financial controls, and continuing with the consolidation of bureaucratic authority over the economy during the Occupation, Japanese financial institutions have been highly regulated. Moreover, the presumption of most regulation, ranging from the Foreign Exchange and Foreign Trade Control Law to the types of liability a financial institution could incur to bank branching, was for many years that what was not explicitly permitted was not allowed.[56] While financial deregulation moved forward considerably in the 1980s and 1990s, it

---

54. The Japanese budgeting system has grown over the years at least partly as a result of strategic gaming among bureaucratic actors and between bureaucrats and politicians, and is thus intentionally nontransparent. On the Japanese budgeting system and FILP, see Campbell 1977; Calder 1993; Shibata, ed. 1993; Miyawaki 1993.
55. Personal interview with private-sector economist.
56. Hoshi 1995; Horne 1985; Rosenbluth 1989; Calder 1993.

did so within the specific historical context of strict regulation by the Ministry of Finance, and more generally in an atmosphere where administrative guidance has been seen as legitimate government action.[57]

Until the 1993 passage of the Administrative Procedures Law, the Japanese political system did not provide for private-sector actors to appeal the actions of regulatory agencies to third parties. Rather, the only arenas of appeal have been the agencies themselves (or occasionally their bureaucratic opponents), or the ruling party. Appeal to the paternalistic instincts of bureaucrats may be effective in some cases, but the scope of such recourse is obviously limited. Moreover, the locus of decision-making authority remains inside the regulatory agency. Appeals to politicians may prove more efficacious,[58] but access must be "purchased"—either literally or through political exchange. The private-sector actor must weigh the costs of appeals to politicians—both the "purchase" price and the possibility of future retaliation by the regulating agency—against possible benefits. The result for many years was an inertial preference for financial sector compliance with ministry directives.[59] On a day-to-day basis the ministry needed to give up relatively little information to its clients to get exhaustive data from them in return.

Finally, the Ministry of Finance has long had effective control over the official economic forecasts of the government, which were officially prepared by the Economic Planning Agency (EPA). (As of January 2001, the EPA has been absorbed by the new Cabinet Office, with unclear implications for MOF control.) MOF retained this control through the mechanism of bureaucratic imperialism—as one Japanese journalist writes, "of the Ministry of Finance's 'colony agencies' the Economic Planning Agency is the most highly valued." By convention, the post of administrative vice-minister alternates between EPA and MOF careerists, with an official from the other agency in the number two slot of director of the secretariat.[60] In addition, MOF officials are generally in control of the Research Bureau, the Price Bureau's Price Policy Division, the Overall Planning Bureau's Planning Division, the Coordination Bureau's Fiscal and Monetary Division, and other staff positions.[61] Control over the EPA is important because budget and tax

57. Vogel 1996.
58. See, for example, Yakushiji 1987; Rosenbluth 1989; Ramseyer and Rosenbluth 1993; Calder 1993; Inoguchi and Iwai 1987.
59. Calder (1993) argues that private-sector actors do not blindly obey the dictates of the ministries. However, even Calder does not deny the bias toward going along with the bureaucrats unless there is some compelling logic against it.
60. Kawakita 1989, 138. This tradition came about in 1969 following a fierce struggle between MITI (which had previously controlled the EPA's top bureaucratic slot) on the one hand and MOF and the EPA on the other. MOF and EPA officials point out that MITI tends to have more expansionary goals for the economy than either MOF or EPA. Therefore, removing MITI from the top two posts was seen as an important way of regaining control over forecasts. Personal interviews.
61. Kawakita 1989, 138.

estimates are based on the EPA's yearly forecasts of economic activity. MOF has on occasion used conservative EPA economic growth forecasts to argue against spending increases or tax cuts; with the economic malaise of the 1990s, it switched to optimistic forecasts of economic growth in order to forestall calls for fiscal stimulus (Table 2.1).[62]

Rational politicians have reason to be suspicious of EPA forecasts and have an incentive to base tax and spending policies on some combination of EPA, MITI, BOJ, and private-sector forecasts, which should tend to decrease the usefulness to MOF of its control over the forecasts. Indeed, suspicion of official numbers on the part of politicians and economic actors seems clearly to have increased over the course of the 1990s. However, even if other actors are suspicious of MOF-biased EPA numbers, they must deal with them in setting fiscal policy.

Bureaucratic Imperialism

"Bureaucratic imperialism" reinforces MOF's information management strategy at each stage. The ministry has amassed considerable resources through its lock on a variety of strategic positions in other agencies, government financial institutions, and government corporations. While the single most important colonized agency is surely the EPA, MOF's control goes well beyond that as well.

In the Defense Agency, MOF men generally include the administrative vice-minister, the directors-general of the Bureaus of Defense Policy and Personnel, and the director of the Finance Division of the Finance Bureau. In the Imperial Household Agency, MOF men are in charge of the finances through the positions of treasurer of the Imperial Household and director of the Accounting Division. Other seconded MOF personnel have included the administrative vice-minister of the Okinawa Development Agency and several key officials in the Management and Coordination Agency. At least as important is the placement of OBs. The biggest prize used to be the governorship of the Bank of Japan, but there are other plums as well. By tradition, a MOF OB is chairman of the Fair Trade Commission. Others head the Japan Bank for International Cooperation (formed in October 1999 as a merger of the Japan Export-Import Bank and the Overseas Economic Cooperation Fund—both formerly headed by MOF OBs), the People's Finance Corporation, and the Development Bank of Japan (all three are major lenders of FILP funds). Other OBs are given directorships in those and other government financial institutions.[63]

62. Personal interviews; also Asahi Shimbun Economics Bureau 1997, 140–144. When Sakaiya Taiichi took the helm of the EPA in 1998, he explicitly criticized the overly optimistic forecasts that persisted in spite of self-evident recession. "Japan Faces Threat of 'Deflationary Spiral': Economy Chief's Warning," *FT*, August 15, 1998, 3.

63. This list, which is meant to be more indicative than comprehensive, was compiled from various sources, including Kawakita (1989); various issues of *Seikan Yōran, Okurashō Meikan,* and *Imidas;* and personal interviews.

Table 2.1

Expected vs. Actual Real GDP Growth, 1987–99

FY	Expected	Actual	Difference
1975	4.3%	4.0%	−0.3%
1976	5.6%	3.8%	−1.8%
1977	6.7%	4.5%	−2.2%
1978	7.0%	5.4%	−1.6%
1979	6.3%	5.2%	−1.2%
1980	4.8%	2.6%	−2.2%
1981	5.3%	3.0%	−2.3%
1982	5.2%	3.1%	−2.1%
1983	3.4%	2.5%	−0.9%
1984	4.1%	4.1%	0.0%
1985	4.6%	4.1%	−0.5%
1986	4.0%	3.1%	−0.9%
1987	3.5%	4.8%	1.3%
1988	3.8%	6.0%	2.2%
1989	4.0%	4.5%	0.5%
1990	4.0%	5.6%	1.6%
1991	3.8%	3.0%	−0.9%
1992	3.5%	0.4%	−3.1%
1993	3.3%	0.5%	−2.8%
1994	2.4%	0.7%	−1.8%
1995	2.8%	3.0%	0.2%
1996	2.5%	4.4%	1.9%
1997	1.9%	−0.7%	−2.6%
1998	2.4%	−1.9%	−4.3%
1999	0.5%	0.6%	0.1%
2000	1.0%	N.A.	N.A.

Sources: Data for expected values from EPA, "Economic Outlook and Basic Policy Stance on Economic Management," issued each fiscal year. Data for actual values from EPA, <www.epa.go.jp/2000/g/qe994-2/gaku994-2e.xls.> Actual value for 1999 is from MOF, *Japanese Budget in Brief 2000*, Table 1.

The resulting bureaucratic empire has important implications for ministry power. One is clearly MOF's ability to influence the actions of the various agencies and institutions in which its bureaucrats and OBs are placed. Second, the empire provides a great deal of useful information about other agencies and about politicians. This information flow is essentially one-way, since there is no reciprocal secondment into the Ministry of Finance above the junior ranks. Finally, it holds implications for independence—because there are so many public-sector organizations in which OBs can be placed, there is less likelihood that the ministry will need to bend policies to suit potential private-sector employers of its retirees. Thus, it is not surprising that in the mid-1990s these public-sector seats became a focus for reformers who wanted to constrain MOF.[64]

BOJ Management of Information

Central to the BOJ's political existence is the management of information. Like any central bank, the BOJ must be able to gather and process information effectively in order to perform its duties. Central banks generally try to keep raw economic data and partial analysis secret from the private sphere; the Bank of Japan has in addition had to try to conceal its intentions from the Ministry of Finance and politicians when disagreement was likely. Information has been a particularly important resource to the Bank because of its lack of direct political ties and resources with which to make effective political trades.

As in the case of the Ministry of Finance, management of information in the Bank of Japan is closely related to its legal jurisdictions and its personnel practices. Since the BOJ is a career bureaucracy, it is not surprising that the basic mechanisms of information gathering, internal use, and external insulation follow a pattern similar to MOF's. Nevertheless, there are important differences, which have tended to reduce its ability to carry out an autonomous monetary policy.

Collection

Effective and prompt knowledge concerning the markets is essential to both of the BOJ's main missions—carrying out monetary policy and maintaining the stability of the financial system. The BOJ gathers information through prudential examination of bank records, its OB network, daily reports on foreign exchange positions of all major players, and its close links with other central banks. To these we may add the bank's official responsibility for collecting a variety of economic and financial statistics, its constant surveillance of and intervention in the financial markets, and the leverage of the discount window. Overall, the BOJ has extensive access to economic and financial information, although its access to political information is relatively limited.

Both the BOJ's prudential responsibilities toward banks and the implicit threat that it might withhold needed credit from uncooperative banks contribute to its ability to gather detailed information about banks' activities and plans. OBs in individual financial institutions and industry associations can similarly provide additional information concerning plans, potential threats, and current prognoses from the perspective of management. This information is most valuable for the oversight of banks and the financial system, but it also holds macroeconomic relevance. For example, the extent of

64. See Asahi Shimbun Economics Bureau 1997; Shiota 1995, chap. 7.

nonperforming loans in the banking system in the 1990s had profound effects on monetary policy transmission.

Another key source of information is the BOJ's own role in financial markets. Not only does the bank monitor activity on the entire range of financial markets throughout each trading day; it also affects the markets directly, primarily through operations during the trading day.

Finally, the bank has good intelligence on overseas developments, including representative offices in New York, Washington, London, Frankfurt, Paris, and Hong Kong. Those offices closely monitor developments in local markets that are of relevance to the bank's missions. Also, along with BOJ representatives at the Bank for International Settlements and the International Monetary Fund, they help to maintain liaison with foreign central banks and international economic organizations. Contacts with foreign central banks are also maintained through regular meetings (such as at the BIS or the G-7) and telephone conversations.[65] These contacts provide important information concerning international economic trends and monetary policies; they also provide the basis for international cooperation in regulatory and monetary policy.

Internal Transmission and Analysis

While some aspects of internal transmission of information parallel those of the Ministry of Finance, others differ in important ways. One of the most important differences is the existence of a highly institutionalized pathway for the diffusion of economic data. The primary organ for this diffusion, as well as for analysis, is the Research and Statistics Department.[66] Considered one of the most important of the BOJ's departments, the Research and Statistics Department is a large and sophisticated producer of economic statistics and analysis. One of its most important tasks is simply collecting and compiling statistics, which are circulated both inside and outside the bank in a number of different publications and (more recently) on the Internet. The department is also responsible for economic forecasting and predicting the future financial needs of the economy—a critical first step in monetary policy making. Finally, it carries out research on the effects of various macroeconomic policy tools, such as the pathways by which they affect inflation and economic growth rates, and fiscal and monetary multiplier effects.

Before the BOJ Law revision took effect in April 1998, the locus of policy-making activity was the bank's internal Executive Board, made up of the governor and deputy governor, seven directors, and four auditors. It

---

65. Ohta Takeshi, the former deputy governor for international affairs, jokingly refers to his old job as "international telephone operator." Lecture at Princeton University, March 1994.
66. Unlike government agencies, the Bank of Japan officially translates *kyoku* as "department," rather than "bureau."

met several times a week, generally with several key department heads (usually Policy Planning, Research and Statistics, and Credit and Management) also in attendance and often making reports. This mechanism appeared to be quite effective in channeling information and analysis to where they were needed, perhaps because of the relative centralization of decision-making power inside the BOJ. The Policy Board, made up of outsiders, was and is the body formally responsible for deciding major policies. It was long derided as the "Sleeping Board," filled with superannuated ex-bureaucrats with little meaningful monetary policy expertise or input.[67] Since 1998, the role of the Policy Board has been strengthened considerably, so that Policy Board meetings have become the main focus.

At the informal level, the Bank of Japan functions very much like the Ministry of Finance. Informal diffusion of information is based on vertical mentor relationships and on horizontal "classmate" ties. As in MOF, a relatively small entering class of elite officials drawn from a small number of university faculties is expected to work in the organization for twenty-five to thirty-five years. Meanwhile, frequent job rotation within and outside the central headquarters offers officials the opportunity to create extensive networks based on vertical relationships. This leads not only to broad expertise on the part of the officials themselves, but also to the ability to access pertinent information through connections in other divisions.

External Communication and Insulation

The Bank of Japan communicates information to the outside world of markets and ministries through a variety of pathways. For example, one of its many important functions is the publication of data and analysis concerning the economies of Japan and its economic partners. The outputs of the Research and Statistics Department offer authoritative numbers and solid economic analysis and contribute to the popular image of the bank as a highly competent, neutral, technocratic organization.

BOJ publications are the public face of external communication; the private side is the problem of maintaining confidentiality. While MOF bureaucrats sometimes deride the Bank of Japan as leak-prone,[68] the true picture is more complex. In general, as in the case of the Ministry of Finance, the internal institutional logic of the Bank of Japan gives individuals within the organization strong incentives to protect information the bank holds to be sensitive. However, the BOJ's environment presents important constraints, which shape the way the bank communicates information to other official and market actors. (Of course, BOJ officials probably do engage in a fair

---

67. Suzuki 1992, 42, among others.
68. Personal interviews.

amount of strategic leaking—a typical weapon of the weak—since few other options are available.)

The only outside official actor of any appreciable importance has been the Ministry of Finance. The ministry has loomed large in virtually all of the BOJ's activities, from bank oversight to monetary policy. There are multiple institutionalized channels of at a variety of levels.[69] Most prominent was the pre-1998 tradition that either the governor or deputy governor would be a MOF OB. This ensured that the ministry would be privy to bank decisions and to the information on which they were based. In macroeconomic policy, MOF's secretariat was in charge of ensuring that monetary policy was properly coordinated with fiscal policy; the highest-level actors were MOF's deputy vice-minister for Policy Coordination and the BOJ's deputy governor.[70] At a more operational level, the head of the BOJ's Policy Planning Department communicated with the head of MOF's Research and Planning Division in the secretariat regarding bank monetary policy intentions.

With regard to the financial sector, several pipelines exist—for example, MOF's Financial (Trust Fund) Bureau is expected to inform the BOJ's Credit and Market Management Department of large-scale market activities (a deviation from the usual direction of information flow, from BOJ to MOF). Until recently, MOF's Banking Bureau communicated both with the MOF OB executive director in charge of bank oversight in the BOJ and with the BOJ's Bank Supervision Department.[71] These ties made for extensive permeation of the bank's informational structure, which denied it the possibility of wielding information as a defense against the ministry when disagreements arose.

The Nature of Monetary Policy Information

The Bank of Japan is also disadvantaged by the nature of monetary policy information. In short, it is unable to carry out meaningful action without the knowledge, and often the assent, of the body politic. While decisions and specific operations are not always public knowledge, most of the key indicators are known to the public immediately. These include short- and long-term interest rates, inflation rates, exchange rates, economic growth rates, and asset prices. Moreover, many of the bank's policy outputs are announced publicly, such as changes in discount rate, reserves policy, and issuance of currency. BOJ intervention in the short-term money markets is less detectable (although even there it is impossible to act invisibly), but changes in interest rates are instantly observable. Whether or not a given change in short-term rates is a result of

69. Personal interviews.
70. Article 3 of the new BOJ Law reduces this role officially ("The Bank of Japan's autonomy regarding currency and monetary control shall be respected"), but it is not yet clear what the pattern will be in the long term.
71. Personal interviews.

BOJ policy, a sustained change over the course of several weeks will tend to suggest either that the bank is either doing something to change the rate or *not* doing something to keep it stable, both of which constitute policy decisions. An exception is credit allocation to individual banks, which is kept very secret. And because of the various uncertainties involved in financial policy, observers cannot be certain of BOJ intentions in the short term (as they could if they had access to complete information on credit allocation).[72] Nonetheless, over the course of weeks or months, concealment of objectives is extremely difficult, if not impossible.

The means by which the BOJ carries out operations in both domestic and foreign exchange markets also tend to lead to information diffusion. The reason is that it must operate through banks or brokers to execute trades on its behalf. While banks are expected to treat buy or sell orders from the BOJ as confidential, it is almost inevitable that information on major BOJ operations will be disseminated beyond the desk of a single trader.[73] There are some ways of mitigating this condition, such as parceling out a number of small operations among a large number of bankers and brokers, but there is no way to eliminate it entirely.

With regard to relationships with financial institutions, however, information asymmetry greatly favors the BOJ: it has access to information concerning their inner workings and plans that they cannot have about it. In areas where information is appropriable and where its collection depends on trust—for example, daily data on the foreign exchange positions of banks and exporters, or evaluations of financial institutions' loan portfolios—the bank keeps its silence. Having such a degree of inside knowledge concerning present and future economic trends gives the bank some room to maneuver when challenged by outsiders on its policy choices; it can plausibly argue, at least over the short term, that confidential information makes those choices necessary.

The World of Elected Politicians

The Diet has a variety of roles that impinge directly and indirectly on the policy-making process. In the areas of fiscal policy and exchange rate management, MOF is legally answerable to the Diet, or more specifically,

---

72. I am grateful to Adrian van Rixtel for reminding me of this point.
73. Most central banks try to manipulate information leakage by financial institutions. For example, some banks or brokers are known to be more close-mouthed than others, and certain of them are closely associated with large trades by central banks. Therefore, if the central bank wants to make the market think that an intervention may have occurred, it will intervene through a more "leaky" bank, or one it is widely known to use. In Japan, a currency intervention can be made even more public by operating through a broker, since by law brokers are required to give the name of the seller. Personal interviews; see also Ghosh 1992.

the Cabinet. Regarding monetary policy, under the revised Bank of Japan Law the BOJ is required to answer questions from the Diet, in addition to twice-yearly testimony by the governor. Until FY 1998, the minister of finance had a veto right over certain monetary policy actions, and he still formally recommends candidates for the top posts of the Bank of Japan. Here I concentrate primarily on the pre-revision years. In general, the most relevant relationships have been with the minister and prime minister, and, except for 1993–94, with various organs of the Liberal Democratic Party.

While political decisions can be decisive, elected politicians have often been ill equipped to shape the substance of macroeconomic and exchange rate policy. In order to intervene effectively in policy making, actors must have access to relevant policy information and the ability to process it independently. To the extent that they do not have ready access to complete information or the ability to use that information to make policy, senior politicians remain dependent on their bureaucratic agents. This is particularly true in crises, when more indirect forms of agency oversight are not suited to the time frame defined by events.[74] As in the bureaucracies, such information management is crucially related to individual career paths and individual incentives as well as to Diet and party organization.

The Diet

Article 41 of the Constitution states that the Diet is "the highest organ of state power and ... the sole law-making organ of the State." In spite of the principles of Cabinet government and Diet control over the budget, however, the Diet has in some ways been the weakest link in macroeconomic and exchange rate policy. This is a result of several factors, including career paths, lack of expertise, the 1980s mandate for fiscal consolidation, and the concentration of MOF OBs in the conservative parties.

By law, the Japanese Diet chooses a prime minister, who in turn forms a Cabinet to carry out the will of the Diet. Each state minister is responsible for the ministry or agency under his or her control, while the prime minister is responsible for all actions of his administration. Thus, his office also carries at least a formal responsibility for coordination among agencies. Under the one-party dominant system that characterized Japanese politics from

---

74. In other words, "fire-alarm oversight," as described by McCubbins and Schwartz (1987). I refer to "senior politicians" rather than backbenchers (à la Ramseyer and Rosenbluth 1993) because they are the ones directly involved, regardless of whether they are simply agents of the backbenchers.

1955 to 1993, the president of the Liberal Democratic Party automatically became prime minister. Other Cabinet posts were divided among LDP Diet members, predominantly those from the Lower House.[75] With the exception of less than a year in 1993–94, the LDP has remained the dominant party even though it has been in coalitions since 1994.

Despite long-term LDP dominance, opposition parties have had considerable power to delay by means of parliamentary rules and custom. Thus, they often have more power to force policy compromises than their minority status might imply. Not surprisingly, processes have developed to facilitate such compromise. For example, if opposition politicians object to a given ruling-party proposal, committee directors (*riji*) will try to come up with a compromise that is more acceptable, or will link discussion of the proposal to some proposal that is of particular interest to the main opposition parties. This management technique allows a bill to move through committees onto the floor of the Diet even if the opposition parties all plan to vote against it. An analogous process exists at the level of each house of the Diet, allowing ruling and opposition parties to agree on the agenda for the Diet in a given session, and to compromise on how to move particularly controversial or important bills through the legislature.[76]

The most important macroeconomic function of the Diet and Cabinet is to pass the budget and the tax laws.[77] Budget bills are usually passed without modification; any compromises between ruling coalition and opposition usually take place before the bill is introduced. Additionally, the Minister of Finance is formally in charge of his ministry and its actions. This means that he is in a position to control appointments to the top ministry posts and is also responsible for appointing the governor and deputy governor of the Bank of Japan every five years. On the international front, he represents the Japanese economic authorities at Economic Summits and at G-7 meetings.

75. Technically speaking (under Article 68 of the Constitution), only a majority of Cabinet members need come from the Diet, but it has been rather rare for non-Diet members to enter the Cabinet. Also, while there is no legal formula for how many Upper House (House of Councillors) and Lower House (House of Representatives) members may be part of the Cabinet, in practice members from the more powerful Lower House dominate. See, for example, Satō and Matsuzaki 1986; Curtis 1988.

76. Krauss 1984.

77. Campbell (1977) argues that the budget occupies a "large space" in Japanese policy making—i.e., that because appropriations precede authorizations, most important decisions are made first within the context of budgeting. The result is that "issues which in other countries would be debated and decided in other arenas ... in Japan are subject to the highly constrained rules of the game characteristic of budgeting" (1977, 3). This is particularly true at the level of microbudgeting.

Career Paths of Politicians

The Diet can best be thought of as a set of actors, centering on the Cabinet and (until August 1993) influential LDP Diet members or (since 1993) coalition party leaders, but building on the incentives and constraints facing individual Diet members. In this section I consider the career paths of Lower House Diet members under the one-party dominant system.[78] Career paths include the requirements of election and reelection and advancement in the party hierarchy.

Election and Reelection Prior to 1996

The basic requirement for any legislative career is the ability to be elected and reelected. Thus, elections are inevitably the central concern for legislators. While this is a universal fact, however, the activities it generates are often highly specific to a given electoral system. Here we consider the unique Japanese Lower House electoral system that existed through the 1980s, mapping out the incentives and constraints it engendered.

The defining features of that system, which held until the 1996 election,[79] were the medium-sized (two- to six-member) electoral district and the single, nontransferable vote. This system had a number of implications, which have been analyzed elsewhere in great detail.[80] One is that election to the Lower House required significantly less than a majority of votes in a given district. At the extreme, a candidate in a six-member district needed a maximum of only about 14 percent of the vote to win.[81] This meant that a relatively small group of hard-core supporters could just about guarantee a candidate election or reelection. Such small groups generally took one of two forms. For the smaller parties, it meant party supporters in the district.[82] For many LDP members, it

---

78. It will not consider the Upper House, because the Upper House is far weaker than the Lower House both in general and particularly on questions involving the budget and foreign affairs. Prime ministers and finance ministers invariably come from the Lower House for those reasons, and the Upper House is regularly ignored by both journalists and political scientists in analyses of budget making. See, for example, Campbell 1977, passim.

79. With the reforms of 1993–94, the Lower House electoral system has completely changed, but it is probably still unique. For more on the changes, see Wada 1996; Kohno 1997.

80. Kohno 1992, 1997; Wada 1996; Inoguchi 1983; Ramseyer and Rosenbluth 1993; Calder 1988a; Curtis 1988.

81. This figure (rounded from 14.29 percent) is obtained by hypothesizing the closest possible vote, with seven candidates all receiving almost exactly the same number of votes. Abstracting away the possibilities of other candidates or a voting total that is not exactly divisible by seven, as long as one candidate received 14.29 percent + 1, the next five could receive exactly one-seventh and still be elected. For districts ranging from five members down to two, the minimum percentage required to win would be 16.67, 20, 25, and 33.33, respectively.

82. These activists might be party members, as was the case with the Japan Communist Party. It also includes *Sōka Gakkai* members for the Kōmeitō, and used to include union members for the Democratic Socialist and Japan Socialist Parties. See for example Curtis 1988, esp. chaps. 1, 4, and 5.

took the form of *kōenkai,* groups of supporters loyal to a particular candidate based on "material compensation for their support."[83] Material compensation is, of course, easiest in distributive areas, such as construction and agriculture, but there are also situations in which regulatory policy can provide for ample compensation to keep small groups active.[84]

Another implication of the electoral system was that, in order for a party to obtain a majority, it had to win, on average, about two seats per district—in other words, candidates from the same party would run *against* each other for the same votes. This fact was significant in terms of both faction-alization within large parties (primarily the LDP, but also the SDPJ in some districts) and the ways in which candidates would seek to differentiate themselves from party colleagues with similar views. Factions (discussed below) offer an institutionalized way for a large party to deal with intraparty electoral rivalries—under the old electoral system, different factions supported different candidates in a given district. Intraparty electoral rivalries also required candidates to differentiate themselves from their party colleagues in the same district. This reinforced the tendency toward *kōenkai* and compensation politics—in other words, forming a strong *personal* organization not necessarily related to party or factional organizations.

A third characteristic of the Japanese electoral system (which remains in place) has strengthened the above tendencies: the set of strict and arcane laws governing campaign behavior. These laws severely restrict both the period during which campaigning is allowed and the practices it can include. The limited duration and scope of legal campaigning in Japanese elections has meant that unofficial activities—the maintenance of "support ... built on personal ties and powerful local personal political machines"—have been far more important than good oratory or sweeping vision in gaining and holding a seat in the Diet.[85] The importance of carefully fostering factional and *kōenkai* relationships is thus reinforced by campaign rules. The extraordinary concentration of second- and third-generation conservative Diet members (of 274 LDP Lower House members just prior to the 1993 party break-up, 96 [35 percent] were second- or third-generation, while only 11 [4.6 percent] of the opposition parties' 238 members were) also points to the importance of *kōenkai* to the electoral fortunes of LDP politicians: the natural advantage of sons, adopted sons, and grandsons appears to have more to do with the heritability of support groups than of political acumen.[86]

83. Calder 1988a, 66.
84. Here I am thinking particularly about regulation of small financial institutions, where grass-roots support groups for LDP Diet members proved extremely important in blocking deregulation of the industry. See Rosenbluth 1989; Horne 1985; and Inoguchi and Iwai 1987 for some of the politics behind financial deregulation attempts from the late 1970s through the mid-1980s.
85. Curtis 1988, 169, 165–175; Calder 1988a, 64.
86. *Seikan Yōran* 1993. These members are virtually all the sons or adopted sons of retired or deceased members. The situation changed somewhat in the election of 1996, due mainly to the

There has also been a high concentration of bureaucratic OBs among LDP Diet members. Before the 1993 election, 73 former bureaucrats were in the Lower House, 70 of them members of the LDP (making up 25.5 percent of the LDP's total).[87] Of these, the 24 former MOF men formed by far the largest single group.[88] Other former bureaucrats gain election to prefectural legislatures and governorships. It seems clear that having served as a career bureaucrat is an advantage in gaining election to public office. Moreover, having served in the Ministry of Finance appears much more helpful in gaining election to the Lower House than having served in any of the other government bureaucracies. The reason for this is presumably the power of the ministry over so many of the levers of government.

Impacts of Electoral System Revision

In 1994, the Diet passed an electoral reform law for the Lower House that provided for a mixed election system.[89] Under the new law, there would be 300 single-member district (SMD) seats and a total of 200 seats (reduced to 180 before the 2000 general election) to be allocated by proportional representation (PR) from eleven regions. The first election under the new system was held in 1996.

The full implications of the new system will probably not be clear for a few more election cycles, but certain characteristics seem likely to change politicians' career paths. The 1996 and 2000 general elections provide at least some preliminary anecdotal support for these hypotheses. The implications are most obvious in the PR districts. Since PR rosters are necessarily drawn up by party leaders (whether regional or national), PR Diet members should have less leverage for building personality-driven *kōenkai* than Diet members under the old system.

As for SMD seats, a couple of effects seem likely. One is that small parties will be forced to form electoral coalitions to jointly sponsor candidates if they want to have any chance of winning. Big party candidates will have much more autonomy relative to their party organizations than their colleagues on the PR rosters; SMD seats are thus already proving to be more attractive to sit-

number of LDP breakaway parties—second- and third-generation members occupied 81 (34 percent) of 238 LDP seats, 20 (13 percent) of 152 New Frontier Party seats, 9 (17 percent) of 52 Democratic seats, and 120 out of the 500 total Lower House seats (13 more than in 1990). *Seikai Jinjiroku* 1997.

87. *Seikan Yōran* 1993. Following the 1996 elections, of 76 former bureaucrats in the Lower House, 52 were in the LDP, and almost all of the rest were in the short-lived New Frontier Party. *Seikai Jinjiroku* 1997, 194.

88. *Seikan Yōran* 1993. The next largest contingents were MITI (12) and the Ministry of Agriculture (10). Following the 1996 elections, there were 24 MOF OBs in the Lower House, followed by 10 from the Construction Ministry, 9 from MITI, and 9 from Agriculture. *Seikai Jinjiroku* 1997, 194.

89. E.g., Curtis 1999, chap. 4; Kohno 1997; Wada 1996.

ting Diet members, especially in the LDP. The degree of autonomy from party organizations is likely to be even higher for those candidates who are jointly sponsored. Also, intraparty rivalries (formerly an important structural cause of LDP factions) are strongly discouraged within an SMD. Finally, in general, SMDs increase the importance of personal appeal, but the standard *kōenkai* strategy of appealing to a very small cross section of voters should become more and more difficult, changing the dynamics of distribution politics.

Career Paths within the Liberal Democratic Party

A major figure in the formation of the Liberal Democratic Party predicted at the party's inception in 1955 that the merger would last only two or three years.[90] By the 1980s, the LDP had not only survived, but thrived politically; along the way, career paths within it had become highly bureaucratized.[91]

The LDP Diet member career path had become clear indeed by the mid-1980s. Satō and Matsuzaki describe a system in which politicians advance through a highly institutionalized set of party and Diet posts, until the fifth election (about eleven to thirteen years on average). The fifth election is the point at which some members would become chairmen of Diet standing committees or get Cabinet positions for the first time, although most would reach the latter level after the sixth election.[92]

Although virtually all LDP Lower House members could expect to reach the Cabinet if they were reelected enough times, reaching the Cabinet a second time was far less common. Nor would most occupy positions of leadership in the party. Those positions, and multiple appointments to the Cabinet, were reserved for members who were powerful in factional or interest-group politics. Moreover, top positions were allocated among factions as a function of their numerical strength, leading to greater emphasis on roles within factions. Thus, advancement to the highest levels of influence in the government and party has ultimately depended on an LDP member's actions on behalf of his faction. This has entailed the development of organizational skills, as well as ability in fund-raising, strategizing, and bargaining.

The Role of Money

Rather than policy agendas or personal ties, the operative principle behind factions has been the ability to get members elected. This essentially has

90. Calder 1988a, 59.
91. According to Satō and Matsuzaki, "One of the most remarkable changes in the thirty years since the merger of the [LDP] has been the progress of institutionalization (*seidoka*) in a range of areas" (1986, 32).
92. For example, in 1986, of the 109 current LDP Lower House members who had been ministers, only 5 had been appointed after being elected fewer than five times. Of 84 members who had been elected 7 or more times only 4 had not been ministers, and no members with nine elections or more had not been ministers. Satō and Matsuzaki 1986, 39–42.

meant the ability to raise and distribute very large sums of money, an ability that is central to success within a faction. While the amount of money needed to maintain *kōenkai* and offices and to survive the semiannual gift-giving seasons is largely a matter for conjecture, it is substantial, particularly for LDP politicians, who have no strong union, religious, or party organization to bring out the vote—a 1989 internal party study was said to have estimated that non-election period district maintenance cost an average ¥110 million (about $800,000 at the time) per year.[93]

The solution to the problem of where to get the money has been to go to those private-sector groups that have benefited most directly from continued LDP dominance. In the distributive areas, these have included construction companies and agricultural cooperatives, while in the regulatory areas the highly segregated financial sector provided considerable support. Of course, major corporations and financial institutions contributed to the LDP party organization, but factional powerbrokers were required to attract additional funds to themselves. Financial flows to politicians went well beyond the legal limits, with favored means including *hagemasukai* ("booster parties," whose expensive tickets are bought in bulk by corporations) and the establishment of shop-front "foundations."

Many of the most successful politicians of the post-war era were particularly effective fund-raisers. Undoubtedly, the basic dynamic of LDP factional politics in the scandal-prone one-party dominant era reinforced the pressure on ambitious individual conservative politicians to raise as much money as possible. This incentive showed no appreciable decline even after the LDP's loss of its singular dominance.

Career Paths within Other Parties

There has been rather less study of non-LDP parties in Japan, and the emergence of new parties beginning in 1992 has only complicated matters. The more established non-LDP parties in Japan—the Japan Socialist Party (JSP, now the Social Democratic Party of Japan or SDPJ), the former Democratic Socialist Party (DSP), the Kōmeitō, and the Japan Communist Party (JCP)—have traditionally had organization-based career paths. These have included labor unions (for the JSP, DSP, and JCP), the Sōka Gakkai religious organization (for Kōmeitō), and party organizations (for JCP and Kōmeitō). Success within those organizations led to sponsorship by the parties in elections, and those organizations in turn provided the bulk of support within a given district. Because of their bases in labor and small business, politicians in the tra-

93. The estimate is cited in Farley 1996. At around the same time, Curtis estimated that "these expenses range anywhere from five to ten million yen per month on average. ... In an election year, these expenses generally double or triple" (1988, 177)

ditional non-LDP parties tended to be less fiscally conservative than their LDP counterparts.[94]

The new parties—including the defunct ones such as Japan Renewal Party, New Party Sakigake[95] (both of them LDP offshoots), Japan New Party, New Frontier Party (NFP—an amalgamation of the Japan Renewal Party, Kōmeitō, Japan New Party, some DSP members, and a number of LDP deserters), and Sun Party (a breakaway from the NFP), as well as the still-extant Liberal Party (comprising NFP members who did not join the LDP, Democratic Party, or the re-formed Kōmeitō following the NFP's break-up), Democratic Party (comprising the former Sakigake and Sun Parties and deserters from the SDPJ and several other parties), and Conservative Party (an offshoot of the Liberal Party)—present a more complicated story. At the risk of oversimplification, I divide their members into three types: political entrepreneurs, the electorally vulnerable, and new entrants.

Political entrepreneurs include politicians like Hosokawa Morihiro (founder of the Japan New Party), Ozawa Ichirō and Hata Tsutomu (cofounders of the Japan Renewal Party and the New Frontier Party, and later rivals), Kan Naoto and the Hatoyama brothers (co-founders of the Democratic Party), and Takemura Masayoshi (founder of Sakigake). A political entrepreneur is an individual who sees opportunities in an environment in flux.[96] He must be willing to risk a respected position within his party (although probably not his seat in the Diet) for the chance to become a central, independent figure in the country's politics. Thus, the political entrepreneur must provide an attractive vision and substantial support for others who would join him. These leaders are the most likely to articulate large-scale plans.

The electorally vulnerable are individuals who hold seats in an established party, but choose to follow entrepreneurs. They tend to be younger, with less secure seats, and thus are more vulnerable if the old order crumbles.[97] While their seats are vulnerable compared to more senior politicians, they have begun to form the kinds of personal support networks that encourage concentration on local needs. Having made the decision to stand with a new party, they must either impress their leaders or jump to yet another party in order to get ahead. While it is difficult to make any meaningful generalizations yet, the electorally vulnerable who have gained the most influence in

94. The "small business" comment refers to the now-defunct Democratic Socialist Party and to the Kōmeitō, although certainly many small businesspeople have been supporters of the LDP. For the standard English-language overview of Japanese electoral politics, see Curtis 1988, esp. chaps. 1 and 4.
95. While Sakigake is not technically defunct, its current strength is only two Diet members.
96. See Otake (1996, esp. 21–22) for an excellent analysis of how unstable institutions provide opportunities for political entrepreneurs.
97. This appears to have been the case with many of the LDP Diet members who followed Ozawa, Hata, and Takemura out of the party in 1993. Kohno 1997, 145–147.

their parties appear to be those who stand out in terms of either their knowledge and experience or their ability to draw public support.

New entrants are the most likely to be drawn to the electoral world by idealism and broad policy ideas. Nevertheless, their seats are the least secure, and in order to be successful they will have to mind the needs either of their constituents or (if they end up in the proportional rosters) of their party leaders. In 1992, when the upstart Japan New Party first ran in the Upper House election, these individuals seemed to be preoccupied with reforms of various sorts, although they were often attracted to the popular calls for activist macroeconomic policy.

Although it is difficult to draw firm conclusions at this point, the individual incentives for members of the non-LDP parties seem to be toward activism; in the face of a recession, we should expect non-LDP politicians to push hard for macroeconomic stimulus.

Party Organizations

Beyond the individual incentives facing Diet members, it is important to consider the structures within which they operate. The most articulated party structures belong to the largest and most established parties. The newer parties are still working to establish viable party structures.

Liberal Democratic Party

The Liberal Democratic Party evolved over the years from an amalgamation of small groups into a complex whole, replete with hierarchy, staff, and cross-cutting networks. Different aspects of LDP organization provide both centralizing and decentralizing forces for its decision making.

Formal Party Organization

By the 1980s the Liberal Democratic Party had developed an elaborate party organization, giving it capabilities in making policy, supporting its members, promoting party unity, improving information management, and adjudicating intraparty disagreements.[98] One of the most important aspects of that organization is the Policy Affairs Research Council. The PARC has historically had a role in increasing the leverage of the party versus the bureaucracy and in strengthening career politicians versus ex-bureaucrats.

The PARC is the party organ responsible for party positions on proposed policy measures. It is composed of seventeen *bukai* (divisions), which essen-

98. Satō and Matsuzaki 1986; Curtis 1988; Baerwald 1986.

tially mirror the Diet standing committees. For the most part, *bukai* are not really research organizations in the way that American congressional committees are. Rather, they rely on information from the bureaucracy, although in client-oriented policy areas private-sector actors provide alternative sources of information. Insofar as macroeconomic policy is not client-oriented, most of the information comes from the bureaucrats of the Ministry of Finance and, to a lesser extent, MITI and the EPA (BOJ officials steer clear of party hearings in order to maintain a stance of political neutrality). *Bukai* maintain contacts with the ministries through formal and informal means. Formally, bureaucrats are often called upon for *bukai* hearings, which are used to review preliminary drafts of bills and the implementation of laws—bureaucrats provide drafts of laws, data, projections, and analysis, and answer questions raised by committee members. Informally, individual members have ample opportunities to meet with bureaucrats on neutral ground, either socially or in study groups of various sorts. The existence of the PARC offers a way for LDP Diet members systematically to review and influence policies; thus, key positions within it are very attractive to politicians. The PARC chairmanship is a particularly influential and prestigious position, considered (along with the vice president, secretary-general, and executive chairman) one of the four key positions in the party hierarchy.

In addition to the PARC, whose mission is explicitly one of shaping policy drafts, there is a range of research commissions and special committees dedicated to the study of a variety of more specific issues; some of these are quite influential. Particularly influential is the Research Commission on the Tax System, in which major tax policy issues are considered before they reach the drafting stage. In general, though, it is the *bukai* that are most relevant to any discussion of LDP involvement in policy formation.

Factions

One of the most striking aspects of the Liberal Democratic Party has been its division into unofficial, but highly organized, nonideological factions. LDP factions exist solely for the benefit of their members, not for any larger policy goals. Factions were originally based on personal loyalty, and were largely divided along the lines of LDP antecedent parties. Over time, those relatively small and personality-driven factions grew, merged, or disappeared, leading to the "four-and-a-half faction system" of the mid-1980s.[99] The factions themselves became large and highly institutionalized—indeed, factions have their own buildings, hold regular meetings, and have official hierarchies. Following a kind of multidivisional corporate structure, they also have subfactional leaders, who compete to recruit the most new mem-

99. See Kohno 1992 for a description and explication of those changes.

bers and raise the most money; it was a feud among subfactional leaders that led to the break-up of the LDP in 1993. Factions throughout the party's history have served two primary functions for their members—they have provided resources for elections, and they have served as the basic organizations for allocating party, Diet, and Cabinet positions. Although the factional structure was shaken by the events of 1993, in the 1980s and early 1990s it was at its most stable.[100]

By the 1970s the LDP had established a norm that key government and party posts would be allocated according to factional strength within the party rather than by a spoils system.[101] Thus, an ambitious Diet member was wise to promote both the strength of his faction and his strength within his faction. On the other hand, since factions had long since ceased to be ideological, he was free to choose his own positions on a broad range of political topics.

Money has been the most important resource for LDP politicians in pursuit of election and reelection, and thus factions have been dedicated primarily to the accumulation and distribution of political funds. Their increasing size has also necessitated increasing the diversity of funding sources and activities.[102] This emphasis in turn hooked into two ongoing trends in post-war conservatism. One was the association of party politicians with financial scandals of various sorts, sources, and sizes, with legal violations ranging from electoral misdemeanors to tax evasion to bribery to insider trading.[103] Indeed, from the mid-1970s through the 1980s (roughly the period of consolidation of large factions), the Liberal Democratic Party saw a marked increase in the incidence and size of major scandals involving top politicians.

A more important implication from the standpoint of actual political relevance was that increasing needs for money led, not surprisingly, to increasing dependence on providers of funds. In other words, the LDP opened itself—even more than the political system already dictated—to interest-group politics and patronage. Factions thus reinforced the emphasis on appeasing economic interest groups through favorable spending and regulation at the sectoral, or even company, level. Not surprisingly, this led factions, and the LDP as a whole, to concentrate on expanding their expertise in distributive and regulatory policy areas.

Zoku

While factions appear to have had relatively little meaning for policy making (as opposed to party management), by the 1980s the Japanese media were hailing a new policy-making pattern within the LDP as the vanguard

---

100. Kohno (1992), for example, assumes that the pattern of the 1980s formed a stable equilibrium.
101. Satō and Matsuzaki 1986, chap. 3. See also Kohno 1992.
102. Kohno 1992; Curtis 1988.
103. Schlesinger 1997; Shimoda 1989.

of politicians retaking control of policy. This was the *zoku* pattern. Generally translated as "policy tribes," *zoku* were groups of LDP Diet members with extensive enough knowledge and networks in a given policy area that they were seen as able to act as a check on the power of the bureaucracies. In other words, bureaucrats could no longer simply make policies for the Diet to rubber-stamp. This led to a new situation described popularly as "party on top, bureaucrats below."[104]

Zoku Diet members are both particularly knowledgeable and particularly influential in given areas of policy, *independent of* their official government roles.[105] *Zoku* have been particularly active in distributional areas like agriculture, construction, and finance, but there are also education and defense *zoku*. The phenomenon of *zoku* changed the calculus of policy making in a number of ways in the 1980s. Most notable was the fact that some Diet members were acquiring real expertise in policy areas that had until then been the exclusive province of bureaucrats. This meant that the locus of policy making was shifting (though not completely) from the highly organized and technocratic bureaucracy to the increasingly bureaucratized Liberal Democratic Party, whose *zoku* members could represent the interests of their supporters more effectively than ever.[106]

A more subtle feature was a shift of power from ex-bureaucrats (including MOF OBs) to career politicians within the LDP ranks. For decades, bureaucrats-turned-politicians had dominated the hierarchy of the LDP and its antecedents, and had essentially held an intraparty monopoly on information relevant to policy by virtue of both their experiences as bureaucrats and their continuing ties with their former organizations. With time, study, and studious cultivation of ties with clients and bureaucrats, career politicians were increasingly able to reduce the informational asymmetry, while maintaining their advantage in areas such as fund-raising and electioneering.[107] The result was a diminution of the power of former bureaucrats, to the point that, following Ōhira Masayoshi's untimely death in June 1980, none of the prime ministers of the 1980s and 1990s other than Miyazawa Kiichi (1991–93) could credibly be termed an ex-bureaucrat.[108]

104. Inoguchi and Iwai 1987, 19.
105. Inoguchi and Iwai 1987; Satō and Matsuzaki 1986.
106. In contrast to this conventional wisdom, Kato (1994) argues that the growing expertise of LDP members in the field of tax policy (i.e., an effective *zoku*) was key to the party's acceptance of MOF-proposed tax reform legislation—in other words, increasing LDP expertise *strengthened* the hand of MOF technocrats. Since many of those tax *zoku* members were former MOF bureaucrats, however, we might well ask whether it was increasing LDP expertise that helped MOF's position, or simply the improved status of specific MOF OBs within the party.
107. Inoguchi and Iwai 1987, 24–28. Not all *zoku* politicians were or are career politicians. Not surprisingly, ex-bureaucrats often fall into the *zoku* pertaining to their former agencies. On the OB-dominated finance *zoku*, see Inoguchi and Iwai 1987, 205–209.
108. Nakasone Yasuhiro, the longest-serving prime minister of the 1980s, had actually joined the Home Ministry immediately following the war, but served less than two years before gaining election to the Diet in 1947.

Finally, *zoku* membership cuts across factional lines. This fact explicitly raises the likelihood of both cross-factional linkages (clearly not a bad thing for party cohesiveness or even the health of factions) and intrafactional rifts. While some foresaw the likely outcome to be a diminution of the power of the factions, what instead occurred was specialization—factions concentrated on funding and allocation of positions, while *zoku* concerned themselves with policy issues, perhaps even constituting a safety valve for intrafactional pressures. Another reason *zoku* have not constituted a rival to LDP factions is that powerful members of important *zoku* tend to have factional power as well. Insofar as the most powerful *zoku* politicians are generally factional power brokers with a specific policy interest, it is an exaggeration to portray the two types of intraparty groupings as rivaling one another. There seem to have been no profound changes in these patterns since the revision of the Lower House election law in 1994.

The prominence of many *zoku* politicians in PARC *bukai* has been a key factor in their influence. Laws and executive orders are drafted and implemented by bureaucrats in the name (or, in the current jargon, as agents) of the Cabinet. There are thus several potential points of intervention for LDP politicians. They may order the bureaucracies to produce a draft law designed to accomplish a given objective. They may offer amendments or criticism to the drafting bureaucrats either before or after the draft is presented to the relevant PARC *bukai*. A minister may require that a draft clear his desk before moving on to the *bukai*. LDP politicians may even push for alterations either in the Diet Management Committee or in the Diet itself, if opposition parties object strongly enough to a proposal.

All of these actions depend on *securing cooperation* from the relevant bureaucrats, whether through direct order or through mutually beneficial political exchange. Few politicians would be in a position to issue direct orders to the bureaucracy on their own individual authority, so most are forced to rely on more cooperative tactics. Effective management of information is as important for *zoku* politicians as for any other political actor. Thus, access to the drafting process before the initial *bukai* presentation gives a politician an advantage over his colleagues. To that end, politicians invest a great deal of time in informal meetings with bureaucrats, from whom they hope to gather information relevant to their specialties. From the point of view of the bureaucrat, revealing information or making a requested change in a draft can be beneficial if the politician is able to promise effective support for a ministry's preferred formulation once the draft is submitted to the PARC.[109]

The activities of *zoku* politicians, although largely carried out through informal means or networks, have both mirrored and reinforced the institutionalization of the LDP. Political power, nurtured in the *bukai*, formed the

109. Kato 1994.

backdrop for a broadening of the field of policy actors.[110] At the same time, it has confirmed the role of the bureaucrat as originator and dispenser of information and of (either favorable or unfavorable) policies. Only lately have other viable sources begun to appear.

Coalition Governments

The advent of coalition governments complicates the question of political organization. Indeed, it is difficult to address this question coherently, given the variety of coalitions that have arisen since 1993, not to mention the break-ups and formations of a sometimes bewildering array of parties. Nonetheless, I offer some general statements about what coalition governance looks like.

First, the non-LDP parties have considerably less well-articulated party structures than the LDP itself. This is particularly true for the smaller and newer parties, and it makes independent policy analysis and formation difficult, particularly in very technical or involved areas such as macroeconomic policy. Thus, even more than the LDP, the opposition parties depend on official analysis, tempered only by personal knowledge and seat-of-the-pants estimation.

Second, only the LDP breakaway parties had any politicians with experience in actually running the government. Most new parties therefore have had less understanding of what is feasible and of how to manipulate the policy process. Without effective networks with bureaucrats, they have had a hard time getting anything done. (Similarly, under the non-LDP coalitions, MOF and other bureaucrats complained that they could not get anything done either, because their own political networks were insufficient.) This has been less of an issue since the LDP effectively shed its SDPJ and Sakigake coalition partners following the 1996 election.

Third, coalitions require coordinating mechanisms. Depending on the number of parties and their relative sizes, consultation could be quite cumbersome—in general, smaller numbers of parties and the preponderance of one power tend to make for easier coordination, although ideological differences can complicate matters. Inexperience and the presence of new faces also make it difficult for actors to have the kind of stable expectations that can make bargaining more effective. Thus, the eight-party non-LDP coalition under Hosokawa (August 1993–April 1994) was more unwieldy than the LDP-led coalition with Sakigake and the SDPJ (June 1994–October 1996), the LDP-Liberal coalition (December 1998–August 1999), the LDP-Liberal-Kōmeitō coalition (August 1999–April 2000), or the LDP-Kōmeitō-Conservative coalition (April 2000–?).

110. Or, as Inoguchi and Iwai put it, *zoku* were born of the "mother" of the committee system and the "father" of Diet members' focus on reelection, were brought up within the PARC, and took center stage with the decline of bureaucratic preeminence (1987, 30–31).

The Role of Politicians in Sum

The Japanese macroeconomic policy-making system tends to limit the short-term options of political leaders for having a meaningful effect on policies. Looking at LDP involvement in macroeconomic and exchange rate policy making, the overall picture has been one of a highly pork-barrel-oriented political party with relatively little expertise and only sporadic interest in macroeconomic impact.

Only with rapid asset price deflation and recession in the 1990s (and with the break-up of the LDP) was this nexus broken. Nevertheless, points of access to the fiscal policy process have been limited. Playing with the budget ceilings in August for the following year is unwieldy and potentially dangerous, and meaningful examination of the budget requires considerable organizational resources (and actually *producing* a budget independently would be impossible). There is more opportunity in terms of fiscal stimulus plans and tax cuts, although these can be tricky as well, and often run into opposition from MOF when it comes to actually drawing them up.

When top leaders do take an active hand in macroeconomic and exchange rate policies, they are forced to act through the Ministry of Finance. That means going up against a formidable array of talent and information; when top politicians have not agreed with the direction in which the ministry wished to lead the country, they have suffered deep organizational and informational disadvantages that have inevitably led to delays and setbacks in regaining control over the situation.

These disadvantages are manifested in several ways. To begin with, almost no one stays very long in any given position in the political world. The average term for a finance minister is slightly over a year, and committee heads both among the standing Diet committees and within the LDP change frequently.[111] This tendency has only been accentuated with the coming and going of coalition governments since 1993. Moreover, there is little incentive for Diet members to specialize in macroeconomic matters—they are far better off becoming specialists in agriculture, public works, or other policies by which constituents are kept happy.[112] The more important means is through tax policy, an area in which a number of Diet members have developed an impressive degree of expertise,[113] and one whose microeconomic implica-

111. The top career levels of the ministry also shift relatively rapidly—the standard time as administrative vice-minister or deputy vice-minister is one or occasionally two years, while vice-ministers for international affairs usually have two years. Nevertheless, there is no question that even a one-year administrative vice-minister has the expertise to address the issues before him. Similarly, given that the structural incentives of the ministry remain generally consistent, it is not surprising that turnover among its top officials produces relatively little change in MOF behavior. (For a contrasting view of the effectiveness of ministers, see Park 1986.)
112. Satō and Matsuzaki 1986; Inoguchi and Iwai 1987. This may be less true for the non-LDP parties.
113. An important example is Murayama Tatsuo, a MOF OB who has been instrumental in tax reform legislation. Inoguchi and Iwai 1987, 114–117.

tions are of obvious interest to many constituents. Even there, tax reform in the 1980s was carried out under a general principle of fiscal neutrality, and based on MOF proposals.[114] The recession years have seen growing political interest in tax cuts, but there again they must deal with MOF's brand of fiscal conservatism in the tax area.

The Minister of Finance is always a top politician (often a faction leader when he is from the LDP), but even so he is unlikely to wield decisive power over the ministry. His tenure tends to be short, and the ministry is adept at controlling information. Also, relatively few finance ministers enter the job with either much expertise or specific goals in mind.[115] They have many other duties to which they must also attend, such as factional or intracoalition politics, constituent service, and party management, and most of these create incentives to concentrate on the same areas as any other Diet member—i.e., pork-barrel and preferential regulation.

Lack of expertise extends beyond just Diet and Cabinet members. Neither Diet members, nor political parties, nor the Prime Minister's Office have the ability independently to analyze or put together fiscal policy. Nor do they have economic forecasting capability. They are thus almost entirely dependent on MOF, the EPA, and other interested ministries for their information. For example, although ministers are often called upon for Diet testimony, by longstanding custom the questions to be asked were submitted beforehand, and the answers prepared by bureaucrats the night before so that the minister would be able to perform the next morning.[116]

Additionally, the presence of a large number of ministry OBs in the Diet, many of whom have significant roles in the ruling party (though reduced in the non-LDP coalitions) has meant that the desires of the ministry cannot easily be ignored. It is certainly true that the presence of these OBs cuts both ways (acting as an LDP influence on MOF at the same time that they are a MOF influence on the LDP), but their experience within the ministry often leads them to adopt similar positions on fiscal consolidation, tax

114. Kato 1994.
115. Miyazawa Kiichi, finance minister from 1986 to 1989 and 1998 to 2001, has been one major exception to that rule.
116. Diet questioning has been a particular bugbear of many bureaucrats, since often the questions are not submitted until late at night. This means that bureaucrats responsible for preparing testimony must work until the early hours of the morning. Although this is not so unusual for MOF officials, one person must be up early the next morning to deliver and explain the answers to the minister, since questioning always takes place in the morning. Personal interviews. Reforms since 1999 have sought to change this pattern by increasing the responsibilities of the minister and parliamentary vice-ministers (deputy ministers after January 2001) in Diet questioning.

policy, and other relevant issues. Even many politicians with no MOF experience have proven to be effective allies for the ministry, including such prominent politicians as Takeshita Noboru, Hata Tsutomu, Ozawa Ichirō, and Hashimoto Ryūtarō. These politicians have recognized the benefits of cooperating with Japan's most powerful and knowledgeable bureaucratic institution. This cooperation naturally depends on trading favors and information, a useful reminder that both politicians and bureaucratic actors operate in a world of mutual constraint and strategic interaction.

3

Macroeconomic Policy Tools

"Show me the money!"

Jerry Maguire

Macroeconomic policy tools and policy making define the ways in which preferences can be and are expressed in actual macroeconomic policies. This chapter begins with fiscal policy, then turns to monetary policy, and finally to exchange rate management.

Macroeconomic Policy: Budgeting

The central area of contention in fiscal policy is the national budget. One of the most important functions of any government is the production and implementation of a budget. Virtually all government functions depend on the mobilization of societal resources, and allocation of those resources cuts to the heart of governing. Nonetheless, in Japan the Diet is almost completely dependent on MOF's expertise in preparing the budget, examining agencies' requests for funds, and putting it all together in the correct legal framework; the main points of political intervention are in the setting of the budget ceiling by the Cabinet in conjunction with MOF, in setting some budget items of particular interest to individual districts, and in setting the percentage increase in the compensation of civil servants. Only in fiscal stimulus plans are politicians clearly dominant.

The General Account

The first step in understanding Japan's fiscal policy is to consider the general account budget. As the second largest economy in the world, Japan has a huge budget (Table 3.1). The Japanese government accounting system divides government bonds into two types: construction bonds and deficit bonds. As the name suggests, money raised through construction bonds

Table 3.1
General Account Budget (¥ trillions)

FY	Spending		Total Bonds	
	Initial	Actual	Initial	Actual
1975	21.29	20.86	2.00	5.28
1976	24.30	24.47	7.28	7.20
1977	28.51	29.06	8.48	9.56
1978	34.30	34.10	10.99	10.67
1979	38.60	38.79	15.27	13.47
1980	42.59	43.41	14.27	14.17
1981	46.79	46.92	12.27	12.90
1982	49.68	47.25	10.44	14.04
1983	50.38	50.64	13.35	13.49
1984	50.63	51.48	12.68	12.78
1985	52.50	53.00	11.68	12.31
1986	54.09	53.64	10.95	11.25
1987	54.10	57.73	10.50	9.42
1988	56.70	61.47	8.84	7.15
1989	60.41	65.86	7.11	6.64
1990	66.24	69.27	5.59	7.31
1991	70.35	70.55	5.34	6.73
1992	72.22	70.50	7.28	9.54
1993	72.35	75.10	8.13	16.17
1994	73.08	73.61	13.64	16.49
1995	70.99	75.94	12.60	21.25
1996	75.10	78.85	21.03	21.75
1997	77.39	78.47	16.71	18.46
1998	77.67	84.39	15.56	34.00
1999	81.86	89.02	31.05	38.62

Sources: MOF, *Ippan kaikei saishutsu kibo no suii* (undated); MOF, *Kōsai hakkō gaku/zandaka nado no suii* (undated); MOF, *Japanese Budget in Brief 2000*, Table 1.

must be applied toward public works;[1] their issuance is legally quite straight-forward. Deficit bonds may be applied to any shortfall in the budget; however, they must be specifically authorized by the Diet for each year, separately from the budget bill itself. Dating back to the days of the Dodge Line in the late Occupation period, the Ministry of Finance has been extremely averse to the idea of financing government spending through deficit bonds.[2]

In spite of MOF's aversion, the 1970s saw the development of a full-scale welfare state and a concomitant full-scale structural budget deficit. There is little question that the introduction and expansion of programs ranging

1. Since the supplemental budget of 1993, the definition of public works has been stretched far enough to include such line items as the purchase of personal computers for schools, but in general public works are exactly what one would expect—construction or improvement of public facilities.

2. Yamaguchi 1987.

from public pensions to socialized medicine to unemployment insurance were a response to intense political pressure on the ruling LDP.[3] Those fiscal deficits are key to an understanding of Japanese budgeting because of both the way they developed and their implications for budgeting and macroeconomic policy in later years. Most notable were their size and the speed with which they developed. From virtually zero in the 1965–70 period, general account deficits rose to an annual average of 1.88 percent of GNP in 1971–75, and to 5.34 percent in 1976–80, peaking at 6.1 percent in the oil crisis year of 1979.[4] In terms of total government spending, the average deficit in 1976–80 was 32 percent and the 1979 peak was 34.7 percent (Table 3.2). An added factor in the early 1970s was Prime Minister Tanaka Kakuei's ambitious public works program known as the "Plan for Remodeling the Japanese Archipelago."[5] Various writers have identified the late 1960s as the point at which vote-conscious politicians wrested effective control over the size of the budget from the austerity-minded bureaucrats of the Ministry of Finance.[6] More importantly, at the same time that government spending commitments were showing a dramatic increase, the Japanese economy slowed down nearly as dramatically (partly due to the oil shock of 1973, and partly due to structural maturation). The implications for the budget became clear in 1973—a year remembered around the world for the OPEC oil shocks of October and December, and known in Japan as Year One of the Welfare Era. It was in that year that a number of national welfare programs were either introduced or dramatically expanded, with major implications for budgeting and macroeconomic policy in general.[7] The result was that tax revenues could not rise quickly enough to cover the shortfall in the general account; this in turn resulted in headaches for the next generation of MOF budget makers.

The budget politics of the late 1970s were preoccupied with the problem of what to do about the deficits. Fiscal conservatives within the LDP such as Fukuda Takeo (MOF OB, and prime minister from 1976 to 1978), Ōhira Masayoshi (MOF OB, and prime minister from 1978 to 1980), and Nakasone Yasuhiro (prime minister from 1982 to 1987) lobbied (albeit not always cooperatively—Fukuda and Ōhira were particularly fierce rivals) to reduce gov-

---

3. Noguchi 1993; Calder 1988a, chap. 8; Curtis 1988, 61–71. Yamaguchi (1987) describes the inability—and desperation—of MOF officials to stop the trend.

4. Lincoln 1988, 93.

5. The five-year plan was issued in February 1973, and called for redistribution of economic activity away from the small group of cities where it was concentrated, and for better public provision of amenities. Lincoln (1988, 22) characterizes it as "the last major policy statement of the high-growth era."

6. Campbell 1977; Yamaguchi 1987. Yakushiji (1987, 40) demonstrates a similar trend in agricultural policy.

7. Calder 1988a, chap. 8; Noguchi 1993; Inoguchi 1983; Yakushiji 1987, Campbell 1977; Curtis 1988, among others.

Table 3.2
Central Government Deficits (¥ trillions)

FY	Total Bonds		Construction Bonds		Deficit Bonds		Bond Dependency (%)	
	Initial	Actual	Initial	Actual	Initial	Actual	Initial	Actual
1975	2.0	5.3	2.0	3.2	0.0	2.1	9.4%	25.3%
1976	7.3	7.2	3.5	3.7	3.8	3.5	29.9%	29.4%
1977	8.5	9.6	4.4	5.0	4.1	4.5	29.7%	32.9%
1978	11.0	10.7	6.1	6.3	4.9	4.3	32.0%	31.3%
1979	15.3	13.5	7.2	7.1	8.1	6.3	39.6%	34.7%
1980	14.3	14.2	6.8	7.0	7.5	7.3	33.5%	32.6%
1981	12.3	12.9	6.8	7.0	5.5	5.9	26.2%	27.5%
1982	10.4	14.0	6.5	7.0	3.9	7.0	21.0%	29.7%
1983	13.3	13.5	6.4	6.8	7.0	6.7	26.5%	26.6%
1984	12.7	12.8	6.2	6.4	6.5	6.4	25.0%	24.8%
1985	11.7	12.3	6.0	6.3	5.7	6.0	22.2%	23.2%
1986	10.9	11.3	5.7	6.2	5.2	5.0	20.2%	21.0%
1987	10.5	9.4	5.5	0.1	5.0	2.5	19.4%	16.3%
1988	8.8	7.2	5.7	6.2	3.2	1.0	15.6%	11.6%
1989	7.1	6.6	5.8	6.4	1.3	0.2	11.8%	10.1%
1990	5.6	7.3	5.6	6.3	0.0	1.0	8.4%	10.6%
1991	5.3	6.7	5.3	6.7	0.0	0.0	7.6%	9.5%
1992	7.3	9.5	7.3	9.5	0.0	0.0	10.1%	13.5%
1993	8.1	16.2	8.1	16.2	0.0	0.0	11.2%	21.5%
1994	13.6	16.5	10.5	12.3	3.1	4.1	18.7%	22.4%
1995	12.6	21.2	9.7	16.4	2.9	4.8	17.7%	28.0%
1996	21.0	21.7	9.0	10.7	12.0	11.0	28.0%	27.6%
1997	16.7	18.5	9.2	9.9	7.5	8.5	21.6%	23.5%
1998	15.6	34.0	8.4	N.A.	7.1	N.A.	20.0%	40.3%
1999	31.1	N.A.	9.3	N.A.	21.7	N.A.	37.9%	43.4%
2000	32.6	N.A.	N.A.	N.A.	N.A.	N.A.	38.4%	N.A.

Sources: MOF, *Kōsai hakkō gaku/zandaka nado no suii* (undated); MOF, *Ippan kaikei saishutsu kibo no suii* (undated); MOF, *Japanese Budget in Brief 2000*, Table 1.

ernment spending and restore fiscal prudence. These efforts ran into a series of roadblocks, including the difficulty of eliminating entitlements, the importance to many LDP politicians of pork-barrel politics, the Bonn Summit of 1978, and the second oil shock. While budget politics in the 1970s make for a fascinating story—and one that badly needs to be written—for our purposes the important thing is that an agreement was eventually reached on how to address the massive deficits.

The "Fiscal Consolidation Agreement"

In 1980, LDP leaders announced the formation of *Rinchō* (*Rinji Gyōsei Chōsakai,* or Provisional Council for Administrative Reform), a blue-ribbon commission charged with studying administrative reform options. Following *Rinchō*'s lead, MOF's 1982 budget proposal included "zero ceilings" on agency budget requests.[8] For most of the rest of the 1980s, all agency budget requests from the general account with the exceptions of defense and foreign aid were required to submit to "zero or minus ceilings," with the goal of issuing no new deficit bonds by 1990. Agencies generally respected the agreement—from 1983 to 1987, all the initial budgets met the zero ceiling on general account spending, and from 1984 to 1987 they also met a 5 percent ceiling on public works spending increases.[9] The result was that by 1990 the government reached its goal of issuing no new deficit bonds (although construction bonds amounted to 10.6 percent of the total FY 1990 budget). Also, using funds from sources that included the privatization of government-owned businesses, by 1987 MOF was buying back ¥2 trillion worth of bonds each year.[10]

Just as the budget deficit was a response to both economic and political imperatives, so was the fiscal consolidation agreement highly influenced by politics. One of its defining characteristics was the "zero" or "minus ceiling" that applied to agencies across the board. This had three major advantages. First, it was a very easy decision rule, and as such was not vulnerable to dealmaking or arguments concerning proper implementation. Second, it gave an impression of fairness, since no agency was given preference. The fairness aspect fit nicely into the Japanese budget paradigm, in which, as Campbell points out, "balance" is highly prized.[11] Third, because the targets were announced early in the process, the Cabinet had every incentive to protect its reputation by enforcing the overall budget ceiling.[12]

As a result of the fiscal consolidation agreement, the role of the Liberal Democratic Party in macrobudgeting in the mid-1980s looked rather different from the pattern that had emerged in the 1970s. This was because the agreement was essentially a series of deficit targets (and a decision rule) for each year until the goal of no deficit-financing bonds was achieved. Those deficit

8. Local finance, debt servicing, funded entitlements, and special accounts were all exempted from the ceilings. Although a good case can be made for the first three, the exemption of special accounts is harder to justify from any standpoint other than that they offered an extremely handy way of camouflaging a great deal of current and future spending. This camouflaging effect helped to increase MOF discretion while providing a safety valve for politically necessary spending. See especially Kato 1994, 268 n. 4.

9. Suzuki (2000, chap. 7) and Kato (1994, chaps. 3–5) offer the best accounts available in English. Kato's view of the exercise is rather cynical, in contrast to Curtis (1988, 71–79). Another creditable account is Noguchi 1993.

10. Those funds were subsumed under the Government Bond Consolidation Fund Special Account (Ohkawa and Ikeda 1993, 138–139).

11. Campbell 1977, 3–4. I say "impression of fairness" because it is not necessarily fair to take funding priorities as given when the policy environment is changing. That particular problem may have been mitigated, however, by the fact that *agencies* rather than *programs* were subject to the ceilings. Therefore, agencies were able to differentiate at least across the range of their functions. McCubbins and Noble (1995) try to dispute the "balance" argument, but in my opinion they do not succeed.

12. Curtis 1988, 78.

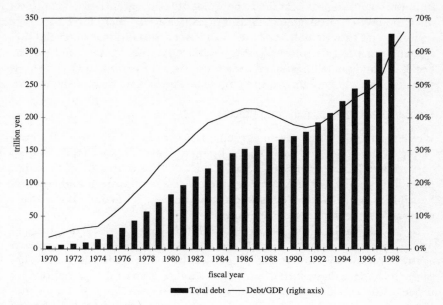

Figure 3.1   Central Government Debt

Note: End-of-year data.
Sources: MOF, *Kōsai zandaka nado no suii* (undated); MOF, *Japanese Budget in Brief 1999.*

targets were actually exceeded on several occasions, but the budgeting goal of "zero or negative growth" for agencies was consistently met. These targets had great legitimacy, as the national debt (and pension obligations) continued to grow despite less severe deficits than in the 1970s[13] (Figure 3.1).

Nonetheless, the fiscal consolidation agreement was always a rather precarious one. From when it first went into effect, the Ministry of Finance and its allies were conscious that any budget growth beyond the zero ceiling could put government finances back on the slippery slope toward deficit. Indeed, the ceilings, if not the agreement itself, came under attack several times, including the Plaza-Louvre period when they were successfully defended. During the stagnation of 1992–2000, the ceilings were breached and then effectively abandoned. An attempt in 1997 to reimpose fiscal consolidation was foiled by the severe economic downturn that resulted. In any event, through the 1980s and into the early 1990s, the agreement was a sort of totem for fiscal conservatives in MOF and the LDP, a monument to the victory of their ideology that was to be protected at all costs.

During the life of the fiscal consolidation agreement, most budget-related activity on the part of LDP politicians was at the margins—either trying to

13. I thank an anonymous reader for Cornell University Press for reminding me of this point.

fund preferred spending at the expense of other programs, or trying to reduce the hit to a given agency. Only if pressures at the micro level grew very
severe would they actually be able to spill over into the macro level. Only
agreement among the most powerful politicians could lead to a decision to
break the budget ceilings; since these were the very people most closely associated with the agreement, the targets were taken very seriously indeed.

The Budget-Making Calendar and Process

While the fiscal consolidation agreement created the framework for budgeting in the 1980s and early 1990s, budgeting itself followed a traditional
course. The Japanese budget-making process adheres to a strict calendar,
providing a handy way of describing the process in an orderly and compre-
hensible fashion. While a complete account of budget making is not really
necessary, some features are relevant here.[14]

By the time a fiscal year begins in April, the budget process has dragged
on for about ten months. In early summer (sometimes even earlier), each
agency or ministry starts putting together the materials it will use in compiling its budget request. This process is a microcosm of the overall budget
process, and constitutes each agency's first attempt to figure out its spending needs and priorities. The formal process begins with the establishment
of the overall and agency budget ceilings in late summer. The ceilings are
officially established by the Cabinet, but are actually negotiated between the
Cabinet and the Ministry of Finance.

By August 31, each agency is expected to have formally submitted its budget request to MOF's Budget Bureau, where it is taken up by the appropriate
budget examiner. The budget examiner and his staff then proceed to work
100-hour weeks questioning, analyzing, critiquing, and trimming those budget requests before putting together an initial draft. The amount of information on other agencies' activities and priorities that passes through the hands
of the budget bureaucrats is staggering; moreover, the examiner can demand
additional information on a given project as he sees fit, and can freely call on
his bureau chief counterpart to answer questions.[15] The budget examiners

14. The most complete account in English is still Campbell 1977; a more recent one may be
found in Kawasaki 1993a. Most Japanese overviews of the Ministry of Finance also contain
detailed descriptions of budget policy making—see, for example, Kawakita 1989.
15. By long-standing tradition, officials of other agencies must go to the Ministry of Finance
as supplicants, where they are treated summarily by officials one or two grades below them
(i.e., deputy budget examiners receive division chiefs, budget examiners receive line ministry
bureau chiefs, and deputy bureau chiefs receive administrative vice-ministers). Thus, the Budget Bureau's power is established doubly—other agencies must come to it, and they are implicitly lower in rank than their juniors in MOF. Stories abound of high-ranking non-MOF
bureau chiefs being made to stand in MOF hallways for long periods of time by budget examiners (see, for example, Kawakita 1989, 40–42).

spend the months of October and November negotiating figures and putting the budget together from the ground up (or "microbudgeting").[16]

Meanwhile, traditionally, higher officials would be involved in "macrobudgeting," deciding on the aggregate size of the budget and any tax cut as well as figuring out the basic allocation across agencies.[17] Since the early 1980s, however, that function has been much attenuated because of the fiscal consolidation agreement and the attendant practice of determining budget ceilings in late summer. This change meant a corresponding change in the role of top officials, whose autumnal technical and political negotiations no longer have much to do with fiscal aggregates.

The month of December is spent integrating the work of the budget examiners to produce a budget draft, which is released in late December or early January. During the years of LDP dominance, at around the same time the party's Policy Affairs Research Council (PARC) would prepare a Budget Compilation Program. Under coalition governments, broad guidelines have had to be negotiated among coalition partners. With the release of MOF's draft, "revival negotiations" begin between ministry and ruling party or coalition officials; by late January, they have produced the official Cabinet draft.[18] The Cabinet draft is almost invariably passed unchanged by the Diet, albeit often over vigorous opposition party denunciations and attempts at modification and delay. Technically, the Diet is supposed to pass the budget in time for the April 1 start of the fiscal year, but often the opposition is able to extend debate so that it is not passed until the end of April or even later. In such cases, a temporary appropriations bill keeps the government in business at previous year levels until the budget is finally passed.

Political Inputs

According to Campbell, "the most striking aspect of Japanese budgeting, to those familiar with other budget systems, is that the majority party organization intervenes routinely at nearly all stages of the budgetary process."[19] The long-dominant Liberal Democratic Party had both good reason to be interested in budget compilation and ample opportunity over the course of its nearly forty-year reign to make its spending preferences known. Indeed, when the LDP has been in power its Policy Affairs Research Council has acted largely as a means of monitoring and channeling party interests regarding the budget. Other parties, including LDP offshoots, have analogous organs, although not nearly as highly articulated. Within coalitions, the various policy chairmen have to meet and negotiate budget priorities.

16. Campbell 1977, chap. 3.
17. Ibid., chaps. 4, 6.
18. Ibid.
19. Ibid., 3.

Although ruling party intervention may be routine throughout the budget process, parties do not necessarily achieve all their goals. The Ministry of Finance bureaucracy has its own incentives concerning the budget, as well as very clear ideas about the benefits of Ministry autonomy. Thus, the Ministry follows strategies that attempt to minimize what it considers to be political meddling on the part of the party organs and influential individual politicians. One of these is strict adherence to the budget-making calendar, which serves to keep politicians out of serious debate on budget items until just a few weeks before the budget draft is introduced to the Diet.[20] And the Budget Bureau makes every effort to ensure that it is the sole repository of ability to produce a comprehensive and legally acceptable budget draft. Probably the most potent weapon in MOF's arsenal in the 1980s and early 1990s was the fiscal consolidation agreement, which reduced the fiscal impact of political intervention to a marginal level once the budget ceilings were set. (Budget hawks attempted to replicate this success in 1997, with disastrous results.) This is not to say that political influence is entirely ineffectual; however, the finance bureaucracy has often been able to restrict the points of intervention through effective management of information, thus reducing the scope of political influence.

Japanese budget practices are confusing. As a result of a long-standing disagreement between the Japanese government and the International Monetary Fund, the IMF for many years did not even publish Japanese budgetary figures, while the OECD attempts to reconcile the figures with its own standards of national income accounting.[21] One of the confusing aspects of Japanese budgeting is the profusion of ledgers—in addition to the general account, there are several special accounts, plus the Fiscal Investment and Loan Program (discussed below). Accounts occasionally overlap, and funding sources are not always clear. Moreover, there is little consistency in accounting for intragovernmental transfers and loan payments (i.e., relations with prefectural and local governments). The result is that it is quite difficult to tell from the outside exactly what the budget numbers mean. In fact, it is possible to have a rather expansionary budget in spite of official claims of fiscal neutrality, and vice versa. This lack of transparency is a central element in MOF's preemptive strategy of information management.

The microbudgeting level is for the most part not the relevant place to look for overall fiscal policy stance.[22] For fiscal impact, the most important

---

20. On these strategies, see ibid., 99–111.

21. Before 1992, the IMF's *Government Finance Statistics Yearbook,* which is its standard text for such statistics, did not even list Japan in the comparative tables section, with the exceptions of 1987 and 1988, when Japan was listed but no data was provided. As of 1992, Japan is listed in that section with full data back to 1981. The *OECD Economic Surveys* reconcile Japanese accounts in their own way, giving data which are at odds with official Japanese figures.

22. This is true in a given fiscal year, but over a slightly longer term a decision to provide a small amount of funding to a new initiative might lead to the establishment of a large and

political questions are the means by which the original budget ceilings are set and the likelihood that those ceilings will hold. As to the first question, the fiscal consolidation agreement provided a blueprint for reducing government deficits at least through the FY 1993 budget, although on several occasions the actual deficits exceeded the targets. These were *political* decisions, made by a strong prime minister and other top LDP leaders, through negotiation with the budgeters of MOF. The making of coalition-era budget ceilings has been a less regimented process, offering potentially greater influence to political parties. The answer to the second question is that, once made, annual ceilings are honored, except when supplemental budgets have been added during the fiscal year.

Thus, only the summer negotiations on budget ceilings and tax revenues are of major import from a fiscal policy perspective. It is possible to make several generalizations about negotiations in the 1980s. First, the fiscal consolidation agreement provided deficit targets that served as the basis of negotiations. Second, both politicians and bureaucrats had made public commitments to the agreement, which made defection more costly. Third, if one side wished to defect from the agreement, the other side had a heightened incentive to prevent that from occurring, since one defection could lead the agreement as a whole onto a slippery slope toward irrelevance. The result was generally cooperative action to meet the stated goals of the agreement[23]; if one side (presumably the politicians rather than the budget bureaucrats) were to attempt to diverge from those goals for whatever reason, the other side would work to keep the final budget as close to the long-term agreement as possible, and would have formidable resources for doing so.

The politicians with the greatest opportunity for meaningful impact on the Japanese budget are those who have early access—the top officials (especially the prime minister and finance minister, but also other party heavyweights who may hold other Cabinet or party portfolios) who negotiate the budget ceilings, and those *zoku* members who have good contacts in MOF's Budget Bureau. This is because they have both foreknowledge and influence. From the point of view of macroeconomic policy, however, only the budget and debt ceilings are really meaningful. In other words, the primary actors are top-level politicians and the MOF bureaucrats who both negotiate with them and provide the data and analysis on which their opinions are formed.[24] Nevertheless, the rigidity of the budget calendar makes fiscal stimulation using the regular budget quite difficult. In particular, since the over-

---

politically charged program. That was certainly the case with certain welfare programs. See Yamaguchi 1987; Calder 1993; Noguchi 1993; Campbell 1977.

23. Game theorists will recognize this situation as a type of Stag Hunt.

24. In other words, forecasts of economic activity, tax revenues, and other essential indicators. These numbers come either from the ministry itself or from the Economic Planning Agency.

all macroeconomic frame is decided around eight months before new spending begins, leaders must be extremely confident of their forecasting ability a year to a year and a half out if they want to take bold steps with it. A more practical means is through supplemental budgets, described below.

Post-1993 Budget Politics

Most of the non-LDP parties that have been involved in governance since 1993 have a natural tendency to prefer activist macroeconomic policy, as a result of the incentives facing individuals within the parties. Again, the key potential points of intervention are the setting of the budget ceilings, examination of the budget draft, and formation of fiscal stimulus plans.

It is the right of the Cabinet to set budget ceilings, although there is invariably considerable input from economic actors and from the ministries, particularly the Ministry of Finance. Insofar as the non-LDP parties have not tended to see themselves as bound by the fiscal consolidation agreement, the setting of ceilings allows major political intervention. The August negotiations over the budget framework are still given central prominence by both participants and journalists, but coalition governments have not felt the same responsibility as the LDP of the 1980s to keep deficit bonds to zero or to stick to a given year's framework when it appeared that a fiscal demand stimulus might be useful. Indeed, after 1993, the fiscal consolidation goals were more or less abandoned. One caveat is that because their own organizational capabilities for analysis are weak, parties must rely on the Ministry of Finance and the Economic Planning Agency for information and analysis regarding the impacts of macroeconomic policy, which could make them more cautious.

As for examining the budget draft, the non-LDP parties do not have the manpower or organization to really comb over it, except in specific areas that are of interest to clients. To go beyond broad aggregates in other areas, they must depend on input from ministries or (increasingly) nongovernmental sources. Thus, their abilities at oversight are limited, raising the possibility that the Ministry of Finance could conceivably reduce the fiscal impact of a nominally expansive budget. Such action should be more likely if there is an expectation that a given party or coalition may not be in power for the long term, because MOF would not need to fear retaliation in case of subsequent detection.

Fiscal stimulus plans and tax cuts offer the best opportunity for parties to involve themselves in fiscal expansion. Fiscal stimulus plans in particular are more straightforward in their accounting for spending (once one gets beyond the often confusing question of funding), and tax cuts are relatively easy to understand and have the virtue of often having private-sector forecasts to rival the official forecasts of revenue impact. Complications remain, of course, but all things being equal, tax cuts and public works are the most practical way of stimulating an economy in the short to medium term. These plans are also more flexible than the cumbersome regular budgeting process. Before turning to fiscal stimulus plans, however, we ought to examine the role of non-budget public funds, which typically form the bulk of such plans.

Activities of MOF's Financial Bureau

An area of MOF's economic policy capabilities that has been little studied to date in the English-language literature is the activities of the Financial Bureau. The Financial Bureau acts like a corporate treasury department, managing government-controlled assets and liabilities and disbursing funds. The assets under the bureau's jurisdiction have been both considerable and wide-ranging—including all state real estate holdings, the bulk of postal savings and life insurance, excess profits of the Bank of Japan, and the government shares of privatized companies such as Nippon Telephone and Telegraph, Japan Railways, and Japan Monopoly Corporation, as well as any surplus or unallocated funds in the general account.[25] As both issuer of government debt and (until 2001) chief investor of postal savings and life insurance funds the Financial Bureau was for many years the largest player other than the BOJ on both the buying and selling sides of the government securities market. As manager of the Fiscal Investment and Loan Program (FILP), the Financial Bureau also has a major role in planning and administering the role of government in the Japanese economy.

Sources of Funds

The funds available to the Financial Bureau that are of importance for Japanese macroeconomic policy come from its function as the "Trust Fund Bureau."[26] Until April 2001 by far the largest source of new funds has been postal savings, whose accumulated balance at the end of 1998 totaled ¥252.6 trillion (nearly $2.5 trillion), making the system by far the largest financial institution in the world.[27] After that came the national pension system, national term life

25. According to Article 7 of the Law Concerning the Funds of the Trust Fund Bureau (*shikin un'yōbu shikin hō*), those funds can only be invested in the debt of national or regional governments, juridical persons as specified by the Diet, and the Electric Power Development Company, or in bonds issued by banks, certain associations of credit cooperatives, foreign governments, foreign government corporations, and international organizations.
26. "Trust Fund Bureau" is purely a legal category that describes the management of trust funds. References to the "Trust Fund Bureau" are actually about trust fund management by the Financial Bureau.
27. Ministry of Posts and Telecommunications, downloadable statistics, <www.zaimu.mpt .go.jp/tokei/eng9802.html>.

insurance (which, like postal savings, is sold and managed by post offices throughout the country), and, from the mid-1980s on, stock and proceeds from the privatization of formerly public corporations.

Japan's postal savings system is often a source of confusion.[28] Essentially, it is a passbook savings program similar to those of banks and credit cooperatives, except that the government has control over deposits. The two other major features that made it different were that until April 1, 1988, postal savings were (ironically) a good way of evading taxes,[29] and that until 1987 postal savings interest rates were set through consultations between MOF's Banking Bureau and the Ministry of Posts and Telecommunications (MPT). Until 1987 interest rates on postal savings tended to be slightly above bank deposit rates. This was because MPT officials saw it in their interest to attract more savings to the postal system, and so resisted demands by MOF to offer rates equivalent to those offered by private financial institutions.[30] The result was that by the mid-1980s, postal savings accounts accounted for about one third of all deposits in Japan. Moreover, since they accounted for an increasing percentage of an increasing savings pool, their absolute size increased dramatically, from ¥103 trillion in 1985 to ¥252 trillion by 1998. Postal term life insurance policies added about a third again as much to those amounts. National pension funds, which increased rapidly from the 1970s onward, were another large contributor of trust funds; as of 1996, total funds equaled ¥116 trillion.[31]

Until 1987, all investment of postal savings and life insurance, as well as national pension funds, was carried out by the Trust Fund Bureau, either through the FILP or in short-term investments. This arrangement changed slightly in 1987 due to a compromise between MOF and MPT according to

---

28. For the best English-language account of postal savings, see Calder 1990a.

29. See, for example, Cargill and Royama 1988, 181–182. Under the *maruyû* system, every individual had a right to tax-free interest in one savings account of up to a specific amount (¥3 million yen in 1987). Because of MOF regulation of banks, it was impossible for an individual to have more than one *maruyû* account in the banking system. However, since each individual post office maintained its own records and was not subject to MOF audit, a single individual could have several tax-free accounts dispersed among various post offices. Moreover, so could that individual's spouse, children, and occasionally even pets—the total number of postal savings accounts was invariably well over the total population of the country, much to the chagrin of MOF Tax Bureau officials (Calder 1990a, 45).

30. It was in MPT, and LDP, interests for several reasons. For one thing, the *maruyû* system was extremely popular. At a more structural level, most post offices in Japan, particularly in rural areas, are actually franchises; franchisees' profits rise with deposits in their branches, and so they are highly sensitive to any move that would tend to reduce deposits. These franchisees are important LDP vote-gatherers in rural constituencies.

31. Saitō, et al. 1992, 186–190; Tamura 1997, 93, 357; MPT, downloadable statistics. Postal savings alone contributed about ¥10 trillion per year to the FILP in 1996 and in the 1997 plan.

which postal savings interest rates would be based on market rates and MPT would be allowed to manage a fraction of postal savings funds (autonomous management). A similar deal was struck with the Ministry of Health and Welfare (MHW) over pension funds.[32] As of April 2001, postal savings, postal term life insurance, and national pension reserves were no longer deposited with the Trust Fund Bureau as part of a broader plan to reform FILP. Until then, MOF managed the bulk of those funds, although autonomous management by MPT and MHW did increase considerably.

Another major source of funds has been proceeds from the privatization of public corporations. NTT and the Japan Tobacco and Salt Corporation (Japan Monopoly Corporation) were privatized beginning in April 1985; privatization of the Japan National Railways began in April 1987. The sale of NTT shares was particularly lucrative for the government—a tranche of 12.5 percent of shares offered in November 1987 went for almost ¥5 trillion, or about 11 percent of total FY 1987 central government revenue.[33] The Trust Fund Bureau is responsible for managing both the dividends from the large portions of each company still held by the government and the proceeds of the public offerings. Of the latter, half was placed in a fund to retire deficit-financing bonds; the rest is available for use in the FILP, special accounts, and portfolio investments.

Short-Term Operations

Most of the funds entrusted to the Trust Fund Bureau are managed by MOF—until 2001, the only exceptions were those returned to the MPT and MHW for autonomous management. One of the main objectives of this fund management has been to pay back holders of postal savings accounts, postal life insurance policies, and pensions, although there have been times when the FILP has had to be bailed out with money from the country's general account; the 1987 MOF-MPT agreement was in fact intended to eliminate that problem.[34] Of course, any institution that takes deposits must

32. Technically, until April 2001, all postal savings (other than those needed for cash on hand and operations) were turned over to the Trust Fund Bureau, which then returned a fraction to MPT for safekeeping. An analogous system was in place for national pension funds as well. Personal interviews, various MOF publications. For accounts of the politics and economics behind the decision, see Calder 1990a; Rosenbluth 1989, chap. 6. As of April 1, 2001, postal savings, postal term life insurance, and national pension reserves are no longer transferred to the Trust Fund Bureau, thus eliminating MOF control over those funds. For a summary, see MOF, "Outline of the 'Bill for the Amendment to the Trust Fund Bureau Fund Act and Others'" (undated), <www.mof.go.jp/english/zaito/zaeo60.htm>.

33. Calder 1990b, 179. Not all of the planned sales of stock were completed in the end because of the depressed stock market of the 1990s.

34. It appears likely, however, that the need for a bailout will arise again. For example, Okue (1996) predicted an "impasse" by FY 1999. FILP in 2000 was losing huge amounts of money through bad loans from government financial institutions and through its holdings of bonds

carry out activities to increase the value of the deposits held while remaining sufficiently liquid to meet its short-term obligations. What is of interest here is the *way* in which short-term operations are carried out, and the effects those operations have on macroeconomic variables.

Ministry of Finance officials deny accusations that their short-term fund management is anything but neutral in its intent and effect on monetary policy, a position with which the Bank of Japan officially agrees. Some individuals within the BOJ disagree, however; as one put it, these operations "can even be regarded as a part of monetary policy conducted by MOF."[35] The reason is that the Trust Fund Bureau is by far the largest player in the government debt market besides the Bank of Japan itself. The Ministry of Finance long resisted expanding the volume of the short-term government debt market for fear of losing control over the interest rates it pays investors. This has inevitably impaired the ability of the BOJ to carry out open-market operations to affect interest rates and money supply. Not until April 1999 were short-term government bill markets truly liberalized.[36] This meant in practice that the Bank of Japan could not completely control interest rates in the government debt market in opposition to the Ministry of Finance.

Fiscal Investment and Loan Program

The FILP is perhaps the most unusual of Japan's macroeconomic policy tools.[37] Also known as the "second budget," the FILP represents long-term uses (five years or more) of government trust funds. In 1985, total planned disbursements under the FILP totaled ¥20.9 trillion; by 1990, that number had grown to ¥34.6 trillion, paralleling the prodigious growth in postal savings described above. By 1997, as the extensive use of FILP funds in fiscal stimulus plans drew ever more Trust Fund Bureau funds, planned FILP allocations reached ¥51.4 trillion, or 65 percent of the general account budget (although only ¥46.6 trillion was actually disbursed—Table 3.3). The money follows several pathways to reach its public works or industrial policy destinations, including government financial institutions, national and regional agencies, public works authorities, and various public policy corporations.

---

of troubled local governments and special corporations (such as the red-ink-hemorrhaging Japan National Railroad Settlement Corporation). The fears laid out in that report are not altogether new, as Miyawaki (1993) demonstrates.

35. Personal interview.

36. MOF mimeo, "*En no kokusaika no suishin ni tsuite*" (Policies to Promote Internationalization of the Yen), December 22, 1998.

37. There is a real dearth of writing on the FILP in English; exceptions include Miyawaki 1993; and Calder 1990a and 1993, chap. 4. Incidentally, the name "Fiscal Investment and Loan Program" has become rather misleading. As Miyawaki notes (1993, 26), 99.8 percent of FILP disbursements in the initial 1993 plan were in the form of loans. For more on FILP investments, see Saitō, et al. (1992, 197–198); updated figures are from Tamura (1997) and MOF's *FILP Reports* from 1998 and 1999.

Table 3.3
Fiscal Investment and Loan Program Disbursements (¥ trillions)

FY	Planned (A)	Revised (B)	Actual (C)	(C) − (A)	(C) − (B)
1980	18.18	18.26	18.10	−0.08	−0.15
1981	19.49	19.62	19.41	−0.08	−0.21
1982	20.29	20.84	20.60	0.31	−0.23
1983	20.70	20.92	20.70	0.00	−0.22
1984	21.11	20.95	19.61	−1.49	−1.34
1985	20.86	20.87	20.49	−0.37	−0.38
1986	22.16	22.23	21.54	−0.62	−0.69
1987	17.08	28.25	27.59	10.51	−0.66
1988	29.61	30.19	29.52	−0.09	−0.66
1989	32.27	33.48	33.01	0.74	−0.46
1990	34.57	36.04	35.81	1.24	−0.23
1991	36.81	39.02	38.15	1.35	−0.86
1992	40.80	46.73	46.13	5.33	−0.60
1993	45.77	54.55	52.46	6.69	−2.09
1994	47.86	52.13	50.32	2.47	−1.81
1995	48.19	52.12	42.19	−6.00	−9.94
1996	49.12	49.12	45.90	−3.22	−3.21
1997	51.36	52.94	46.64	−4.72	−6.30
1998	49.96	60.39	54.37	4.41	−6.02
1999	52.89	N.A.	N.A.	N.A.	N.A.

Sources: BOJ, *Zaisei Kin'yū Tōkei Geppō*; *FILP Report '98*; *FILP Report '99*. Actual value for 1998 is the estimate from the *FILP Report '99*.

The initial FILP budget is prepared in the Financial Bureau in a process analogous to the compilation of the general account budget. The various agencies, financial institutions, public corporations, and other designated organizations of the FILP tender their requests to the Financial Bureau. Like the general account, the FILP draft is presented to the policy affairs research councils of the ruling party or coalition, and then to the Diet, where it must be approved. Several characteristics distinguish the FILP process from that of the general account budget, however. Most fundamentally, FILP allocations do not constitute free money—in principle, FILP loans must be paid back. This fact significantly reduces the intensity of political wrangling over the contents of FILP line-items. Second, the bulk of FILP funds are disbursed through government financial institutions, or through local or regional authorities.[38] Thus, FILP line-items tend to be much broader than those found in the general account, meaning both considerably less work in analyzing and compiling the draft, and considerably less room for politicians to push particular projects. Finally, the Ministry of Finance is empowered to increase FILP disbursements up to 50 percent above the initial budget without Diet approval, which offers MOF bureaucrats added flexibility in using the FILP as they see fit.[39]

38. Government financial institutions tend to be controlled by the many MOF OBs on their executive boards and (often) in their governors' chairs.
39. Saitō, et al., 1992, 7–8.

Since the early 1970s, the Fiscal Investment and Loan Program has concentrated mainly on housing, public works, and public amenities.[40] In some ways, the FILP is a means of centralizing control over projects that in a federal system would be decentralized—for example, financing the building and maintenance of a toll road. Partly because of the heavy component of public works, not to mention the greater flexibility MOF enjoys in allocating and changing FILP lending and the fact that it does not contribute directly to the budget deficit, the FILP has emerged as the major instrument of fiscal stimulus in postwar Japan. In particular, fiscal stimulus packages are predominantly made up of increased FILP allocations.

Despite its emphasis in fiscal stimulus packages, however, exactly how effective the Fiscal Investment and Loan Program might be as a fiscal stimulant is very much open to question. Like the OECD and IMF, the U.S. Treasury has questioned FILP's economic effects,[41] and even prominent Japanese economists claim not to know how to analyze it. There are two essential questions from the macroeconomic standpoint.[42] First, since additional FILP lending is simply drawn from short-term holdings of the Financial Bureau, does it constitute increased public borrowing? This question is actually somewhat more complicated than it sounds. It breaks down into the dual question of whether postal savings itself is simply a case of massive public-sector borrowing, and whether drawing money out of short-term holdings for long-term uses will mean that private investors must take up the slack in the government debt market, thereby leading to private-sector dissavings. Moreover, it would be easy to retire bondholdings of the Trust Fund Bureau with a loan from FILP, which would have absolutely no macroeconomic impact in the short run (unless the interest rate were significantly different).

The second question is whether, assuming that the FILP operates as a fiscally responsible financial institution, there is any meaningful difference (other than size) between its activities and those of any other financial institution. Ministry of Finance officials claim that the particularly stimulative effects of public works spending mean that it is unnecessary to consider the effects on macroeconomic aggregates. Even if they are correct, however, the point is irrelevant if a given public investment merely substitutes for potential private investment. Finally, it must be borne in mind that the FILP components of fiscal stimulus plans are often *not fully disbursed,* especially when

40. See Saitō, et al. 1992; Calder 1993, chap. 4; and Johnson 1982, chap. 6, esp. 210–212.
41. That confusion was expressed by U.S. Treasury Undersecretary Lawrence Summers when he was reported in early 1993 to have sent a list of questions concerning Japanese fiscal policy to the Ministry of Finance. While MOF officials I interviewed at the time denied the specifics of the report ("there is no list, but there are questions," as one put it), they admitted that Summers had requested among other things an explanation of how the FILP works at the macroeconomic level. It is not clear that he ever received satisfaction.
42. The standard macroeconomic formula suggests that a fiscal stimulus is only meaningful to the extent that (1) spending increases more than revenue, or (2) the multiplier effects of increased spending exceed zero. While the second statement is technically correct, the first is a fairly reliable indicator and is most often used, as in Posen 1998.

introduced late in the fiscal year—thus, grand pronouncements of fiscal stimulus based on planned FILP lending are more symbolic than substantive (see Table 3.3).

Fiscal Stimulus Packages

Twice in 1986–87, six times in 1992–97, and three times in 1997–99 (with a fourth expected in autumn 2000), the Japanese government passed fiscal stimulus packages to deal with either continuing international economic imbalances or domestic recession. In each case, the government announced a total amount that was significant—¥3 and ¥6 trillion in 1986–87, ¥6–15 trillion in 1992–97, and ¥12–17 trillion in 1997–99—and in each case, the number attached clearly inflated the likely impact of the package.[43] Here we consider the constitution of such packages.

Fiscal stimulus packages are made up of three main components, the largest of which is typically increases in FILP allocations. The second part, the part with which most outsiders are familiar, is a supplemental budget (*hosei yosan*). The third is tax cuts, about which little need be said, except that there is an important difference between temporary and permanent cuts, and also that some packages have counted already agreed-upon cuts as a new contribution.

In principle, a supplemental budget reopens the general account in order to deal with some unforeseen event or fiscal circumstance that requires additional spending. Although fiscal stimulus packages were relatively rare until 1986, supplemental budgets have not been—in fact, there is usually at least one per year, following the annual negotiation on government salaries.[44] Events like natural disasters are also often covered by supplemental budgets, if there is not sufficient money in reserve to cover them. Funding for supplemental budgets typically comes in one of two forms: reserve funds (*yobikin*) or unused funds (*tsumitatekin*). Because the Ministry can usually estimate fairly accurately how much salaries will rise, and because there are reserve funds explicitly set aside for special needs, such existing funds generally suffice. In other words, in the normal course of events, supplemental budgets do not really constitute new spending in the sense that total government spending for the year increases; rather, they constitute a reallocation of previously budgeted funds. This was true even for some "fiscal stimulus" plans from 1985 to 1999, notably those in fall 1986, spring 1992, and fall 1993.

Supplemental budgets that are part of a fiscal stimulus plan focus almost entirely on public works of one sort or another—particularly projects in

43. See Posen (1998, esp. chap. 2) for an extensive analysis of the 1992–95 packages.
44. Each year, the National Personnel Authority makes recommendations regarding how much government salaries should be raised. Since the salary increases are negotiated after the ministry's draft budget is presented, and become effective in the fall, a supplemental budget is necessary to cover the shortfall.

which funds can be allocated quickly—since these are the sorts of activities believed to have the strongest short-term effect on overall economic activity. The relatively narrow focus of supplemental budgets adds to the ability of the government to respond quickly to the requirements of a given situation. Budget examiners need only consider a small number of projects, and in fact usually just provide accelerated allocation of funds to projects that are already being funded.

The relative speed with which supplemental budgets can be compiled leads to the ironic situation that current-year spending can be altered more easily than the next year's. Precisely because the budgeting calendar for the general account is extremely rigid, the supplemental budget is a necessary instrument in the Japanese government's fiscal policy toolbox. Nonetheless, it is not clear that supplemental budgets often have very meaningful macro-economic impact. As in the case of increases in the FILP, supplemental budgets often amount to merely expenditure switching—they do not represent a significant increase in either spending or public-sector borrowing unless they include bond issues. (In several cases in the 1990s, such bond issues have actually been forced mainly by shortfalls in revenue rather than by increased spending.) If they have any macroeconomic effect, it is through a multiplier effect associated with public works, which some MOF officials estimate to be a factor of about 1.5 (compared to 0.5 for tax cuts).[45]

The magnitude of fiscal stimulus plans can be manipulated in other ways besides FILP padding, use of existing reserve funds, and expenditure switching. Plans often double-count: by including expenditures that are for purposes other than fiscal stimulus (for example, disaster relief), by including the bond funding needs for previously approved expenditures when there is a revenue shortfall, and by conflating current and future fiscal year expenditures. Plans have also been known to include the full amount of guaranteed loans rather than the value of the guarantees themselves and to count suggested spending by prefectural and regional governments as actual spending.

Politics of Supplemental Budgets and FILP

The budget calendar raises a major obstacle for the ruling party or coalition in any attempt to fashion a fiscal response to any unforecast economic development. When then–finance minister Miyazawa went to the Louvre meeting in February 1987, for example, he could not publicly offer a fiscal expansion—the FY 1987 budget draft was then under review in the Diet, and any attempt to revise it would have made for an untenable mess.[46] Thus, responses to emergencies or shortfalls are made through changed allocation of FILP money or through passage of a supplemental budget.

45. Personal interviews and statements at public lectures.
46. See Funabashi 1989, 193–195, and personal interviews.

The input of politicians on the FILP is similar to their actions regarding the budget, though somewhat more limited. This is true for several reasons. Most important is the demand side. Since FILP funds are not "free money," they are simply less attractive to politicians than straightforward spending from the general account. Also, since the funds are owed to postal savings and pension holders, there is greater need to allow the technocrats to manage them. Third, it is harder to keep track of FILP funds because so much of the money moves through (MOF-controlled) government financial institutions, which are expected to evaluate borrowers, and which in any event cannot force economic actors to borrow more (even if that were a good idea). Finally, MOF enjoys a greater legal right to use FILP moneys as it sees fit—FILP line items are broad enough to allow the Ministry to shape the allocation of funds, and besides, MOF can expand FILP outlays 50 percent over the Diet-approved blueprint without seeking permission.

Supplemental budgets can be introduced and passed at any point in the fiscal year, and tend to cover a very small range of spending—when designed for fiscal stimulation, they concentrate on public works. The process of compiling a supplemental budget is also significantly less institutionalized than that of compiling a regular budget, which offers a more substantial role to politicians in shaping the budgets. Supplemental budgets presumably look very attractive to politicians, in that they allow a second shot at funding (with "free money") electorally beneficial projects that were rejected or postponed during the regular budgeting process. This is certainly true to an extent, but when one actually looks at fiscal stimulus plans, it is apparent that most of the funding goes through the FILP. The fiscal impact of politicians' input on supplemental budgets is further reduced because the sources of funds are in the end determined by the Ministry of Finance; the ministry's favored sources are unspent or reserve funds. Nonetheless, the ruling party policy committees (and construction *zoku* when the LDP is involved) are closely involved in putting together these packages.

Finally, from a strategic point of view, supplemental budgets are an important means of shifting fiscal policy power from MOF to politicians. As already noted, they constitute a reopening of the budget battle, usually at a time when politicians have been able to gain some empirical knowledge of the effects of the initial budget. This reduces the effectiveness of bureaucratic obfuscation. Moreover, practically speaking, the size of supplemental budgets has increased over the course of the 1990s, particularly in 1995 and 1998–99. Only with the reappearance of moderate growth in FY 2000 did fiscal stimulus plans begin to recede in their importance relative to Japan's overall fiscal stance. As the share of these relatively politically manipulable budgets rises within overall fiscal policy, the politically controlled element of overall fiscal policy also expands. For all these reasons, supplemental budgets in the context of fiscal stimulus plans are considered highly unwelcome by MOF's fiscal conservatives.

Monetary Policy Making

Any discussion of the implementation of Japanese monetary policy should begin with a caveat. Since the 1970s the autonomy of the private sector vis-à-vis the economic bureaucracies in Japan has grown progressively as a result of financial deregulation,[47] and major private-sector firms have developed increasingly globalized strategies. This has made bureaucratic direction of the economy ever more difficult. The reduced number and type of policy instruments available to economic bureaucrats restrict their ability to carry out policies. The main features of financial liberalization as it pertains to the transmission of monetary policy are the decontrol of interest rates, increased securitization, and international capital flows. Liberalization has forced monetary policy to follow more indirect routes, such as interest rate management, rather than direct control of credit availability. Open market operations have also become progressively more important as markets in government debt have continued to develop (albeit slowly). The more arm's-length relationship that results between the BOJ and the banks means reduced BOJ leverage at the same time that it has made the application of monetary policy less exact. More than previously, intervention to further monetary policy goals must conform to market forces if it is to be effective.

Policy Tools

The tools of the Bank of Japan are essentially the same as those available to any other central bank—they include manipulation of the discount rate, operations in the interbank market, open market operations, and reserves policies.[48] While unexceptional in and of themselves, the bank's policy tools have often been used differently in Japan than elsewhere. The overall picture of Japanese monetary policy implementation is one of a system that is only gradually catching up with the country's sophisticated and increasingly deregulated financial sector.

In particular, the official discount rate has played a more prominent role in Japan than it does in other countries. Movements of the discount rate are rare, and both financial markets and the popular press make much of them. The

47. A variety of reliable works describe the gradual liberalization that began in the late 1970s, culminating in the "Big Bang" of 1998–2001. These include Suzuki 1990; Cargill and Royama 1988; Eijffinger and van Rixtel 1992; Nakakita 1999; and Horiuchi 1999, among others.
48. I will not discuss "window guidance," a kind of credit-rationing that has long been identified as uniquely Japanese. By the time period covered in this study, it was no longer a major policy tool in the BOJ's arsenal, and it was finally formally done away with in 1992 (Calder 1993).

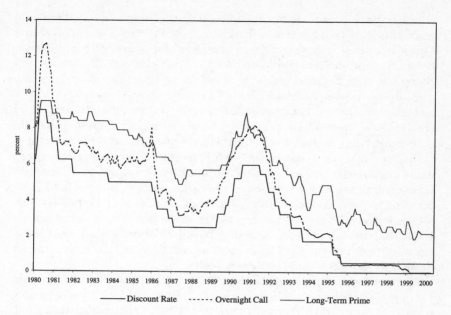

Figure 3.2   Interest Rates

Note: Monthly average.
Source: BOJ downloadable statistics.

discount rate is often described as a *nishiki no mihata* (the traditional Imperial battle standard). In other words, it symbolizes the intentions and authority of the central bank, and is expected to carry other interest rates with it—there are relatively narrow bands above the discount rate in which various market interest rates are expected to move. (Since late 1995, overnight rates have stayed below the discount rate.) The BOJ uses market operations to ensure that interest rates stay within the desired ranges and to prepare the way for changes in the discount rate.[49] Until the late 1980s, however, commercial bank lending rates were still set by an advisory council on which representatives of financial institutions sat alongside current and former officials of the Ministry of Finance and the Bank of Japan[50] (Figure 3.2).

49. Mieno 2000, 260–261.
50. The Interest Rates Adjustment Advisory Committee (*kinri chōsei shingikai*) was an advisory organ to the minister of finance. It was chaired by the deputy governor of the Bank of Japan and included the directors-general of MOF's former Banking Bureau and EPA's Co-ordination Bureau, and representatives from finance, industry, and academia. (See *Shingikai Sōran,* various years.) Until 1988, it set an upper limit on bank interest rates, while the MPT set an effective lower limit until 1987 by virtue of its veto power over changes in postal savings rates. According to a former MOF participant, authority over interest rates was split, necessitating coordination between MOF and the MPT, but the opinions of the BOJ were not a major factor in that coordination (personal interview). For a lament by a former top BOJ official, see Ogata 1996, 114–116.

Just as the discount rate has been unusually meaningful in Japanese monetary policy, market operations have traditionally been a less central tool. This is because Japanese capital markets were for many years tightly regulated, a condition that still has not been entirely eliminated. Discount rate changes remain the most important symbolic policy change, but short-term rates are the key intermediate target. They have become even more important since the discount rate was reduced to 0.5 percent in 1995. Market operations have traditionally focused on the interbank market rather than the government debt market due to the relatively small volume of short-term securities in the latter. In particular, the BOJ likes to manipulate the overnight uncollateralized call rate, because it is the easiest to control. Also, since the short-term prime rate is now set on the three-month CD rate, that has become an important instrument.[51] With regard to open market operations, MOF's Financial Bureau is a major player in the government debt market. While BOJ officials formally deny that Trust Fund Bureau short-term activities affect monetary policy implementation at all, some informally describe those activities as a form of monetary policy.[52]

A key constraint on the ability of the Bank of Japan to carry out open market operations was finally lifted in 1999. As of that year, the short-term government debt market instruments—finance bills (FBs) and treasury bills (TBs)—are now being auctioned to the market, rather than purchased by the BOJ at below-market yields. Also, the lifting of withholding tax for most foreign investors may in time vastly increase the bill market's potential size.[53] While the impetus for these changes came from a desire to make the Tokyo money markets more attractive to foreign central banks in order to promote "internationalization of the yen," they promise to have major effects on the Bank of Japan's ability to implement monetary policy decisions.

The least-used tool of monetary policy (as in any country) is altering reserves requirements. As a matter of law, banks and other deposit-taking financial institutions are required to keep interest-free deposits with the Bank

---

51. Personal interviews with BOJ officials. Professional "BOJ watchers" in securities firms and investment banks confirm that they concentrate on the unsecured call rate (Oshio and Kishimoto 1996, 27–35).

52. In formal interviews, BOJ officials argue that Trust Fund Bureau operations do not constitute intervention, since the bureau is only one market participant. They give the example that Nōrin Chūkin (a financial institution that services agricultural credit cooperatives) and the Trust Fund Bureau both do about ¥10 trillion in operations a day, but no one talks about the interest rate interventions of Nōrin Chūkin. "It does have an effect," but the BOJ can always neutralize that effect it if it wants. More informally, some BOJ officials point out that regardless of the total amounts of daily trading, the Trust Fund Bureau can take large positions that affect interest rates in the relatively small government debt market (personal interviews). This will likely change following the recent expansion and liberalization of the short-term government bill market.

53. Foreign Exchange Council 1999.

of Japan for a specific percentage of their own liabilities.[54] By altering the percentage, the authorities can make lending more or less profitable and can cause banks to expand or contract their lending portfolios. In practice, this tool is hardly ever used, perhaps partly because before 1998 changes in reserves requirements needed the approval of the minister of finance but probably mostly because it is a very blunt instrument.[55] Also, reserves requirements are seen as having more to do with prudential regulation of financial institutions than with monetary policy.

Basic Patterns

By looking at the basic flow of policy making and operational goals, and then considering again the constraints on the BOJ, we can see how the elements of information management and personnel patterns shape the bank's strategic interaction with the Ministry of Finance and politicians.

Authority in the Bank of Japan has been centralized in the person of the governor. Technically, the Policy Board (of which the governor is the chairman) has had to approve major policy changes; practically, that requirement has been toothless. Perhaps the strengthening of the Policy Board found in Articles 14–20 of the revised BOJ Law will have major effects on its role, but in 2000 the full impact of that change was not yet apparent. The final decision for any action of the bank has resided with the governor. Of course, this could also be said of government ministries, where the minister has ultimate responsibility for the actions of his or her ministry, but the similarity is only superficial. To begin with, as a former BOJ or MOF career official, the BOJ governor has both the expertise and the access to information necessary to understand and direct the actions of the Bank. Perhaps as importantly, the job of governor is a full-time position, unlike that of a minister in a parliamentary system, who must tend to his political bases and factional and party politics in addition to his ministerial duties. Finally, the BOJ governor serves five years—five times the typical term of a cabinet minister—and in many cases has served the previous five years as deputy governor.[56] These facts decrease any potential internal principal-agent problem

---

54. These liabilities include deposits, debentures, bonds, and so forth (Article 2 of the Law concerning the Reserve Deposit System). The percentage may be no more than 20 percent, except for yen-denominated deposits by nonresidents, the maximum for which is 100 percent (Article 4). The exact amounts vary by the size of institutions' liabilities, and follow a progressive scale.

55. Mutō and Shirakawa, 1993, 72–73. The MOF approval provision was found previously in Article 4 of the Law concerning the Reserve Deposit System. Article 15 (3) of the revised Bank of Japan Law supersedes the old law.

56. Prime ministers typically reshuffle their Cabinets on an annual basis, although key positions like finance minister tend to change hands less quickly. In the forty years from 1960 to 2000, twenty politicians served a total of twenty-seven terms as finance minister, an average of less than eighteen months (*Ōkurashō Meikan* 1999, 313–314).

in the Bank of Japan in terms of both information and monitoring. This situation stands in contrast to the ministries, where the minister himself is
likely to have at best a tenuous hold over his subordinates.

The centrality of the governor's role means that information flows effectively in a vertical fashion as well as horizontally, and that bank policies are
coordinated at the highest levels. Changes in monetary policies generally
begin in the Research and Statistics Department. Having detected a change
in one or more indicators, the Research and Statistics staff pass along their
interpretation of the meaning of the change to the Policy Planning Department (monetary policy is considered by the eponymous Policy Planning Division). Policy Planning then develops a recommendation as to how to move
the economy back toward the BOJ's preferred equilibrium. Under the old
law, those recommendations were presented to the bank's Executive Board
in one of its four-times-weekly meetings; following discussion among members of the board, the governor would make a final decision. In the case of
market operations, the decision process would end there, although Policy
Board approval was technically required (it was invariably and unanimously
given) for other policy changes, such as altering the discount rate. Under
the revised BOJ Law, the Policy Board is meant to have an active role in all
policy decisions. At each stage in the process, contacts with MOF become
more likely, especially with regard to policies that require the approval of
the Ministry of Finance.

Operational Goals

The basic operational goals of the Bank of Japan do not differ in any meaningful way from those of other central banks—they include stable prices,
sustainable economic growth, stable currency, the integrity of the financial
system, and organizational autonomy.[57] From the monetary policy standpoint, bank officials claim to place more emphasis on prices than on
growth. Like many central banks and economists, the BOJ officially denies
the existence of any trade-off between inflation and growth.[58]

Operationally, there remains plenty of room for ambiguity. For one thing,
as most economists agree, while there is no trade-off between growth and inflation in the long term, there certainly is one in the short term, before wage
demands begin to take into account expectations of continued inflation.[59]

---

57. It may seem odd to include "organizational autonomy" in the list of operational goals of
a central bank, but research backs up the argument that some central bank policies are made
to assert political independence even as they address other operational goals. See, for example, Woolley 1984; or the essays in Mayer, ed. 1990.
58. That conclusion is often justified through self-criticism of its own role in the high inflation of 1973–74, as in the semi-official Mutō and Shirakawa, 1993, 106.
59. Cargill, Hutchison, and Ito (1997, 156–157) offer evidence that Japan's Phillips curve
is unusually steep, which weakens the justification somewhat.

Thus, central banks are justified in acting to smooth out short-term deviations from the long-term full-employment equilibrium. Second, what constitutes a long-term equilibrium or a short-term deviation is a matter of judgment and interpretation on the part of policy makers. Third, the questions of how to rectify short-term disturbances or to maintain long-term equilibrium are highly controversial among economists; solutions might include measures to alter interest rates (discount rate changes, open and interbank market operations), quantitative restrictions (reserves policy or old-fashioned window guidance), or the development of a monetary rule that uses price or quantity measures as intermediate goals.

Clearly, even in theory, there is considerable discretion left to economic authorities in their management of monetary policy. Like many other central banks, the BOJ takes this discretion very seriously—for example, it has always rejected the use of a straightforward monetary rule of thumb that would make its actions completely transparent.[60] Indeed, the most important monetary policy measures, market operations, are not announced, and can be carried out with varying degrees of secrecy. Publicly announced policies such as those concerning the discount rate or reserves policy are accompanied by an official explanation, but even these actions are not transparent *ex ante*. Only since FY 1998 has the Policy Board been required to publish its minutes. The secretiveness with which monetary policy is conducted tends to reinforce both organizational and economic goals. Organizationally, a discretionary policy with less than complete disclosure provides a much more difficult target for potential adversaries or competitors.[61] From the policy point of view, a number of economic studies have found utility in secrecy on the part of central bank market operations in both domestic interest rates and foreign exchange.[62]

Japanese monetary policy has tended to be rather proactive, in spite of the praise it received from American monetarists in the 1980s and early 1990s, and it has responded to economic growth as well as to inflation. Moreover, it has been quite sensitive to foreign exchange rates, as evidenced by the unwillingness to raise interest rates in 1988 and 1989 amid fears of an uncontrolled rise in the value of the yen, even though asset price inflation had become apparent by at least mid-1988.[63]

---

60. Mieno 2000, 24 and chap. 6. This was true even when U.S. monetarists such as Hutchison (1986) were lauding the BOJ's monetary orthodoxy. BOJ officials emphasize the discretionary aspect of monetary policy and generally state that rather than following a specific principle (such as the public emphasis on price stability), it is necessary to deal flexibly with changes in inflation, growth, and exchange rate (Ogata 1996, 105–107; personal interviews).

61. For a development of this line of thinking in the case of the Federal Reserve System, see Woolley 1984, 104–108, 150; Hetzel 1990.

62. Ghosh (1992) offers the case for foreign exchange market intervention; citations for the domestic policy implementation literature can be found in his footnote 3.

63. Cargill, Hutchison, and Ito 1997, 74–80.

Politics of Monetary Policy

As a general rule, the Cabinet has had relatively little input regarding monetary policy, other than the appointment of the governor, deputy governor, and Policy Board. Since FY 1998, new rules requiring periodic reports to the Diet have taken effect; nonetheless, the Diet has no direct role in the determination of monetary policies. Legally, the locus of most monetary policy decisions is outside the world of electoral politics, although before the revision of the BOJ Law the minister of finance had the legal rights to postpone discount rate actions and to issue direct orders to the Bank of Japan "when necessary."[64] Nonetheless, it is generally the ministry, rather than the minister, of finance that Bank of Japan officials have seen as the primary constraint on their actions.[65]

The result is that, while the Bank of Japan would have a hard time resisting strong LDP policy preferences, such situations rarely arise. When they do, they become part of BOJ lore—an informal collection of anecdotes that tend to show the bank losing out to stronger interests.[66] In later chapters I look at two BOJ stand-offs with the political world, one a dispute between Governor Mieno and Finance Minister Hashimoto in December 1989 over the timing of a discount rate hike, and the other a highly publicized threat by LDP powerbroker Kanemaru Shin against Mieno in spring 1992. Both cases demonstrated clearly that the bank had little choice but to take political considerations very seriously.

Constraints on Monetary Policy Makers

Regardless of what BOJ goals are, or how they are arrived at, the bank operates in a world of constraints. These constraints take the forms of market forces, law, custom, and political expediency.

One constraint can be found in the markets themselves. While countercyclical monetary policy can smooth out business cycles, the extent to which either the fiscal or the monetary authorities can change fundamentals is limited, as the doldrums of the 1990s showed. Moreover, at times a central bank has to "buy" credibility when market actors doubt its commitment to a given policy or target.[67] In addition, changes in market conditions can directly affect the usefulness of specific policy tools—since the mid-1980s, some of the key trends have included increasing disintermediation, increased access by corporations and financial institutions to the Euroyen

---

64. The latter can be found in the old Bank of Japan Law, Articles 42 and 43.
65. Personal interviews. As one former high-ranking BOJ official put it, the bank seldom gets private guidance from politicians, although there are occasional public criticisms. In general, pressure comes from MOF and the markets.
66. For more details, see Grimes 1995, 305–308.
67. Blinder 1999.

markets, and continued MOF control over the size of the T-bill market and over bank and FILP lending and deposit rates. These changes cut in several ways, but the net result has been a decreased ability on the part of the economic authorities to exert control over the financial sector.[68]

Legally, several points are relevant. Certain policy actions by the BOJ have required either the approval of the minister of finance or MOF acquiescence to be effective. For example, market interest rate changes did not manifest themselves directly in bank lending rates until FY 1988, because those rates were set by a MOF-dominated advisory committee. More importantly, before FY 1998, a change in the discount rate required notification of the finance minister (who could demand a one-month delay in implementation) and the approval of the prime minister. (Under the revised BOJ Law, the only requirement is notification of the finance and prime ministers, who cannot overrule it or force a delay.) The BOJ also needs MOF approval to expand limits on currency in circulation.

Custom and political expediency (often two sides of the same coin) constitute the last set of constraints. The most important set of customs was the need to form consensus with the Ministry of Finance before carrying out even monetary policy actions that did not require MOF approval. Nor is political expediency easily avoided—monetary policy is never completely independent of political context.[69] Since the BOJ cannot conceal intentions or actions over the course of more than a few months, it has had little choice but to accept those legal and customary constraints.

Exchange Rate Intervention

The instrument most closely associated with international monetary policy and international economic coordination is exchange rate intervention—in other words, buying assets in one currency with assets in another currency in order to raise the value of the former currency. Intervention in the foreign exchange markets remains the first (and often only) line of defense against excessive depreciation or appreciation of the national currency.

This is not the place to review the vast and often technical literature on the effectiveness of intervention, but one finding is clear: intervention itself has no ability to affect markets in the long or even the medium term in con-

---

68. For example, disintermediation increased the importance of open and interbank market operations, and access to the Euroyen markets meant that Japanese monetary policy was far more subject to international forces. Liberalization of financial regulation contributed to all of these effects. MOF control over bank and FILP rates made the flow-through of discount rate and other interest rate policies less direct. Finally, MOF control over the TB market made open market operations less effective than in other advanced countries.
69. Woolley 1984; Mayer, ed. 1990.

travention of economic fundamentals.[70] While it might appear puzzling that states are willing to speculate with billions of dollars in operations that are not effective in any sort of economically meaningful way, there is one great benefit to intervention: it does not subvert key domestic goals for the sake of international activities. Therefore, it remains far more popular among policy makers than altering monetary or fiscal policy for the sake of satisfying international markets.

Jurisdiction and Process

The basic principle of exchange rate intervention in Japan (technically known as "equilibrating operations")[71] is direction by MOF's International Bureau and actual execution by the BOJ—the bank is very explicitly only an agent in the intervention process. As one MOF official forcefully put it, the BOJ has no responsibility at all for the value of the currency, and no influence over what gets done. It simply collects information on the state of the market, which it transmits to the ministry. The ministry makes decisions about intervention not "based" on this information, but using this information as one input.[72]

Intervention is carried out under the rubric of the Foreign Exchange Fund Special Account (FEFSA), a balance sheet entry that represents the ability to use up to a specific amount of government funds for international operations. As the executor of the FEFSA, the BOJ Financial Markets Department's Foreign Exchange Division (until May 2000, the division was part of the International Department) is responsible for carrying out currency trades ordered by MOF's Foreign Exchange and Money Market Divi-

---

70. This is not to say that intervention cannot be effective at some level. One possibility is that intervention may be a signal that a state is willing to defend the currency with more fundamental macroeconomic policy tools (particularly but not exclusively monetary policy) if exchange rates continue to move in an unfavorable direction, as argued by Dominguez (1989) and Ghosh (1990) Another possibility, raised by Dominguez and Frankel (1993), is that forceful intervention by monetary authorities when market psychology perceives a possible bubble can turn the tide of speculation; this hypothesis suggests short-term effects.

71. While retired officials seem generally willing to discuss "intervention" (*kainyū*), at least regarding past operations, current officials are much more careful to use the technical legal term "equilibrating operations" (*heikō sōsa*) (personal interviews). The first time I encountered this was in a 1993 interview with an International Finance Bureau official who started the interview by denying the very existence of intervention in a flexible-rate currency regime. When asked what on earth the Ministry was using its Foreign Exchange Fund Special Account for, he responded by reading the definition of "equilibrating operations" out of a book of statutes! In fact, there is not the slightest difference between what economists and newspapers call "intervention" and what the ministry calls "equilibrating operations"—MOF simply prefers not to use a term that suggests less-than-free markets.

72. Personal interviews. There are times when the ministry leaves tactics to BOJ discretion, but at other times it maintains very firm control over even minor details.

sion.[73] In the Tokyo market, these trades are executed either by banks or by brokers. If intervention is carried out in other markets, such as London or New York, it is done through swap lines (standing agreements in which a foreign central bank acts as the agent of the home central bank in the foreign market, with the understanding that the home central bank will buy back the proceeds at the same price) or bond repurchase agreements. Regardless, the BOJ is not allowed to carry out operations without a direct order from the Ministry of Finance.

There does not appear to be any consistent pattern as to when MOF managers are hands-on, and when they leave the execution to their BOJ agents.[74] What is consistent is communication between the responsible division chiefs in MOF and the BOJ regarding tactics, goals, and amounts of dollar buying or selling. During an intervention, MOF officials monitor markets themselves to supplement the analysis provided by the BOJ. The more urgent a given intervention is considered to be, the more often the two sides communicate—the bank will report on the effects of intervention and perhaps recommend changes in tactics or quantities, and the ministry will consider those reports in making decisions on whether to change direction or hold the course. In even a routine intervention, officials from the two sides will confer by phone several times during the day; on a particularly active day, such communication will be nearly continuous.[75]

In recent years, the Japanese government has become more sensitive to charges that it manages the economy, leading both to an insistence on non-interventionist terminology ("equilibrating operations") and to an official reticence about the goals of its interventions. (In this respect as in many others, Sakakibara Eisuke, the vice-minister for international affairs from 1997 to 1999, was a major exception.) In the mid-1980s, and again with the ultra-high yen of 1995, however, officials made no bones about what the government's intervention goals were at any given time. This is not to say that they admitted to any given intervention or any specific target rate—indeed, one of the enduring characteristics of Japanese intervention policy is intense secrecy re-

---

73. There have been name changes in both MOF and the BOJ since 1985. I use only the names in use as of 2000 to eliminate confusion.
74. Tactics can actually vary greatly in foreign exchange intervention. One issue is the degree to which the interveners want the market to know what they are doing. Another is the question of how to divide intervention—should one intervene all at once to show the strength of the government's intentions, or divide it up so as to be able to hit the market whenever it appears to be turning away from the desired direction? Finally, how does one gauge the psychology of the market—at what points are indecision and a fear of getting caught overextended strong enough for intervention to be decisive? These are questions in which academics have shown some interest (e.g., Dominguez and Frankel 1993), but which central bankers and government officials often negotiate by the seat of their pants. To give the interveners credit, academic research offers little concrete or reliable guidance in answering any of these questions.
75. Personal interviews.

garding goals, strategies, tactics, amounts, and any other specifics.[76] Interestingly, MOF officials deny the existence of any formal means of testing the effectiveness of intervention, and in fact do not appear to have carried out such tests, preferring a "we know it when we see it" approach.[77]

Funds for Intervention

From January 1985 to April 2000, Japan's foreign exchange reserves rose from $22.35 billion to $324.1 billion, by far the largest in the world (Figure 3.3). Whether or not the ministry and the Diet are simply proceeding on faith, they implicitly accept (or at least do not challenge) the usefulness of large-scale intervention—the proof of this is that they consistently allow the Foreign Exchange Fund Special Account to expand when it is running low. Like the general account, special accounts of the national budget require Diet approval; the FEFSA seems to be a particularly uncontroversial one, probably because all major actors in Japan consider the yen-dollar exchange rate a national priority.[78]

Most discussion of Japanese foreign exchange intervention focuses exclusively on the Foreign Exchange Funds Special Account, but BOJ funding is also critical, in three ways. One is through the funding mechanism for the FEFSA. Foreign currency purchases are carried out with yen that the Ministry of Finance obtains through the issuance of short-term financing bills (FBs). Until 1999, when FBs began to be offered at public auction, the BOJ was essentially constrained to absorb all new issues of FBs, at below-market rates. This made intervention appear even less costly to MOF bureaucrats and politicians than it already would have.[79]

The second way BOJ funds can affect intervention policy is through the management of its own foreign reserves, which as of September 30, 1999, totaled about $33 billion (as compared to FEFSA totals of more than $273 billion at the time). Foreign reserves are held in interest-bearing deposits

---

76. Such secrecy is, in fact, the international norm. A theoretical justification is offered by Ghosh (1992), but a more important reason is that central bankers are highly pragmatic people. The general idea seems to be that if they do not announce their actions, financial players who are nervous about the current level of the currency will be more skittish about any apparent intervention, thus making for a kind of multiplier effect. A more cynical interpretation is that making no announcement provides for plausible deniability in case the intervention fails. The major exception to the rule is the U.S. Federal Reserve Board, which has long published monthly intervention aggregates several months after the fact, and which in 1991 began releasing daily intervention data after three months had passed. Regardless of the secrecy principle, however, Dominguez (1989, 1999) shows that markets are often able to detect intervention (especially when it is in large amounts) with rather high accuracy.

77. Personal interviews.

78. See, for example, Kojo 1993. Komiya and Suda's (1991) substantial account of Japanese exchange rate policy from 1971 to 1982 underscores the importance of exchange rates in the view of the government and private-sector experts in Japan.

79. Personal interviews.

Figure 3.3   Foreign Exchange Reserves

Note: End of month.
Sources: MOF downloadable statistics (9/96-); MOF, International Finance Bureau *Annual Reports;*
Japan Economic Newswire.

or securities, the proceeds of which must be reinvested. While it may not be strictly correct to think of the decision to use those proceeds for either domestic or foreign assets as intervention, it clearly affects the central bank's net foreign exchange position. When foreign-denominated securities mature, the central bank must decide whether to replace them with securities denominated in the same currency, a different foreign currency, or the home currency. This is another area where the Bank could quite legally have at least some effect on intervention (especially because such reserves are generally held in short-term securities that mature often). Again, participants and observers offer no evidence that that ever occurs—rather, the consensus is that the BOJ's management of foreign reserves complements MOF intervention policy.[80]

The final, and certainly most important, area in which BOJ funds figure in intervention is "sterilization," or preventing currency interventions from affecting the domestic money supply. Like most central banks, the Bank of Japan routinely provides or absorbs money in the domestic market to counteract any

80. Personal interviews.

potentially inflationary or deflationary effects of foreign exchange intervention. Unsterilized intervention has long been recognized to have a greater effect on exchange rates than sterilized, because it directly affects domestic money supply, while sterilized intervention is presumed to have an effect only through either signaling channels or temporary psychological impacts.[81] In reality, however, the question of whether a given intervention is sterilized is largely an academic distinction—monetary policy operations respond to market conditions, and intervention is but one of many factors that lead to disturbances in money markets. In other words, intervention will be sterilized *de facto* if it causes a change in supply or demand for funds that officials in the BOJ's Market Operations Division consider significant, even though those officials may well be completely ignorant of the fact that a specific intervention has actually occurred.

Information

In foreign exchange intervention as in other areas, access and control over information is a key dimension of institutional power. One part of the intervention process in which the BOJ has meaningful leverage is data collection and analysis. Most directly, the BOJ's Foreign Exchange Division (which carries out currency intervention) collects daily reports from all of the major Japanese foreign exchange banks on their own current positions and buy and sell orders, as well as those of their clients (particularly importers and exporters). These data are enormously important to any understanding of where foreign exchange markets are likely to head in the short term and therefore to any decision about how to respond.[82] The data allow the authorities to plan their intervention tactics and strategies more effectively—BOJ officials describe their counterparts at international central bankers' meetings as frankly envious of their figures.[83] However, the aggregated form in which the BOJ provides this data to MOF means that often MOF must depend on the BOJ analysis.

Politics of Exchange Rate Intervention

What role do politicians play in exchange rate intervention? Although intervention is the area of international economic policy in which direct ac-

---

81. The distinction between sterilized and unsterilized intervention is clearly made in the so-called Jurgensen Report (Working Group on Exchange Market Intervention 1983). For theorizing on signaling, etc., see Ghosh 1990; Dominguez 1989; and Dominguez and Frankel 1993.
82. Personal interviews with current and former BOJ and MOF officials. It is claimed that in particularly hectic intervention periods, the BOJ receives three or four such reports per day.
83. Personal interviews. Of course, how much of a difference even such detailed figures make is open to question, given the hit-or-miss nature of intervention.

cess may well be weakest, political actors can play a major role in times of crisis—which are, after all, the times when intervention really matters. There are two mechanisms through which politicians can affect intervention behavior: by direct order, and by budgeting for the Foreign Exchange Fund Special Account from which the BOJ intervenes.

On a day-to-day basis, the finance minister (and sometimes the prime minister) are notified of intervention, but in keeping with the principle of secrecy regarding intervention, other politicians are not informed. In times of crisis, however, political leaders are quite capable of making their wishes known. According to Gyohten Toyoo, a former vice-minister of finance for international affairs, then–prime minister Nakasone demanded in June 1986 that he stabilize the yen at a lower level before the July election. Clearly, the only policy instrument readily available in such a time frame was intervention, and MOF intervened accordingly, although Gyohten was aware that it would likely be ineffective.[84] Of course, a great deal of intervention occurs without the demands of political leaders, but insofar as intervention can offer a concrete measure of MOF responsiveness to their concerns, it is a useful (and low-cost) method of appeasement.

As for the possibility of cutting off funding to the special account, it appears never to have been threatened; in any event it would be an empty threat. First, if intervention were actually approaching the special account's limit, it would undoubtedly be doing so in the direction favored by the ruling party or coalition; if addressing exchange rates is at all urgent, neither ruling nor opposition parties are likely to protest an expansion. Second, even if the special account were to become temporarily unavailable, MOF and the BOJ could use other funds to intervene.

---

84. Volcker and Gyohten 1992, 257. A range of personal interviews also support the view that when the prime minister or finance minister gets exercised about the exchange rate, the ministry responds by carrying out interventions as called for.

4

Plaza-Louvre Period, 1985–87

International Influences on Domestic Policy

[I]n view of the present and prospective changes in fundamentals, some further orderly appreciation of the main non-dollar currencies against the dollar is desirable.

Plaza Agreement communiqué, September 22, 1985

From 1985 to 1987, Japanese macroeconomic politics revolved around the problem of choosing an appropriate domestic policy mix in the face of international economic shocks. It was a period of intense discussion of economic policy coordination among the world's leading economies. In the name of reducing international imbalances, the Japanese government was pressured to allow the yen to appreciate rapidly and to promote domestic demand. It responded with a policy mix that was fundamentally unsound, and that set the stage for the ruinous bubble economy. But to understand that response, an examination of external pressure is not enough—we must also look at the domestic policy-making structure.

The period breaks down naturally into four phases, each of which presented Japanese policy makers with a different set of challenges. From spring 1985 until the end of the year, the emphasis was primarily on lowering the level of the dollar through foreign exchange market intervention. From January to June 1986, *ad hoc* monetary policy coordination emerged as the centerpiece of international coordination efforts, even as the U.S. team was pushing for a more formalized, comprehensive framework. From the appointment of Miyazawa Kiichi as finance minister in July 1986 until just before the Louvre Accord in February 1987, signs of more comprehensive bilateral U.S.–Japanese coordination began to appear. Finally, from the Louvre Accord until the end of 1987, there was a shift to coordination of domestic demand management. I begin, however, with the initial context, provided by the policies of the U.S. and Japanese governments in the early 1980s.

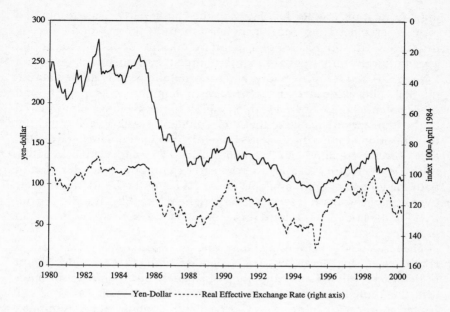

Figure 4.1   Exchange Rates

Source: BOJ downloadable statistics.

Past as Prologue: The Early 1980s

In November 1980, voters in the United States elected Ronald Reagan president on a platform of tax cuts and more forceful American leadership in the world. The experiment known as Reaganomics began in earnest the following year, with unprecedented tax cuts accompanied by increases in government spending. The unsurprising result of the experiment was massive budget deficits at the same time that corporate and personal savings rates began to decline. Coupled with the anti-inflationary program of the Federal Reserve Board, the resulting high interest rates drew massive foreign investment and raised the value of the dollar (Figure 4.1).

Meanwhile, in Japan there was a growing consensus against the loose fiscal policies that had produced staggering deficits in the 1970s. The consensus included many of the most influential actors in Japanese politics—big business, the financial industry, the Ministry of Finance, and several LDP faction leaders. With the country entering a period of slower economic growth, they realized that rising revenues could no longer be expected to cover the growing budgetary gap.

At the same time, political pressures for higher entitlements spending and the need to buy votes with pork-barrel programs made targeted spending cuts unappealing for legislators in the ruling party. They responded with an agreement to reduce the deficit to zero by the end of the decade by freezing current government spending (except for certain items that were politically important at the international level, such as defense and foreign aid) and privatizing government corporations. This allowed for traditional political tussles over apportionment of public works spending and other potential pork, but made them subject to strict ceilings administered by the Ministry of Finance so that they would not systematically affect the fiscal position of the national government.[1] Off-budget financing from the Fiscal Investment and Loan Program provided another cushion to public works-dependent legislators, and the early 1980s saw an acceleration in both the growth of funds available to the FILP and the trend toward their use for public works and social welfare-oriented spending. But the general trend of the budget was toward fiscal consolidation, seen in a reduction in fiscal deficits.

The result was that government dissavings decreased, while private savings continued at a high level—exactly the opposite of the U.S. economy. Almost by definition, this led to a ballooning of Japanese bilateral trade surpluses with the United States and a corresponding flow of capital back to the United States, as Japanese savings covered public and private consumption and investment in the United States.[2] While other events and trends of great significance to the international financial system also played out in the early 1980s—the most obvious being the Latin American debt crisis and the increasing international mobility of capital—for our purposes, the 1980s can best be described as the interplay between the growth of U.S.–induced imbalances and international attempts to counteract them.

The consequences of national macroeconomic policies began to appear early in the 1980s. At the Ottawa Summit in 1981, German chancellor Helmut Schmidt complained that U.S. monetary policy had brought Germany "the highest real interest rates since the birth of Christ."[3] The following year, at the Versailles Summit, France's president Mitterand pushed for more coordinated intervention to stabilize exchange rates in the face of the surging dollar and sagging franc. Bilaterally, the United States and Japan embarked on the ill-fated Yen-Dollar talks in autumn 1983.[4] Begun at the initiative of Treasury Secretary Donald Regan and Undersecretary

1. Capital spending and special accounts—under which most construction spending falls— were not directly subject to the agreement (Kato 1994, 144).
2. The definition to which I refer is the national income accounting identity $(S-I) + (T-G) = (X-M)$. I say "almost by definition" because the U.S.-Japan bilateral balance could conceivably have remained the same, while U.S. deficits and Japanese surpluses with the rest of the world grew instead. Nonetheless, at the aggregate level it still meant massive current account imbalances and Japanese financing of U.S. budget deficits. The latter kept U.S. interest rates from rising higher than they already had by preventing crowding out.
3. Putnam and Bayne 1987, 130.
4. For an excellent, concise account, see Frankel 1984.

Beryl Sprinkel, the negotiations were based on the flawed assumption that more open capital markets in Japan would make the yen a more attractive medium of investment, and thus raise its value relative to the dollar. While the Yen-Dollar Agreement may well have had some implications for Japanese financial markets, it did nothing to fix the major imbalances in the world economy.[5]

By the beginning of 1985, unease over the trade balance, and by extension over the value of the dollar, had reached unprecedented heights. Not only was the United States regularly pressed by its G-5 and Economic Summit partners to do something about the problem, but domestic pressures were growing as well. According to one analysis, four hundred protectionist bills were submitted to the Congress in that year alone[6]; meanwhile business and labor groups supported the efforts of legislators such as Sen. Bill Bradley and Sen. John Danforth to force the administration to reduce the value of the dollar.

Economists too added their collective voice: although some, such as Beryl Sprinkel (by 1985 the chairman of the President's Council of Economic Advisers), continued to toe the "strong dollar" line, mainstream analysis found the dollar to be overvalued by at least 10–20 percent. Some even worried about the problem of "sustainability": they feared that the U.S. economy would be unable to pay off the debts it was amassing, and that when markets finally realized it investors would flee dollar-denominated assets.[7] This would lead to a "hard landing," in which the dollar would drop precipitously and the U.S. public and private sector would find themselves unable to obtain the funds they needed without paying prohibitively high premiums. This in turn would lead to recession in the United States and in the world economy in general. Japan additionally feared that the United States—by far its largest single export market—might impose exclusionary trade policies in order to protect domestic firms hurt by an overvalued dollar. It was in this atmosphere that the rescue attempts of the Plaza-Louvre period were to begin.

Dealing with Dollar Anxieties, June–December 1985

The dollar reached a peak on February 26, hitting DM3.469 and ¥263.65 to the dollar. America's G-5 partners continued to complain loudly about lack of cooperation. In January and again in February Germany inter-

5. Rosenbluth (1989, 5) argues that the negotiations were not a major cause of market liberalization.
6. This figure was quite popular among Japanese at the time—for example, see Volcker and Gyohten (1992, 249).
7. For example, Marris 1985; Krugman 1985; and Ishii, McKibbin, and Sachs 1985.

vened in large amounts with some support from its EC brethren but without significant support from either the United States or Japan. In subsequent G-5 meetings, its representatives complained bitterly about that inaction but were unable to get commitments for coordinated intervention in the future.[8]

Increasing U.S. Flexibility

In spite of what appeared to be continued unwillingness on the part of the United States to intervene, in April 1985 Assistant Secretary of the Treasury for International Affairs David Mulford began talking in earnest with Vice-Minister for International Affairs Ōba Tomomitsu about trying to get the two countries to agree on a strategy to lower the value of the dollar.[9] Ōba finally approached Finance Minister Takeshita with the idea of coordinated intervention in June.[10] Takeshita in turn broached the subject privately with U.S. Treasury secretary Baker following the fractious G-10 meeting in Tokyo that month. Baker agreed that coordination might indeed be a good idea—in fact, he wanted to expand the idea beyond simple exchange rate intervention to include macroeconomic and structural policies as well, to which Takeshita demurred. Nonetheless, they agreed to leave it to Mulford and Ōba to discuss the plan in greater detail.

Ōba and Mulford quickly agreed upon a strategy of cementing a bilateral plan first, and then letting the Europeans in on it.[11] According to a number of former MOF officials, the Treasury was pushing for rather wide-ranging policy coordination, while MOF was steadfast in wanting to discuss only exchange market intervention.[12] In the end, the more narrow plan won out. By early August, they had solidified a plan for large-scale, coordinated intervention and presented it to the other G-5 deputies. The G-5D (G-5 deputies) forum specifically does not include central bank representatives—the finance ministries wished to keep central bankers out of the decision-making process until their cooperation was clearly needed.[13] By early September, deputies had completed the basic document for ministerial negotiation, with spaces in those spots that might involve specific commitments by the members of the G-5; other com-

---

8. See Funabashi 1989; Iida 1990; Ohta 1991.
9. Personal interviews.
10. Takeshita does not remember it exactly that way—in his memoirs, he takes full credit for coming up with the idea, and for initiating the Plaza process (Takeshita 1991, 153). According to Funabashi (1989, 88), Nakasone also took full credit. Other observers, however, are almost unanimous in their opinion that Ōba was responsible. Personal interviews.
11. Personal interviews.
12. Other officials state that both Ōba and Mulford saw exchange market intervention as the first step (or even a test case) in an evolutionary process toward more comprehensive coordination. Personal interviews.
13. Personal interviews.

mitments included in the eventual communiqué were simply restatements of existing policy plans.[14]

The circle of people with foreknowledge of the Plaza plans was extremely small. In Japan, only Ōba, Takeshita, and Prime Minister Nakasone Yasuhiro knew about them until a little more than a week before the meeting was to occur, when BOJ governor Sumita Satoshi was finally informed. In the United States, the circle was just as small, comprising Baker, Undersecretary Richard Darman, and Mulford. Baker finally informed the president, and received his approval, the Tuesday before the meeting. Federal Reserve Board chairman Paul Volcker was brought in the next day.[15] Secrecy was considered so important that on the day he was to go to New York, Sumita actually faked a cold, and went to the airport in a surgical mask so that he would not be recognized. Similarly, on Saturday morning, Takeshita loaded his golf clubs into the trunk of his car and played nine holes; during his break, he ducked out and sped off to the airport in his golf clothes.[16]

The Plaza

The meeting went as planned,[17] and the resulting communiqué followed the draft text very closely, with two exceptions. First, Volcker, fearful of the prospect of a hard landing, insisted on changing the phrase "further appreciation of the non-dollar currencies" to read "further *orderly* appreciation of the non-dollar currencies." Second, in the face of opposition by central bankers protective of their territories, all mention of interest rates was deleted. The negotiations themselves thus dealt mainly with coordinated intervention. The central question was how much of the intervention burden each country would take on.[18] There were also technical questions concerning where and when to intervene. Surprisingly, in spite of the multiplicity of issues discussed by various combinations of officials and the fact that altering exchange rates was the whole reason for the exercise, most par-

14. These include, for example, commitments by the United States to reduce its deficits and by Germany to reduce some taxes. For the text of the communiqué, see Funabashi (1989, 261–266). As Volcker puts it, "To the best of my knowledge, no budget, trade, or structural policy was changed as a result of the Plaza" (Volcker and Gyohten 1992, 245).
15. Funabashi 1989; Volcker and Gyohten 1992; Sumita 1992; personal interviews. For the best account of the Plaza meeting and the events leading up to it, there is no substitute for Funabashi's work. Incidentally, the Plaza was a rare case in which the central bank deputies (Ogata Shijūrō in the case of Japan) participated in the final preparatory meeting for a G-5 meeting.
16. See Sumita 1992; Takeshita 1992; Volcker and Gyohten 1992; and Funabashi 1989.
17. As Ohta Takeshi put it, "it was a very beautiful, well-arranged political show." Lecture at Princeton University, March 22, 1994.
18. If the ministers had really had confidence in the exercise, they should not have thought of intervention as a burden at all—if they had expected the dollar's value to go down, they should have been happy to sell their dollar holdings. Ghosh (1992) mentions this paradoxical point as well.

ticipants and third-party accounts agree that target rates were never set or even discussed.[19]

The main event was the news conference to announce the agreement. While some accounts suggest that that show of unity was sufficient to move the market,[20] a closer look at both contemporary analyses and market responses shows a different picture. Several contemporary observers pointed out that there was no explicit commitment to changing the level of the dollar, and no mention of intervention; rather, they saw simply a restatement of announcements that had been made time and again in the past and had never been acted upon. A particularly pungent example came from the *Economist:* "Finance ministers would like to think that they just have to buy simultaneous tickets to New York, and that then markets will do their bidding. But most investors are not hurrying to believe the Plaza cabal."[21]

The markets appeared similarly unconvinced. Because Monday, September 21, was a national holiday in Japan,[22] the first markets to open were in Europe, and the dollar did indeed lose ground against the other G-5 currencies with the encouragement of considerable intervention. However, the dollar soon stabilized as market participants engaged in profit-taking. When the Japanese market opened the next morning, MOF intervened aggressively, and the reverse trend soon ended. MOF officials point to the success of that intervention with some pride as being the action that guaranteed the success of the Plaza Agreement, and in fact it certainly coincided with the end of the dollar's rally.[23] Nevertheless, market acceptance of a lower dollar was not really complete until the following week, suggesting that governments had to purchase credibility through intervention.

19. The major exception, however, is Funabashi (1989), who is seldom faulted on matters of fact—he writes of a broad agreement to lower the dollar by 10–12 percent in the first six weeks, with no agreed targets thereafter. In any event, Germany soon claimed the right to stop intervening once the dollar had depreciated 7 percent against the mark in the space of two weeks.

20. For example, Destler and Henning 1989, 42.

21. *Economist,* September 28, 1985. The *New York Times* and *Washington Post* showed similar skepticism. Japanese newspapers were more straightforward in their news coverage, and because of a newspaper holiday the first editorials in the *Nikkei* and *Asahi Shimbun* did not appear until September 25, at which point the yen had already risen to ¥228 to the dollar. Both of those publications welcomed a "return to common sense" (*jōshiki no kaifuku*) but concentrated more on a now forgotten trade address given by President Reagan on September 23.

22. The holiday is the autumnal equinox. Funabashi without irony describes Ōba as having carefully looked up the proper English translation and come up with "vernal equinox" (Funabashi 1989, 28). His counterparts were presumably forgiving of the mistake.

23. Personal interviews.

BOJ "Support"

Within a couple of weeks, the Europeans stopped intervening, with Germany claiming that the dollar had depreciated sufficiently, but the United States and Japan were not quite satisfied with the extent of the depreciation. Late in October, the Bank of Japan allowed short-term interest rates to rise in order to stop the dollar from stabilizing at the then-current rate of about ¥218.[24] The maneuver worked, but it brought on the wrath of both Japan's G-5 partners and the Ministry of Finance. At a meeting convened in early November under the auspices of the OECD, BOJ representative Ohta Takeshi (the new deputy governor for international affairs) was roundly criticized by the representatives of both finance ministries and central banks, although his MOF counterpart Ōba offered token support. The BOJ publicly denied that the move had any international significance at all, claiming that it had been taken as a response to "technical matters." By mid-November, the episode was over, to the relief of all of the participants. However, it had been effective in breaking the yen-dollar rate out of its rut, and the dollar continued to depreciate against the yen through the rest of 1985.

Other actors' resistance to the BOJ's effort to raise interest rates seems strange at first glance. First of all, decreasing the value of the dollar versus the yen was still very much a part of both U.S. and Japanese policy, and there is no more effective way of altering exchange rates than altering the interest rate differential between two countries. Moreover, the Plaza Agreement had said nothing about interest rate management or even about exchanging information on planned monetary policies, so the Bank of Japan was correct in its assertion that it had not violated the Agreement. If the interest rate action had violated neither the letter nor the intent of the Agreement, then what was the basis for these objections?

From the U.S. side, they were twofold.[25] First, Volcker remained exceedingly nervous about the possible impact of a free fall in the value of the dollar and feared that higher Japanese interest rates might trigger a run. More importantly, the greatest fear of most of the participants in the process, including Baker and Volcker, was that the decline of the dollar might lead to recession in other countries, endangering both the international economy and the positive effects on the U.S. current account of dollar depreciation.[26] Thus,

24. While the BOJ has never publicly acknowledged that it in fact made such a decision, interviews with MOF and the BOJ officials, as well as observers from the press and the markets, confirm that it did in fact take place. Among former BOJ officials, Ohta's memoirs state quite clearly that it occurred (1991, 104), as do Ogata's (1996, 23) and Mieno's (2000, 191–192). As both Ohta and Mieno explain it, long-term rates suddenly dropped as a result of U.S. interest rate declines, which stalled the rise of the yen. The BOJ stepped in at that point to raise long-term rates by tightening short-term rates, which both authors see as having been decisive in breaking the market psychology that was keeping the dollar from dropping further. See also Funabashi 1989; Volcker and Gyohten 1992.

25. See Funabashi 1989, 33. Also personal interviews.

26. Volcker and Gyohten 1992, 246; Funabashi 1989, 33.

a rise in Japanese interest rates would only be counterproductive. The Ministry of Finance similarly feared the deflationary effects of yen appreciation. It is also possible that MOF bureaucrats worried about the country's fiscal position.[27] In any event, with the Bank of Japan subdued, the dollar continued a gentle downward trend through November and December. The year 1985 ended with the dollar at ¥200.60.

Rising Yen and Falling Interest Rates, January–June 1986

January 1986 opened with Finance Minister Takeshita saying to reporters, "How much of a difference is there between ¥201 and ¥199?"[28] The markets accurately interpreted this to mean that Japan would not intervene against the yen if it broke the ¥200 mark, and it quickly moved into the upper ¥190s. While the Ministry of Finance and Bank of Japan seemed satisfied with the new level, Japanese exporters were less pleased, even though it at least seemed to offer the promise of stability. Small- and medium-sized corporations were particularly worried about their ability to retain their foreign markets.

At the same time, the likelihood that such a rapid appreciation might be extremely recessionary for the Japanese economy became increasingly obvious. In spite of the foreknowledge from September that the value of the yen would be much higher, however, neither the Economic Planning Agency's economic forecast nor MOF's final budget draft showed any sign of trying to counteract the deflationary effects of a higher yen. Former officials of both the Ministry and the BOJ point out that the deflationary effects of an appreciated currency are counteracted by the expansionary effects on spending of lower import prices, and that in previous experiences of steep yen appreciation recession had in fact not been a problem. Also, they considered it a bad precedent for the forecast or budget draft to contain exchange rate predictions.[29] In any event, once deflationary pressures began to show themselves in early 1986, it was clear that only monetary policy could address the problem, and on January 30 the Bank of Japan lowered the discount rate from 5 percent to 4.5 percent. This action went along with the wishes of all major actors—the Treasury and the Fed were relieved that Japan was taking steps to increase its domestic demand, which they thought would be helpful for the world economy; the Fed and Japanese exporters (and presumably their Diet representatives) could breathe easier

27. Slower economic growth would directly lower tax revenues, and perhaps increase outlays for entitlements. Indirectly, slower growth might also have prompted calls for fiscal loosening.
28. Takeshita 1991, 159.
29. Personal interviews.

about the possibility of a free fall in the dollar; and the Ministry of Finance felt no pressure to compromise its commitment to fiscal consolidation for the sake of domestic demand.

Coordinated Discount Rate Cuts

Despite the discount rate change, the yen continued to rise against the dollar, the U.S. trade deficit continued to increase, and the U.S. economy remained relatively slack. Most members of the Federal Reserve Board, including Volcker, were basically in favor of lowering interest rates to deal with lagging domestic demand. However, Volcker argued that such action was likely to hurt confidence in the dollar, and should be postponed until the central banks of Germany and Japan acted to lower their interest rates as well. A minor rebellion among some board members in February provided a strong impetus for Volcker to pursue coordinated interest rate cuts,[30] which he immediately did. Bank of Japan officials were apparently not aware of Volcker's political situation, but they were generally receptive to the arguments presented. German officials also decided that their domestic economy could use a monetary infusion, as did France. On March 6 and 7, the four countries cut key interest rates, although they did not admit publicly that the cuts were coordinated.

On April 21, the United States and Japan again carried out simultaneous interest rate cuts following a G-5 meeting in which Baker and Volcker pressured Governor Sumita for a discount rate cut. Unlike the March action, most of the Executive Board of the Bank of Japan was not pleased with the April cut. They felt that it followed too closely on the heels of the March cut, and that it would hurt the credibility of the bank as an autonomous, nonpolitical actor. Most of all, they felt that there was no economic need to loosen monetary policy at that point, and that if anything were to be done it should be a fiscal stimulus. Nevertheless, Sumita had made a commitment to Japan's G-5 partners, and the Bank had little choice but to live up to that promise.[31] There are undercurrents of a MOF role as well. First, Sumita is unlikely to have made such a commitment at a G-5 meeting (where both Takeshita and Ōba were in attendance) without encouragement from his MOF counterparts, and there is no evidence that the ministry objected to the cut. Second, MOF had positioned itself as the conduit for all international negotiations, and the Treasury and even the Fed generally talked with ministry officials before bringing up cuts with the Bank of Japan.[32]

30. See Funabashi (1989, 48–49) for an excellent third-party account of the so-called Palace Coup. Volcker and Gyohten (1992, 274) also touch on it.
31. Personal interviews. See also Ohta 1991, 107. Mieno (2000, 205) points to "international commitments" as the reason for what he considers excessive rate cuts.
32. According to Hosomi Makoto (a former MOF vice-minister for international affairs),Volcker always contacted the international vice-minister to seek his opinion before approaching

The "Policy Mix" Question

By this time, BOJ officials were complaining that the macroeconomic "policy mix" was skewed in the direction of monetary policy and that well-balanced adjustment required active fiscal policy measures as well. Miyazawa Kiichi, an LDP faction leader and high-ranking party official, was also calling for a fiscal stimulus to stem what appeared to be the possibility of a full-fledged "high-yen recession" (*endaka fukyō*). Meanwhile, the yen continued to appreciate in spite of continued Japanese efforts against it, and the mass media produced dark, almost hysterical forecasts that the high yen would ruin Japan's economy.[33] And Baker continued to talk down the dollar. The result was massive pressure on the Japanese government to do something. However, the policy mix argument was anathema to career MOF officials, particularly those in the Budget Bureau, because it threatened the drive for fiscal consolidation. They also argued that monetary loosening was the optimal policy because it would tend to lower the value of the yen at the same time that it stimulated the economy.

Adding to the growing debate on suitable economic policies was the publication in April of the Maekawa Report.[34] The Maekawa Commission was a blue-ribbon panel of elder businessmen, former bureaucrats, and academics headed by Maekawa Haruo (a highly respected former governor of the Bank of Japan) empaneled in autumn 1985 by Prime Minister Nakasone to produce a blueprint for making Japan's economy more open and efficient. The general focus of the report was on structural reforms, reflecting the belief that barriers to competition were reducing opportunities for foreign exporters and investors. Nevertheless, the former bureaucrats on the commission kept close contact with their respective agencies, ensuring that nothing objectionable to those agencies would appear in the report.[35] In the end, the report faithfully reflected the views of the Ministry of Finance regarding macroeconomic policy—it called for flexible monetary policy to deal with domestic demand and continuation of the policy of fiscal reconsolidation.

---

the Bank of Japan. If the vice-minister told him that such matters were the concern of the Bank of Japan, it was taken as MOF approval to go ahead with the initiative. Personal interview. Perhaps even more revealing, the official interpreter at the time for the BOJ governor in G-5 meetings was the MOF deputy vice-minister for international affairs!

33. BOJ governor Sumita even began to receive threats and crank calls at home, and was given police protection (Sumita 1992, 113–114).

34. Formally, the report was called *The Report of the Advisory Group on Economic Structural Adjustment* (1986).

35. Personal interview with Hosomi Makoto, the MOF OB participant on the Commission.

The Tokyo Summit

In the midst of this ferment, Japan hosted the Tokyo Summit in May. The Japanese participants lobbied hard for relief from the still-rising yen, but their wishes were thwarted. Instead, the Summit concentrated on two issues. The more minor one from the perspective of policy coordination was a demand from Italy and Canada to shift the finance ministers' club from G-5 to G-7. What appeared to be the more important debate was over Baker and Darman's proposal for "multilateral surveillance with objective indicators." This proposal, which was agreed upon at the Summit, would have made countries' commitments at the G-7 subject to evaluation based on indicators such as GDP growth, unemployment rates, and inflation. If a given country were seen not to be fulfilling its pledges, it would be expected to rectify its economic policies. Understandably, this proposal made countries like Germany and Japan nervous since they felt they might be forced to sacrifice autonomy; to their eventual relief, the objective indicators exercise never came to much.[36]

Despite Japan's failure to get action on the yen at the Tokyo Summit, the yen's value remained a major obsession. Perhaps the greatest impulse behind actions to slow the rise of the yen was the "double election" of June 1986, Nakasone's gamble to reverse a two-decade-long trend of flagging LDP support by holding the Lower House election on the same day as the scheduled Upper House election. In Japan, a country where exchange rates are front-page news, the unabated rise of the yen was a major political albatross for the government; in fact, as the election approached, it became a fixation of Nakasone's. As Gyohten Toyoo, MOF vice-minister for international affairs in 1986–88, later wrote:

> Right after the summit meeting [May 1986], I told Prime Minister Nakasone I thought the market was still not convinced the dollar had fallen sufficiently, and that we had better wait, let the dollar slide somewhat more, and then hit the market with a massive, surprise intervention. Nakasone sounded very understanding and said, "I know you experts know much better than I do about the exchange rate." But then he added, "You have to restore it to one hundred and seventy yen before the election.[37]

Urgent signals were received in Washington as well. In response, Baker temporarily stopped talking down the dollar, and even testified to Congress

36. As one MOF official who had occasion to deal with the objective indicators put it, the only real effect was to put extra reams of paper into the hands of each finance minister, none of whom save Miyazawa was really able to process them. Therefore, once the managing director of the IMF left the room, the numbers were ignored. Personal interviews.
37. Volcker and Gyohten 1992, 257. Since Gyohten does not give a date, it is hard to know just what the rate was at the time of the conversation. It was probably in the low to mid-¥160s, and falling.

that the administration was satisfied with the current level. Meanwhile, the Ministry of Finance continued to intervene on behalf of the dollar, apparently unilaterally[38] (see Figure 3.3). However, the Bank of Japan steadfastly resisted repeated requests from the United States to lower interest rates, and even began raising short-term interest rates in preparation for a discount rate hike in the fall.

First Fiscal Responses, July 1986–February 1987

The double election was a huge success for the LDP—it won more seats in the Lower House than it had at any other time in its thirty-one-year history, and expanded its commanding majority in the Upper House as well. It also afforded Miyazawa Kiichi the opportunity to become finance minister, as Takeshita Noboru moved to a party post from which he would concentrate on making himself the next prime minister. Miyazawa was both knowledgeable about economic matters (as a MOF OB) and the most prominent LDP politician supporting fiscal loosening. In fact, he had been publicly calling for a fiscal stimulus for months, much to the annoyance of Ministry of Finance officials and some of his fellows in the LDP. In July 1986, he was given the chance to try to put his ideas into policy.[39]

The Baker-Miyazawa Agreement

Miyazawa's public statements suggested to Treasury officials that resuming negotiations on stimulating Japanese domestic demand would be profitable, and a meeting between Miyazawa and Baker was quickly set up. As it turned out, the scheduled meeting was leaked (in his book, Gyohten seems to imply that the source of the leak was in MOF) and quickly called off. Another meeting was scheduled more secretly, and on September 6 the two met in San Francisco.[40] While Miyazawa was impatient to implement a fiscal stimulus in Japan, he also realized its utility as a bargaining chip to get the American side to stop talking down the dollar and to restrain its fiscal deficit. The career officials at the Ministry of Finance concurred on the need to change U.S. behavior, if not necessarily on the desirability of a fiscal stimulus.

---

38. Funabashi 1989, 152–155.
39. Ibid., 98–99.
40. The finance minister worked hard to remain incognito. Once the news leaked that Miyazawa was in San Francisco, Japanese newspapers tried desperately to find where he was staying. One paper even sent bouquets to every hotel in the city in hopes of smoking him out (Volcker and Gyohten 1992, 264–265). While charming in itself, the story also shows the deep distrust Miyazawa held for his underlings in the Ministry of Finance, since he planned his trip through the consul-general in San Francisco (a Ministry of Foreign Affairs official). Miyazawa did bring Gyohten with him, however.

In negotiations at both ministerial and deputy levels, the Japanese pushed hard to get the Treasury to agree to cooperate to stabilize the dollar, while the Americans called for stimulation of Japanese domestic demand.[41] Following extensive negotiation, that is exactly what was agreed to. The Baker-Miyazawa Agreement, announced October 31, included a cut in the Japanese discount rate to 3 percent (the fourth cut that year) and a commitment to fiscal stimulus, in exchange for an explicit statement by Baker that the exchange rate was at a satisfactory level and a restatement of the U.S. intention to reduce the budget deficit.

As it turned out, however, the agreement satisfied no one. To start with, the U.S. negotiators felt that the Japanese had deceived them on the question of the exchange rate. They had agreed to the language "the exchange rate realignment ... is now consistent with the present underlying fundamentals" on September 26. At that time the exchange rate had been ¥153–154 to the dollar, but by the time of the announcement the yen had weakened to ¥161–163. A number of officials strongly suspected that the Ministry of Finance had manipulated the exchange rate during that period in order to force the Treasury to defend a higher value of the dollar than it had intended. Accordingly, Mulford insisted on inserting the word "broadly" before "consistent" in the communiqué.[42] More importantly, the Treasury made no effort to intervene to defend that level, although Baker's talking down of the dollar did subside temporarily. Soon after the agreement was announced, the yen resumed its upward trend, with no hint of U.S. countermeasures.

Not surprisingly, Miyazawa and the Ministry of Finance were unhappy with the U.S. unwillingness to defend the exchange rate. They denied that MOF had had any role whatsoever in the weakening of the yen, and objected that the Treasury had not lived up to its side of the bargain. The Treasury's passivity in the face of the rise in the yen was particularly damaging to Miyazawa, who had hoped to get political mileage out of the agreement and thus had touted it highly.

The Supplemental Budget of 1986

Although in the end he promised both sides far more than he could deliver, Miyazawa's commitment to fiscal stimulus as a means of reducing international imbalances and bringing the Japanese economy out of recession did lead to the compilation of a ¥3 trillion supplemental budget. However, reaction from the United States, the Bank of Japan, private-sector analysts, and

41. However, according to former MOF officials knowledgeable about the negotiations, the Treasury never crossed the unwritten diplomatic line by suggesting specific policies by which Japan should do so, nor did it suggest targets (personal interviews). This approach contrasts sharply with coordination attempts under the Clinton administration.
42. Funabashi 1989, 156–164. His account is confirmed by various personal interviews.

the press was swift: *"mamizu ga nai"* (literally, "no fresh water"—in other words, there was no substance to it). While many current and former MOF officials dispute that assessment, they concede that the Ministry worked hard to minimize the size of the stimulus.[43]

In the United States, the supplemental budget only worked to reconfirm the Treasury team's suspicions that the Japanese had bargained in bad faith. It also caused considerable consternation in the Bank of Japan, where the discount rate cut had been accepted only because it was seen as part of a deal to improve the macroeconomic policy mix. In the Bank's analysis, MOF had once again taken advantage of it, leaving the BOJ to deal with any possible complications.[44] The remaining piece of the agreement was to prove a bust thereafter—neither Gramm-Rudman nor the U.S. deficit reduction agreement of December 1986 would prove to have the desired impact on the U.S. budget deficit.

By January 15, the yen had passed the ¥150 barrier, and was still climbing. The situation brought about panic in Tokyo and an unplanned and urgent trip by Miyazawa to Washington on January 21, where he received no satisfaction at all—not even reassurance that the Treasury was taking the situation seriously.[45] He returned to Tokyo with nothing to show for his visit, unable to do anything but watch the dollar continue to plummet in the face of massive Japanese intervention. By February, however, the Treasury team had decided to return to multilateral negotiations. The result was the Louvre Accord, which signaled the beginning of the next phase of coordinated action.

From the Louvre to the Christmas Agreement, February–December 1987

On February 21, 1987, the G-5 convened again to discuss the problem of the dollar, this time in the offices of the French Ministry of Finance in the Louvre.[46] In some ways the circumstances were similar to those surround-

43. Personal interviews. On the other side, several current and former MOF officials offer the opinion that *mamizu* is a function not only of government borrowing, but also of the specific types of spending or tax cut undertaken. Since they believe that public works spending has a higher multiplier effect than other fiscal actions, they argue that the 1986 program had at least some effect.
44. Personal interviews. Former BOJ official Ogata also says as much (Ogata 1996, 26–27).
45. The visit did occasion some sarcasm, however. Funabashi quotes a Treasury official as saying, "When the sharp move came, he was in very bad shape. He came back here, you know, very fast" (1989, 162). The visit was entirely at Miyazawa's initiative. Former MOF officials report that they hardly had enough notice to schedule the proper meetings in Washington, much less arrange for any sort of substantive discussions. Personal interviews. The visit seems to fit what Cohen (1991) describes as Japan's "supplicant" mentality in negotiations with the United States.
46. The incidental politics were almost as interesting as the agreement itself. The accord was to be officially proclaimed on February 22 by the G-7, after the G-5 had already made

ing the Plaza meeting a year and a half earlier: current account imbalances were still at politically dangerous levels, U.S. budget deficits had shown no sign of decreasing, European economies were still growing slowly, and everyone was concerned about the dollar. The differences, however, were striking. The most obvious was that the central urgency was not an overvalued dollar, but rather a dollar seemingly in free fall, which threatened the international financial system.

Perhaps equally important was that over the previous ten months the G-5 had developed a framework for macroeconomic and exchange rate policy coordination. The centerpiece of formal mechanisms was multilateral surveillance with objective indicators, meant to add a discipline that previous coordination efforts had lacked. Despite the high hopes of American negotiators—and the misgivings of the Japanese and Germans—however, objective indicators added little to actual G-7 proceedings.[47]

While certain pieces of that framework were clearly not functioning as advertised, G-5 coordination had in some ways followed an evolutionary path as Mulford and Ōba had originally envisioned. It had begun with just coordinated intervention in exchange rate markets, and then progressed to *ad hoc* monetary policy coordination. The Baker-Miyazawa Agreement constituted an attempt at bilateral coordination that addressed fiscal, monetary, and exchange rate policies all at once. The Louvre Accord seemed the logical next step in a progression whose practical successes were becoming less and less apparent.

The Louvre Accord

The February 1987 Louvre Accord called for comprehensive macroeconomic policy coordination as the only means to solve global economic imbalances while ensuring world growth. Like previous G-5 and Summit communiqués, it declared its goal to be "stable, non-inflationary growth," but unlike those statements, it defined the means by which that was to be achieved. It also established, for the first time since 1973, a set of exchange rate targets among the seven largest market economies. That the assembled

---

its decisions. The Italian government found that arrangement to be unacceptable, with the result that Finance Minister Goria did not attend, and the accord was announced by what amounted to a G-6. Both Funabashi (1989) and Volcker and Gyohten (1992) contain colorful accounts of the blow-up.

47. According to one Japanese official who was involved in the process of preparation, the results of multilateral surveillance were "extremely disappointing." The indicators were all contradictory, which meant that there could be no automatic intervention—just more debate about what should be done. At least as important was the severe lag in getting statistics: it is impossible to know what the present growth rate is, for example. This view corresponds to the general consensus. Personal interviews. See also Volcker and Gyohten 1992, 276–279; Funabashi 1989, chap. 6.

finance ministers did so with impressive delicacy should not detract from a sense of the importance of that step.

Even at the Plaza, where the agreement was directed solely at exchange rates, there had been no explicit agreement over what those rates should be. At the Louvre, the participants agreed to set the current rates as informal targets, within an unannounced "reference range" around the current dollar exchange rates—¥153.50 and DM1.825. There would be an internal band of 2.5 percent within which countries were expected to try to keep rates, while between 2.5 percent and 5 percent countries were held to be obligated to intervene. If rates were to exceed those bands, the Accord called for consultation and possible rebasing.[48]

Beyond the important step of coming to an agreement again on exchange rate policy, the participants for the first time affirmed publicly the principle of policy coordination for the purpose of demand management. Moreover, the Louvre Accord called for a *systematic* approach to policy coordination, building on the practice of multilateral surveillance. Had it been successful, the accord would have produced a nearly constant process of consultation and adjustment based on mutually agreed-on targets and objective indicators.[49] In other words, national economic policy makers would have forfeited a considerable degree of discretion in pursuing their domestic agendas. However, even though the focus had turned in principle from exchange rate management to domestic demand management, coordinated intervention continued as a major policy instrument, as authorities in both the United States and Japan continued to prefer it to more difficult and costly fiscal policy measures.

Effects of the Louvre

The policy coordination exercise was damaged before it even began. The United States offered nothing more than its usual optimistic projections to show that this time the budget deficit was sure to decrease.[50] Meanwhile, bound by Japan's legislative agenda (the budget draft was still under consideration in the Diet), Miyazawa was unable to commit formally to a fiscal stimulus. The apparent reluctance on the part of the two states with the largest imbalances to contribute to their remediation had a predictably negative effect on the willingness of other states to change their policies. As usual, the burden was borne (to the extent that it was borne at all) by monetary policy, and record-low interest rates continued in Japan and Germany. Coincident

48. For details, see Funabashi 1989, chap. 8.
49. As Gyohten notes drily, adherence to the agreement would bring "economic fundamentals in line with the existing exchange rate regime. This was indeed a very hopeful interpretation" (Volcker and Gyohten 1992, 267).
50. Volcker and Gyohten 1992, 283.

with the Louvre Accord, the Bank of Japan lowered the country's discount rate for the fifth time in little over a year, to 2.5 percent.

Despite the high hopes and rhetoric of the Louvre Accord, and in spite of substantial coordinated intervention, the original reference ranges lasted only a couple of months.[51] On April 7, the yen-dollar rate was "rebased" at the prevailing rate of ¥146 to the dollar, and Secretary Baker soon resumed talking down the dollar, in direct contravention of the U.S. commitments in the Louvre Accord.

The Supplemental Budget of 1987

In March, as the Japanese budget for FY 1987 languished in the Diet,[52] the Ministry of Finance began work on a ¥6 trillion fiscal stimulus plan. The government introduced the package in the Diet in May, after the budget had finally been approved. Despite the unprecedented decision to introduce a supplementary budget so soon after the regular budget had been approved, the new plan again drew accusations of *"mamizu ga nai."* Ministry of Finance officials admit their unhappiness with having had to put together another stimulus package when in their view the recession was over, but object to the claim that there was nothing to the new package.[53] Indeed, unlike the 1986 package, there was some new money attached to the program in the form of a ¥1 trillion tax cut.[54] Nonetheless, the real stimulative impact was again far less than Japan's G-7 partners had hoped for.

Regardless of the effect of the package on the international economy, the ministry was clearly correct in its assessment that the economy had turned the corner. The first quarter of 1987 showed annualized GNP growth of 4.1 percent and the second half of the year saw a certifiable boom.[55] Asset prices began to soar, egged on by loose monetary policy, while consumer and wholesale prices remained stable. To finish out the equation, Japanese exports of goods and services remained competitive on world markets. In response to the upswing, the Bank of Japan acted once again to raise interbank lending rates over the summer as a prelude to raising the discount rate in the autumn.[56]

---

51. From March 23 to April 6, the New York Fed bought about $3 billion worth of yen, while observers estimate Japanese intervention in the first quarter of 1987 at $16 billion (Funabashi 1989, 188).
52. The reason for the delay in voting on the budget had to do with tax reform bills, treated in detail in Kato (1994, chap. 5).
53. Personal interviews.
54. This tax cut, like so many economic policy measures offered by various countries as their contributions to coordination, was the result of domestic political processes completely unrelated to international negotiations (Kato 1994, chap. 5).
55. Adjusted annual growth figures for the second, third, and fourth quarters were 3.0, 4.3, and 5.4 percent, respectively (*Nihon Tōkei Geppō*, no. 323, May 1988).
56. Personal interviews. It would have been difficult to raise rates more quickly, given the continued fragility of the dollar.

Black Monday and Aftermath

In the United States, Alan Greenspan replaced Paul Volcker as Fed chairman in August, and promptly raised interest rates to dampen inflationary pressures. This action helped stabilize the dollar, and seemed to clear the way for the Bank of Japan to carry through on its own plan to raise the discount rate. As it turned out, events were to intervene in the form of Black Monday, October 19, 1987, when the Dow Jones Industrial Average lost more than 20 percent of its total value. The Fed and its counterparts in other countries reacted quickly, providing a huge volume of liquidity to prevent the crash from spreading and leading to a worldwide financial crisis.

The first major market to open following Black Monday was the Tokyo Stock Exchange, and officials at the Ministry of Finance and the Bank of Japan worked overnight to prevent a continuation of the crash. It appears that discussions with MOF contributed to the decision by major institutional investors not to sell their holdings, thus stopping the crash from causing worldwide financial chaos. While markets remained somewhat unsettled, the story essentially ended in Tokyo on October 20.[57]

The cause of the crash will probably be debated for years, but it clearly showed the uncertainty of financial markets concerning economic policy. Following the crisis management by the Fed and other central banks, macroeconomic policy coordination was put on hold, and economic policy makers (including Baker) became very quiet about international economic matters. The G-7 finally issued a statement in December (by which time the dollar had dropped from October's average of ¥143.5 and DM1.81 down to a monthly average of ¥128.6 and DM 1.63)—the so-called Christmas Declaration—that essentially restated previous G-5 and G-7 communiqués. It did so without meeting, however, out of fear that an inconclusive G-7 meeting would send a destabilizing signal to markets that were already jittery.[58] In spite of its confident wording, the Declaration in fact signaled the demise of the Louvre strategy.

Analysis

Analysts of the Plaza-Louvre period have used a variety of theoretical perspectives to explain Japan's actions in the period—economic, international realist, regimist, and domestic politics.[59] While each of these perspectives offers some insight into the actions of the Japanese government, no satisfac-

---

57. The fullest account I have found of this episode is by Hanson (1996, chap. 3).
58. Ohta 1991, 115–116.
59. Realism argues that differences in power offer the best explanation for actions in the international sphere. Regime theory argues that power politics can be mitigated through

tory explanation can be made without considering the structure of Japanese macroeconomic policy making. While external political and economic pressures often prompted reactions by Japanese authorities, those responses were not predictable based solely on the pressures themselves. Examining the characteristics of G-5 and G-7 cooperation (the regimist approach) or domestic interest groups provides even less leverage on understanding events. Only by combining domestic structure with internal and external pressure are we able to come up with a consistently satisfactory explanation.

June–December 1985

The primary problem facing policy makers in 1985 was "bringing down superdollar."[60] Both economists and policy makers by then recognized that the U.S. dollar was very overvalued, particularly vis-à-vis the yen, and shared a consensus view that a cheaper dollar was necessary to reduce current account imbalances. Nobody should be surprised that major international problems for the world's largest economy brought about concerted action on the part of the community of industrialized states. Nor is the policy reaction itself surprising. Insofar as the strength of the dollar was linked closely to market expectations, massive government intervention would be the obvious first choice from an economic point of view; moreover, coordinated, publicly announced intervention was widely agreed to be the most effective kind of sterilized intervention.

From a realist power perspective, it was logical that the United States took the lead in organizing the Plaza. Also, the continuing problem of U.S. credibility in the international monetary sphere practically required that the U.S. government be out in front in intervention. From the Japanese perspective, the extraordinary degree of trade friction and the importance of bilateral U.S.–Japanese trade made authorities eager to embrace and even strengthen U.S. resolve on the dollar problem. Similarly, the BOJ's October interest rate action was consistent with efforts to strengthen the yen further (and deter heightened trade frictions). Realism also helps us to understand why U.S. and Japanese negotiators planned the Plaza strategy in secret even though they could be confident that other countries would be amenable to it—as the two most powerful national economies, they could choose a strategy that

---

agreements, international organizations, or even shared norms among policy makers of different states. The economic perspective is represented by various economists and policy makers, the realist by such authors as Iida (1990) and Funabashi (1989), the regimist by Dobson (1991) and Keohane (1984), and domestic politics by Kojo (1993) and Kawasaki (1993a). Both the domestic politics perspective and my own domestic structures argument are variants of Putnam's (1988) two-level game approach, which looks at how international negotiators must seek to satisfy both domestic constituencies and international counterparts.

60. This is the title of Volcker and Gyohten's (1992) chapter 8, which gives their account of the events of 1985–86.

would be most beneficial to them without interference, but with the full expectation that others would comply with their *fait accompli.*

Events were also generally consistent with regime theory. The existence of the G-5 offered the opportunity to confer on important matters of international monetary policy, but it would be difficult to talk of that group as a meaningful "regime." There were no set rules or procedures, and no mechanism to enforce any decisions at which the participants might arrive. What *did* exist was a long-standing resolution to support sustainable exchange rates, as well as international swap lines that facilitated intervention. In effect, the G-5 did exactly what it was able (and meant) to do. Moreover, the intentions of Mulford and Ōba that the Plaza Agreement might lead to more ambitious coordination suggests an evolutionary model of regime building.

But there are problems with such an interpretation. First, there is little evidence to suggest that the G-5 provided much more than a negotiating forum: the Plaza Agreement was essentially an agreement between two sovereign countries with the accession of another three. The weakness of the G-5 as an institution and the Plaza as an agreement was confirmed by the BOJ's October action and the Bundesbank's early withdrawal from the intervention process.

While all the international forces were aligned in favor of coordinated action, the macroeconomic policy-making structure helps us to understand the specifics of Japanese actions. The preparatory process, for example, fits the basic pattern of MOF information management. The process began with discussions between high-ranking MOF and Treasury officials (Ōba and Mulford) in March; these discussions were kept as a close secret inside the Ministry of Finance, even from Finance Minister Takeshita and Prime Minister Nakasone. Political leaders were only brought in when it was time for a face-to-face meeting between Takeshita and Baker (who had been kept fully informed). BOJ officials were kept even more in the dark than politicians—Governor Sumita (a MOF OB) was informed only about ten days before the Plaza.

Structure also offers the best explanation of the BOJ's move to raise short-term interest rates in October. That action makes the most sense as an instance of bureaucratic rivalry between the BOJ and MOF, dealt with as a technical matter without the involvement of politicians. Thus, the BOJ decided to carry out a policy that would contribute to the yen's revaluation, but that MOF would oppose.[61] Not only did the bank choose the instrument over which it had the most autonomous control, it did so in a way in which it could have plausible deniability—the Executive Board left discretion over how to deal with market fluctuations to the Credit and Market Management Depart-

---

61. As to why the bank did so, there are differing opinions. Some MOF and BOJ officials argue that the BOJ was simply trying to contribute to an international effort with which it

ment, which acted by *not acting* to stem rising short-term rates.[62] Despite the secretiveness of the action, the ministry (predictably) detected the changes almost immediately. After several weeks of denying any action to an increasingly impatient MOF and to its international counterparts, the bank was forced to take remedial action in the marketplace.

January–June 1986

Looking at the first half of 1986, it becomes more and more difficult to justify Japan's actions through economic rationality. This is especially true of the steadfast refusal of the Ministry of Finance—and its bureaucratic vassal, the Economic Planning Agency—to address even the possibility that the high yen might have recessionary effects for which fiscal stimulus might be a necessary remedy. It is understandable that the Ministry would not want to set the precedent of debating foreign exchange policy and goals as part of the budget debate in the Diet; more striking, however, is the fact that even internal analysis refused to deal with it. Also, as the recessionary effects of the high yen became more and more apparent in 1986 (with elections approaching), and some politicians began calling for a fiscal stimulus, MOF made no effort to draw up even tentative plans for such a stimulus. Instead, it continued to fight a rear-guard action against Nakasone's proposed income tax cut.[63] While Japanese policy makers were certainly in a difficult position, the policy mix they chose carried real dangers for the Japanese economy.[64] It is true that fiscal consolidation had considerable political and economic legitimacy, but MOF's unwillingness to consider contingency plans at all was clearly geared more to fears that such plans might be used than to a belief that no contingency was likely.

Realists fare better in explaining the actions of Japan and its partners. In particular, the actions of the U.S. Treasury Secretary make sense—Baker's continued talking down of the dollar constituted a simple way of keeping

---

agreed, and that the interest rate hike was an important step in moving the yen toward the desired level of ¥200/$1. A less charitable opinion voiced by some MOF officials and observers was that the BOJ leadership felt that the ministry had not adequately consulted with the bank, and so decided to push the process in a logical direction of which MOF would disapprove. Personal interviews. Either the "contribution" view or the "autonomy assertion" view is consistent with my argument.

62. Mieno 2000, 191–192.
63. For details, see Kato 1994, chap. 5.
64. This is not purely after-the-fact analysis by an American political scientist. Bank of Japan economists, as well as several private economists, were worried about the implications of this over-reliance on monetary policy as of the April discount rate cut (personal interviews). For after-the-fact analysis by Japanese economists, see Tachi, et al. 1993 and Noguchi 1992. What is surprising about these analyses is their sources—the Tachi group was commissioned by MOF's Institute of Fiscal and Monetary Policy, while Noguchi is a former MOF bureaucrat with continuing strong bureaucratic connections.

pressure on Japan to take up more of the burden of adjustment, either through macroeconomic policy measures or trade concessions.[65] The emphasis on foreign coordination with U.S. rate cuts also points to a pattern in which foreign authorities were forced to respond to U.S. actions. But while Japanese accommodation was predictable from realist theory, it is not clear what *kind* of accommodation was to be expected.

Events seem in some ways to fall equally well into a regimist framework. In this story, coordinated interest rate cuts were a recognition that domestic demand had to be managed, and only monetary policy could be effectively coordinated in the existing international monetary regime (based on long-standing central bank contact and the immediate detectability of any defection from an agreement). The objective indicators exercise constituted an attempt to begin to build a mechanism whereby effective coordination of exchange rate and macroeconomic policies could be directed and enforced. However, the exchange rate policies of Japan and the United States make this story somewhat less plausible—continued Japanese intervention (counter to, although not actually violating, G-5 consensus) concurrent with continued "talking down" of the dollar by the U.S. Treasury do not suggest serious efforts at confidence-building.

Looking at the interaction between domestic politics and international pressures presents a mixed picture in explaining Japanese actions in the first half of 1986. There is no question that domestic politics militated strongly in favor of a moderation in the appreciation of the yen, which fits well with both Japan's unilateral foreign exchange market intervention against the yen and the continued loosening of monetary policy. However, the lack of any fiscal stimulus measures (or even an official government call for them) does not make as much sense, since fiscal measures were preferred over inaction by both the United States and domestic business interests.[66]

In order for domestic politics to be really helpful in explaining the policy mix in the first half of 1986, we must consider the power structure in macroeconomic policy making. As we have seen, the Japanese macroeconomic policy-making structure automatically prefers exchange rate intervention over other responses to international imbalances. The steadfast refusal of the Ministry of Finance to mount, much less prepare, a fiscal stimulus package also looks familiar. Moreover, MOF's monopoly on budget-making expertise prevented stimulus-minded politicians like Miyazawa from putting together credible proposals of their own with which to woo voters and political con-

65. This is in some ways similar to Kirshner's (1995) "currency manipulation," although he argues that it is highly unlikely that the United States, Japan, or Europe could effectively exploit monetary power against one another.
66. In particular, small- and medium-sized exporters (an important LDP constituency) were being hit hard by the yen appreciation. This resulted in public calls by MITI and some politicians for fiscal stimulus on their behalf. Nevertheless, the government pledged no action, and following the election even ended up scaling back the tax cut it had promised.

tributions. Finally, the dissatisfaction expressed by BOJ Executive Board members over the April discount rate cut suggests that MOF pressure at the G-5 meeting (finance ministers and their deputies, plus central bank governors without deputies) led the MOF OB Governor Sumita to commit to a rate cut with which career officials of the Bank disagreed.[67] Additionally, according to some sources, U.S. authorities went through the Ministry of Finance before putting pressure on the BOJ to reduce rates. If true, this provides even stronger evidence of the importance of policy-making structure.[68]

On a related point, the structure I describe suggests that foreign exchange intervention will signal monetary rather than fiscal policy change, *even though intervention is controlled by the Ministry of Finance*. This appears to have been the case. According to a paper written in the Bank of Japan's Institute for Monetary and Economic Studies, "the amount of intervention is positively correlated with future growth rates of money supply but is uncorrelated or negatively correlated with past growth rates of money supply. From this we may confirm that changes in intervention tend to precede changes in money supply."[69]

Similarly, intervention proved to be an effective signal of discount rate changes.[70] The paper found these effects with little change across the period 1973–91. More specifically, it found that both of the coordinated rate cuts of spring 1986 (as well as the two following cuts of November 1986 and February 1987) were signaled by exchange market intervention. This provides yet more evidence of domestic structures affecting Japan's macroeconomic policies—there is no other good reason why a MOF action should signal a BOJ policy shift.

July 1986–February 1987

Given that a reduction of international economic imbalances was a widely accepted goal within the Japanese government (though ironically, not necessarily within the Bank of Japan), the events of the subsequent eight months are difficult to explain as a rational economic response to the needs of the economic system, although the Baker-Miyazawa Agreement at least paid lip service to the most important issues. By summer 1986, it was becoming apparent that ex-

67. Mieno, who was Sumita's deputy governor at the time, is circumspect in all his mentions of Sumita's policy decisions. He does allow, however, that international coordination made for bad monetary policy (Mieno 2000, 205–206, 216–217).
68. Personal interviews with Hosomi Takashi and others.
69. Watanabe 1992, 36. It is extraordinary that this analysis was done by a BOJ official and was published in an official BOJ organ. (In fact, after I got hold of a draft of the paper in English, I was told by another BOJ official that it would *not* be published. Perhaps what he meant was that it would not be published in English.)
70. Watanabe 1992, 34. Cargill, Hutchison, and Ito (1997, 74–80) also find that exchange rate intervention was an important factor in monetary policy (because it was not fully sterilized).

change rate changes alone were not bringing about the desired changes in trade balances and that substantive macroeconomic policy changes were needed in Japan and the United States.[71] In other words, Japan had to save less compared to investment, and the United States had to save more; the most practical way of bringing about that result would be fiscal stimulus in Japan combined with a direct stimulus to investment (i.e., monetary stimulus), and fiscal deficit reduction in the United States.[72] In Japan, it was particularly important to have a reasonable mix of monetary and fiscal policy, since the former had already been loosened considerably. What actually occurred was further monetary loosening with only a token fiscal stimulus on the Japanese side, and a deficit reduction plan on the U.S. side that would prove to have no teeth.

Again, the realist perspective offers a more satisfying explanation. As Funabashi shows, the United States was growing impatient with European (specifically German) reluctance to act more aggressively, and attempted to follow a "G-2" strategy of first making an agreement with Japan, and then jointly trying to push it on the Europeans.[73] Perhaps more importantly, the Baker-Miyazawa Agreement can be seen as constituting hardball politics on the part of the United States. The substance of the U.S. side of the agreement was to stop talking down the dollar, a weapon that cost very little for the United States to use but was perceived as extremely costly by the Japanese. In other words, Secretary Baker's words prior to the agreement had no other purpose than to put pressure on Japan. The effectiveness of that pressure is shown by the willingness of the Japanese to take actions for which the U.S. side had been pushing. There are two problems with this story, however. First, Miyazawa *wanted* a fiscal stimulus, and there is no evidence that political leaders were responsible for gutting the fiscal stimulus. Second, a substantial fiscal stimulus to balance the discount rate cut was in the interests of the most affected domestic interest groups regardless of what the United States did.

71. Up to that point, many observers still believed that the so-called J-curve was responsible for the continuing, indeed rising, imbalances. The J-curve is an economic phenomenon whereby a depreciation in the home country exchange rate causes a short-term worsening in the trade account because prices rise on foreign goods that have already been ordered, or because alternate suppliers are not immediately available. The effect is assumed to wear off in a few months as home companies change their sourcing and increase their exports, more than overriding the temporary worsening. Getting a handle on the J-curve was somewhat more difficult than usual in 1985–86, because the dollar kept sliding, making it difficult to know whether an upswing was actually occurring. Nevertheless, by summer 1986, relatively few observers thought that trade balances would be equalized simply by more dollar depreciation.

72. In defense of the Ministry of Finance, economic simulation suggested that Japanese fiscal policy would have a relatively minor effect on current account imbalances, while U.S. deficit reduction would have a huge effect. Thus, it was far more important for the United States to change its policies than for Japan to do so (Yoshitomi 1986; Takenaka, et al. 1986, 1987; McKibbin and Sachs 1991).

73. Funabashi 1989, chap. 7.

Regimes add little to the story. Neither the negotiations leading to the Baker-Miyazawa Agreement, nor the agreement itself, nor its aftermath built upon any of the established cooperative mechanisms. Rather, it appears to have been an ad hoc attempt by the two finance ministers to move their governments and central banks in their own desired directions. Moreover, the assumption on both sides that the other had acted in bad faith could only be an impediment to future cooperation. The best a regimist explanation can do is to say that the failure of coordination in autumn 1986 proved the need for a regime that could facilitate broad and effective coordination—in other words, the Louvre Accord.

Looking at the policy-making structure again provides a better explanation of actual events. Miyazawa (and possibly Baker) seem to have used their international agreement to force the government or central bank to act in a way that it would not have chosen without the commitment. However, without an understanding of how the Japanese macroeconomic policy-making system works, it makes no sense to speak of a finance minister needing outside pressure to force his own subordinates to put together a fiscal stimulus plan. The compilation of such a plan requires no societal interests whatsoever (and in any case, virtually all appeared to be on the side of Miyazawa)—it simply requires a degree of agency control that Japan's political leaders do not always have. The fact that the plan that was actually compiled proved not to contain what the finance minister believed it did similarly requires an understanding of how the Ministry of Finance manages information.[74]

February–December 1987

From the economic point of view, Louvre certainly addressed the major problems facing the international monetary and trading system. First, by calling for coordination on fiscal and monetary policies, the accord promised to get to the heart of the sustainability problem, while trying to prevent worldwide recession. Second, the reference range system was designed to prevent destabilizing movements and speculative attacks in exchange rates in a flexible way. There was a difference of opinion among economists (particularly in the United States) on how best to do so, or whether it was even a good idea to consider exchange rates a target of economic policy, but both the intent and the mechanism fell well within the mainstream of economic thinking. If the commitments made at Louvre were economically rational, though, why did countries not stick to them? Indeed, such basics of the agreement as a better policy mix in Japan and deficit reduction in the United States would have been in those countries' interests even *without* concrete commitments from other par-

---

74. Miyazawa was reported to be furious that the package did not contain what he announced it did (personal interviews). It certainly did not help his reputation as an expert who was on top of policy.

ticipants. Thus, it is in implementation that the economic interpretation breaks down, although it is perfectly sufficient to explain the effective coordination of G-7 actions following Black Monday.

Regimists can point to the Louvre Accord as a major step in the development of "principles, norms, rules, and decision-making procedures around which actor expectations converge in a given issue-area"[75]—in this case, international monetary relations. The meeting at the Louvre was presented as a culmination of more than a year and a half of efforts to make the major economies more complementary. The accord itself offered specific rules concerning exchange rates, and macroeconomic policy coordination was conducted in the context of multilateral surveillance with objective indicators, an institutionalized mechanism that provided for a common informational base and the potential for enforcement. The problem was that the regime was not respected—for example, U.S. officials felt free to offer statistics that were blatantly wrong, accompanied by pledges they could not fulfill. On the Japanese side, Miyazawa was constrained by the domestic political process from offering anything concrete at all even though he fully intended to carry out a fiscal stimulus as soon as the FY 1987 budget was approved. This also reduced the credibility of the effort. The lack of commitment to the agreement was shown by the waning interest in defending the reference ranges, even after they had been rebased scarcely a month and a half after they had first been set. The failures of the Louvre Accord suggest a more modest view of the importance of the international monetary "regime": perhaps the G-7 simply overreached the abilities of the existing regime. If so, the true extent of regime capabilities could be seen in the coordinated response to Black Monday—useful in an emergency, but not for day-to-day management of the international economy.

The breakdown in cooperation makes good realist sense, of course. The ambitious coordination plans were clearly put in place because nearly a year and a half of *ad hoc* coordination measures had not solved the basic problems of the international economy. Only by gaining concrete commitments could participants be locked into courses of action they knew to be mutually beneficial. However, the actual actions of the participants suggest more of an attempt to minimize their own costs than to realize adjustment in the most efficient way possible. What is more surprising is the willingness of states to incur reputational costs—European countries quickly lost their enthusiasm for positive measures when confronted at the Louvre by politically manipulated U.S. economic forecasts and Japanese unwillingness to commit any more in the way of fiscal stimulus than a vague offer that something might be done once the FY 1987 budget was passed.

Looking at events from a two-level perspective suggests that the ultimate failure of the Louvre strategy was that international-level commitments ex-

75. This is the standard definition of a regime. See Krasner 1983a, 1.

ceeded what domestic actors were willing to accept.[76] In other words, national leaders failed by miscalculating the political calculus in their own countries. At the same time, the policy changes that did occur—in particular, the May 1987 Japanese fiscal stimulus plan—were presumably aided by the existence of an international agreement.

In this case, there is an interesting twist, however. There was no major domestic constituency in Japan resisting a fiscal stimulus package except for the Ministry of Finance; MOF could only do so because of the specific structure of macroeconomic policy making that existed in Japan. A similar story can be told about the United States, in which Secretary Baker was playing a game against the Federal Reserve Board. In this interpretation, Baker and the administration attempted to use an international agreement to force the Fed to take on the burden of adjustment. This would have been especially pressing for Baker, insofar as he had little meaningful input into fiscal policy.[77]

On the Japanese side, we again see the reluctance of the Ministry of Finance to use the fiscal policy tool, and its ability to block politicians from using it. As an unpublished BOJ analysis tactfully put it, "the Japanese Ministry of Finance might pay little attention to the consequence of fiscal policy on the exchange rate."[78] In particular, MOF's use of the fiscal consolidation agreement and budget calendar to fend off calls for greater fiscal stimulus showed very effective gamesmanship. Budget makers resolutely refused to modify the FY 1987 budget framework in response to Miyazawa's calls for fiscal stimulus. Moreover, MOF only began compiling the May stimulus plan after a resolution was passed within the LDP to that effect; the delay made political inspection far more difficult.

76. Putnam (1988) uses the term "win-set" to mean the range of alternatives that are politically acceptable to domestic political actors (usually defined as the legislature in democratic states).

77. Volcker and Gyohten 1992, 276. The U.S. Treasury Department has no jurisdiction over the budget, which is prepared in the executive branch by the Office of Management and Budget. It does prepare administration tax proposals, although such proposals inevitably come out of the Congress significantly altered.

78. This quotation appears at the end of an English-language draft of Watanabe (1992, 15). It is omitted in the published Japanese version.

5

Inflating and Bursting the Bubble, 1988–92

Hesitation and Overshooting

"Though the evaluation will be made by future historians, I believe that
the policies I carried out were not in error."

Mieno Yasushi, BOJ Governor 1989–94

The year 1988 opened with a weak dollar and a lack of consensus
among the G-7 countries on questions of coordinated action. As it turned out,
1988 would see a stabilization of the dollar against the yen in the mid-¥120s
and a relatively stable firming against the DM. In spite of a series of coordinated interventions,[1] the main factors appeared to be continuity in national
economic policies and a resultant stabilization of market expectations. Stability
at the international level—exchange rate stability (or movement within a comfortable range) and a reduction in U.S. trade deficits—continued through
1988 and into 1990. While no one forgot the macroeconomic stresses and
crises of the Plaza-Louvre period, it appeared that policy makers had in general achieved their objectives with a minimum of permanent damage to the
world and national economies. Thus, macroeconomic politics were directed
toward the demands of the domestic economy. In this period of relative calm,
the policies that resulted were to have serious negative repercussions on the
Japanese economy.

Over most of the period 1988–92, Japan experienced stable consumer,
wholesale, and producer prices, strong growth, high investment in fixed capital and research and development, stable exchange rates, and declining trade
imbalances. In many ways, it appeared to be a golden age, a renaissance for the
Japanese economy. As it turned out, however, the period held a more ominous
parallel to the "Gilded Age" of the 1920s than just excitement and prosperity—it was built on shaky foundations that were to lead to the crash of the
1990s.

Much of the prosperity of the late 1980s was based on a speculative bubble. The bubble was fueled by rapid increases in the money supply caused
by the continuation of the Bank of Japan's low-interest-rate policy until May
1989, at least a year beyond the point at which it had ceased to be econom-

1. Ohta (1991, 115–121) is one of the rare sources to describe those interventions.

136

ically justifiable. The series of interest rate hikes that began in 1989 both cut money supply growth and increased costs for would-be speculators and investors; the result was a bursting of the bubble, a dramatic fall in asset prices, and eventually weakness throughout the financial world and the real economy. Despite rapid reductions in interest rates as recession became manifest, by mid-1992 it was apparent that they would not be effective in staving it off.

Monetary policy both encouraged and ended the bubble, but it was not able to put the economy back on track in the recession that resulted. This chapter examines both the economic policies that caused prosperity and then led to disaster and the macroeconomic politics behind them. The see-saw pattern of Japanese monetary policy from 1988 to 1992 fits closely the model of macroeconomic policy making laid out in chapter 1. The failure of fiscal policy to respond in any way before August 1992, or effectively even then, also looks sadly familiar.

Speculators' Paradise—1988–89

The strength of the Japanese stock market in the face of the U.S. stock market crash seemed to give the Japanese economy a large dose of confidence and optimism. Between the very low real interest rates and increased ease of raising money in equity markets, firms' cost of capital was extremely low or even negative. In all the major cities, ambitious construction projects continued or were conceived, while throughout Japan companies increased investment in fixed capital and research and development and households began to put their savings into the stock market in unprecedented amounts.[2] Enormously successful stock offerings connected to privatization of government-owned industries added both to the exuberant mood and to the desire on the part of households not to get caught behind the big gains that were available to them.[3]

This exuberance continued into 1988 and 1989, as many of the greatest fears Japanese held for their economy were alleviated. Exchange rates stabilized, albeit at a much appreciated rate, and current account surpluses, as well as the politically all-important bilateral trade surplus with the United States, declined slowly but (apparently) surely. Within Japan, inflation as measured by all the conventional price indexes—consumer, wholesale, and

2. Investment by firms was fueled not only by the low cost of capital, but also by wages that had risen rapidly relative to those of international competitors. While rising wages certainly increased offshore production, domestic investment and R&D were also affected because higher labor costs created an incentive to increase the share of capital and technology in total value-added.
3. The first tranche of the sale of the national telephone carrier, NTT, was the best example, although the first sales of Japan Monopoly Corporation and Japan Railways stock also occurred around this time. The privatization issues may have helped bring more households into the stock market, due to restrictions on initial purchases—such as quotas on shares—that favored small investors. Calder (1990b) analyzes Japan's privatization effort.

producer—stayed near or even below zero. Meanwhile, the rapid economic growth and the successful issues of privatization stocks were fast making the dream of fiscal consolidation a reality (see Table 3.2). The declining trade balance did not even seem to be hurting Japanese producers, as a result of both higher domestic demand and their increased ability to invest abroad.

Despite the halcyon haze of prosperity, however, there were clear warning signs for the economy, of which policy makers were well aware. These were the rapid increase in the money supply and, more importantly, the rise in asset prices. Asset prices are not captured in standard price indexes, but their rapid rise alarmed many policy makers, especially at the Bank of Japan. Indeed, officials and publications of the BOJ had begun publicly warning of the dangers of overly loose monetary policy in autumn 1986.[4] Money supply, however measured, was growing at a very rapid rate from mid-1986, with particularly striking increases in 1987. While the trend was particularly true of M_1 growth, the more important $M_2 + CD$ growth rate also rose markedly in 1987, remaining at a high rate through 1990 (Figure 5.1).[5] (It is also true, however, that the volatility of various monetary aggregates had increased markedly throughout the 1980s due to increased financial liberalization and international openness, and thus the effects of specific monetary policy tools had become much more difficult to predict.)[6]

In concert with the increasing liquidity in the economy, asset prices rose rapidly. Stock prices are the most obvious example (Figure 5.2). The Nikkei Index does not tell the whole story, however, since the period also saw a considerable broadening of Japan's equity markets. New listings included many Japanese companies and increasing numbers of foreign firms, but they are probably most popularly symbolized by the great privatizations of Japanese government–owned corporations—most famously, three tranches accounting for 34.6 percent of NTT stock netted the government ¥10.2 trillion (approximately $70 billion) in 1986–88.[7] Meanwhile, the total valuation of stocks on the first tier of the Tokyo Stock Exchange rose from ¥169 trillion (52 percent of GDP) in mid-1985 to ¥527 trillion (131 percent of GDP) in mid-1989.[8] Small investors entered the stock markets in droves for the first

---

4. Particularly noteworthy in this regard was an October 1986 statement to the Diet by Deputy Governor (later Governor) Mieno, which laid out the case for an interest rate hike (NHK 1996, 127).

5. While the BOJ has never followed a strict monetarist rule, the two indicators of M_1 and $M_2 + CD$ are important factors in making policy. $M_2 + CD$ emerged as a particularly important indicator in the 1980s, as financial deregulation broadened the types of liquid financial instruments available to savers (particularly corporations). CDs, first introduced in Japan in the 1970s and increasingly liberalized in the 1980s, have been important in the Japanese money supply as a favored savings vehicle for corporate savers.

6. Mieno 2000, chap. 6.

7. Takano 1992, xiii.

8. Noguchi 1992, 23. The choice to use mid-year numbers is Noguchi's.

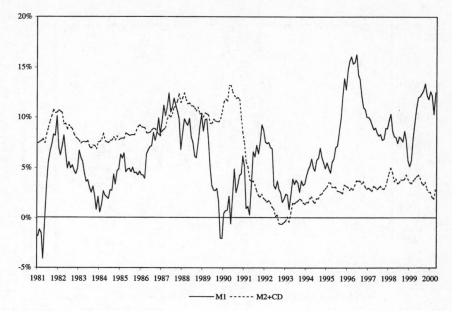

Figure 5.1 Money Supply Growth

Note: Year-on-year growth.
Source: BOJ downloadable statistics.

time in Japan's postwar history, as stories circulated concerning the money to be made by canny investing.[9]

With low interest rates, rapidly increasing stock prices, and strong export earnings, companies' cost of capital dropped to an extremely low level. In response, they redoubled investment in fixed capital and research and development and raised increasing percentages of the necessary funds through securities issues and retained earnings. Convertible bond and stock warrant issues became a particularly popular way of borrowing at very low rates on the assumption that most investors would choose to convert their principal to company stock before the company would have to pay back

9. A variety of figures with more or less explicit ties to the underworld also became big-time speculators. In Osaka, a tea house owner named Onoue Nui managed to borrow ¥3.2 trillion (over $25 billion) for stock and bond speculation from the Industrial Bank of Japan, Tōyō Shinkin (a credit association that ended up in bankruptcy from the affair), Sumitomo Corporation, Sanwa Bank, and other financial institutions. She was finally sentenced to twelve years in jail in March 1998 (*Japan Digest*, March 9, 1998, 14).

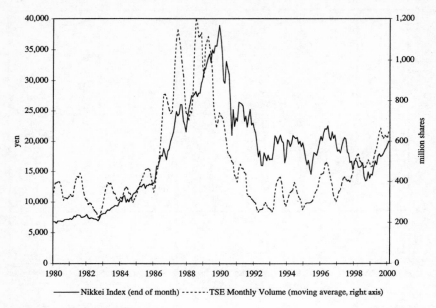

Figure 5.2   Tokyo Stock Exchange

Note: Monthly volume on a six-month moving average.
Source: BOJ downloadable statistics.

principal.[10] Faced with the loss of traditional customers to the securities markets, banks began looking to new customers for their loans, only to find that the greatest increase in demand could be found among speculators in real estate and equities.[11]

While the rise in stock prices seemed to produce no losers, land was becoming a major social issue, as values in major urban centers soared. Here the degree of speculation was, if anything, clearer even than in the stock market—many rental properties were selling for more than the present discounted value of their rental income, even assuming continued low interest rates.[12] As land values soared, the value of companies holding desirable properties increased as well, allowing them to borrow more for expanded speculation.[13] Thus, land and stock prices joined in an upward spiral, fueled largely by the easy availability of cheap money (Figure 5.3; see also Figure 5.2).

10. A convertible bond is a bond that can be exchanged within a certain time period for company stock. A stock warrant is essentially a call option for company stock that is attached to a corporate bond.
11. Taniguchi 1993, 18–19.
12. Tachi, et al. 1993, appendix.
13. See Taniguchi 1993 for a concise discussion.

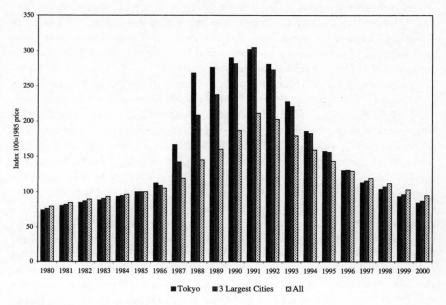

Figure 5.3 Commercial Land Prices

Note: Beginning-of-year prices, indexed to 1985.
Source: National Land Agency downloadable statistics.

Monetary Policy Response, 1989–90

While 1988 saw increases in interest rates by the United States and Germany (Japan's primary partners in the Plaza-Louvre coordination process), the Bank of Japan held back. The policy of easy money was popular during those years: corporations and individuals were benefiting as their paper wealth increased, exporters appreciated the dampening effect it had on the value of the yen, MOF officials appreciated the opportunity to restrict fiscal policy and to start attacking the government's debt problem through the sale of assets at high prices, and politicians were happy with both the prosperity and the opportunity to expand political funds through stock-ramping deals or early purchases of new equity offerings.[14]

In addition to the troubling asset price inflation and money supply growth, 1989 saw the first signs of the long-expected increases in CPI and WPI inflation. With concern within the Bank of Japan and among growing numbers of economists on the rise, Governor Sumita finally announced an

14. The most public of these was the Recruit scandal, which included pre-IPO share offerings to a number of LDP politicians at discounted prices. Shimoda (1989, 120–121) describes those and other payoffs to politicians and bureaucrats.

increase in the discount rate from 2.5 percent to 3.25 percent on May 31, 1989, immediately after the passage of the FY 1989 budget. This was followed in October by an increase to 3.75 percent. These actions were met with general approval from economic and journalistic actors, as consensus had built that Japan's economy was overheated.[15]

In December 1989 Governor Sumita's term ended, and he was replaced, as expected, by his deputy, Mieno Yasushi. While Sumita had originally been a career MOF bureaucrat who had had relatively little experience in the field of monetary policy before he took the deputy governor post at the BOJ in 1979, Mieno was a BOJ careerist. He was known as an inflation hawk and an advocate of more aggressive action to slow money supply growth. Almost immediately, he acted to raise interest rates for the third time in seven months. Mieno's first major policy action as governor did not proceed smoothly, however. For reasons that remain unclear, Mieno's proposal irked the powerful finance minister, Hashimoto Ryūtarō, who exercised his legal prerogative to postpone any change in the discount rate.[16] As word of the dispute leaked, financial markets reacted nervously. In the end, however, the overwhelming force of market expectations that the rate hike would go through forced Hashimoto to drop his position, and on December 25 the discount rate was increased to 4.25 percent. Four days later, the Nikkei peaked at ¥38,915.87, approximately triple its value at the time of the Plaza Agreement.

The BOJ under Mieno would act to raise interest rates twice more, with discount rate hikes put into effect on March 20 and August 30, 1990. From a level of 2.5 percent on May 30, 1989, the discount rate rose to 6 percent by the end of August 1990, a mere fifteen months later. (The final rate increase was meant to head off possible inflationary pressures due to Iraq's invasion of Kuwait.)[17] As usual, the discount rate defined the lower end of a band within which the bank sought to maintain short-term rates, and the overall rate structure closely followed the changes in the discount rate (see Figure 3.2). The last of the rate hikes was particularly striking, coming as it did in the middle of a rapid decrease in stock prices—on August 30, 1990, the Nikkei had fallen to about ¥26,000 from a level in early June of over ¥33,000.

---

15. While Mieno, like his predecessor Sumita during the high-yen recession, would later receive multiple death threats for his policies (Mieno 2000, 245), it was easy at first for many people to feel satisfaction at the losses of unscrupulous speculators even if there were serious impacts on their own wealth.

16. Two explanations are usually put forward. One is that Hashimoto felt slighted by Mieno, either because Mieno announced his decision to the Cabinet without prior consultation with him or because Mieno acted arrogantly in that meeting. The other is that Hashimoto was annoyed that the intended decision had been leaked to the newspapers, perhaps before he knew of it. While the debate may have some relevance for understanding Hashimoto's character or his relationship with Mieno, there seems to have been no fundamental disagreement over the policy (Suzuki 1992, 52–54).

17. Mieno 2000, 210.

While Mieno writes that the first four rate hikes were meant to return monetary policy to a "neutral stance,"[18] the rapid rate rises were the monetary equivalent of driving a truck into a brick wall. Growth in M_1 plummeted in 1989 and 1990, and the broader aggregate of M_2+CD followed suit within two years (see Figure 5.1). Despite vigorous attempts to loosen monetary policy since 1991 (evidenced by the high growth of M_1 at several points in the interim), M_2+CD growth has never recovered to pre-1990 levels. The effects of this rapid monetary deceleration made clear that the bubble had indeed been primarily a monetary phenomenon.

The August rate hike was the last major macroeconomic policy action of 1990. Four months later, as the year closed, stock prices appeared to have stabilized at a little under two-thirds of their previous year's peak, while inflation had been addressed proactively. Real GDP showed a more than respectable growth rate of 5.1 percent, and Japan's macroeconomic authorities were able to congratulate themselves for having headed off disaster, despite the considerable loss of nominal wealth in the economy and the pain experienced by many investors. Governor Mieno gained the nickname "Onihei" (a fearsome Edo-period magistrate in a popular TV series), as the slayer of the bubble.[19]

Fiscal Policy? The Structural Impediments Initiative

As befitted a rapidly growing economy with large official debts, the government's fiscal position in the years 1988–90 was conservative. MOF bureaucrats worked hard to ensure that deficit ceilings mandated by the fiscal consolidation agreement were met, and they were helped considerably by rising tax revenues. Indeed, both the economy and tax revenues grew faster than expected, allowing the government to achieve its goal of no new deficit bonds by FY 1990 with relative ease (see Table 3.2). Privatization efforts were also bearing fruit. Not only were large-scale offerings of NTT and Japan Monopoly Corporation stock creating major windfalls that could be used to retire long-term government debt, but MOF budget hawks were relieved finally to be getting rid of the perennially money-losing Japan National Railways. While the stock of government debt continued to rise, the improving fiscal situation provided a clear beacon of hope for all concerned.

Although the state of the economy appeared to many Japanese officials to be an opportunity to get their fiscal house in order, it appeared to many

18. Ibid., 209–210.
19. The term was first applied (admiringly) by a columnist in *Shūkan Gendai* on February 2, 1991. At the time, there was also a less flattering list of those responsible for the drop in stock prices: "Number one is [Saddam] Hussein; number two is Mieno; there is no number three or four; and number five is [then–prime minster] Kaifu." One journal soon reported that BOJ staffers were worried that Mieno might become obsessed with living up to the "Onihei" appellation (Mizuno 1997, 196–198). Mieno now laughs at the nickname (2000, 279–280).

U.S. officials to be an opportunity to increase Japanese purchases of U.S. goods and services. The new Bush administration, determined to follow a new path in dealing with U.S.–Japanese bilateral economic disputes that would avoid the rancor of previous negotiations over semiconductors, fighter planes, and other issues, proposed that the two governments enter into talks that would address the root causes of the disputes. In September 1989, those negotiations began, under the rubric of the "Structural Impediments Initiative" (SII).[20]

The SII negotiations encompassed a huge array of issues in many sectors, and involved multiple Japanese ministries. For our purposes, however, only two issues are really relevant—construction and attempts to alter the savings-investment balance at a structural level. The question of the S-I imbalance quickly became bogged down in ambiguity, since there was little agreement on either the causes of overly high Japanese savings or even whether such a macroeconomic question should be addressed in a bilateral forum. Thus, the most concrete aspect of the S-I negotiations as they pertained to Japanese fiscal policy proved to be attention to government finances, in the form of construction spending.[21]

The U.S. effort to get Japan to spend more on public works was odd on its face. Given the closed nature of the Japanese construction industry, it seemed relatively unlikely that expanded funding for projects would carry any meaningful benefits for U.S. firms. Close ties between government and domestic companies clearly compounded the problem.[22] There was a feeling that increasing the pie might make the domestic industry more willing to accept changes in practices, but the primary reason for the focus on construction seems to have been as a back-door means of loosening fiscal policy.

This back door was an attempt by U.S. ambassador Michael Armacost to circumvent MOF by dealing directly with Kanemaru Shin, a major LDP powerbroker and strong ally of construction interests.[23] Kanemaru in turn lobbied the Ministry of Finance and its minister, Hashimoto Ryūtarō (his factional subordinate), for greater spending. In the end, Japan pledged ¥430 trillion in public investment over the next ten years.[24] While that result was touted as a triumph by the U.S. administration, it was actually not a very profound increase, and in any event included very little additional spending over the first three to four years. Most of that spending was to be in the form of loans from the Fiscal Investment and Loan Program. Also, the pledge was just a pledge—like many government budgeting systems,

20. Schoppa 1997.
21. Noguchi 1995, chap. 10; Krauss 1993; Schoppa 1997.
22. Woodall 1996.
23. Armacost 1996, 69. Also, MOF interviews.
24. According to Noguchi (1995, 336), the initial offer of ¥400 trillion was reached by taking the total from the past ten years and adding 50 percent. A quick calculation demonstrates

Japan's has no provision for a binding commitment for such a long period of time. In short, despite the fondest hopes of the U.S. administration, Japanese fiscal policy remained, correctly, conservative.[25]

Side Effects, 1990–92

If the brief stock market rally in June 1990 had increased fears of a reinflated bubble among monetary policy makers, then the August 1990 discount rate hike effectively relieved them. Indeed, stock prices dropped dramatically, with the Nikkei hitting a post-peak low of ¥20,221 on October 1, 1990. Thereafter, the Nikkei bounced around erratically between the low and mid-¥20,000s through most of 1991—essentially the same range in which it moved in 1987 and early 1988. Land prices continued to rise through 1991, however, before starting a long-term decline in 1992 (see Figure 5.3).

Economically, this shift in the value of stock prices had two short-term effects. The first was the obvious decrease in wealth for virtually all investors. In cases where most of the assets had been purchased prior to 1988, this meant mainly a decrease in "paper" wealth; for those who had purchased significant proportions of their portfolios from about mid-1988 to mid-1990, it also meant a real loss of principal.[26] Soon, there was also a dramatic drop in sales of real estate. This second effect presaged the severe financial crisis that was to come: as assets such as stocks and land lost value, speculators who had borrowed money to buy those assets no longer had strong incentives (and in some cases were soon unable) to continue servicing those debts. The heavy use of land as loan collateral exacerbated the problem.

The importance of this trend was not obvious in 1990, but by 1991 bank regulators began to realize some of the possible implications. Soon, rumors began to swirl that MOF had issued administrative guidance to the effect that banks should not be too quick to sell off the land they had acquired either on their own or through actual or de facto defaults.[27] The regulators worried

---

that this is equivalent to a 4 percent rate of growth over the previous period (roughly equivalent to Japan's trend rate of growth in the 1980s), which does not suggest that the sky was falling on fiscal conservatives.

25. Schoppa (1993, 1997) has characterized the construction agreement as a victory for the United States. Needless to say, I disagree with that assessment. I am more in agreement with the assessment of Noguchi, who argues that while the public works component of SII had relatively little impact, MOF's intransigence on fiscal policy meant real victories for the United States in other areas, such as the Large Store Law and the land tax system (Noguchi 1995, 335–365).

26. Low dividends and the short recovery period imply that dividends did not even begin to provide an effective offset of the capital gains losses. Aoki (1988, 115) shows that the dividend/price ratio was in the 1–2 percent range and dropping in the early to mid-1980s.

27. I remember well a number of conversations at the time with a friend who was working with a predominantly Japanese clientele at a commercial real estate agency in New York. He regularly bemoaned the effects of that guidance.

about the effects of declining capital-asset ratios on banks' ability to continue providing credit[28]; because banks were allowed to value assets at book value, not selling them off seemed a viable means of staving off a credit crunch. Both banks and regulators were keenly aware that a large amount of banks' capital adequacy was built on unrealized gains in their stock and land port-folios. Moreover, the relatively high percentage of real estate and other spec-ulative lending in banks' portfolios meant that keeping land prices stable was also important for the banks' income. By 1992, the problem had become clear enough that Japan even petitioned the BIS to ease capital require-ments; the petition was rejected in June 1992, leaving the banking system with no easy way out of its predicament.[29]

If the banks were running into problems, the situation of the so-called *jūsen* (housing loan corporations) was even worse, albeit smaller in scale. These nonbanks had first come into existence in the 1970s, at a time when large banks had neither the interest nor the administrative capacity to ser-vice small real estate–based loans.[30] By the mid-1980s, they were well estab-lished and had expanded beyond the field of lending for personal homes. In 1988, when the National Land Agency head called for an end to real es-tate speculation and the Ministry of Finance issued guidance that banks should not lend money for speculative purposes, the *jūsen* were in the right place at the right time (albeit not in retrospect) to give the banks access to that forbidden zone. In essence, banks lent money through nonbank affili-ates—most notoriously the *jūsen*—which in turn lent to real estate specula-tors.[31] The schemes had the benefit of nominally obeying MOF dictates while turning the actual administration of real estate loans over to non-banks, over which MOF possessed much more ambiguous authority.[32]

By the early 1990s, the results of the aggressive use of *jūsen* for real estate lending were becoming clear. Having vastly increased their loan portfolios based on post-1987 real estate transactions, the *jūsen* saw the value of their loans plummet along with the actual value of the loans' collateral. By No-vember 1992, the MOF-related Discussion Group on the Non-Bank Issue

---

28. Capital-adequacy was of particular concern for any bank involved in international finance. The 1988 Basle Accord, to which Japan was signatory, had decreed a minimum capital-adequacy ratio of 8 percent for all international banks by the end of FY 1992 (see Kapstein 1991 for more details). This left Japanese banks whose capital was declining in value in a very tough place, as described by Taniguchi (1993, 28–34).
29. Taniguchi 1993, 28.
30. Adachi 1997, chap. 1; Mabuchi 1997, 8–12.
31. Mabuchi 1997, 12–15; Taniguchi 1993, 24–28.
32. In order to gain more control over the actions of the *jūsen*, the Ministry of Finance arranged for several retired officials to take leadership positions in them. This proved to be an ineffective method of ensuring responsible lending. Later, the conspicuous presence of MOF OBs in the top tier of the failed institutions led to considerable public resentment over MOF's role in the debacle.

was warning that 20 percent of *jūsen* loans were nonperforming.[33] This semi-official estimate proved to be highly over-optimistic; by 1995, MOF estimated that 76 percent of the seven housing loan corporations' loans were nonperforming and nearly 60 percent were unrecoverable.[34] The failures of the *jūsen*, other nonbanks, and many real estate companies were to have profound effects on banks, since many of the loans made to these economic actors (often for the purpose of speculation) could never be repaid, and in any event were effectively nonperforming. The basic problems were compounded by the fact that the *jūsen* were owned by consortia of the banks themselves, so their woes in turn threatened the value of banks' capital.

Policy Responses—BOJ

Macroeconomic and banking policy makers naturally responded to these disasters and potential disasters. As it became evident that the rapid rise in interest rates was having severe side effects throughout the economy, the Bank of Japan acted to reverse its contractionary policies. On July 1, 1991, it took the modest step of lowering the discount rate from 6 percent to 5.5 percent. Nonetheless, bank lending continued to decline, and by fall the BOJ was loosening policy in earnest. On October 1, it announced that it would lower banks' reserve requirement ratio—by 40 percent, effective October 16—for the first time since December 1986.[35] (Changing this ratio required the approval of the minister of finance.) On November 14, and again on December 30, the Bank announced cuts of 0.5 percent in the discount rate, which ended the year at 4.5 percent.

Traditionally, there has been an unofficial taboo against altering interest rates between the submission of the Cabinet's budget draft in late December or early January, and its final passage in late March.[36] This taboo was honored in 1992, but on the first day of the new fiscal year, April 1, the BOJ again cut the discount rate (this time by 0.75%).[37] The fifth consecutive dis-

---

33. "*Nonbanku nenkan rieki o karuku fukitobasu furyō saiken*" (Nonbank Nonperforming Loans Easily Blow Away Annual Profits), *Ekonomisuto*, November 9, 1992, 100–103.
34. Of ¥10.72 trillion in loans (about 2 percent of Japan's outstanding private loans), MOF estimated that ¥8.13 trillion were nonperforming, and of those ¥6.27 trillion were unrecoverable (Milhaupt and Miller 1998, 90).
35. Economic Planning Agency 1997, 751.
36. The reasoning is that changing interest rates would void some of the official assumptions concerning government finances and economic outlook, thus offering an opportunity for opposition parties to slow the passage of, or even force changes in, the budget.
37. Mieno himself offers a different interpretation of why there was no action prior to April 1. He claimed that a widely publicized threat (discussed below) by the Takeshita faction's number two man, Kanemaru Shin—that if Mieno did not act to cut the discount rate immediately he should be fired—forced him to put off a planned cut so as not to look as if he was being bullied. The fiscal stimulus plan announced at the end of March gave him political cover (Mieno 2000, 213; Mizuno 1997, 200).

count rate cut in a little over a year occurred on July 27, 1992, bringing that benchmark rate down to 3.25%, its lowest level since May 31, 1989.

Despite the BOJ's aggressive reversal of its bubble-bursting policies of 1989–90, the growing financial mess proved difficult to reverse. The fall of asset prices had led to a large increase in bankruptcies (not only in the real estate sector), which inevitably had impacts on creditors and suppliers; perhaps more importantly, the bubble psychology also changed. No longer did investors believe that prices could only go up. This boded ill for holders of loans whose collateral had dropped considerably in value, as well as for economic actors' perceptions of wealth. Thus, neither speculation nor consumption was likely to revive the economy. And on top of the increasing pessimism concerning the nation's economic prospects,[38] the stock of bad loans continued to rise. These ills were finally being reflected in stagnant economic growth figures: the blithely optimistic official forecast for FY 1992 of 3.5 percent growth was rapidly being proven unattainable.

Macroeconomic Policy Responses—MOF

Predictably, the macroeconomic response of the Ministry of Finance came considerably later than that of the Bank of Japan. Fiscal conservatism was symbolized by the government's decision to pay for its $13 billion contribution to the Gulf War effort with a special tax in 1991 rather than with bonds. Conservatism initially made economic as well as political sense. Overall economic growth started to slide in the second and third quarters of FY 1991, but was strong again in the fourth quarter (January–March 1992).[39] In any event, it was reasonable to wait for the effects of monetary policy loosening.

Nevertheless, there were several signs that the game of macroeconomic politics was alive and well. For one thing, the FY 1992 official forecast, and consequently the budget, gave no indication that policy makers were very worried about the warning signs that were clearly appearing already, such as the fourfold increase in the magnitude of business failures in 1991 (from ¥2 trillion to ¥8.1 trillion) and the dramatic drop in stock prices.[40] No one better understood the precarious situation of financial institutions than the inspectors in MOF's Banking and Securities Bureaus, who had full access to

38. All components of the BOJ's *Tankan*, which surveys business confidence, had dropped into negative territory by early 1992. Except for a brief period in early 1997 when the principal manufacturers' number broke zero, the *Tankan* numbers remained negative from 1992 at least through fall 1999. (Downloadable at <www.boj.or.jp / en / dlong_f.htm>)

39. After a very weak figure for the fourth quarter of 1991 (third quarter of FY 1991), first-quarter growth in 1992 showed a surprising recovery to 3.4 percent for GDP and 4.3 percent for GNP ("Special Factors Boost Japan's Economy to 4.3% Rate," *Japan Economic Newswire*, June 16, 1992). That recovery was only short-lived, however.

40. Even using yearly averages, which flatten out the spike in late 1989, the Nikkei's value in 1991 (¥24,296) was still 29 percent below the 1989 average (¥34,059). These averages as well as the figures on business failures are in IFMP 1996.

their books. Nonetheless, MOF bureaucrats may have felt that just as monetary policy had created and burst the bubble, so could it set things right again.

Amazingly, in the aftermath of the Gulf War tax hike MOF's Budget Bureau even teamed up with some LDP fiscal conservatives including Ozawa Ichirō to propose a new "International Contribution Tax," the proceeds of which would be saved in a special fund for future (unspecified) international contingencies.[41] Supporters followed an unusually stealthy strategy to try to minimize contact with the usual LDP review process, but when politicians on the party tax committee finally saw the proposal in December 1991, they put it on indefinite hold. This is a good example of the veto power politicians hold over new initiatives. The decision was no doubt buttressed by the slowing of the economy that had become apparent in autumn 1991.[42] Ironically, MOF was seeking to respond to economic slowdown with higher taxes! Despite the name, it is evident that the tax hike plan was meant to address the possibility of a revenue shortfall in FY 1992—even the bill's supporters were unable to enunciate clearly the kind of contingencies in which the proposed fund could or should be used.

More evidence that the policy game was still in effect can be seen in MOF's resistance to political calls for aid to distressed sectors and companies. While there was by no means a consensus in favor of fiscal expansion within the ruling party, a number of powerful Diet members wanted compensation for constituents. In these petitions ministry bureaucrats detected the scent of fiscal stimulus and so acted in the standard ways to hold it off— these included the above-mentioned optimistic official forecast, as well as strict secrecy in autumn microbudgeting and adherence to the budget ceilings set that summer. The result was another government revenue and spending plan that furthered the cause of fiscal consolidation, despite the ominous signs on the horizon.

As 1992 progressed, it became increasingly evident that the authorities in the Bank of Japan and Ministry of Finance had underestimated the effects of the bursting of the bubble and overestimated the effects of monetary loosening. Politicians were, not surprisingly, increasingly frustrated—one sign of this was LDP kingmaker (and macroeconomic neophyte) Kanemaru Shin's widely reported comment in February 1992 to the effect that "the discount rate should be lowered even if it means the prime minister firing

41. See the following articles from the *Nikkei: "Kokusai kōkenzei kettei"* (Decision on International Contribution Tax), December 14, 1991, 5; *"Posuto-baburu kinkō seichō e shiren"* (Looking for Balanced Post-Bubble Growth), December 15, 1991, 1; *"Kokusai kōkenzei miokuri, tō zeichō no hanpatsu tsuyoku"* (International Contribution Tax Postponed, Strong Reaction from Party Tax Council), December 17, 1991, 3.
42. *"Keiki wa akirakani kakō kyokumen ni haitta"* (Economy Has Clearly Turned Downward), *Nikkei*, December 17, 1991, 2.

the governor of the BOJ."[43] The comment was aimed at the Bank of Japan, but was also meant to push Prime Minister Miyazawa to use fiscal expansion. Business organizations also supported more government action, although perhaps less crudely than Kanemaru.[44]

The prime minister was indeed listening to such criticisms, and even tried to make the FY 1992 budget more expansionary, albeit without revising the budget itself, which would have been procedurally very difficult. Instead, in March the government decided on what it called a "fiscal stimulus package" to take effect as of the start of the new fiscal year on April 1. Unlike most such packages, however, this package did not have any additional funds whatsoever attached. Rather, it called for a cut in the official discount rate (although indirectly, because monetary policy is supposed to be a BOJ prerogative), increases in FILP lending to small and medium-sized enterprises, and a front-loading of public works spending, so that 75 percent of spending would be done in the first two quarters of the fiscal year.[45] The plans also called for private-sector action, with MITI requesting that public utilities expand investment in the first two quarters. Subsequently, MOF officials "suggested" to long-term credit banks that they keep long-term interest rates low.[46] At the time of its announcement, however, many politicians and observers suggested that it was a prelude to a more ambitious fiscal stimulus package. Even the chief EPA official in charge of making such assessments, Coordination Bureau director-general Yoshitomi Masaru, suggested that a plan later in the year might be necessary, despite his confident claim that the public spending in the first half of the year of ¥1.5 trillion would stimulate at least ¥4 trillion in economic activity.[47] Such announcements had the effect of putting pressure on MOF later in the year.

Surprisingly, the soft economic growth and stock market weakness did not appear to hurt the LDP in the Upper House election on July 26. Its respectable seat totals meant that with cooperation from the Kōmeitō or DSP and independents, it could win votes in the Upper House. In general, economic actors appeared to be waiting for an August stimulus package for which Miyazawa

---

43. Quoted in Suzuki 1992, 2. The comment created a considerable buzz throughout Japan at the time. According to his 1996 speech in London, Mieno took the threat seriously at the time (*mattaku esoragoto dewa nakatta*), although as noted above he felt he had to stand up to it (Mizuno 1997, 200; see also Mieno 2000, 213).
44. See, for example, the comments of the head of the Japanese Chamber of Commerce and Industry in "Ishikawa Seeks Fiscal Stimulus to Economy," *Jiji*, March 5, 1992.
45. MOF mimeo "*Kinkyū keizai taisaku*" (Urgent Economic Measures), March 31, 1992.
46. The first inkling of this plan appeared in early March ("MOF Considers Fiscal Steps Under Govt Package," *Jiji Ticker Service*, March 5, 1992). The details were announced March 31. The calls for private action were rather extraordinary for a macroeconomic plan and suggested that interventionist thinking was still alive and well in the bureaucracy. Indeed, an unidentified senior MOF official was quoted as saying, "We will instruct, or I should say, make suggestions, to them" ("MOF Official Confident about Growth Target," *Kyodo*, April 20, 1992).
47. "Government Announces Package to Boost Economy," *Kyodo*, March 31, 1992.

had called in the run-up to the election. However, with the election over, there was no particular pressure on the government to act right away.

In terms of real action, the first response was more monetary loosening. However, more knowledgeable politicians had begun by the spring to realize the need for fiscal stimulus to get the economy back in gear. Finally, on August 28, under orders from the Miyazawa Cabinet, the Ministry of Finance announced the largest fiscal stimulus plan ever. Officially valued at ¥10.7 trillion, like most plans it consisted mainly of FILP allocations and unspent funds; but it also included an unprecedented ¥2.26 trillion bond issue.[48] It also promised to move forward a number of public works projects that were planned for later in the year, raising the possibility of another stimulus plan before the end of the year to pick up the resulting slack.

There was considerable speculation leading up to the plan. By May, the Industrial Bank of Japan was predicting that growth for FY 1992 (officially predicted as 3.5 percent, as Table 2.1 shows) would be unlikely to top 2 percent, even though it also predicted that a fiscal stimulus plan would be introduced in the fall.[49] The United States and other G-7 nations also renewed pressure for a stimulus in response to the doubling of Japan's current account surplus from FY 1990 to FY 1991. Meanwhile, unidentified MOF officials were quoted in the press as saying that no further fiscal stimulus was necessary, and that indeed such a stimulus might only serve to reignite inflation.[50]

Even if the direct macroeconomic impact was in doubt, the plan appeared to appease stock market participants at least temporarily. The Nikkei's August 28 close was ¥17,971, up more than 10 percent from the previous day's close; more strikingly, it had been in the ¥15,000s for more than a month before the announcement, and only ten days earlier had dropped as low as ¥14,309 until rumors of the plan sparked an upsurge in prices starting around August 20. The index stayed in the high ¥17,000s–low ¥18,000s range for the next month (see Figure 5.2).

48. *"Saikin no keizai taisaku"* (Recent Economic Plans), undated MOF mimeo. Prime Minister Miyazawa was a former MOF man, but he had long since been disowned by the Finance bureaucrats because of his self-confidence and Keynesian tendencies. Moreover, he had been tricked by fiscal stimulus plans before (in 1986 and 1987), and was insistent on having real money attached. Then–finance minister Hata was also generally seen as a liberal in matters of economic policy.

49. "FY '92 Economic Growth at Only 2.0 Pct: IBJ," *Jiji Ticker Service*, May 11, 1992.

50. See, for example, "MOF Official Cautions on More Fiscal Stimulus," *Jiji Ticker Service*, May 7, 1992. The official quoted in the article warned that stimulus would likely lead to inflation and then to instability in world currency markets. Two weeks earlier, an unidentified "top official" had criticized U.S. calls for monetary and fiscal stimulus with the argument that "suggesting further monetary easing would spoil the effects of previous interest rate cuts by creating expectations in the market for another cut and leading companies to delay borrowing money for investments" ("Official Snubs Call for More to Boost Japan's Economy," *Kyodo*, April 26, 1992).

Microeconomic Policy Responses—MOF

Macroeconomic stimulation was not the only focus of MOF response in 1990–92, however. Three microeconomic interventions stand out as well. By early 1990, annoyance over excessive bank lending to land speculators was once again addressed by policy makers, as it had been in 1988. On March 27, just before the end of the fiscal year, the ministry issued an administrative directive titled "Regarding the Restraint of Land-Related Lending." This directive called on banks not to increase their real estate–related lending at a faster pace than their overall lending, and requested reports on all lending to real estate and construction firms and to nonbanks.[51]

The intention was to cut off funds to land speculators, but whatever effectiveness it had in that regard, it also offered some perverse incentives. In particular, agriculture-related financial institutions were exempted from the directive, thus making it attractive for them to act as middlemen between banks and *jūsen*.[52] This was to lead to considerable problems for the agriculture-related financial institutions later, when they were particularly exposed to the *jūsen* disaster. The second microeconomic intervention was the rumored informal directive to Japanese financial institutions not to sell off foreclosed assets that had fallen in price. The purpose was to put a floor under real estate prices and to keep banks' books looking good. Both directives were typical of the techniques of the Ministry of Finance, which was never one to shy away from intervention in the activities of financial institutions.[53]

The most audacious of the microeconomic interventions began in autumn 1992, in response to the distressing slide in stock prices. As a result of asset price deflation, both bank capitalization and loan collateral had fallen dramatically in value. The result was that by late 1992, journalists were beginning to warn of huge stocks of nonperforming loans at financial institutions of all sizes, and the growth of bank lending fell from more than 10 percent in 1990 to around 2 percent in 1992.[54]

While nothing could be done to change the past, it was apparent that further depreciation of asset prices would mean further depreciation of collateral and bank capital, which would translate into less new lending and more bad loans, and so on, in a continuing downward spiral. Monetary policy was

---

51. Mizuno 1997, 195. The Japanese title of the directive is *"Tochi kanren yūshi no yokusei ni tsuite."*
52. Mizuno 1997, 195.
53. On the interventionist nature of MOF, one can find innumerable accounts. These include Vogel 1996; Mabuchi 1997; Asahi Shimbun Economics Bureau 1997; and Ishizawa 1995. See Katō (1997) on interventionism among bureaucracies in general.
54. *"Nonbanku nenkan rieki o karuku fukitobasu furyō saiken"* (Nonbank Nonperforming Loans Easily Blow Away Annual Profits), *Ekonomisuto*, November 9, 1992, 100–103. At around the same time, a director of Sumitomo Bank was quoted as saying that ¥200 billion worth of capital had been "thrown into the sewer." "*'Ginkō fushin' no jidai ga yatte kita"* (The Era of "Non-Confidence in Banks" Has Arrived), *Ekonomisuto*, October 6, 1992, 24.

already responding to the need of borrowers for lower interest rates, but asset prices remained a major problem. The declines in bank capital were particularly troubling given that Japanese banks were expected to meet the new BIS capital-adequacy standards by January 1993.[55] As the unrealized gains made on investments in the bubble market evaporated, many of Japan's internationally active banks ran the risk of dropping below the BIS standards and having to call some existing loans while severely curtailing new loans. Thus, in addition to the potentially dire direct effects of the decline in asset prices, if stock prices dropped low enough a very serious credit crunch could result. (One common assessment put the danger zone in the ¥14,000 to ¥15,000 range of the Nikkei average, into which the index had briefly dropped in July and August.)

It was under these circumstances that MOF embarked on a crusade to lift equity values back up toward the ¥20,000 level. The August fiscal stimulus plan had been temporarily helpful in stemming a sell-off of equities, but by October and November values were again dropping into potentially dangerous territory. In response, MOF and BOJ officials tried to increase confidence in the market through a variety of announcements and leaks to the press, as well as through informal guidance to major market players to hold onto large capital positions.[56] In addition to indirect measures such as announcements and guidance, the ministry had begun by late summer to act directly as well, through the so-called "PKO," or "price-keeping operation" (a pun on UN "peace-keeping operations").

In the PKO, government trust funds were placed in investment trusts (managed by trust banks), which in turn invested in the stock market.[57] The scheme did not require Diet approval, insofar as the management of trust funds is legally the responsibility of the Trust Fund Bureau (MOF Financial Bureau). The twist in this case is that short-term trust funds are supposed to be used only in the debt instruments of certain types of institutions, most of them government or government-related. However, the 1987 deal that had returned a portion of funds to the MPT and MHW for "autonomous management" also allowed those ministries to put their funds into investment trusts. The total value under autonomous management—not all of which was going into the stock market, of course—totaled ¥37.86 trillion (over

55. Under the terms of the Basle Accord, the capital-adequacy standards for internationally active banks (i.e., the "BIS standards") divided bank capital into two "tiers." Tier-one capital is shareholder equity. Tier-two capital consists of loan-loss reserves and various other assets. Most importantly for our story, unrealized gain on securities can account for up to 45 percent of tier-two capital (Kapstein 1991, 22). Japanese banks had seen their tier-two capital, and thus their ability to lend new money, expand rapidly in parallel with Japanese stock prices in the late 1980s (Taniguchi 1993, 28–34).

56. Nihon Keizai Shimbunsha 1994, 68–69.

57. For a good overview of how the PKO worked, see *"'Kabuka seishi' o sasaeru PKO"* (PKO Supporting "Stock Price Quietude"), *Nikkei*, February 25, 1993. The article also contains

$300 billion at the time) by the end of February 1993, out of total trust funds of ¥298 trillion.[58]

The plan was designed to have a dual effect on stock prices—directly, by increasing effective demand, and indirectly, by signaling to investors that downside risk would be minimized by government intervention. The signaling was more than just informal or through rumors, however. The August 1992 fiscal stimulus plan actually contained ¥2.8 trillion (approximately $22.5 billion at the time) explicitly earmarked to go into investment trusts, with the stated purpose "to vitalize the securities market,"[59] although it is generally understood and acknowledged that considerably more funds have gone into the operation, which apparently continues to this day.[60]

Despite the apparent unlikeliness of such a ploy working, many observers and participants credit the PKO with bringing the Nikkei back up to the ¥20,000 mark by April 1993. Nonetheless, the stabilization of the stock market did not eliminate the pressure on macroeconomic authorities to fix the shattered economy, as most other economic indicators showed declines. Even the stock market did not look extremely healthy despite the higher prices, as trading volume dropped dramatically, sending many smaller brokers out of business (see Figure 5.2). As in the case of currency intervention in the Plaza-Louvre period, the ministry tried to solve the problem without hurting its core values of fiscal consolidation and financial control. But while the plan was generally credited with putting a floor under stock prices, it did not succeed in creating conditions for long-term growth in the market.

Postscript

While government briefers confidently predicted that the 1992 fiscal stimulus plan and the PKO would move the economy off the path of slowdown and financial difficulty, many observers disagreed with that assessment. It turned out

some speculation that the action had been prompted by a member of the LDP's Policy Affairs Research Council, but that version seems to be a minority opinion. Nihon Keizai Shimbunsha (1994, 67–71) also discusses the PKO.

58. Ministry of Finance, Financial Bureau, *"Zaiseitōyūshi kankei shiryō"* (Materials Related to the Fiscal Investment and Loan Program), mimeo, April 1993. The accounts used in both autonomous management and the PKO are the Postal Savings Special Account, the Post Office Life Insurance and Annuities Welfare Corporation, and the Pension Welfare Service Public Corporation. ¥37.86 trillion was the equivalent of about $300 billion at the contemporaneous exchange rate of approximately ¥125 / $1.

59. These provisions can be found in the MOF summary for the plan. The quotation in the text is from the English-language press release for the FY 1993 regular budget, "The Budget and the Economic Management for FY 1993" (embargo date of December 21, 1992; 5), which confirms the continuation of stock price maintenance. " *'Kabuka ...*" (*Nikkei*, February 25, 1993) also makes explicit mention of the ¥2.8 trillion from the August 1992 fiscal stimulus plan.

60. In autumn 1998, Minister of Posts and Telecommunications Noda Seiko announced publicly her opposition to continuing the plan with MPT-administered funds. "No Postal Funds to Bolster Stocks: Noda," *Jiji* , August 28, 1998.

that the latter were right, as business confidence, stock prices, lending, and economic growth all continued to show disappointing numbers in the final months of 1992, despite the upturn in the stock market in the immediate wake of the plan's announcement. The one bright point was the moderate rate of change in the value of the yen, which, despite increasing dissatisfaction over macroeconomic policy in both Japan and the United States (where presidential candidate Bill Clinton was campaigning against Japanese trade surpluses, particularly in high value-added goods), moved gently from the mid- to the low ¥120s between summer and the end of the year.

Thus, the hope of MOF bureaucrats that the 1992 fiscal stimulus plan would be enough to satisfy critics of continued fiscal conservatism proved to be in vain. As the economy continued its stagnation, sniping increased between the BOJ and MOF over responsibility for the situation, while market participants, politicians, and (after the November 1992 election) the incoming U.S. administration all raised their voices in favor of a more activist response by the Japanese authorities. As it turned out, the continuation (and indeed, worsening) of the situation opened the door for these nonbureaucratic actors whom the ministry and the bank had for so long sought to exclude from policy making. The airily optimistic official forecast of 3.3 percent growth for FY 1993 and its accompanying conservative budget were to be the last absolute victories for the ministry's vision of fiscal consolidation above all other considerations.

Analysis

Although authors have pointed to a variety of distortions in the Japanese economy as contributing to the bubble, it is evident that loose money fueled asset price inflation.[61] Therefore, we must explain why the BOJ maintained its easy money policy for so long. The next question is, given the apparent preference for easy money by politicians (in general) and the Ministry of Finance (in the interests of fiscal consolidation), why was the fiscal tightening of 1989–90 so dramatic? The resolute stand against the bubble appears to contradict the image of a BOJ dependent on others' favor. Finally, how can we best understand the pattern of macroeconomic response that arose once the adverse effects of bursting the bubble became apparent?

Explaining Easy Money

As we have seen, from January 1986 to February 1987 the BOJ's discount rate had been lowered from 5 percent to 2.5 percent, where it remained un-

---

61. Cargill, Hutchison, and Ito (1997, chaps. 4–5) demonstrate this rigorously. Some of the distortions often cited include land-use laws, poor prudential bank regulation, and poor price pass-through on imported goods.

til May 1989. Meanwhile, money supply growth (as measured by the BOJ's own preferred aggregate, M_2 +CD) outstripped economic growth by an average of more than six percentage points between 1986 and 1990.[62] Of all of Japan's economic policies of the post-Louvre period, the failure to raise interest rates in 1988 is perhaps the most difficult to explain from an economic standpoint. That is certainly true in retrospect. Even at the time, however, knowing what policy makers knew then, Japanese authorities were playing a dangerous game—then–deputy governor Mieno said in 1987 that it was "like sitting on a powder keg" that was "getting drier and drier by the day."[63] Published BOJ analysis from that time also consistently warned of asset price rises and a money supply that was rising much more quickly than GNP growth. These concerns were real despite the fact that consumer, producer, and wholesale prices remained stable. Thus, the Bank of Japan was aware of the dangers of continuing its lax monetary policy stance (although certainly no one predicted problems of the magnitude that actually arose). The only way the policy could have made sense is if the Japanese authorities had placed so much emphasis on the exchange rate that domestic policy paled in comparison.[64] From an economic standpoint, Japan's unwillingness to rein in the money supply in 1988 remains a puzzle.

Other approaches do not contribute much to our understanding either. International-level explanations (even in looking at the macroeconomic aspects of SII) seem to add little, given the stabilized exchange rates, the declining current account imbalances, and the cautious treatment by U.S. officials of macroeconomic and exchange rate questions following Black Monday.[65] Mieno does cite international "commitments" and the financial fragility following Black Monday, as do many authors. These "commitments" were not binding, however, and in fact had not deterred Germany in 1988 (nor even the BOJ for a few brief weeks in fall 1985) from easing up interest rates. Also, there is considerable evidence that the low interest rate policy was causing distress within the bank. Only by focusing on domestic factors do we gain insight into the extended low interest rates.

Japanese actions in 1988–89 are most consistent with both political control over bureaucracies and with my description of the macroeconomic

62. Calculated from BOJ figures (money supply) and EPA figures (GDP growth).
63. Ohta 1991, 113. Mieno (2000, 195) has it as "sitting on dry kindling."
64. Cargill, Hutchison, and Ito (1997, 68–80) make a version of this argument. It also calls to mind McKinnon and Ohno's (1997) assertion that the yen-dollar exchange rate is a "forcing variable" for Japanese monetary policy. However, McKinnon and Ohno argue that it consistently forces *restrictive* monetary policy, leading Japan into a series of liquidity traps. In the late 1980s, monetary policy was creating *excess* liquidity.
65. This is not to deny any U.S. pressure—David Mulford (promoted by the new Bush administration to undersecretary of the treasury) frequently admonished Tokyo to deal with bilateral imbalances, and there were continuing trade frictions. But the urgency of the Plaza-Louvre period had clearly abated.

policy-making structure. As suggested by its published reports and in personal interviews, the BOJ was interested in raising interest rates at several points between February 1987 (if not earlier) and May 1989. The first clear instance, just prior to Black Monday, was understandably jettisoned for fear of roiling the markets further. By mid-1988, however, there was no longer a major fear of worldwide financial collapse, and BOJ officials were again interested in tightening monetary policy. The Ministry of Finance and LDP were unwilling to accept that, however. In the case of the LDP, the short-term prosperity brought about by the boom made politicians unwilling to believe that monetary policies were too lax, especially since prices were stable and the yen was strong. The motivations of MOF were apparently more complicated. For one thing, the fiscal consolidation effort was still in full swing, in combination with the introduction of a new consumption tax; with such battles continuing, any move to slow economic activity would only have made MOF's political task harder. Moreover, the higher tax receipts that accompanied rapid growth brought the goal of fiscal consolidation a step closer. Finally, the ministry had no appetite for a stronger yen, which might have rekindled demands from affected industries for compensation from the national budget.

The BOJ's institutional setting was thus decisive in determining the direction of Japan's macroeconomic policies. However, it is not possible to disentangle the respective roles of the Ministry of Finance and ruling-party politicians.

Explaining BOJ Overshooting

Analysts now agree that in its belated efforts to subdue the asset inflation that two years of ultra-low interest rates had produced, the Bank of Japan overshot considerably in its quest to end the bubble. The five discount rate hikes between May 1989 and August 1990 proved to have more far-reaching effects than anyone imagined at the time. In this case, it is impossible to dismiss the importance of economic uncertainty—while some observers (and especially speculators) felt by early 1990 that monetary tightening had gone too far, many if not most policy makers and observers thought that it was essential to break market expectations that could lead to a recurrence of the bubble. The simple fact is that even very sophisticated econometric methods cannot accurately predict the course of such a complex phenomenon.

What is clear is that international pressures for a higher yen were *not* driving interest rate hikes, as McKinnon and Ohno's analysis would suggest.[66] Not

66. This may seem a bit unfair to McKinnon and Ohno, who after all manage to avoid discussing the causes of the 1989–90 interest rate hikes even as they affirm the importance of the effects (1997, chap. 5). However, if their model is to have any validity at all, it should have at least *some* relevance to the most pronounced example of credit constriction in the period of their study.

only were U.S.–Japan trade balances improving, but the yen actually weakened briefly during the period of the interest rate hikes, and ended August 1990 at approximately the same level as it had ended May 1989, and weaker than it had ended April 1989. Moreover, the major U.S.–Japan trade negotiation of 1989 and 1990, the Structural Impediments Initiative, specifically excluded exchange rates from consideration.

We cannot dismiss as easily the possibility that political leaders were directing their bureaucratic agents to cool down the economy. Despite the many benefits that accrued to the ruling party from the bubble years, as a long-term dominant party it also had to think about the future, and by mid-1989 it was undeniable that asset price inflation threatened the Japanese economy.[67] The markets also seemed to see the LDP as having turned against the bubble—on the day after the LDP's resounding Lower House election win on February 18, 1990, the Nikkei experienced its second largest dip ever (after the 1987 crash). Market participants identified the party with the likelihood of more interest rate hikes, despite the open conflict between Mieno and Finance Minister Hashimoto in December 1989.[68]

Thinking about matters from the standpoint of domestic structures gives a different set of motivations, which I believe provides greater insight into both the overshooting and the BOJ's subsequent actions in 1991–92. As argued above, the bank's leadership was already chafing at the long period of low interest rates and the extraordinary run-up in asset prices. According to top officials of the time, Mieno and others on the Executive Board had wanted to raise interest rates in 1987 (only to be deterred by the U.S. stock market crash in October) and again in 1988 when Germany's Bundesbank started tightening German monetary policy.[69] When the LDP and MOF finally became alarmed over the asset price problem in 1989, the BOJ was at last able to do what its leadership had wanted since the summer of 1987. However, the long-term weak structural position of the bank in relation to other official actors meant that if pain were to result, it might have to pull back, thus risking the resurgence of a speculative bubble. In the brief window offered it by LDP and MOF alarm, the bank took extremely aggressive action. It is difficult to prove that the BOJ's monetary tightening would have been more gradual (particularly in 1990) if it had greater assurance of its autonomy, but that is the logic of the structural argument, and it certainly fits the facts. (Mieno Yasushi, BOJ governor for the last three rate hikes, argues that he simply wanted to return to a "neutral" discount rate of around 5 percent as quickly as possible.[70] Nonetheless, the extreme haste of the actions, which

67. The after-effects of the Recruit scandal and the ensuing Upper House election loss in summer 1989 may have made the LDP less eager to continue to be associated with the bubble. On Recruit, see Shimoda 1989.

68. On the effects of the Lower House election, see Hanson 1996, 178.

69. Personal interviews.

70. Mieno 2000, 209–210. Also, personal interview with Mieno in November 1999.

gave no opportunity to gauge each one's effects, seems rather reckless even for an inflation hawk like Mieno.)

Explaining Responses to Financial Crisis

The final set of policies to consider are those of 1991 and 1992. The key ones here are the series of discount rate cuts, the fiscal response (both the initial reluctance and the August 1992 fiscal stimulus plan), and the start of the PKO. In each case, we can see the standard patterns of behavior described in chapter 1.

The most significant response to the financial crisis can be seen in monetary policy, where the discount rate was cut from 6 percent in July 1991 to 3.25 percent in July 1992. Cutting interest rates was the obvious first response to the crisis, both economically and politically. It was apparent that excessive tightening in 1989–90 had led to a series of ominous economic statistics, and it seemed apparent that the liquidity crunch that resulted from that tightening would have to be addressed with a looser monetary policy. Also, only monetary policy could respond quickly and flexibly enough to such a sudden change. Politically, the discount rate was conveniently symbolic of the policies that had led to financial turmoil.

At the same time, not everyone was convinced that the bubble would not return. One retrospective offers a series of quotations from Governor Mieno that suggest that the Bank of Japan was resistant to the idea of interest rate cuts over the 1991–92 period. These include statements in May 1991, September 1991, and January 1992 that the bubble was not yet over, as well as specific denials in March and April 1992 that slow money supply growth was bad for the economy and that financial institutions were in even short-term difficulties.[71] While some of these statements no doubt constitute attempts by the central bank governor to reassure markets, they are also very public statements that seem often to contradict the BOJ's actions in the monetary field. In fact, it is generally agreed that Mieno was (wrongly, in retrospect) very reluctant to abandon his attack on the bubble.[72] In the end, however, despite the concentration of BOJ decision making in the hands of the governor, Mieno was unable to hold out against political and social pressure without the support of the Ministry of Finance.

MOF was similarly reluctant to loosen in the area under its jurisdiction—i.e., fiscal policy. MOF's resistance proved to be more effective than that of the Bank of Japan, however. FY 1991 and FY 1992 both saw conservative budgets that reflected the fiscal consolidation trend of the previous decade. For our purposes, there is not much to analyze in the FY 1991 budget,

71. Mizuno 1997, 193–194.
72. Mizuno 1997; personal interviews. Mieno (2000, 212–213) says he feared excessively rapid loosening because that would leave unfinished the structural adjustment that had begun in the economy.

which was issued when the economy was still growing briskly. The FY 1992 budget is more interesting. It was based on a Pollyanna-ish official forecast of 3.5 percent growth, despite the evident slowing down of the economy and what ministry officials—with their intimate knowledge of banks' account books—surely knew was an expanding bad loan crisis. Despite increasing political sentiment in favor of more stimulatory fiscal policy, the budget primly stuck to the budget ceilings agreed to the previous summer. The budget draft effectively ended any hope for a fiscal stimulus before late summer 1992, particularly given the political unpalatability of amending the budget draft. Despite the upcoming Upper House election in July, MOF exploited a lack of consensus on stimulus by making no effort to start preparing a supplementary plan.

The fiscal conservatism that characterized most of 1992 is an excellent example of how a determined bureaucracy can take advantage of structural and informational tools to push its own agenda. One part of the story is the extremely optimistic official forecast, which suggested that no changes needed to be made to the established budget ceilings. Even though many politicians and market participants doubted the forecast, the ruling party was unwilling to challenge the more knowledgeable Ministry of Finance on such a sensitive issue, one it had little independent ability to discredit. MOF also made good use of the budget calendar, which provided an effective means of stalling. And, of course, the recently achieved goals of fiscal consolidation added considerable legitimacy to MOF's efforts. Nonetheless, whatever the economic basis for MOF's preferences (and it is not difficult to argue that it was sensible for fiscal policy to adopt a wait-and-see attitude, given the considerable loosening of monetary policy), an observer of bureaucratic politics can only be impressed at its ability to prevent serious consideration of a policy it feared.

It might be argued that the government's conservative stance came to an end in August 1992, with the introduction of the largest fiscal stimulus plan ever. We must, however, bear in mind that—like most fiscal stimulus plans—this one too bore inflated estimates of actual size and likely impact.[73] Indeed, general account spending in FY 1992 actually *fell short* of the initial budget, despite the alleged additional spending of the August stimulus plan (see Table 3.1). Also, a considerable portion of the plan was dedicated to moving planned public works spending forward, a calculated gamble that growth would pick up and another stimulus plan would not be necessary to cover new public works spending in the final quarter of FY 1992 (January–March 1993). While it is again impossible to dismiss the importance of considerable economic uncertainty, it is difficult not to conclude that the ministry took advantage of that uncertainty to reduce the size of the fiscal stimulus. It did so

73. Posen makes this clear (1998, chap. 2).

in the face of the personal advocacy of Prime Minister Miyazawa, a Keynesian whose suspicion of his own former ministry went back at least to the days when it had effectively neutralized the fiscal stimulus plans he had championed as finance minister in 1986 and 1987.[74]

The final policy in question was the PKO intervention. It is unclear how involved politicians were in the decision to prop up the stock market with trust funds, but it is generally interpreted as a MOF-initiated operation. The preference for informal intervention that would have a minimal impact on the government's fiscal position is reminiscent of the preference for currency market intervention over fundamental policy changes. Like other policies that do not require Diet approval, the decision to intervene in the equity markets suggests both the strengths and the weaknesses of the ministry vis-à-vis the legislature. The ability to carry out major policies involving the large-scale outlay of public funds demonstrates considerable autonomy. On the other hand, the need to use administrative measures shows the hesitancy of the ministry to take its chances in the legislative process.[75]

74. Former MOF budget officials I interviewed in 1993 felt that MOF had fought the good fight against Miyazawa in 1986 and 1987, and that he was resentful as a result.
75. This parallels Haley's argument about bureaucrats' "authority without power" (1991, esp. 139–168).

6

Dealing with Stagnation, 1993–97

The Shift toward Activism

The Japanese government got what it paid for in the 1990s—one good
year of growth and little else.

Adam Posen, *Restoring Japan's Economic Growth*

As Japan entered 1993, important new forces seemed poised to
affect macroeconomic policy. Internationally, the inauguration of U.S. president Bill Clinton augured much more pressure from the United States to
stimulate the domestic economy, as was made clear in statements by prominent members of his economic policy team. The United States' pugnacious
trade stance and its emphasis on bilateral trade figures raised the political
stakes in U.S.–Japanese economic relations, and increased the likelihood
that fiscal policy might be needed to check American protectionist measures, as it had in the Plaza-Louvre period. Officials at MOF and the EPA
may or may not have had this Washington audience in mind when they projected a very optimistic 3.3 percent growth rate for FY 1993, but at least
within the Ministry of Finance, officials were bracing for heavy pressure.[1]

At the same time, the Japanese economy did not seem to have been very
stimulated by either of the discount rate cuts of 1992 or by the August fiscal
stimulus plan. The stock market remained soft, land prices began to drop, and
more and more reports were surfacing in the media concerning the bad loans
held by financial institutions. And while the yen had remained steady, the current account had again ballooned, from 1991's $72.9 billion to $117.6 billion
in 1992, an increase of more than 60 percent.[2] Public resentment of the
macroeconomic authorities' conservatism was beginning to take hold as well.

Finally, we cannot ignore the major Japanese political story of 1993: the
break-up of the Liberal Democratic Party and the subsequent installation of
the first non-LDP government since that party's formation in 1955.[3] This is
not the place for a full account, but in a nutshell, a power struggle inside the

1. I base this statement on both interviews at the time and casual conversations in early 1993
when I was a visiting researcher at MOF's Institute for Fiscal and Monetary Policy.
2. IMF (various years).
3. Kohno 1997, chap. 8; Schlesinger 1997, chaps. 21–22; Curtis 1999, chap. 2.

largest (Takeshita) faction fused with popular calls for electoral reform, lead-ing to the exit of more than thirty members of the party and then to an LDP loss in a Lower House election in July. The popularity of electoral reform was probably at least indirectly linked to public dissatisfaction over economic conditions, although that is difficult to prove; in any event, the breakup of the LDP clearly had implications for the politics of economic policy.

Prior to the July 1993 election, political pressure surely compounded the pressure on the Miyazawa administration for economic policy change. Sub-sequently, the non-LDP coalition governments of Hosokawa Morihiro and Hata Tsutomu faced pressures to fix the problems of the economy. After the passage of political reforms, and with the return of the LDP to power (at first in formal coalition with the Socialists and Sakigake, and later in infor-mal coalition) in June 1994, economic recovery once again became the cen-tral problem for the Japanese government.

In the period 1993–97, then, continuing economic problems and politi-cal uncertainty were intimately intertwined. Meanwhile, along with changes in the world of elected politicians came changes in the interactions between politicians and bureaucrats. Bureaucrats in general, and MOF officials in particular, became targets of political and media attacks alleging incompe-tence, arrogance, and even corruption, damaging their ability to act as de-cision makers. Nonetheless, the Ministry of Finance demonstrated surpris-ing resilience and strength in the face of politicians' attempts to assert their authority over their putative agents.

What this meant in practical terms was that fiscal policy did become more expansive, at least until FY 1997, but never to the extent claimed by the vari-ous governments, which announced a variety of stimulus plans and tax cuts. In line with the logic of chapter 1, those fiscal plans included less and less window dressing over time, as optimistic official projections of their effec-tiveness lost credibility. Interestingly, the increasing responsiveness of fiscal policy appeared in tandem with a variety of attacks on the recognized bases of MOF power, particularly in terms of personnel. As chapter 7 shows, these included efforts to eliminate public corporations that had offered sinecure *amakudari* positions for retiring bureaucrats, an attempt by Finance Minister Takemura in 1994 to name a non-MOF governor of the Bank of Japan, and media denunciations and even arrests of MOF bureaucrats for overly cozy (and lucrative) relations with financial institutions under their supervision.

Meanwhile, monetary policy was, predictably, loose—by September 1995, interest rates were so low (the discount rate was 0.5 percent) that nominal short-term rates could hardly be lowered any more. Throughout the period, as usual, monetary loosening preceded fiscal stimulus, until it had ceased to be effective as an expansionary macroeconomic policy tool.

The period ended with a final twist. Prime Minister Hashimoto's FY 1997 budget proved to be extremely contractionary, leading to an all-out, irrefutable recession. One of its key components—a hike in the consumption tax from 3 to 5 percent—was the fulfillment of a deal made between Prime Minister Murayama and MOF bureaucrats two years earlier, but other facets constituted an alliance between MOF and LDP budget hawks alarmed by Japan's ballooning public debt. That fiscal intransigence held—even in the face of recession and the failures of several major financial institutions—until December 1997, at which point the government shifted to large-scale fiscal stimulus. Thus, the budget hawks' triumph in setting the FY 1997 budget was a pyrrhic one. I argue that the extraordinary overreaching by budget hawks in the preparation of the FY 1997 budget was, like the BOJ's overshooting in tightening monetary policy in 1989–91, at least partly caused by the perception among MOF officials that their powers were limited. This led them to force through large-scale and (apparently) permanent steps toward fiscal consolidation when the opportunity presented itself.

The Waning Days of the 1955 System

The politics of the LDP breakup constitute a fascinating topic on their own, though describing and analyzing them would take us far afield. Nevertheless, the situation surely made the leadership more desperate for a convincing solution to Japan's economic woes. Because political conditions and policy-making processes could be expected to change considerably under subsequent coalition governments, this section covers the brief period from the end of 1992 until June 1993, when a no-confidence vote forced new Lower House elections.

Fiscal Policy

From summer 1992, the Japanese fiscal stance began to change, most evidently in the August fiscal stimulus package.[4] As usual, the bulk of the funding was increased FILP lending and reserve funds, but it did contain ¥2.26 trillion in new bonds. Having trumpeted their success in eliminating the issuance of deficit bonds by 1990, the LDP and MOF ensured that borrowing for the package would be in the form of construction bonds. Despite the plan's stated aims, much of the spending could be expected to have little impact on either domestic demand or international imbalances.[5]

4. Ironically, despite its claimed urgency, the plan was not actually approved by the Diet until December 11, although some of the projected spending had apparently already begun before the official approval.
5. As one U.S. economist argued in autumn 1992, "A quarter of the total will take the form of land purchases by the state, which will not boost GNP and will have minimal repercussions abroad. Japan's fiscal package needs to be front-loaded and redirected away from land transactions and toward purchases of goods and services" (Eichengreen 1992, from Internet—no page number available).

After the introduction of the fiscal stimulus package, no new macroeconomic policy actions were taken until the introduction of the ¥72.35 trillion FY 1993 budget. Following standard procedure, the MOF budget draft stayed within the budget ceilings established that summer. With spending increases of only 0.2 percent and no tax cuts, it was generally regarded as fiscally conservative.[6] This was a natural stance to take, given the healthy (but excessively optimistic) economic growth forecast of 3.3 percent. Despite disapproving analyses in newspapers and by the new U.S. administration, the budget draft fulfilled the hopes of the budget/tax bureaucrats in MOF, who remained committed to fiscal reconsolidation. The 3.3 percent forecast was over-optimistic not only in hindsight, but also at the time. It fits in with the general tendency to use the official forecast to minimize budget deficits.[7] Even as the budget draft was announced, however, Prime Minister Miyazawa and other top bureaucratic and political officials were making clear that further fiscal stimulus was likely.[8]

Despite the general lack of enthusiasm that greeted it, the budget draft was passed without change by the Diet in March 1993, before the end of FY 1992. At first glance, this may appear odd, since opposition parties have traditionally held up budgets they do not like until well into the new fiscal year, with only short-term spending agreements keeping the government working in the interim. In this case, however, Miyazawa had promised a supplemental budget, which could only be submitted *after* the original budget was passed.[9] Therefore, in order to get supplemental spending in place as quickly as possible, it was necessary to pass the budget as quickly as possible.

Miyazawa soon made good on his pledge, introducing "New Comprehensive Economic Measures" with a stated value of ¥13.2 trillion (equivalent to 18 percent of the initial general account budget), including a ¥2.2 trillion supplemental budget and a ¥2.25 trillion tax cut.[10] As usual, most of the rest was made up of FILP-financed public works spending. Also as usual, the package contained a number of curious items (¥41 billion in aid to Rus-

6. A contrary view was expressed by Robert Feldman, then chief economist for Salomon Brothers in Tokyo. He argued that, "Apart from politics and theatrics, an analysis of the actual numbers in the budget suggests that it is already quite expansionary in nature" (1992, 4). He based this analysis partly on the fact that debt service payments would be 2 percent lower than in the previous budget, leaving more room for real fiscal spending, and partly on increased FILP spending. The report also predicts a fiscal stimulus package in the form of a tax cut later in the year.

7. Indeed, only a few months later, a mid-level economist from the Economic Planning Agency complained to me that MOF was skewing EPA forecasts to blunt calls for fiscal stimulation (personal interview).

8. Feldman 1992, 3–4.

9. See, for example, "Pressure for Japan Growth Package," *FT,* February 15, 1993, 5.

10. Figures are from a MOF press release entitled " '*Shin sōgō keizai taisaku' no pointo*" (Main Points of the 'New Comprehensive Economic Measures'), and from a MOF mimeo entitled "*Heisei 5-nendo hosei yosan furēmu*" (FY 1993 Supplemental Budget Framework).

sia and contributions of ¥25 billion to the National Debt Service Special Fund could hardly be expected to stimulate the domestic economy), but it was generally greeted as a major pump-priming measure. Indeed, this was a notable and even unprecedented fiscal action on the part of the Japanese government. While the numbers were certainly exaggerated—and the FILP money to be lent through government financial institutions would still be at the discretion of the Ministry of Finance–dominated management of those institutions—the package clearly included considerable new public investment.[11] Moreover, its timing (like that of the 1987 fiscal stimulus plan) increased the announcement effect. Finally, the statement that 75 percent of public works would be completed in the first half of the fiscal year suggested that if growth had not picked up by fall there might be an additional stimulus plan. All in all, it represented at least a partial victory for Miyazawa's Keynesian preferences.

MOF's press release also emphasized the exceptional nature of the plan, pointing out that it was "the largest in history" and that its introduction immediately following the passage of the regular budget was "extremely unusual."[12] Virtually all ministry officials I interviewed at the time made it clear that they believed the package was very substantive, although they opposed the use of deficit financing for fiscal stimulus in general.[13]

Nevertheless, one must be careful not to exaggerate the fiscal impact of the plan. For one thing, ¥11 trillion (more than 2 percent of GDP) came from FILP in a year in which FILP was already budgeted at ¥45.8 trillion. Since FILP's use of funds can be legally increased by 50 percent at the finance minister's discretion and without Diet approval, strictly speaking, the FILP portion of the plan was essentially a public relations gesture. Moreover, increased FILP lending is problematic as a means of stimulating growth. Even if we assume that substitution effects do not eliminate the stimulative nature of increased FILP lending, we must not forget that sources of trust funds were expanding very rapidly (for example, postal savings were growing at more than 10 percent per year following the bursting of the bubble), so a considerable chunk of the FILP increases in both the initial FY 1993 plan and the fiscal stimulus plan can be understood as paralleling the natural growth of available funds. Finally, as Table 3.3 shows, FILP activity for FY 1993 totaled only ¥6.7 trillion more than the initial plan—a substantial sum, but much less than claimed.

In short, the 1993 plan does suggest that political will on the part of the political leadership changed Japan's fiscal position noticeably despite the strong consensus that existed around the fiscal consolidation movement.

---

11. Feldman (1993) estimated that it would add ¥8.2 trillion (1.7 percent) to GNP, assuming all funds were actually used.
12. MOF, " 'Shin sōgō keizai taisaku' no pointo," 1. The phrase was "kiwamete irei."
13. Personal interviews.

However, it also suggested limits even on the government of a dedicated Keynesian who was facing strong external political challenges, and thus had particularly strong motivation to stimulate the economy rapidly.

Monetary Policy

While fiscal policy remained rather conservative, at least until the FY 1993 fiscal stimulus plan, monetary policy continued its reversal from Mieno's bubble-bursting days. On February 4, 1993, the BOJ announced the sixth discount rate cut in seventeen months. This one brought the discount rate back to 2.5 percent—a level the Japanese economy had not seen since the long period of monetary laxness that ran from February 1987 until May 1989.

There is not a great deal to be said about the economic judgments behind this particular retreat—with a stagnant economy, a rising stock of non-performing loans, and a slumping stock market (the monthly average for January 1993 was back down into the ¥16,000s), the decision to lower interest rates would seem to be overdetermined. What is more notable is the timing. It has been rare for the Bank of Japan to change the discount rate in the period between introduction and passage of the budget—Cabinets object to actions that would tend to change the assumptions under which the budget was made, because of the danger of opposition parties holding up the budget in debate.[14] In 1993, the timing was not made an issue, because everyone knew that delaying the passage of the FY 1993 budget also meant delaying the fiscal stimulus plan Miyazawa had promised.

The other point to be made on timing is that it appears that a number of BOJ officials (incorrectly, in retrospect) were worried that monetary policy was being loosened too far, too fast.[15] Monetary policy is known to operate with long and variable lags, and there had not been sufficient time to evaluate fully the effects of earlier interest rate cuts, but the continuing decline in growth in lending and GDP in spite of earlier monetary stimulation removed much of the force of this argument. There may also have been some officials who worried about the political impact on the BOJ of returning to the bubble rate of 2.5 percent. In any event, none of these fears were enough to seize the day, especially given the groundswell in favor of vigorously attacking economic and financial stagnation.

14. The most famous case of this was BOJ governor Maekawa's action to raise rates in February 1980, in the midst of the second oil shock. Even under such clearly urgent circumstances, it only went through on appeal to Prime Minister (and MOF OB) Ōhira Masayoshi (Sumita 1992, 97–98; Mizuno 1997, 155–158). After 1980, there were two instances during the Plaza-Louvre period—January 1986 and February 1987—when the discount rate was cut prior to approval of the budget. In general, loosening monetary policy should be less controversial than tightening it, since by reducing debt-service costs it actually gives the government more slack.

15. Mieno (2000, 212–213) implies as much.

Macroeconomic Policy under Non-LDP Coalitions, August 1993–June 1994

Following a successful vote of no confidence against Prime Minister Miyazawa's administration on June 18, 1993, and the subsequent Lower House election on July 18, Japan's first non-LDP prime minister since 1955, Hosokawa Morihiro, was elected by the Lower House on August 6. Hosokawa entered office at the head of a coalition of seven parties, ranging from the Social Democratic Party of Japan, which still had a number of self-identified Marxists in its left wing, to the quirky reformers of the Japan New Party, to the conservative reformers and political opportunists of the LDP breakaway Japan Renewal Party.

This eclectic mix inevitably meant complications in policy making. In economic policy, the progressive parties in the coalition were in favor of greater fiscal expansion and abolition of the consumption tax, while Japan Renewal Party mastermind Ozawa Ichirō was on record as calling for raising the consumption tax rate from 3 to 10 percent (following a 50 percent cut in income and residence taxes, and a smaller cut in corporate taxes) and cutting back on the overall size of government.[16] Divided by differences over economic policy, but united under a clear mandate to enact sweeping political reform, the Hosokawa government concentrated primarily on political issues in autumn 1993.

This does not mean that it completely ignored economic policy, however—that would have been impossible, given a yen that had spent the summer hovering just above the ¥100/$1 mark, MOF's July announcement that tax revenues for FY 1992 had been ¥3.2 trillion under its revised estimate, and other worrisome economic news.[17] The continuing economic crisis had fractured the consensus in support of fiscal consolidation, and in any event most of the new coalition was not a party to the original agreement. Politicians' visions of economic crisis inevitably clashed with MOF fears of fiscal crisis (shared by many politicians, including Ozawa), and a new set of interactions arose that led to an interesting new pattern of macroeconomic policy.

Personnel and Networks

While Japanese politics was undergoing unprecedented upheaval, the central bureaucracies were not. In the Bank of Japan, Governor Mieno and Deputy Governor Yoshimoto's five-year terms continued and rotations below the top level went on undisturbed. At the Ministry of Finance, Budget Bureau director-general Saitō Jirō was, as expected, promoted to the post of administrative vice-minister on June 25, exactly one week after the success-

---

16. Ozawa 1994, 177–179.
17. "Finance Ministry Seeks Tight Spending Controls," *DY,* July 14, 1993, 6.

ful vote of no confidence against the prime minister.[18] As usual, there was a full-scale reshuffling of personnel; at the bureau-chief level, only the director-general of the Banking Bureau remained in place.[19]

The changes at MOF reflected the ascendancy of the most conservative of the budget/tax bureaucrats. This was best exemplified by Saitō himself, who told reporters upon his appointment, "I think that my greatest duty is not to issue deficit bonds. If we issue them again, having worked to return deficit bond issuance to zero, all our efforts to this point will have been for naught." Saitō was not alone in this sentiment: key budget and administrative positions were occupied by his bureaucratic allies.[20]

Saitō's arrival at the top post was welcomed in an organization that feared the erosion of fiscal consolidation. Single-mindedness in the pursuit of fiscal consolidation was already a hallmark of Saitō's career. Not only had he spent the bulk of his career in the Budget Bureau, including three years as a budget examiner; he was also known for having sought to introduce the so-called "International Contribution Tax" to make up for an expected deficit in FY 1992 when he was director-general of the Budget Bureau, and he was associated with the 1991 decision to finance Japan's contribution to the Gulf War through a special tax increase rather than through bonds.[21] Current and former MOF bureaucrats who feared the reemergence of large budgets knew that Saitō would fight hard to prevent that; indeed, he was popularly known within the ministry as a "once-in-a-decade vice-minister."[22] Saitō had also had the opportunity to work closely in 1991 with the fiscally conservative Ozawa Ichirō (when the latter was secretary-general of the LDP) during the failed attempt to introduce the International Contribution Tax; with Ozawa as the apparent power behind the throne in the new government, that connection was seen as beneficial to MOF power.

To MOF's budget hawks, the new Cabinet looked promising, despite the inclusion of Socialists. Ozawa was sure to have considerable informal authority to shape the coalition's agenda, and indeed he quickly made clear his opposition to a new large-scale fiscal stimulus package.[23] Moreover, Prime Minister Hosokawa's own economic policy views focused on deregulation rather than macroeconomic stimulus, and he had announced in July that "Over two years have passed since the bursting of the bubble, and in that time, the Miyazawa Cabinet devised various stimulatory policies. However,

18. Presumably, approval of a new slate of bureaucratic postings was not foremost in the outgoing prime minister's mind. In any case, the top jobs had all been decided much earlier.
19. *Ōkurashō meikan* 1997, 333–342.
20. Shiota 1995, 13, 23–25.
21. Ibid., 20–23; Kishi 1996, 93; Noguchi 1995, 8; *Ōkurashō meikan* 1993, 42.
22. This nickname (*jūnen ni hitori no ōmono jikan*) is mentioned in virtually every book or article I have read by reporters when discussing Saitō (see, for example, Kishi 1996; Noguchi 1996; Shiota 1995).
23. "High-Ranking Coalition Leader Says No Bold Economic Moves Will Be Taken," *Asian Wall Street Journal Weekly*, August 9, 1993, A7.

the economy has not recovered at all. If whatever we do has no effect, then it would be better not to carry out short-term stimulatory policies, but instead to move toward long-term structural reform."[24] Chief Cabinet secretary Takemura Masayoshi was also generally an advocate of fiscal conservatism (and even more so of deregulation and administrative reform); Finance Minister Fujii Hirohisa was a former budget examiner in MOF. Thus, although the emphasis of coalition leaders on deregulation and political leadership may have given many bureaucrats pause, on the fiscal end there was considerable identity of purpose between MOF and key coalition policy makers.

The Hosokawa government's emphasis on structural reforms in Japan's economy and government represented the return of a position that had dominated domestic policy discourse in the early and mid-1980s under Prime Minister Nakasone. Advocates were driven by a Thatcherist-style ideology as well as frustrations with existing inefficiencies (the latter neatly encapsulated in Hosokawa's own struggle with the central government to have a traffic light installed when he was governor of Kumamoto Prefecture). But just as in the late 1970s and early 1980s when the administrative reform movement first started gaining ground, fears concerning Japan's fiscal position became more and more compelling as deficits mounted through the 1990s.[25] Structural and administrative reform were increasingly presented as an *alternative* to fiscal stimulus as a means of bringing growth back to the Japanese economy. (Ironically, despite Hosokawa's importance in reviving the debate, the influence of the structural reform idea actually peaked under the 1996–98 administration of LDP prime minister Hashimoto Ryūtarō.)

Meanwhile, LDP Diet members were finding that their personal access to MOF officials was drying up. All of a sudden, they were being treated like members of the opposition (which, of course, they were). Even former *zoku* Diet members were not forewarned about relevant policy proposals, and the rank of officials sent to the party to provide explanations was downgraded from the bureau chief or deputy bureau chief level to the deputy division chief level—a serious slap in the face, as well as a loss of valuable information on top-level policy planning.[26] Katō Kōichi, a prominent LDP leader, was inspired to say, "Until now, we thought it was a parent-child relationship, but it's actually more like distant relatives."[27] The cold shoulder was all the more galling due to Saitō's close relationship with the LDP turncoat Ozawa.

24. Shiota 1995, 36.
25. I am grateful to an anonymous reviewer from Cornell University Press for pointing this out.
26. See, for example, Mabuchi 1997, 127–131; Shiota 1995, 32.
27. Mabuchi 1997, 129.

Macroeconomic Policy

Despite the fiscally conservative proclivities of key coalition figures, public calls for stimulus remained strong. These calls were supported by the Social Democratic Party, the largest single party in the coalition, and it soon became evident that some sort of plan would be required. Given the lack of enthusiasm on the part of Hosokawa, Ozawa, Takemura, and Fujii, however, it was not difficult for the Ministry of Finance to produce a plan with very little substance in macroeconomic terms.

On September 16, the coalition announced "Urgent Economic Measures." Much of the text of the plan called for liberalization of regulations and greater internationalization of the economy—clearly not of immediate usefulness—but it also offered ¥6 trillion in public spending. Of the total, only ¥709 billion came from the general account; the rest was FILP.[28] It was as equivocal a package as could be constructed while still keeping the total number relatively high. Less than a week later, the Bank of Japan announced a discount rate cut of 0.75 percent, to 1.75 percent. This was generally understood to be a reaction to a summer-long high yen/dollar exchange rate, combined with the need to support the new government's economic policies.

Around the same time, policy makers began to take on the question of major cuts in direct taxes that Ozawa had already raised in his *Blueprint for a New Japan,* a political manifesto published in June 1993.[29] Actually, agitation for these tax cuts fit in nicely with established MOF opinion, which had for at least a decade and a half favored changing the balance between direct and indirect taxes.[30] Advocates of indirect taxes, conscious that their position was exceedingly unpopular, were willing to trade large-scale direct tax cuts for an increase in the consumption tax. Thus, a deal was politically feasible, and behind-the-curtains negotiations began. In order to make the package politically palatable, coalition leaders made clear that the direct tax cuts would come into effect *before* the consumption tax hike.

---

28. *"Kinkyū keizai taisaku"* (Urgent Economic Measures), MOF mimeo, September 16, 1993; *"Saikin no keizai taisaku no kibo"* (Scale of Recent Economic Measures), undated MOF mimeo. Despite Hosokawa's and Takemura's honest commitment to deregulation, the proposals were very general. As Shiota points out (1995, 40), one of the few specific deregulation measures actually announced was to allow home brewing of beer.

29. Ozawa 1994, 177–179.

30. For the complete story of the three major attempts to introduce a large-scale indirect tax in the late 1970s and 1980s, see Kato 1994. The final triumphant introduction of a 3 percent consumption tax in 1988 under the Takeshita government met with widespread anger, and the tax remains highly unpopular outside of policy-making circles. The reason MOF officials were so adamant about changing the balance between direct and indirect taxation was their realization that an aging society would put an unfair burden on those of working age if most taxes were income-related rather than spending-related.

While the fiscally conservative core among MOF bureaucrats would rather have seen a simultaneous tax cut/hike, they were willing to accept the compromise for the sake of long-term fiscal structure. The idea also offered something to both advocates and opponents of further fiscal stimulus. Advocates in the coalition would be able to claim that they had carried out a major stimulative tax cut, while opponents would be assured that the fiscal drain would be only temporary. (In terms of their actual stimulative effect, temporary tax cuts are as a rule less effective in changing consumer behavior than permanent ones.)[31]

There remained two major questions. The more fundamental one—the size and timing of the tax cut/hike—was for negotiators to figure out over the course of the succeeding months. The other question was how to fund the temporary deficits that would necessarily occur. For a really large-scale switch between direct and indirect taxes, construction bonds would not do the trick, since there were only so many justifiable public works projects in the pipeline, even with an extremely flexible definition of public investment. At the same time, the Ministry of Finance and other fiscal conservatives took very seriously the principle of zero issuance of deficit bonds and feared that authorizing deficit bonds again would be a dangerous first step down a slippery slope toward fiscal irresponsibility. In September, Finance Minister Fujii announced that the gap would be covered by a new sort of bond—what he termed "continuance bonds" (*tsunagi kokusai*)—which was contained in the draft bill announced by the Tax Commission of the prime minister's office on November 16, the last step before Cabinet sponsorship. Although self-evidently a way of disguising new deficit bonds, the new label also offered fiscal conservatives some assurance that their use would be temporary.

The tax cut/hike remained the primary macroeconomic issue on the coalition's agenda through 1993, although it inevitably took a back seat to the quest for comprehensive electoral reform.[32] The tax issue was apparently also the central issue within the Ministry of Finance—the budget draft was not submitted until February 15, 1994, an unprecedented delay. Officially, Prime Minister Hosokawa had requested the delay in order to iron

---

31. According to economic theory, rational individuals will save a much larger percentage of tax cuts that are known to be temporary, thus reducing the potential multiplier effect. Insofar as the tax cut / hike idea constituted a temporary tax cut, it was really not very much of a victory for the stimulus advocates, unless the consumption tax hike component lacked credibility—in other words, if consumers believed that the tax hike could be postponed if economic growth had not picked up by the planned date of its introduction. Of course, the fiscal conservatives required a credible commitment in order to agree to the compromise, so hopes of not experiencing the agreed tax hike were probably very weak among consumers. In other words, rather than offering the best of both worlds, economic theory would suggest that neither stimulus nor consolidation would be served by such a compromise.

32. The reform bill passed the Lower House in November 1993, but did not make it through the Upper House until February 1994.

out funding issues, but more conspiratorial explanations also abounded.[33] Insofar as both the coalition government and the Ministry of Finance needed each other's cooperation, the motivation was most probably to save electoral reform and defend the tax hike from log-rolling.

While the FY 1994 budget was still being prepared, or at least held back, by the Ministry of Finance, MOF was also busy compiling another fiscal stimulus plan. The "Comprehensive Economic Measures" plan was announced on February 8 and passed by the Diet on February 24. Touted as totaling ¥15.25 trillion—the highest value ever for a stimulus plan—it contained ¥5.85 trillion in tax cuts, about ¥5.5 trillion of which was in the form of temporary income tax cuts that reflected the expected first step of the tax cut/hike deal. Most of the rest (¥7.2 trillion) was FILP spending on public works. In addition, there was ¥2.19 trillion yen in supplemental general account spending (funded by ¥2.18 trillion in bonds), aimed mainly at aid to small and medium-sized enterprises.[34]

Although a large-scale income tax cut had clearly been in the offing as part of the tax cut/hike planning, the fiscal stimulus plan constituted a major loss for the Ministry of Finance in the battle for fiscal consolidation. Tax revenues did not recover to their FY 1993 level until FY 1997, and deficits began to balloon (see Table 3.2) In a miscalculation that was apparently at the urging of Vice-Minister Saitō and the Japan Renewal Party's Ozawa, Prime Minister Hosokawa had called a midnight press conference on February 3 to announce his plan to introduce a new "People's Welfare Tax" as of FY 1996. The new tax was really nothing but a surtax on the consumption tax, which would have raised it from 3 to 6 percent. The justification (and origin of the name) was that the tax would ensure that sufficient funds would be in hand to deal with the aging population. It was clearly a case of poor preparation—only days earlier, Chief Cabinet secretary Takemura had told reporters, "It's okay if a tax cut must rely on deficit bonds. I don't intend to approve a consumption tax hike."[35] In response to Hosokawa's announcement, Takemura threatened to resign and the SDPJ threatened to withdraw from the coalition. Only by postponing discussion on the tax hike and agreeing to the 20 percent income tax cut did the parties patch over the dispute. In an ensuing press conference, Ozawa was quoted as saying, "I give in totally and without conditions in this matter."[36]

33. For a summary of these claims, see Shiota 1995, 55–57.
34. *"Sōgō keizai taisaku"* (Comprehensive Economic Measures), MOF mimeo, February 8, 1994; *"Saikin no keizai taisaku no kibo."*
35. Shiota 1995, 58. Takemura still describes the consumption tax incident as his biggest policy conflict under the Hosokawa government (personal interview, August 1999).
36. This bare-bones account is condensed from a much more colorful one by Shiota (1995, 60–66), in which the Ozawa quotation appears (1995, 66).

The saga had an ironic epilogue. Despite the retreat of the budget hawks and the compilation of a budget with an expected bond-dependence ratio of 18.7 percent (including ¥10.5 trillion in construction bonds and ¥3.1 trillion in "continuance bonds"),[37] the FY 1994 budget was not actually approved by the Lower House until June 8, and by the Upper House until June 23. This was not due to the budget itself, however; it was the result of political jockeying and splintering among the Diet's various non-Communist parties and factions. These forces had already led to Prime Minister Hosokawa's resignation in April, which was followed by the minority administration of the Japan Renewal Party's Hata Tsutomu. The SDPJ refused to support Hata formally, and it was only a matter of time before they withdrew even their informal support. On June 25, almost immediately after the final passage of the budget, Prime Minister Hata resigned, bringing to an end the brief era of the non-LDP coalitions.

The Return of the LDP: The *"Ji-sha-sa"* Coalition Years, 1994–98

Four days after Hata's resignation, SDPJ leader Murayama Tomiichi was elected prime minister by both houses of the Diet, with the support of the Liberal Democratic Party and Takemura's LDP splinter party, Sakigake. Thus was born perhaps the most surprising government of the postwar era—the so-called *"Ji-sha-sa"* coalition, which brought together the two great rivals of postwar Japanese electoral politics under one unsteady roof.[38] The new coalition had no clear mandate, although LDP leaders touted it as a return to responsible leadership. And there was inevitably pressure to reinvigorate the economy.

Personnel and Networks

In reaction to their treatment by MOF officials during their months in opposition, LDP Diet members had no qualms about venting their spleen once they were back in power. Indeed, by November 1994, Katō Kōichi (then

---

37. IFMP 1997, Table 3.3. Despite the polite fiction of the "continuance bonds," MOF publications simply place them in the category of "deficit-financing bond issues."
38. *"Ji-sha-sa"* is a contraction of the first syllables of each party's name in Japanese. I will omit the fascinating story of how this unlikely coalition came to be, but I should point out that it required a special SDPJ vote to change its official policy platform by eliminating its long-standing principled opposition to the Self-Defense Forces, the U.S.–Japan security alliance, the national flag, and the national anthem. On the "no-principle coalition," see, for example, "Japanese Leader Ditches Socialist Platform to Accept Role of Military," *WP,* July 21, 1994, A19. The price of abandoning these unpopular principles was the wholesale loss of Diet seats—by 1998 the SDPJ had fallen from being the primary challenger to the LDP to being little more than a marginal party. Sakigake's life course has been similarly dismal.

chairman of the LDP's Policy Affairs Research Council) actually barred MOF deputy vice-minister Komura Takeshi from entering his office, because of both Komura's perceived impertinence and what Katō saw as MOF foot-dragging in carrying out orders to reorganize government financial institutions and to reduce the percentage of Tokyo University graduates in MOF entering classes. That particular rift was not healed until Komura and Saitō were replaced and their successors made peace with Katō.[39] The barring of Komura was an extraordinary snub, symbolizing the desire to put bureaucrats in their place.

As worrisome to ministry officials as the LDP's animosity was the appointment of Sakigake's Takemura Masayoshi as finance minister. Throughout his tenure in that post (June 1994 to January 1996), Takemura sought to make good on his political platform of making key decisions at the ministerial level, rather than simply ratifying the decisions of career officials. Despite his earlier stance of fiscal conservatism, in January and February 1994 Takemura had rejected the proposal to increase the consumption tax, while still supporting an income tax cut. Moreover, as the leader of a small (and dwindling) LDP splinter party, Takemura was playing a dangerous game vis-à-vis both the LDP and the electorate. Having managed to stake out the position of finance minister despite his party's very marginal utility to the LDP, Takemura sought both to maximize his power through his ability to control the Ministry of Finance and to appeal to voters as a reformer unwilling to accept business as usual.[40] On a personal level, he was said to have felt slighted by MOF's courtship of Ozawa and Hosokawa and inattention to himself when he was chief cabinet secretary in the Hosokawa administration.[41] And finally, if Sakigake stood for anything, it stood for administrative reform, which was at least partly aimed at reducing the power resources of the major ministries.[42]

In terms of bureaucratic personnel, the new coalition faced the regular turnover of central government officials in June and July, as well as the need to appoint a new governor and deputy governor of the BOJ for a five-year term that would begin in December. Japanese central bureaucracies plan

---

39. Kishi 1996, 87–92. Komura was a close associate of the unpopular Vice-Minister Saitō. As deputy vice-minister, he would also have been responsible for deciding which officials to dispatch to various parties to answer questions—and LDP members were understandably resentful of the significant downgrading they had experienced in that respect during the non-LDP coalition period.

40. Sakigake's votes were not needed for a majority in either chamber, but Takemura had played an important role in bringing the parties together (Yayama 1994). Also, Sakigake provided some cover for both the LDP and SDPJ against criticisms that their cooperation was purely cynical.

41. This was particularly true in the "People's Welfare Tax" episode. Shiota quotes a Sakigake Lower House member as saying that Takemura had a "desire to retaliate against the bureaucrats who slighted him" (1995, 91).

42. Nakano 1998b.

their own personnel shifts as a matter of course (a significant source of solidarity), and the Ministry of Finance in 1994 was no different. By May, the secretariat had put together the new starting lineup and submitted it on June 23. Actually, the new line-up offered by the career bureaucrats differed little from the old one—except for the Customs, Financial, and Banking Bureaus, there were no changes from the bureau chief level up.[43] While there were strong feelings against Saitō among coalition party leaders, the slate was accepted. Despite this victory for the principle of autonomy in personnel matters, Saitō would remain in a weak position.[44] With regard to the BOJ, tradition demanded that the new governor be a MOF OB and the deputy governor a BOJ man, but since Finance Minister Takemura had pledged to go his own way, the bureaucrats had reason to expect a fight. (See chapter 7.)

Macroeconomic Policy

Politics of coalition-building aside, several major economic issues faced the incoming government. One of these was clearly the still stagnant economy—despite the major stimulative actions of the Hosokawa and Hata governments, it soon became clear that the economy would not grow at anywhere near the 2.4 percent rate predicted. (As Table 2.1 shows, real GDP growth for FY 1994 proved to be only 0.7 percent.) Another issue was the burgeoning bad debt problem. The situation of the *jūsen* was particularly spectacular, but throughout the banking system, much larger problems with portfolios and capital adequacy were squeezing lending. Broader monetary aggregates were showing the resulting contraction, despite the sustained extremely low interest rates (see Figure 5.1). A third issue was the unresolved question of tax system reform. The Hosokawa-Hata budget had finessed it by declaring a one-year income tax cut for FY 1994, but that was clearly not a permanent fix. Tax system reform was also connected to the long-term issue of fiscal consolidation that motivated so many MOF officials as well as a sizable number of conservative politicians.

While the banking system problems are logically separate from the question of macroeconomic policy making, a brief digression on the subject is in order. A key reason why loose monetary policy was ineffective in spurring growth or even mild inflation was that the banking system was not able to turn that ready money into lending.[45] This was partly because of the sorry

---

43. *Ōkurashō Meikan* 1997, 333–342. In other words, seven of the top ten positions were not rotated, including the three with ministry-wide authority (administrative vice-minister, vice-minister for international affairs, and deputy vice-minister) and the two most important bureau chiefs (Budget and Tax).
44. Shiota 1995, 87–92.
45. Sasaki-Smith 1999.

state of many loans (and potential borrowers). It was also largely due to the fact that many banks' capital adequacy in the late 1980s and early 1990s had been built on unrealized capital gains on assets that had since depreciated considerably. Closing out nonperforming loans threatened to reduce nominal owned capital even more. Admitting the loss, and therefore officially cutting into capital, would require banks to cut back lending or to use actual capital to cover deposits. The woes of the *jūsen*—while a relatively small part of the overall bad loan crisis—only compounded the difficulties facing the banks that had lent to them. Therefore, the microeconomic issue of how to fix the financial sector was until at least 1999 one of the most important factors in Japan's macroeconomic stagnation. Politically, it was also relevant to MOF's position in all areas of policy making—such an immense policy failure could not help but color all of the ministry's dealings. Nonetheless, I do not deal here directly with efforts to resolve the bad-debt situation, since until 1998 policy makers did not treat it as a macroeconomic policy issue *per se*.[46]

The main macroeconomic issue confronting the new coalition government was how to deal with tax revision. It might seem strange that leaders of a state that was confronting economic stagnation, a faltering financial system, and the threat of a renewed high yen (see Figure 4.1) should have been spending large amounts of time and political capital on the proportions of direct and indirect taxes—a question of little obvious relevance to any of those major problems. However, they had little choice, given that MOF and the Hosokawa government had opened the debate. Actually, both of the major proposals (the Tax Commission-approved MOF draft and the "People's Welfare Tax") also offered a convenient way to deal with demands for both fiscal stimulus and fiscal consolidation. Since the established proposals both called for an initial (permanent) income tax cut followed at some later point by a permanent increase in the consumption tax, everyone could go home happy, assuming that the time lag would be sufficient to get the economy back on track.[47]

Nevertheless, many leading actors in the coalition remained opposed to the plan.[48] These included Takemura as well as several influential SDPJ leaders, including former party leader Doi Takako and Secretary-General Kubo Wataru (who would replace Takemura as finance minister in 1996). The

---

46. Horiuchi 1998.
47. This arrangement constitutes a temporary tax cut in macroeconomic terms, and as such would be expected to have considerably less effect than a permanent tax cut of equivalent magnitude. (There is, however, a certain speciousness to that argument, since it is highly unlikely that the government would have passed permanent tax cuts of such magnitude without thought to future deficits.) If the subsequent tax hike were expected to be smaller than the initial tax cut, then rational individuals should indeed have been expected to handle a portion of the tax cut as a permanent reduction.
48. Takahashi (1999) argues that MOF had already effectively neutralized media opposition.

Socialists had a particularly difficult time accepting a large increase in the consumption tax—not only did they feel that it was regressive, but opposition to the tax had been a major plank of their economic platform since before the introduction of the tax in 1988. On top of these formidable barriers, the basic proposal was also inextricably linked to Ozawa—a particular bugbear of all three coalition members—and with the increasingly unpopular Vice-Minister Saitō.

It appears that top MOF officials tried to keep the proposal alive by renewing ties with the Liberal Democratic Party.[49] This was understandably difficult, given Saitō's close partnership with Ozawa in the non-LDP coalition period. One author writes that these efforts at first centered on Takeshita Noboru—former prime minister and long-time finance minister, and *eminence grise* in the party—using officials (especially Tax Bureau chief Ogawa Tadashi and Budget Bureau chief Shinozawa Kyōsuke) who were not tainted by political cooperation with Ozawa. Ogawa was particularly well suited to this role—not only was he not directly associated with the Saitō clique, but he had also served twice as Takeshita's personal secretary.[50]

Even Takeshita's help was not enough to swing the coalition, however, and MOF was forced to change tactics. The new effort focused on the coalition parties' policy councils, sending officials from the deputy division chief level up to make a unified call for a simultaneous resolution of the tax cut and tax hike questions, and to avoid a straight income tax cut.[51] By concentrating on the working level, the ministry could bypass Takemura and Socialist leaders like Doi and Kubo. Moreover, since Prime Minister Murayama had called for "bottom-up" decision making, he could compromise on a major party plank while still saving face and staying in power.[52]

After considerable politicking, a final compromise was submitted to the prime minister on September 22, 1994. It looked considerably different

49. This story comes from Shiota (1995, 94–108).
50. Both the finance minister and the prime minister typically have one secretary on loan from the Ministry of Finance. These jobs are given to up-and-coming career officials and help cement effective communication between the ministry and political parties (i.e., the LDP for most of the postwar period). Ogawa's relationship with Takeshita was clearly special—he had served under Takeshita both in 1979–80 when Takeshita was finance minister, and in 1988–89 when Takeshita was prime minister. (For Ogawa's full curriculum vitae in MOF, see *Ōkurashō Meikan* 1997, 3.) His dates in those positions match exactly with Takeshita's, even though they do not jibe with the normal intra-ministry rotations, suggesting that Takeshita had hand-picked him. Shinozawa *was* closely associated with Saitō's budget clique, but had not been involved in Saitō's overtures to politicians.
51. Shiota (1995, 105–108) identifies LDP Policy Affairs Research Council Chairman Katō Kōichi (a budget hawk, but not a MOF fan), LDP Tax System Research Council Chairman and MOF OB Murayama Tatsuo, coalition tax council chairman Sekiyama Nobuyuki of the SDPJ, SDPJ Policy Council Chairman Hino Ichirō, and coalition tax council director Igarashi Fumihiko (concurrently Sakigake's Policy Research Council vice-chairman) as the main targets of the MOF persuasion campaign.
52. Shiota 1995, 106.

from the original MOF proposal. First, the ¥5.5 trillion income and residence tax cut would include a permanent across-the-board cut of ¥3.5 trillion and an across-the-board temporary income tax rate cut of 15 percent.
Second, the consumption tax would be raised only to 5 percent (below both
the 7 percent MOF proposal of fall 1993 and the 6 percent proposed as the
"People's Welfare Tax"), and the time lag between income tax cut and consumption tax hike would be stretched from two years to three.[53] Third, a
"New Gold Plan" welfare program for senior citizens would be introduced
in FY 1995 with budgeted funds of ¥300 billion over the first two years, in
effect moving forward an SDPJ-proposed program that was at that point
only under consideration. Finally, half of the incremental increase in the
consumption tax would be transferred to local and regional governments.
Igarashi Fumihiko, Sakigake's point man on tax reform, proudly declared
that "the Ministry of Finance was utterly defeated."[54]

The truth is not actually that obvious. From the start, there had been no
question that MOF would have to compromise—that is simply the way tax
policy works. Presumably, that realization was incorporated into the initial
proposal, particularly in terms of numbers. In any event, along with the tax
reform announcement, Takemura and other officials immediately announced the need to cut government spending in order to maintain long-
term fiscal solvency. As for the "New Golden Plan," it did not constitute a
huge amount of money compared to the other measures being considered,
and moreover, it would be provided jointly by the central and regional governments (with no guarantee that regional governments would go along
with the plan). Finally, the regional allocation of half of the consumption
tax hike, while clearly insulting and an intrusion on MOF prerogatives,
could easily be dealt with by reducing the other funds transferred to regional governments. Indeed, given that approximately half of all taxes col-
lected centrally already went to regional governments, it was not likely to
make much of a dent at all.[55]

But while much of the plan could thus be dismissed as not particularly difficult to swallow from the point of view of the budget/tax mainstream in the
ministry, other aspects were more worrisome. One of these was clearly the
time frame for the consumption tax increase. According to newspaper reports, there had been considerable pressure from the United States (par-

---

53. "Three years" means three *fiscal* years. The tax hike would actually take place in two and
a half years, as of the beginning of the 1997 fiscal year.

54. Shiota 1995, 111–114, 118.

55. Yonehara (1993) describes the regional revenue system. Shiota (1995, 113–114) writes
that the idea of guaranteeing regional governments a share of the consumption tax had already been an issue between MOF and the Ministry of Home Affairs, and the September
1994 plan essentially decided it in favor of the latter. Interestingly, Takemura himself was a
former MHA bureaucrat, and Prime Minister Murayama had started his career in the All
Japan Prefectural and Municipal Workers' Union, which may be a comment on the benefit
of having OBs in high places.

ticularly Treasury Secretary Lloyd Bentsen and Deputy Secretary Lawrence Summers) to draw out the gap between cutting and raising taxes to at least three years in order to continue to stimulate domestic demand.[56] Indeed, Summers had even met with Takemura in Tokyo on September 20, at the last stages of putting together the tax reform package.[57] The continuation of large cuts in tax revenue also created concern, though not as much as the additional year before the consumption tax hike.

On the other hand, the decision to consider the tax cut and tax hike simultaneously was a great relief for MOF. Over the course of the summer, Prime Minister Murayama and other coalition leaders including Finance Minister Takemura had made statements that it would be better in terms of economic stimulus to pass the tax cut first and put off a decision on the consumption tax until the Japanese economy had strengthened.[58] Such an outcome would have been a nightmare for fiscal conservatives, who did not believe a tax hike was possible without a tax cut—indeed, it would have upended the entire strategy of calling for an income and residence tax cut in the first place.

Moreover, the "permanent" tax cut itself showed clear signs of compromise on the part of the more devoted Keynesians. For one thing, the ¥5.5 trillion agreed upon did not constitute an expansion of the existing Hosokawa-Hata cuts. Also, only ¥3.5 trillion was actually permanent, and it was in the form of broadening tax brackets for middle-income citizens and raising the minimum taxable income, the effects of which would naturally fall off over time if the economy were growing or prices rising. The remaining ¥2 trillion would come from a temporary 15 percent reduction of tax rates that would expire as of FY 1997, at the same time that the consumption tax hike would kick in.

Continuing Economic Headaches

With the final decision over tax system reform out of the way, the budget-making process for FY 1995 proceeded smoothly. In December, the Cabinet accepted the MOF draft, which called for total expenditures of ¥70.987 trillion, a 3 percent reduction from the FY 1994 initial budget. Surprisingly, the new budget actually called for less bond issuance than had its predecessor—

---

56. This pressure was widely reported at the time. See, for example, "Fear of Fractured Tax Reform: Three-Year Prior Tax Reduction Agreed Upon Out of Concern for United States," *Sankei Shimbun,* September 11, 1994, 11 (FBIS translation); "Hashimoto Phones Brown," *Kyodo,* September 20, 1994; "U.S. Influenced Consumption Tax Hike Decision," *Kyodo,* September 21, 1994.
57. "U.S. Influenced Consumption Tax Hike Decision."
58. "Tax Cuts to Be Financed with Deficit Bonds," *Kyodo,* July 4, 1994 [FBIS translation]; "Further Reports on Issues Related to Tax Reform—MOF on Coalition Leaders' Remarks," *Mainichi Shimbun,* August 30, 1994, 9 [FBIS translation].

¥12.6 trillion total and ¥2.9 trillion in continuance (deficit) bonds, compared to FY 1994's ¥13.6 trillion total and ¥3.1 trillion in continuance bonds (see Table 3.2) Also in December, the Cabinet accepted the optimistic EPA estimate for FY 1995 growth of 2.8 percent, and adopted a supplemental budget that actually *reduced* FY 1994 spending by ¥673.5 billion.[59]

Despite the apparent efficiency and cooperation with which those important items were handled, however, symptoms of serious macroeconomic problems were again on the rise in the October–December quarter. The most severe, of course, was the financial system mess, symbolized by the increasingly obvious collapse of the *jūsen*. Meanwhile, the Ministry of Finance was acting to contract spending, as had been implicitly agreed in the September compromise. What was not yet apparent was that real GDP growth in the quarter would end up at –1 percent (annualized), a poor performance that was surely not helped by attempts to constrict government spending.

At the same time, both the firmness of the stock market and the steadiness of the yen were reassuring. In particular, the Nikkei had held steady at the ¥19,000–¥21,000 level since February 1994, which suggested that there was renewed confidence in the economy and that many banks' capital-adequacy ratios would be healthy enough to carry out new lending. On the international front, the yen had held in the high ¥90s/$1, with occasional forays to just over ¥100/$1, since the beginning of July. Although the level seemed high, at least it was stable. (In fact, on a real effective basis, it had weakened slightly in value due to low Japanese inflation.) Also, U.S.–Japanese comprehensive trade talks had concluded on October 1, with only the issue of autos and auto parts left unresolved; combined with the earlier signing of the final agreement of the Uruguay Round on April 15, this seemed to indicate that serious trade frictions had been managed successfully.

Tremors Large and Small, January–April 1995

On January 17, 1995, Kobe and surrounding areas were hit by an earthquake with a magnitude of 7.2 on the Richter scale. The Great Hanshin-Awaji Earthquake killed more than 5,000 people, reduced much of Kobe to rubble, and created havoc in the regional economy. Perversely, it also created expectations that economic growth would accelerate—the result of the need to rebuild and the accompanying government spending. Before the end of FY 1994, the government did indeed pass one more supplemental budget, this one for an increase in general account and FILP spending of ¥1.022 trillion; the measure

59. The 2.8 percent figure was widely seen as optimistic—see "Officials Project Rosy '95; Revise '94 Figures Sharply Lower; 2.8% Growth Guess Well above Forecasts of Private Think Tanks," *Nikkei Weekly*, December 19, 1994, 1. *"Ippan kaikei sainyū saishutsu yosan hosei kakuchō"* (General Account Revenue and Expenditure Budget Supplements), undated MOF mimeo.

was adopted in February 1995. The beginning of rebuilding probably did expand the economy to some extent, but real GDP growth for the quarter would come out to only an annualized 0.3 percent.[60]

Other events also shook Japan. On March 9, the chairman of Tokyo Kyōwa, one of two recently failed credit cooperatives (ironically, the other was called Anzen, or "safety"), testified in the Diet to having lavishly entertained two elite MOF officials at the same time that his cooperative was going bankrupt. Several top officials were reprimanded for failing to supervise their subordinates properly, even as the credit cooperatives' operations were taken over by the Tokyo Kyōdō Bank, a newly formed institution that received about half its funding from the Bank of Japan.[61] The revelations were to have severe repercussions on MOF's legitimacy.

Then, on March 20, members of an eccentric cult known as Aum Shinrikyō staged a nerve gas attack on the Tokyo subway, concentrating on stations used by bureaucrats and party officials. While the attack fortunately killed relatively few people, the event seemed to fit into the country's general pessimism. Also, it tended to erode confidence in the police, especially when it was revealed that a similar incident using the same poisonous gas had not been vigorously or competently investigated.[62]

At the same time, the yen had begun to appreciate rapidly, showing an upward trend starting in February. From a weekly average of ¥99.85 for the week ending February 3, the exchange rate raced up to a peak of ¥79.75 on April 19 in Tokyo. This 20 percent increase in the space of only a few weeks created a crisis mentality in the currency markets as well. Particularly alarming was the fact that the strengthening continued despite a cut in the discount rate from 1.75 percent all the way down to 1 percent (other interest rates fell in parallel, as seen in Figure 3.2) and the announcement of a stimulus plan by the government, both on April 14. The exchange rate stayed in the low ¥80s through June, and did not break ¥90/$1 again until August.

Several factors were coming together to create this extraordinary movement in the exchange markets. The Mexican currency crisis reduced confidence in the U.S. economy, Japan's relatively high real interest rates (albeit low nominal interest rates) were attracting money from the United States, and the Japanese financial crisis and Kobe earthquake were compelling many Japanese firms and financial institutions to repatriate dollars. Continuing high U.S. trade deficits contributed as well at various points.[63]

60. "Experts Discuss Nation's Economic Growth," *Ekonomisuto,* May 2–9, 1995, 26–31 [FBIS translation].
61. On the establishment of the Tokyo Kyōdō Bank, see "Tokyo Kyodo Bank Opens," *DY,* March 21, 1995, 8. Of the new bank's approximately ¥40 billion in capital, ¥20 billion came from the Bank of Japan, the remainder from commercial banks. "Mieno Denies Political Pressure over New Bank," *Jiji,* March 30, 1995.
62. Kaplan and Marshall 1996.
63. Sakakibara Eisuke, "*Kokusai manē no kōbō: Chō doruyasu no kiki*" (International Money Games: The Ultra-Low Dollar Crisis), *YS,* September 2, 1999, 1.

In response to the initial currency movements, Japanese authorities intervened immediately to stem the rise of the yen. Newspapers reported that the Bank of Japan was intervening on a daily basis; while there was no official confirmation, Japanese official foreign reserves did rise more than $30 billion from January to May, including more than $15 billion in March and $12 billion in April when the yen was at its strongest.[64] The United States began to get involved in March, and there was even a coordinated intervention in support of the dollar by the United States, Japan, and a "dozen or more" European central banks on March 3. As the coordinated intervention was proceeding, U.S. Treasury Secretary Rubin (who had replaced Lloyd Bentsen on January 10) said that "a strong dollar is in our national interest."[65] U.S. intervention continued and there were a number of statements by officials such as Rubin and Fed chairman Alan Greenspan. Nonetheless, U.S. authorities were not willing to do more than that since they feared that raising interest rates could choke the economy.[66]

The job therefore fell largely to the Japanese, who were taking the situation very seriously. By March 6, as the rate eased into the ¥93 level, Finance Minister Takemura suggested to the Upper House Budget Committee that he might call an emergency G-7 meeting to support the dollar.[67] Days later, BOJ governor Matsushita Yasuo[68] publicly ruled out an interest rate cut for the sake of the exchange rate (although the BOJ was actually lowering market rates even as it remained—for the moment—adamant about the discount rate). Meanwhile, leaders of Japan's four major business groups underscored the significance of the situation for Japanese industry by jointly visiting the prime minister at his office. On the same day, Takemura admitted to the Lower House Finance Committee that there was a "certain limitation to concerted intervention," and the Cabinet decided to have the Ministry of Finance start preparing countermeasures.[69]

On Friday, March 31, the government announced a deregulation proposal it hoped would stem the rise of the yen. The proposal was extremely vague, however, and was seen as a desperate attempt to reverse the market without pledging anything of substance. The following Monday, April 3, U.S. and Japanese authorities were forced to intervene again, in an amount estimated at the time at $2–3 billion. Secretary Rubin even took the unusual

64. Compiled from contemporaneous news reports. Also, see Figure 3.3.
65. *NYT,* March 4, 1995. Analysts estimated that the U.S. contribution was about $500 million, following a solo intervention of approximately $250 million the previous day. (For previous day, see *WP,* March 3, 1995.)
66. In support of the position that macreoconomic policy should not be sacrificed for the sake of the dollar, the *New York Times* ran an editorial entitled "Let the Dollar Drift," March 8, 1995, A20.
67. *DY,* March 7, 1995.
68. Matsushita, a former MOF administrative vice-minister (1982–84), took over from Mieno in December 1994. For more on his appointment, see chapter 7.
69. "Currencies in Turmoil," *FT,* March 9, 1995; *DY,* March 9, 1995.

step of announcing the intervention, and Finance Minister Takemura made a late-night announcement that Japan had decided "to show its strong determination to ensure currency market stability."[70] Nonetheless, the dollar ended the day at the ¥86 level. With the Nikkei plunging toward ¥15,000 and even the domesticist Vice-Minister Saitō of MOF expressing worry, MITI minister Hashimoto announced that Finance Minister Takemura was putting together a fiscal stimulus package. Meanwhile, Takemura and other Cabinet members were calling for the BOJ to cut interest rates.[71]

The practical effects of those calls were announced on Friday, April 14. The Bank of Japan lowered the discount rate from 1.75 percent to 1 percent, an extraordinarily low nominal interest rate, and the Ministry of Finance announced "Emergency High Yen Economic Countermeasures." Nonetheless, there was little positive response to the Japanese moves in the currency markets, which apparently agreed with an article in *The Independent:*

> Any American tears over the surging yen will be crocodile tears. The private view in the Clinton administration is that the superyen has handed the U.S. just the crowbar it needs to lever open the protected domestic markets of Japan. The Americans and the Japanese are currently at loggerheads over the issue of opening up the Japanese car market. The U.S. Trade Representative, Mickey Kantor, would be unlikely to thank Treasury Secretary Robert Rubin if he lets the Japanese off the hook of an over-priced yen.[72]

Investors' muted reaction to the drop in interest rates was surprising. Less surprising was their lack of reaction to the fiscal plan, although it was claimed to contain ¥4.62 trillion in new spending, including ¥2.73 trillion from the general account. This was sensible, since virtually all the new spending would be to repair damage from the Kobe earthquake rather than for stimulation to counteract yen appreciation. Also, the plan was announced with no specific spending plans—those would have to wait until June 27.[73]

Even a meeting of the G-7 finance ministers in Washington, D.C., on April 25 had equivocal effects—in the end, no one was surprised that the ministers

---

70. "Federal Reserve Intervenes to Curb Dollar Decline," *FT,* April 4, 1995, 40.

71. "Takemura Indirectly Seeks ODR Cut," *DY,* March 28, 1995, 1; "Kamei Urges BOJ to Cut Base Rate to Tame High Yen," *Japan Economic Newswire,* March 28, 1995; "Govt Sees Discount Rate Cut as One Option," *Jiji,* April 3, 1995.

72. "G7 Has No Answer to Currency Woes: Markets, Not Governments, Will Decide the Yen's Fate," *The Independent,* April 20, 1995, 33. This fits the general perspective of McKinnon and Ohno (1997). For similar views from a variety of sources, see "Yen Casts a Godzilla Shadow over Talks," *Wall Street Journal,* April 13, 1995, A10; "U.S. Wielding Limp Dollar in Trade Talks, Analysts Say," *JC,* April 21, 1995, 1A; "Dollar Will Resume Fall after Pause that Failed to Refresh, Analysts Say," *JC,* May 8, 1995, 2A.

73. MOF mimeos, "*Kinkyū endaka-keizai taisaku*" (Emergency High Yen Economic Measures), April 14, 1995; "*Kinkyū endaka-keizai taisaku no gutaika-hokyō o hakaru tame no shoshisaku*" (Policies to Carry Out and Reinforce the Emergency High Yen Economic Measures), June 7, 1995.

had agreed only to get their own fundamentals right and "to continue to co-operate closely in exchange markets."[74] While it remains somewhat unclear why a blow to Japanese exporters should increase the value of Japan's currency, market participants were widely reported to be focused primarily on the trade talks. Despite reports of continued BOJ intervention and perhaps some coordinated intervention, the yen-dollar rate remained at unprecedented levels until after the final resolution of the auto negotiations in late June.

The Yen Crisis Eases, June–December 1995

Besides the termination of U.S. trade threats, the yen crisis was eased by several symbolic and substantive acts. On June 20, Prime Minister Murayama instructed the Economic Planning Agency to put together a fiscal plan for the second half of the year in recognition of the significant front-loading of public works projects that had been legislated in the April stimulus plan.[75] In early July, Japanese and U.S. central bankers cooperated in exchange rate intervention while almost simultaneously reducing overnight interest rates.[76] A little later, on August 2, the Japanese government announced new guidelines to encourage outward investment. Along with the easing of the high yen pressure, stock prices also began to improve, with the Nikkei showing an increase from its June average of ¥15,039 to ¥16,189 in July and ¥17,411 in August.

All was not rosy, however. The attention on international finance had not helped to restore the fortunes of failing financial institutions, and several had gotten into serious trouble. In addition to the Tokyo Kyōwa and Anzen Credit Cooperatives cited above, two other credit cooperatives (Cosmo in Tokyo, and Kizu in Osaka) had to close down in July and August. Most shocking of all was the August 30 decision to close Hyogo Bank, the first bank in the postwar era to be allowed to shut down without being merged into a stronger institution.

Meanwhile, a Japanese banking scandal was developing across the Pacific Ocean as well. On September 18, it was revealed that a young trader for Daiwa Bank in New York, Iguchi Toshihide, had hidden trading losses of $1.1 billion from U.S. bank examiners over an eleven-year period, in violation of U.S. law.[77] To add insult to injury, the Ministry of Finance was accused of trying to conceal the crime from U.S. authorities (as well as from

74. *FT,* April 26.
75. "Murayama Orders Economic Stimulus Package," *Kyodo,* June 21, 1995. On June 27, the EPA offered the outline of a plan to be announced in September, but with no numbers attached.
76. "Japan Joins U.S. to Block Fall by Dollar," *NYT,* July 7, 1995, 33. The interest rates in question were the Federal Funds rate in the United States and the uncollateralized overnight call rate in Japan.
77. For summaries, see Asahi Shimbun Economics Bureau 1997, 100–107, and the particularly useful chronology on 103; Hanson 1996, 261–268; Mabuchi 1997, 7–8.

the BOJ). Although Iguchi had confessed on July 24 in a letter to Daiwa's chairman, who had in turn informed the MOF Banking Bureau chief on August 8, ministry officials did not see fit to inform bank examiners at the Federal Reserve Bank of New York until after the scandal had broken.[78] Daiwa Bank lost its privilege to operate in the United States and was assessed $340 million in fines, and the Ministry of Finance lost considerable face. The obvious implication was that MOF was not in control of the problems in the Japanese financial sector—or perhaps even worse, that it was in fact responsible for the rapidly worsening situation.

With growth still slow, reconstruction in the Hanshin area still necessary, and financial institutions in ever more precarious straits—not to mention the very fresh memory of the ultrahigh yen—there was still pressure on macroeconomic policy makers to act to accelerate the economy and de- crease the burden on shaky lenders and borrowers. Accordingly, on Sep- tember 9, the Bank of Japan finished what it had started in its open market operations in July by lowering the discount rate to the unheard-of level of 0.5 percent. In addition to easing interest rates, the BOJ poured massive amounts of funds into the market in the form of bond purchases.[79]

A week and a half later, on September 20, the government announced the fiscal stimulus plan Murayama had called for in June, containing a record ¥14.2 trillion (more than 3 percent of GDP) in new spending—what it called a "drastic impetus to domestic demand."[80] Again, a certain amount of the plan was padding—¥3.2 trillion was for land purchases, most of the plan's funding was accounted for by FILP or reserve funds, and it included an unenforceable call for ¥1 trillion in spending by local governments—but it did constitute a significant departure from the government's initial spend- ing plan. The ¥5.3 trillion in additional general account spending was equal to about 7.5 percent of the initial budget. Also, the plan was accompanied by a ¥4.9 trillion ($49 billion) bond issue.[81]

By the end of FY 1995, government bond issues for the year totaled ¥21.25 trillion, as compared to the initially budgeted ¥12.6 trillion; the gov- ernment's bond dependence was 28 percent. It is also true, however, that, for all the hype, general account expenditures in FY 1995 only expanded by

78. A director of Daiwa Bank who was present at the meeting between MOF officials and Daiwa Bank executives quoted the Banking Bureau chief as telling them, "Right now the tim- ing is really bad"—in retrospect, an obvious reference to the impending collapse of Hyogo Bank (Asahi Shimbun Economics Bureau 1997, 102).
79. Reported in *Japan Digest,* October 30, 1995, 12.
80. *Saikin no keizai taisaku;* "Economic Measures toward Steady Economic Recovery," Sep- tember 20, 1995 (downloaded from Economic Planning Agency internet site). The "drastic impetus" heading comes from the English version—the original Japanese is the less dramatic *"naijū shinkō saku"* (domestic demand promotion policy).
81. "Ministries Submit 2nd Supplementary Budget Proposal," *Kagaku Kōgyō Nippō,* October 2, 1995, 1 (download from FBIS).

¥4.95 trillion, to a total of ¥75.939 trillion, despite the ¥7.44 trillion sup-
posedly added in the fiscal stimulus plans (although some of the spending
increases appear to have shown up in FY 1996). Also, actual FILP allocations
in FY 1995 were in fact lower than the initial plan, despite the approximately ¥12 trillion in extra allocations in the two fiscal stimulus packages
(see Tables 3.1, 3.2, 3.3). Politicians, bureaucrats, and voters alike had been
alarmed by the excessive movement of the yen and its implications for the
domestic economy, not to mention the devastating Kobe earthquake and
the burgeoning financial crisis, and the year's actual fiscal position reflects
that alarm. Nevertheless, the stimulus plan numbers, as usual, significantly
overstate the truth.

The rest of the fiscal year found policy makers grappling with the thorny
and politically charged problem of resolving the *jūsen* situation.[82] They also
agreed on a new budget for FY 1996, with an increase in expenditures of 5.8
percent over the previous year's initial plan, ¥12 trillion yen in deficit bonds,
and an overall bond dependence ratio of 28 percent.[83] The accompanying official economic forecast called for a real GDP growth rate of 2.5 percent for FY
1996—an optimistic figure based at least partly on the expansive budget plan.

Healthy Growth and the Move toward Fiscal Reconsolidation

FY 1996 was a good year for the Japanese economy. After a weak first quarter, real GDP growth for the year came out to an astounding 4.4 percent,
with neither inflation nor deflation as a threat to the economy. Fiscal deficits
did rise considerably, but it looked like the fiscal stimulus was finally jump-
starting the economy on its way to long-term growth. Ironically, however,

82. The history of *jūsen* resolution calls for another book, but here a brief description of the
process is in order. (The following is drawn from Mabuchi 1997, 16–19.)

Leaving aside technical issues, the major *political* argument was over who would be expected to pay for cleaning up the mess. Taxpayers did not want to pay for *jūsen* manage-
ments' incompetence and / or corruption; the banks that owned and lent to the *jūsen* felt
they should not have to cover other creditors; and the agricultural credit cooperatives that
had lent huge amounts of money to the *jūsen* felt they had been hurt by a MOF directive
against lending to the *jūsen* by nonagricultural financial institutions in early 1990. Thus,
when a plan was announced on December 19 that included ¥685 billion in public money,
¥3.5 trillion from parent banks, ¥1.7 trillion from lender banks (in the form of abandoning
40 percent of their claims), and ¥530 billion from agricultural financial institutions (in the
form of abandoning less than 10 percent of their claims), everyone was angry.

While parts of the story are amusing—for example, the agricultural financial institutions
refused to pay unless their contribution was called a "donation" (*zōyo*) rather than an "obli-
gation" (*futan*)—it had real implications for Japan's financial system. Also, even if the New
Frontier Party's three-week Diet sit-in seemed overly dramatic at the time, the delay on the
jūsen plan, the FY 1996 budget, and other legislation did nothing to dampen the feeling of
unease concerning the financial system.

83. Posen (1998, 50–51) points out that in comparison with *final* FY 1995 spending and revenue, the FY 1996 initial budget was somewhat contractionary.

one of the major boosts to the FY 1996 economy was the impending tax increase in FY 1997 (i.e., the consumption tax hike that had been agreed upon in 1994)—private-sector spending, especially in consumer durables, soared in the second half of the year, as consumers sought to avoid paying the higher tax. Meanwhile, a strong showing in the October 1996 Lower House election gave the LDP much greater leverage vis-à-vis its SDPJ and Sakigake "partners," both of which had been humbled in the polls and by defections to the newly formed Democratic Party. (The coalition became an informal one, with a completely LDP Cabinet.)

Budget hawks now had the upper hand. This was partly because of the increasing strength of the economy, but also because the main opposition parties had called in their election platforms for postponing the consumption tax increases. The LDP's victory could thus be interpreted as a repudiation of such fiscal "irresponsibility." And as a final guarantee for advocates of fiscal consolidation, there was the already-decided consumption tax hike, which could only be blocked by passing another law. This gave the budget hawks the power of inertia.

Fall 1996 saw a resurgence of interest in fiscal consolidation, and the FY 1997 budget reflected that interest. In particular, the MOF Tax Bureau predicted an increase in tax revenues of ¥5 trillion from the planned consumption tax hike, while the lapsing of the temporary portion of income tax cuts would provide an additional ¥2 trillion. General account spending actually increased by a modest 3 percent (from FY 1996's initial budget figure of ¥75.1 trillion to ¥77.4 trillion), but the increase of ¥2.3 trillion did not even begin to compare with the expected rise in tax revenues of approximately ¥7 trillion. The upshot was an expected reduction in bond dependence from 28 to 21.6 percent—in other words, an extremely contractionary budget for a still fragile economy.[84] The overall fiscal picture was actually even more contractionary, as it included a cut in non–general account public works and a premium hike in the national health insurance plan.

Also by fall 1996, the MOF-related Fiscal System Advisory Council was holding hearings on how and when to again eliminate deficit bonds. In December, it published its final report, which gave specific debt and deficit targets: bringing the deficit-to-GDP ratio of national and local government below 3 percent, balancing expenditures (not including debt service) with revenues, and eliminating new deficit bonds, all by the year 2003. In the meantime, it called for holding the growth of national and local government expenditures below the economic growth rate.[85] The report was im-

84. Posen 1998, 50–51. Posen actually locates the beginning of contraction in the FY 1996 budget, and argues that the FY 1997 budget only compounded the contraction.

85. *"Zaisei kōzō kaikaku tokubetsu bukai saishū hōkoku ni tsuite"* (On the Final Report of the Special Committee on Fiscal Structure Reform), MOF, December 12, 1996. On the Internet in Japanese at <www.mof.go.jp / singikai / zaisin / tosin / 1a105.htm>.

mediately taken up by a newly formed council headed by Prime Minister Hashimoto himself and including four former prime ministers, three former finance ministers (not including the three prime ministers on the council who had also held that position), all the top officials of the LDP, and the key policy personnel of the SDPJ and Sakigake.[86] The Conference on Fiscal Structure Reform started its deliberations in January 1997. In March, Hashimoto presented the Conference with his "Five Principles of Fiscal Structure Reform," which bore a strong resemblance to the recommendations of the MOF advisory council:

1. To achieve fiscal structure reform (deficit-GDP ratio below 3 percent, no new deficit bonds) by the year 2003, and no later than 2005.
2. To make the final three years of the twentieth century a "period of intensive reform," in which there would be "absolutely no sacred ground" preserved against spending cuts and reforms and in which major spending items would be targeted for specific reductions.
3. To limit discretionary general account expenditures in the FY 1998 budget to less than those of FY 1997.
4. To cut the long-term (ten-year) capital investment plan considerably, and to agree not to draw up a new one involving expenditures.
5. To manage government finances such that the "national burden ratio" (*kokumin futanritsu*)—the total of taxes paid by people plus social welfare premiums plus government deficits divided by national income—would not exceed 50 percent.[87]

The conference's final report, titled "On the Promotion of Fiscal Structure Reform," was issued on June 3, 1997, and was immediately accepted by the Cabinet. It essentially followed the Five Principles, making 2003 a firm target date for achieving fiscal consolidation and extending the existing FY 1995–2005 capital investment plan by three years (thus reducing the ten-year amount from ¥630 trillion to ¥470 trillion), as well as stipulating specific measures in almost every area of government activity.[88] The elements of the Cabinet Resolution were compiled and presented as a bill to the Diet on September 26. The Fiscal Structure Reform Law passed the Lower House on November 6 and secured final passage in the Upper House on

86. Conference on Fiscal Structure Reform name list at <www.kantei.go.jp / jp / zaiseikouzou / meibo.html>.
87. This is a summary of *"Zaisei kōzō kaikaku go gensoku"* (Five Principles of Fiscal Structure Reform), March 1997, <www.kantei.go.jp / jp / zaiseikouzou / 5gensoku.html>.
88. Cabinet Resolution, *"Zaisei kōzō kaikaku no suishin ni tsuite"* (On the Promotion of Fiscal Structure Reform), June 3, 1997, <www.kantei.go.jp / jp / 0604zaisei-kaku.html>. In 1994, the government had replaced the ¥430 trillion 1990–2000 plan agreed to under SII with the much larger 1995–2005 plan. "EPA Group Calls for Rise in Public Works to 630 Trillion Yen," *DY,* October 7, 1994, 1.

November 28, 1997—ironically, only days after the historic collapses of Hokkaido Takushoku Bank and Yamaichi Securities.

The passage of the reform law was quite extraordinary. By November, the Japanese economy and financial system were in a state of crisis, which normally would have called for some sort of stimulus plan. Providing a credible commitment not to resort to fiscal stimulus plans in response to short-term crises was, of course, exactly the point of the law, but one might imagine that a severe crisis would weaken the case for passing the law in the first place. (Certainly, the opposition parties believed that). Indeed, one reason that late FY 1996 had been such an ideal time to begin deliberations on fiscal reconsolidation was that the economy was looking so healthy for a change. In the end, we can only speculate that either the leaders (career MOF officials, as well as LDP members such as Prime Minister Hashimoto, Finance Minister Mitsuzuka Hiroshi, PARC chairman Yamasaki Taku, and LDP secretary-general Katō Kōichi) who pushed consolidation so hard in the fall fervently believed in it, or that they had so tied their political credibility to the plan when the economy was in better shape that they felt they could not back down without conceding a serious mistake.[89]

As the previous paragraph suggests, FY 1997 rapidly turned into a sort of *annus horribilus* for the Japanese economy. As Posen demonstrates, "This reversal from the solid growth of 1996 can only be attributed to the Japanese government's fiscal policy."[90] Just as the prospect of a FY 1997 consumption tax hike had created a surge in consumer spending in the second half of FY 1996, the reality of the tax hike put a freeze on spending. On September 11, the EPA announced that GDP growth for the first quarter of the fiscal year was −2.9 percent, a stunning 11.2 percent annualized drop—the kind of decline that usually requires a war or an oil shock. Consumer spending was particularly hard hit, with a drop of 5.7 percent (24.8 percent annualized).[91] Despite the plunge in economic activity, official government briefers repeated that the economy was on the track to recovery, and MOF officials grimly insisted that the country's fiscal situation would not permit a fiscal stimulus plan. With interbank interest rates at around 0.5 percent, a monetary stimulus was not in the cards either.

With the rapid slowdown in growth, many firms that had been on the edge of financial trouble plunged into *de facto* or *de jure* bankruptcy. The decrease in firms' ability to pay back loans, combined with the Southeast Asian

89. In support of the latter interpretation, a MOF official pointed out to me that the legislative process can be as rigid as the budget calendar. Thus, once the advisory council's report had been approved by the Cabinet, it would take a conscious (and conspicuous) decision *not* to introduce legislation that codified the council's report. Nonetheless, if there was ever a good time to break with tradition for the sake of reducing future pain, this was probably it.
90. Posen 1998, 51.
91. The original, unrevised numbers can be found in full in "Japan April–June Real GDP Shrinks 2.9 Pct Qtr / Qtr," *Jiji*, September 11, 1997.

currency crisis that began in July, wreaked havoc on a number of financial institutions. The inevitable result was increased bankruptcies in the financial sector, of which Hokkaido Takushoku and Yamaichi were only the most obvious. By December, it had become apparent that the problem was so severe that government action was urgently needed, and resistance to any policy that would cut into fiscal consolidation began to erode.

From the point of view of macroeconomic policy, the rest of FY 1997 was essentially an attempt to deal with the horrendous side effects of failed fiscal and financial policies. It included a February 1998 plan to provide ¥13 trillion to major banks as needed to increase their tier-one capital (an action that should have been taken years before) and ¥17 trillion to shore up the ailing deposit insurance system, as well as a ¥12 trillion fiscal stimulus plan. The failure of the fiscal consolidation effort was officially confirmed in the decision to amend the Fiscal Structure Reform Law in April 1998. The revision pushed back the target year from 2003 to 2005 and changed the spending guideline for FY 1999 from "will not exceed an overall increase of 2 percent" to "an increase minimized to the extent possible." Perhaps most significantly, it vitiated the procedural centerpiece of the law, changing the phrase "the issuance of special public bonds [i.e., deficit bonds] will be reduced in each fiscal year" by inserting the wording: "except when it creates a serious hindrance to carrying out measures to address serious consequences on citizens' standard of living due to the occurrence of markedly abnormal and extremely catastrophic natural disaster, or marked stagnation in economic activity."[92] "Marked stagnation in economic activity," the revision stipulated, was to be determined by Cabinet Order. Since the example given in the MOF draft is two consecutive quarters in which annualized real GDP growth is less than 1 percent, however, this amendment constituted a clear defeat for the anti-Keynesian MOF budget brigade.

Analysis

Despite consistently strong citizen and market sentiment for fiscal stimulus, the years 1993–97 instead saw a stop-and-go approach to fiscal policy. For the most part, and to a surprising extent, the policies of the increasingly unpopular Ministry of Finance carried the day. Only the 1994 tax cut (part of a MOF strategy to hike indirect taxes) and the fiscal stimulus plans of 1995 really had substantial stimulatory effect, and even the 1994 tax cut was partly offset by large spending cuts. The 1997 Fiscal Structure Reform Law

---

92. Committee on Fiscal Structure Reform, "*Zaisei kōzō kaikaku hō no ichibu kaisei hōan ni tsuite*" (On the Bill to Partially Revise the Fiscal Structure Reform Law), April 24, 1998, <www.mof.go.jp / gijiyosi / 1a001c3.htm>.

in particular was a MOF victory, if short-lived. It wrote into law an updated version of the 1980s' fiscal consolidation agreement.

What is most striking in the period is the extent to which macroeconomic policies failed to address the actual needs of the Japanese economy. In looking at the failed policies of 1993–97, several possible explanations come to mind. These include, at various points, alternation of coalition governments, economic contingency, economic beliefs, and the role of the United States. Each is plausible for one or more subperiod, but only the policy-making structure appears to have consistently affected fiscal policy outcomes in relatively predictable ways. Monetary policy outcomes, in contrast, are overdetermined—the economic situation, MOF preferences, political preferences, and even U.S. government preferences all pointed toward easy money. Therefore, the following analysis focuses on fiscal policy.

The most striking characteristic of the period was the elimination, or at least disruption, of LDP one-party dominance. There were five prime ministers, representing four different party or coalition configurations. Moreover, even within the LDP-SDPJ-Sakigake coalition—by far the longest lasting of the period—there was a drastic change in the configuration of power following the LDP's success and its partners' setbacks in the 1996 Lower House election. (The formation of the Democratic Party a month earlier was probably even more disastrous for SDPJ and especially Sakigake than the 1996 election.)

We might expect two types of effects. One would be changes in policy outcomes in tandem with the changes in coalition. The other is the general point made in chapters 1 and 2 that alternation of governments should lead to political entrepreneurialism and greater activism—during a period of economic stagnation, this will tend to mean preference for fiscal stimulus.

Looking back over the arc of events, it is more or less impossible to discern any clear macroeconomic policy pattern that coincides with governmental composition. The Miyazawa government was committed to fiscal stimulation, but with little effect. The Hosokawa government showed a commitment to fiscal consolidation, but actually put into motion—at least temporarily—larger deficits with its decision to cut income taxes in return for a future consumption tax hike. The Murayama cabinet, with its odd combination of LDP and SDPJ, created moderate expectations of fiscal expansionism, but maintained the status quo. It only delivered real stimulation in the context of the high-yen crisis. Only Hashimoto's administration seems to have had strong feelings on fiscal policy that ended up actually being implemented, albeit with disastrous results. (I leave out the Hata government, because it did not last long enough to have any meaningful effect.)

Although alternation of coalitions had no clear effect on macroeconomic policy, we do see greater political activism over time in trying to shape MOF decisions. Chapter 7 provides additional evidence of that activism, but for now it is worth noting that politicians increasingly used personnel decisions and informational networks to reduce their dependence in the budget-making process. Although the policy outcomes themselves are often unpredictable based on that dynamic, it is evident that politicians were becoming more involved in overall fiscal policy. And generally speaking, we do see increasing budget deficits and the abandonment of the old fiscal consolidation agreement, despite the resistance—and often the apocalyptic warnings—of MOF bureaucrats.

Turning to the international level, contemporary news reports regularly pointed to the role of the United States in pushing for fiscal expansion, as does a recent scholarly book by Takaaki Suzuki.[93] The Clinton administration was often strident in calling for Japan to increase domestic demand. And in interviews at the time, a number of MOF officials made clear their opinion that the spring 1993 fiscal stimulus plan was meant only to dampen the new administration's aggressive stance.[94] This is not entirely convincing, however. After all, Prime Minister Miyazawa himself was seen to prefer stimulus, and the economy was clearly slowing considerably. In any event, the 1993 stimulus plan had little if any effect from a macroeconomic perspective. Even the spring FY 1994 fiscal plan, which had considerable Keynesian meaning, primarily reflects the deal for a higher consumption tax rather than U.S. pressure.

The best evidence for a U.S. role in Japanese stimulus plans in the period can be seen in the two plans of 1995. In those cases, however, it is far more believable that the economic situation itself was driving Japanese policy— the rapid 20 percent rise in the value of the yen was having serious effects on both exporters and those capital-constrained financial institutions that had major holdings of international assets. In other words, the ultrahigh yen threatened the Japanese economy through both a diminution of external demand (at least in yen terms) and the possibility of domestic credit contraction. Certainly the United States played an important *indirect* role by doing so little to ease the situation for Japan until the auto negotiations were cleared up. But the case for direct influence is weak. (It is not necessary to consider a U.S. role in producing more expansionary regular budgets since, as Posen makes clear, the regular budgets were in fact not expansionary.)[95]

What of economic contingency? The macroeconomic situation of 1993–97 gave rise to a variety of economic analyses and prescriptions, both over time and in specific subperiods. It is probably fair to say that macroeconomic policy was broadly responsive to economic contingency. Increasing deficits and length of stagnation correlate roughly, at least until 1997. The role of economic contingency was particularly clear in 1995, when the yen crisis made for great clarity of purpose. And the great fiscal contraction

93. Suzuki 2000, esp. chap. 9.
94. Personal interviews.
95. Posen 1998, chap. 2.

of 1997 occurred in the midst of what appeared to be an improvement in the economy; moreover, the desire to address the long-term economic problem of excessive debt provides a clear rationale for the direction—if not the radical scale—of the changes.

There are some aspects of the story that give pause, however. For one thing, as already noted, clear consensus existed only in the extreme situation of 1995. At other times, expansionary policies met MOF resistance and led to struggles among politicians as well as with bureaucrats. (MOF resistance was not purely cynical—officials were seriously worried about the long-term effects of deficits on Japan's fiscal situation, and not without reason. The irony is that the contractionary policies of 1997 were themselves to become the cause of much larger deficits over at least the next three years.) Meanwhile, fiscally conservative administrations received the avid support of the ministry when they sought to rein in the budget, and by far the largest movement in fiscal policy that cannot be attributed to a specific current crisis was the 1997 contraction. We can also discern a process of learning in 1992–94, as politicians gradually realized how bad the economic situation was, and how serious was the need for a policy response.

Turning back to a structural explanation, MOF bureaucrats were clearly aware of their deteriorating political position over the course of the period and moved from outright resistance and delay to both subtler and more drastic tactics. The "subtler" tactics to which I refer are the courting of leading politicians and attempts to persuade them of the rightness of MOF analysis.[96] Bureaucrats were particularly successful in gaining Hashimoto's attention in this regard. As for more drastic measures, the attempt by MOF budgeters and their allied LDP deficit hawks to codify their preferences into law was (after considerable wooing, of course) almost spectacularly successful, as seen in the 1996 passage of the Fiscal Structure Reform Law. Although soon eviscerated in the aftermath of the FY 1997 fiscal contraction, the law was a conscious attempt by the deficit hawks to return to the good old days of the fiscal consolidation agreement of the 1980s. In this case, however, the attempt was both more legalistic *and* more ambitious. Both the legalism and the ambition ironically reflected the weakening of MOF's structural political situation. Top ministry bureaucrats knew that they might not have another chance to push forward their fiscal agenda—as chapter 7 makes clear, politicians were already threatening the structural power of the ministry. Only by locking the door to the treasury and throwing away the key could MOF's budget and tax mainstream prevent what they perceived as long-term ruin. And this was their last, best chance—last because of the increasing attacks on MOF structural integrity, and best because of the pliable attitude of Prime Minister Hashimoto.

96. The process recalls Kato's (1994) argument.

In the end, if we step back and look at the trend of Japan's revenues and spending it is evident that loosening did occur, and that it was far beyond the scale of 1986–87. It seemed to be strongly associated with increased political involvement, particularly after the policy-savvy LDP recovered the reins from the anti-LDP coalitions in 1994. Ironically, strong LDP influence appears even in the catastrophic policies of 1997; Prime Minister Hashimoto's leadership was particularly evident in the Fiscal Structure Reform Bill (which, of course, also enjoyed great support from MOF).

The overall strategy by LDP and other politicians to contain MOF included extremely heavy political pressure, as the next chapter demonstrates. By 1995, the MOF goal of maintaining autonomy was under fire from a number of new directions, and the budget compromises discussed in this chapter were a major response. Following the catastrophic failure of the 1997 fiscal consolidation, the ministry again found itself the scapegoat, contributing to fundamental structural change and a substantial weakening in its policy-making influence.

7

Structural Changes, 1997–2000

The Dismemberment of MOF and the Rise of the BOJ

> The Bank of Japan's autonomy regarding currency and monetary control shall be respected.
>
> Bank of Japan Law, Article 3 (revised June 1997)

By the mid-1990s, politicians were gaining a degree of power at the expense of the Ministry of Finance while playing within the existing rules of the game of macroeconomic politics. But by 1996, they were beginning to map out a new set of rules that would fundamentally change the game. Spurred on by the magnitude of the policy failures of the 1990s, leading politicians carried out a direct attack on some of the key structural bases of MOF power. The changes that resulted are already having profound effects on macroeconomic policy making—and by extension, on macroeconomic policies.

In June 1997, the Diet approved a wholesale reform of the Bank of Japan Law, giving the BOJ more autonomy and responsibility, and thus altering the legal structure of its relationship with MOF. Simultaneously, the Diet acted to remove financial oversight responsibilities from the ministry by establishing a new Financial Supervision Agency as of June 1998. And turning to personnel matters, in January 1998 a series of arrests of MOF banking supervisors forced the resignation of the administrative vice-minister and the head of the Banking Bureau. To add insult to injury, the new administrative vice-minister was a former MOF man who had been dropped off the elite budget/tax track.[1]

The story begins several years earlier, when the Ministry of Finance began to come under increasing scrutiny and criticism from all sides. The resulting vigorous public debates led to widespread calls to weaken MOF's power by addressing the very issues this study emphasizes—breadth of legal jurisdiction and autonomy of personnel and *amakudari* management. The

---

1. The new vice-minister, Tanami Kōji, had been on the fast track until July 1996, at which point he was moved from the post of director-general of the Financial Bureau (often a stepping stone on the way to administrative vice-minister) to chief Cabinet councilor for internal affairs—a prestigious post, but the end of a MOF career.

changes and tumult of the late 1990s are varied and fascinating, but this chapter sticks closely to the themes of structural power and structural change by concentrating on personnel and organizational change. Following that analysis, it turns to actual macroeconomic policies and shows how structural change promoted policy change.

Continued Attacks on MOF's Personnel Power Base

At the same time that MOF and politicians were butting heads on tax and budget issues, not to mention financial regulation and bailouts, politicians and the media put the ministry on the defensive in terms of personnel practices as well. Perhaps no agency had manipulated personnel to its advantage quite to the extent that the Ministry of Finance had, but all have used control over pre- and post-retirement jobs as a key pillar of bureaucratic autonomy. Political reformers realized this, and starting with the Hosokawa government, they began to attack the insulation that allowed the bureaucracies to resist political control. The non-LDP coalitions were not able to mount a really effective attack on this key perquisite due originally to their concentration on other matters (particularly political reform) and later to their weakening power base. However, the *Ji-sha-sa* coalition homed in on the issue soon after its establishment. We see this broader strategy in a series of events, including the appointment of a new BOJ governor in 1994, ethics accusations against officials, and the unprecedented forced resignations of three MOF administrative vice-ministers, as well as the structural changes described in the next section.

BOJ Governorship

As we have seen, there was a well-established pattern dating back some twenty years in which the position of governor of the Bank of Japan alternated between former MOF officials and BOJ officials, with the deputy governor coming from the other bureaucracy. With Governor Mieno's term coming to a close in December 1994, the *Ji-sha-sa* coalition had on its hands another major decision with macroeconomic implications. Since Mieno was a BOJ man, the assumption was that the governorship would be taken by a MOF OB. However, Finance Minister Takemura clearly recognized that personnel policy constituted one of the major strengths of the career bureaucracies, and that the BOJ governorship was the biggest prize among MOF bureaucrats' post-retirement jobs.[2]

2. Shiota 1995, chap. 6; and personal interview with Takemura Masayoshi, August 1999.

Therefore, he made clear that he alone would have final say over this key appointment. In this quest, he did have some advantages. First, the finance minister is empowered to make a recommendation for governor to the prime minister. Second, unlike most years, MOF and its OBs had not yet come to a conclusion on whom to put forward.[3] Both the indecision and the division created political opportunities for Takemura.

Takemura made clear that his preference was for a private-sector economist.[4] This threat served to unite current and former MOF leaders, who agreed to back Matsushita Yasuo (chairman of Sakura Bank and a retired administrative vice-minister). Takemura instructed his underlings to come up with a full list of candidates, only to be told that the decision was his alone. Governor Mieno also backed Matsushita. As Mieno's retirement neared with Takemura still unable to come up with an appropriate candidate from the private sector, the finance minister allegedly even broached to Mieno the possibility of nominating a BOJ man (either the prospective deputy governor, Fukui Toshihiko, or even a repeat term for Mieno), but Mieno demurred.[5] Takemura's inability to take advantage of MOF-BOJ rivalry is not surprising—the tradition of alternating positions between MOF and the BOJ had arisen as an equilibrium solution to a nasty rivalry, and also served to keep other actors out of contention. In the end, Takemura settled on the slate of Matsushita and Fukui, perhaps taking solace in the fact that, although a MOF man, Matsushita had spent the better part of a decade in the private sector.[6] Although it had achieved its basic aim, MOF was on notice that it could no longer rely on tacit political approval for business as usual.

In March 1998, there was finally a break in the old pattern, when Governor Matsushita and Deputy Governor Fukui were both forced to resign. The Hashimoto Cabinet appointed as governor Hayami Masaru, a long-retired BOJ OB who had been chairman of Nissho Iwai trading company. It appointed two deputy governors as well: BOJ "prince" Yamaguchi Yutaka, and Jiji Press economic reporter Fujiwara Sakuya.[7] For the first time since 1969, MOF retirees were completely excluded from the top ranks of the bank.

3. Shiota 1995, chap. 6.
4. He told me in an interview in August 1999 that he had been particularly interested in an economic commentator named Tanaka Naoki.
5. See Shiota (1995, chap. 6) for this story. As late as November 1, Takemura told a press conference, "There is a custom that BOJ career employees and MOF OBs alternate at the job, but I don't think such a rule exists" (1995, 170)
6. When I asked him in August 1999 about the nomination process, Takemura said that neither the bureaucracies nor the markets were prepared for a governor who broke the pattern, so in order to maintain stability he appointed Matsushita (whom he saw as an able candidate). Personal interview.
7. Profiles can be found at <www.boj.or.jp/about/about_f.htm>.

Scandals

Meanwhile, as financial system troubles continued, the Ministry of Finance started to come under increasing pressure from the media, the public, and politicians. Part of this scrutiny had to do with the self-evident policy failures of the country's elite economic policy makers, but increasingly the bureaucrats' greatest asset—the perception of integrity—became a major focus.[8] Japanese citizens had long discounted the ethics of politicians, but a series of disclosures made clear that bureaucrats were by no means immune. In the early 1990s, various "loss compensation" schemes by securities firms were revealed. These schemes, which favored large account-holders (and, it later turned out, *sōkaiya*—corporate blackmailers), turned out to have been sanctioned by MOF inspectors.[9] Perhaps more damaging was the spectacular failure of the *jūsen* and the indelible image—broadcast throughout the country—of Diet members questioning the failed *jūsen*'s MOF OB leaders.[10] In many cases, these nonbanks had lent large amounts of money not only with poor judgment, but to some very shady characters.

Even by 1993, evidence of lavish entertainment of MOF officials—especially bank examiners—by financial institutions had begun to come to light. Reports focused on nights at expensive restaurants and drinking establishments, golf outings, and the like. There was nothing new about these activities—they had long been an integral part of Japan's informal regulation, in which close relationships between regulators and the businesses they regulated were believed to allow effective but cooperative supervision, unlike the adversarial American model of regulation. What had changed was the willingness of the public to accept such behavior as "business as usual," especially given the overwhelming evidence of policy failure in the supervision of financial institutions.

On March 9, 1995, Takahashi Harunori, the chairman of the failing Tokyo Kyōwa credit cooperative, testified before the Diet about large-scale entertainment of Taya Hiroaki (then director-general of the Tokyo Customs House, and previously director of the Budget Bureau's Coordination Division) and Nakajima Yoshio (deputy director-general of the Budget Bureau, and formerly a secretary to Prime Ministers Kaifu and Miyazawa). This entertainment included, in Taya's case, a free flight to Hong Kong in Takahashi's private jet. It later turned out that Nakajima's wrongdoing was considerably more extensive, involving no-interest loans and money under the table from a variety of financial institutions.[11] The official response on

---

8. See, for example, Mabuchi 1997, 1–36; Horvat 1998.
9. Hanson 1996, chaps. 7, 8, 10; Ishizawa 1995, 159–162; Laurence 1999.
10. Mabuchi 1997, 19–22.
11. Ikuta 1996, 27–35; Mabuchi 1997, 6–7. Ikuta writes that while the venerable *Nikkei* first reported Nakajima's financial shenanigans on August 28, 1995, it did so in order to preempt the weekly magazine *Friday* from getting the scoop. If so, the publication follows a long pattern of "respectable" newspapers getting involved in government scandals only when the more sensational weeklies force the issue (Farley 1996).

March 13, 1995, did not satisfy many observers. Both Taya and Nakajima received official reprimands, but were neither fired nor prosecuted. Vice Minister Saitō was given a strict warning for having allowed such things to happen, and his salary—along with those of the deputy vice-minister and the directors-general of the Budget and Customs Bureaus—was docked 20 percent for one month.[12] Nakajima was moved from his line position as deputy director-general of the Budget Bureau in May, and resigned with full pension at the end of July, when his more extensive dealings became public. Taya, who was demoted to a job in the secretariat, held out until December 27, at which point he too left the ministry.

While these two individuals, especially Nakajima, had undoubtedly received ethically unacceptable benefits from the financial sector, their being singled out in public appeared to be both an effect of and a stimulus to citizens' anger with the special privileges enjoyed by public servants. Indeed, comparing books and articles about the Ministry of Finance before 1995 with those after the Tokyo Kyōwa scandal reveals a marked difference in the way MOF bureaucrats are seen by popular authors—the post-Tokyo Kyōwa writings depict an organization of people whose arrogance exceeds their competence and who are interested in power for their own personal aggrandizement, while the earlier writings concentrate mainly on the power MOF holds in the political world.[13] That reaction dovetailed with rising doubts about the competency of the central bureaucracies, leading to an erosion of their traditional legitimacy and to the increased popularity of calls for administrative reform, political accountability, and elimination of *amakudari*.

By calling into question the motivations of individual officials, the scandals and rumors also cast doubt on the motivations and integrity of their organizations as a whole. The pattern recurred during the macroeconomic crisis period of 1997–98. After prosecutors shifted investigations into high gear in late 1997, several MOF bank examiners were arrested in January and February 1998, and scores of officials were disciplined for having accepted excessive gifts from banks and in some cases for having forewarned banks of upcoming "surprise" inspections.[14] Amazingly, on January 26,

---

12. See Shiota 1995, 242–247. The term I have translated as "official reprimand" is *kunkoku shobun,* and "strict warning" is *genjū chūi shobun.*
13. For pre-Tokyo Kyōwa writings, see Nihon Keizai Shimbunsha 1994, 1992; Ishiwatari 1989; Ishizawa 1995; and Kawakita 1989. For post-Tokyo Kyōwa, see Shiota 1995; Ikuta 1996; Kishi 1996; and all the articles (some of them quite scurrilous) in *Kanryō kyokuhi jinjiroku.* When the earlier writers address scandals, they seldom single out individuals, and never elite-track bureaucrats; rather, MOF is generally presented as a monolith. The later writers go after individuals, preferring to home in on elite-track bureaucrats and often dissecting personal networks to suggest that other (generally more powerful) individuals are guilty by association.
14. There are copious reports and analyses to be found in newspapers and magazines of the time. In English, see, for example, "A 'MOF-Tan' Casts Light on Japan's Murky Collusion," *Christian Science Monitor,* February 6, 1998, 1; "Japanese Aghast as Murky Secrets Emerge," *FT,* January 31, 1998, 2.

1998, prosecutors actually raided the Ministry of Finance itself to arrest the director of the Financial Inspectors Office in the secretariat. None of the officials arrested were elite-track, but many elite officials were disciplined. At least two suicides resulted (one of a bank examiner, and one of a MOF OB Dietmember), and several top MOF officials were forced to resign. Similar stories came to light concerning BOJ bank audits, and when the chief of the BOJ Capital Markets Division was arrested in March for accepting bribes from banks, both Governor Matsushita and Deputy Governor Fukui resigned as well.[15]

Vice-Ministerial Resignations

A final set of attacks on the personnel system of the Ministry of Finance can be seen in the forced resignations of two consecutive administrative vice-ministers in 1995. While there were, of course, reasons for politicians going after the individuals in question, MOF's autonomy was a central issue in both of the 1995 resignations. In 1998, there was yet another forced resignation of the administrative vice-minister in connection with the bank examination scandals; in that case, the vice-minister seemed even less like the central target, and more like collateral damage from a full-bore assault on the ministry itself.

The first early retirement was that of the beleaguered Saitō, on May 26, 1995, only about one month shy of his full term.[16] After nearly two years of intense public scrutiny and criticism, Saitō finally agreed to resign to take responsibility for the scandals and problems that had emerged under his watch. In return, the internally planned personnel rotation was left intact, with no political meddling.[17] The benefits for the (mainly LDP) politicians involved were both revenge at a personal level and a warning to the new MOF leadership that no one would be allowed to defy political leaders with impunity.

A little more than half a year later, on December 29, 1995, Saitō's successor, Shinozawa, turned in his resignation as well, taking responsibility for the *jūsen* problem and the continuing effects of the scandals over entertainment of MOF officials. Coming after the massively unpopular unveiling of MOF's *jūsen* liquidation proposal, Shinozawa's unexpected resignation probably helped improve the chances of dealing effectively with that vexing problem. His replacement on January 5, 1996, by Ogawa Tadashi, the commissioner of the National Tax Administration, meant that the top position belonged to someone outside both the budget bureaucrats in general and

15. "Senior Central Bank Official Arrested: BOJ Figure Accused of Accepting Entertainment from IBJ, Sanwa Bank," *YS*, March 12, 1998, 1.
16. For the entire story of Saitō's time in office, see Shiota 1995, passim.
17. Ibid., 256–260.

the Saitō line in particular. (Ogawa was close to LDP powerbroker Takeshita Noboru, which could only have been seen as useful in bringing about a smooth, effective, and politically sensitive resolution to the *jūsen* and other problems facing MOF.) Although neither Ogawa nor his successor, Komura Takeshi, was ever personally the lightning rod for criticism that Saitō had been, severe economic conditions and new revelations of MOF officials' misconduct forced Komura's resignation in January 1998 anyway.

Reasons

The attacks on MOF had multiple reasons. For one, the Ministry of Finance was under fire for having protected weak and corrupt financial institutions. That protection was illustrated in the expression "convoy system," which meant that the most competitive banks were prevented from moving forward aggressively in order to prevent the least competitive ones from failing. The central MOF tenet that no bank be allowed to fail ended up increasing the systemic risk in Japanese finance. Although the Bank of Japan was involved in prudential regulation as well, its officials had been saying publicly for some time that the role of regulators was to prevent systemic failure rather than individual failure.[18] Thus, in financial regulation too the BOJ looked more competent than MOF, even as it was constrained in its actions by the ministry.

In addition to the scandals discussed above, the Ministry of Finance was also tarred in the public eye with the labels of incompetence and arrogance. But while public opinion is important in politics, it is not necessarily enough to break apart decades of inertia. However, the relationship between the ministry and the ruling LDP had changed considerably from that of the pre-coalition period.[19] The days of the Saitō-Ozawa alliance had demonstrated that the ministry was happy to provide support to whichever politicians seemed the most useful, and was willing to leave its old LDP partners out in the cold if necessary.

At least some ruling party politicians were probably motivated by revenge for the slights of the non-LDP coalitions period, although it seems unlikely that personal grudges alone could account for major policy change. More importantly, politics had changed structurally as well. The emergence of a credible (or at least somewhat credible) opposition meant that the LDP had to take public opinion seriously. The move to both single-seat and proportional districts also increased the need to identify the party with specific, popular policies, and then to stick with them.

With the elements in place of widely recognized policy failure, public disapproval, a weakened relationship with ruling politicians, and politicians' increased sensitivity to public opinion, the ministry was vulnerable.[20] On the

---

18. Mieno (2000, 55) mentions a specific speech of his to that effect in October 1994.
19. Mabuchi 1997, chap. 2.
20. Ibid.

other hand, it retained considerable strengths, including its *amakudari* network in the political and economic worlds and the fact that many individuals or firms still depended on MOF's cooperation for their livelihood. Nonetheless, the political atmosphere and the failings of the existing system set the stage for substantial structural changes.

Reorganization

The reorganization ideas being floated by 1996 were extremely worrisome for the Ministry of Finance, even as they promised to give considerable new responsibilities to the Bank of Japan and perhaps even to the politicians who were pushing them. These included the reform and reduction of government financial institutions, as well as the revision of the Bank of Japan Law and the establishment of new financial regulatory bodies. Another idea that constituted an even more profound attack on MOF prerogatives—a plan to move budgeting functions from the ministry to the Prime Minister's Office—ended up not being put into effect, although it appeared to be taken very seriously by both politicians and MOF bureaucrats.

Government Financial Institutions

Even as the Ministry of Finance was resisting usurpation of its influence in the Bank of Japan and trying to minimize the fiscal impact of stimulus and tax plans, it and other ministries were also fighting a rearguard action against a reorganization of public corporations (in MOF's case, particularly public financial institutions). Public corporations have been a major source of secure *amakudari* posts for ministries, and stable *amakudari* posts are essential to organizational autonomy—without such "reserved seats," retiring bureaucrats are at the mercy of private-sector corporations or politicians, thus forcing them into either clientelism or capitulation. With that in mind, politicians such as Takemura had been calling since 1993 for the reorganization of public-sector corporations, both to make them more efficient and to reduce bureaucrats' ability to use them as employment agencies or as instruments of bureaucratic policy preferences.

Finance Minister Takemura and his Sakigake party were personally associated with the idea of administrative reform, and he launched a crusade to rationalize the existing system of public corporations, with a particular emphasis on the financial institutions. By the 1990s, many public corporations had outlived their original purposes. Others were redundant or were only benefiting a small group of clients and employees. A considerable part of Takemura's tenure as finance minister was spent trying to achieve this rationalization, although in the end bureaucratic stalling and squabbles among various politicians pushing various schemes meant that the only decisions made were to merge the Export-Import Bank with the Overseas Economic Cooperation Fund to form the Japan Bank for International Cooperation and to merge the Japan Development Bank and the Hokkaido-Tohoku Development Finance Public Corporation to form the Development Bank of Japan, both as of October 1, 1999 (four years hence). Neither change made for any diminution of functions. When the agreement was announced in March 1995, Takemura took credit, saying, "Based on my political decision, we chose the merger of the Ex-Im Bank and the OECF."[21] Takemura's overall failure to make major changes can be attributed partly to bureaucratic resistance, and partly to the LDP's growing annoyance with him and desire to cut him down to size.[22] Nonetheless, senior MOF officials had been forced to expend real political capital to defend the financial institutions.

BOJ Law Revision—The End of an Era?

The most significant check on the ministry's power in macroeconomic policy making was the revision of the Bank of Japan Law, which was passed by the Diet on June 11, 1997, and went into effect the following April.[23] The structural weakness of the BOJ, as we have seen, resulted primarily from its limited legal jurisdiction and the tradition of placing former MOF men in its top positions. While BOJ officials had long chafed under MOF's paternalistic influence, they were not really in a political position to effect change, due to the ministry's great advantages in dealing with politicians. The result was that earlier attempts to increase the BOJ's autonomy had failed, or in some cases had never made it off the pages of the books that advocated them.[24]

The self-evident failure of macroeconomic and financial policy in the 1990s presented a rationale for increased autonomy. Although former Governor Mieno had been the focus of anger in the years immediately following the bursting of the bubble, by 1997 many observers had absolved the

---

21. Shiota 1995, 250. His chapter 8 covers the whole story in detail.
22. Takemura, like Ozawa, had led an LDP breakaway party, which obviously did not increase his popularity with his erstwhile colleagues. He also annoyed many by trying to gain personal power and public support at the expense of more experienced LDP members—he had only been elected three times, not even enough for a normal LDP Lower House member to attain the post of Diet committee chairman, much less the most powerful non–prime ministerial position in the Cabinet. With only a small party to support him and having made many enemies among both politicians and the bureaucrats under his authority, it is not surprising that Takemura was not a long-lived political commodity. The defection of almost his entire small party to form the Democratic Party in September 1996 confirmed his fall from grace.
23. I hope at some point to do a more in-depth study of the BOJ Law revision, its political and intellectual antecedents, and its effects, but this book is not the place to do it. This section only hits the high points. Undoubtedly the best existing account is Mabuchi 1997.
24. Mabuchi 1994, chap. 2.

BOJ of any guilt for its role in the creation and bursting of the bubble, arguing that its weakness had given it no choice. Instead, they began to blame the Ministry of Finance for having forced those policies on its weaker cousin—essentially my argument here.[25]

Nonetheless, few early predictions were optimistic that the BOJ Law revision attempt would be any different from past episodes. One seeming difference was that this time coalition members were specifically aiming to weaken the Ministry of Finance and saw MOF reform and BOJ Law revision as "two sides of a single coin."[26] The process followed three stages, beginning with deliberations by a high-level coalition "Project Team," set up in February 1996 with a broad mandate to address financial regulation, the fiscal system, and MOF reform. The team came up with a strong proposal in favor of BOJ autonomy and expanding the bank's financial oversight capabilities. (The next section describes the team's proposals concerning MOF reorganization.)

Following the team's report, Prime Minister Hashimoto formed an academic committee called the Central Bank Study Group, whose final report on November 12, 1996 (about three weeks after the LDP's major Lower House election victory) echoed the Project Team's call for BOJ autonomy and transparency. It recommended the publication of minutes of Policy Board meetings and abolition of the cabinet's right to disband the Policy Board, among other things, but left in place the cabinet's right to postpone major BOJ policy decisions.[27]

At that point the matter was officially passed on to the MOF-affiliated Financial System Research Council, following the standard pathway for changes in financial law. The Council's February 6, 1997, report in several ways reflected the views of its MOF secretariat. While calling for autonomy and transparency, it also recommended that the finance minister retain the right to approve the BOJ's budget and to request postponement of policy changes. These recommendations were based partly on a constitutional argument—that the Diet could not forfeit its role as the "highest organ of state power" (Article 41) in any area of policy, and thus must maintain supervision over any agency established to advance public purpose.[28] The Financial System Research Council's report was immediately endorsed by BOJ Governor Matsushita (a MOF OB), despite some criticism of the continuing role of the Ministry of Finance in BOJ affairs.[29] Finance Minister

25. For example, Nakakita 1999, 33–36.
26. Ibid., 45.
27. Ibid., 52–56; Mabuchi 1997, chap. 5.
28. Nakakita 1999, 56–59.
29. "Panel Report Gets Green Light from Bank of Japan Gov.," *DY,* February 7, 1997, 14. Other reports had him somewhat more reserved, saying only that "The report approaches the level of global standards." "Bill to Give Bank of Japan Policy Control: Provision Allowing Nonvoting Government Members Raises Concerns about Central Bank's Independence," *Nikkei Weekly,* February 10, 1997, 13.

Mitsuzuka took the unusual step of insulting his own agency, saying, "It was a total defeat for the Finance Ministry bureaucrats."[30]

Surprisingly, on February 20, 1997, the ruling coalition rejected what the newspapers had started to call the "MOF-drafted" bill, and on March 11 it submitted a stronger version to the Diet (with the Cabinet right to postpone policies removed). The Cabinet's BOJ Law revision draft passed the Lower House on May 22 and the Upper House on June 11, without further modification. The new law enshrined for the first time the primacy of the Bank of Japan in monetary policy, eliminated MOF's formal responsibility for coordinating monetary and fiscal policy, instated a requirement to report directly to the Diet, strengthened the role of the Policy Board, and freed the board from an archaic selection process that had long guaranteed that voting members other than the governor would be superannuated government and BOJ OBs. It was indeed a near total defeat for MOF, if not a total victory for the strongest advocates of central bank independence.

The process of BOJ Law revision was striking not only for its results, but in itself. Most important, the revision process was actually started—and framed—by politicians.[31] The Project Team did not have a bureaucrat-dominated secretariat, nor did it depend primarily on the bureaucracy for proposals and information. The Ministry of Finance, which clearly had the most to lose both from BOJ Law revision and from the team's other focuses, tried hard to convince team members of the dangers of the various changes being considered. The Project Team chairman, Itō Shigeru, was moved to say that MOF officials "come so often to explain that we practically need to bar the door."[32] LDP backbenchers were another major target. MOF argued especially against excessive haste. Indeed, delay probably would have helped MOF's cause, given the heavy Lower House losses sustained in the fall by both Sakigake (the most gung-ho advocates of radical reform) and the SDPJ, but there was also plenty of resentment of the ministry among top LDP politicians such as Katō Kōichi and Yamasaki Taku.

In contrast to MOF, the BOJ establishment was strangely silent. Mabuchi argues convincingly that the BOJ's silence reflected top officials' fear of MOF reprisal in the event of failure and suggests that the MOF OB governor Matsushita may have been less enthusiastic than BOJ career officials. (Indeed, Mabuchi writes that a secret BOJ task group formed to encourage the Project Team's work specifically excluded the governor.)[33] The financial world also kept a low profile, so public discourse was dominated by reformist politicians and the media on the one side and MOF alone on the

---

30. "Is Bank of Japan Ready to Be Weaned?" *DY,* February 19, 1997, 7.
31. Mabuchi 1997. Mieno (2000, 100) also emphasizes this point—as well as his surprise at the efforts' success.
32. Mabuchi 1997, 173.
33. Ibid., chap. 3.

other. Because the process came in the midst of financial scandals and the *jūsen* bailout, the ministry was in an unenviable position, which reformists used to their advantage.

Dismembering MOF—The New Shape of Financial Supervision

Along with the BOJ Law revision, the Cabinet also submitted a bill to establish a new Financial Supervision Agency to take over MOF's role as supervisor of the banking, securities, and insurance sectors.[34] The bill also passed in June, and the agency was established the following year, on June 22, 1998. The 1997 Diet session thus dealt the most serious blow yet to MOF's institutional bases of power.

As in the case of BOJ Law reform, the idea of separating financial regulatory functions from financial rule-making functions had both political and theoretical appeal. Among intellectuals a strong argument had developed that making and enforcing policy were two logically distinct categories. Combining the two under one agency inevitably created severe conflicts of interest—for example, rule makers might draft regulations that allowed enforcers to profit in some way from their role, or that justified greater resources being devoted to the organization as a whole. Critics also suggested that an agency that combined both functions might be more prone to informal styles of control and clientelism—precisely the problems manifested in the Japanese financial system.

In addition to this theoretical argument was the political one: MOF's extremely broad jurisdiction allowed it great political power, and only by removing one or more functions could its overall power be reduced.[35] In other words, reducing its role in the financial system might have the side benefit of weakening its ability to set budget or tax policy. By the same token, separating the budget function from MOF's other existing functions (another idea much in vogue, for reasons similar to those that led to the establishment of the Office of Management and Budget in the United States) would weaken its ability to have its way in financial policy.[36]

Thus did MOF's organizational integrity come into play in 1996 and 1997. While both approaches to the dismemberment of MOF appear to have had similar doses of logic on their side, in the end the idea of only stripping financial functions won out. It is impossible in this short treatment to provide anything approaching a definitive answer as to why, but we may offer some plausible hypotheses. One is obvious—the financial system prob-

34. Mabuchi 1997 is by far the best source on this, especially chaps. 1, 3, and 4.

35. Some were skeptical about both arguments and argued that there would be very little effect on MOF power or regulatory transparency (*"Shinsetsu kin'yū kantokuchō no towareru dokuritsusei"* 1997).

36. Mabuchi (1997, 25–28) presents a somewhat different justification for such a division, based on Mabuchi 1994.

lems were being managed far less skillfully than the budget-making problems, and many people felt that new ideas and new blood were needed to
carry out new policies credibly. Another is that the Ministry of Finance
fought to maintain its most central function—budgeting—and mobilized all
its OBs and other resources to ensure that the more severe option would
not come about.[37]

For whatever reason, the idea of separating rule making from enforcement won out in 1997. There is some irony in that victory, however, insofar
as the two functions have been reunited—outside MOF—in July 2000, in
the Financial Services Agency (originally comprised of the former Financial
Supervisory Agency and MOF's former financial system planning functions,
and taking on the functions of the former Financial Reconstruction Commission and control over the Deposit Insurance Corporation in January
2001). This seemingly contradictory decision suggests that the political argument was more important than the theoretical one, although it does appear that the new agency will be operating with greater transparency than
MOF ever did.

Another financial regulatory body was formed in October 1998 to address the inability of existing institutions to make decisions regarding financial institution solvency and to dispose of failed institutions' assets in an
orderly and efficient way.[38] This was the Financial Reconstruction Commission, the head of which was given the rank of Cabinet minister. The FRC officially oversaw the FSA and the Deposit Insurance Corporation. Its role was
strengthened by the simultaneous passage of revised bankruptcy laws that
made it much easier for the government to declare a firm bankrupt and
then nationalize it. Again, the establishment and functioning of the FRC
constitute too large a topic to take on here, including as they do a variety of
new laws and an initial allotment of ¥43 trillion for the purposes of dispos-
ing of assets and strengthening banks. However, the establishment of the
FRC, like that of the FSA, points to the failure of the old informal system of
dealing with bank failures, and by extension with the system stewardship of
the Ministry of Finance. Moreover, it constituted the removal of yet another
function from the ministry.

Both the FSA and FRC have been surprisingly effective and autonomous.
This can be seen in the strict accounting rules and enforcement by the FSA,
as well as in the FRC's nationalization of two of Japan's largest banks and the
sale of one of them to foreign interests. So far, then, financial supervision is
definitely not proceeding as usual. In line with the analysis in chapter 1, the
continued autonomy of the agencies and their successor will depend on

37. There is at least anecdotal evidence for this—for example, one MOF OB Diet member
subtly suggested to me in 1997 that MOF needed to be punished but not eliminated (personal interview).
38. Kobayashi 1999.

questions such as personnel and information management.[39] The decision
to establish a new Financial Services Agency combining the functions of the
FRC, FSA, DIC, and MOF Financial System Planning Bureau as of January
2001, along with adoption of an informal principle that all personnel transfers from MOF above the division chief level will be permanent and one-
way,[40] suggest that the new agency will be relatively independent from MOF.

Other Changes, in Brief

Two other government actions promise to reduce the ability of MOF and
other agencies to use administrative guidance and opaque procedures to
keep informal control. The 1993 Administrative Procedures Law (which
went into effect in October 1994) requires that government agencies make
their procedures explicit and provide written explanations and appeal procedures for all rejected applications and administrative punishments, while
the 1999 Information Disclosure Law (effective in 2001) requires that agencies make internal documents available at the request of the public.[41] These
legal changes should have profound effects on the patterns of information
management described in this study.

Subsequent Attempts at Stimulation

As we have seen, the fiscal consolidation law and contractionary fiscal
policies of 1997 were a pyrrhic victory for MOF budget hard-liners. Not only
did the 1997 policy U-turn create recession and financial institution bankruptcies, it also aggravated a political climate that had turned against the
ministry and its conservative budget line. That political climate contributed
to existing efforts to weaken the ministry by stripping it of important regulatory and macroeconomic policy functions while strengthening the Bank
of Japan. But what effect did these structural changes have on policy outputs? While it may still be too early to make a definitive statement, the
macroeconomic policy outputs we have seen since late 1997 do seem to fit
the analysis of this book—in particular, there has been much more flexibility in fiscal policy, and much less in monetary policy.

Fiscal Plans

Since the events described above, there has been a series of aggressive fiscal
stimulus plans and expansionary budgets, turning the fiscal reconsolidation

39. Also, "*Shinsetsu kin'yū ...*" 1997; Mabuchi 1997, 46.
40. Personal interviews.
41. There has been a fair amount of commentary on the Administrative Procedures Law—
see, for example, the roundtable discussion in "*Gyōsei tetsuzuki hō no seitei to kongo no kadai*"
1994. I have come across less commentary on the Information Disclosure Law, but one brief
overview can be found in Efron 1999.

effort on its head. Ironically, the first of these was announced in December 1997—less than a month after the final passage of the Fiscal Structure Reform Law—and passed in February 1998. April 1998 saw not only the amendment of the Fiscal Structure Reform Law, but also a ¥12 trillion fiscal stimulus plan to augment the stingy FY 1998 budget. Beyond whatever new money it added to public spending, the most important effect of the stimulus plan was to front-load public works for the fiscal year. Following a smaller supplemental budget, in November the government announced a ¥17 trillion plan in addition to a ¥6 trillion permanent tax cut. (The plan actually extended into the first half of FY 1999, which of course reduced its immediate stimulatory effect.) The FY 1999 budget, whose ceilings had been announced in summer 1998, was the most expansionary ever, and was supplemented by another ¥17 trillion fiscal stimulus package (¥5.6 trillion from the general account) in November 1999. The FY 2000 budget was similarly expansionary, and a substantial stimulus plan (albeit much smaller than the 1999 plan) was being prepared in autumn 2000.

All of these plans contain considerable padding, and their numerical values cannot be taken at face value. But we can say that their fiscal effect has been dramatic. Actual FY 1998 spending exceeded the initial budget by more than ¥10 trillion (almost 13 percent), and tax revenues were ¥12 trillion below the budgeted amount, leading to an extraordinarily high bond dependency ratio—when the effects of the various stimulus plans in FY 1998 are taken into account, a staggering 38.6 percent for the year (see Tables 3.1, 3.2). The expected value for FY 1999, based on the initial budget, was 37.9 percent; with the fall fiscal stimulus plan and weak second and third quarter growth, it ended up at 43.4 percent. By the year 2000, Japan had the highest current budget deficit of any OECD country and the highest accumulated public debt of any major economy except Italy, which it was set to surpass.[42] Whatever one's position on the appropriateness of fiscal expansion in Japan, for the first time in the crisis of the 1990s there can be no question that it is happening—in large amounts, and without an agreed ending date.

As is often the case, it is difficult to disentangle the exact causes of each of these plans. For one thing, the Japanese economic situation in 1997–99 was more dire than at any previous point. These years included not only Japan's first real recession (negative GDP growth in two consecutive quarters) in years, but also its first full year of contraction since 1974—actually a year and a half of unbroken contraction before positive growth numbers

---

42. On the deficit, see for example "Japan Passes U.S. as Top Issuer of Public Debt," *FT,* March 4, 2000, 6. According to 1999 OECD projections, Japan's debt-to-GDP ratio was expected to hit 114 percent in calendar year 2000, just shy of Italy's 115 percent (MOF, *Japan's Budget in Brief 2000,* section I-2). Subsequent OECD figures project that the ratio will hit an alarming 130 percent by the end of March 2001. "Tokyo Liabilities Far Exceed Government Assets," *FT,* October 5, 2000, 16.

appeared briefly in the first quarter of FY 1999. Given the seriousness of the situation, it is not surprising that leaders chose to make aggressive use of fiscal stimulus. An apparent return to growth in the first two quarters of 2000 set the stage for a smaller fiscal stimulus that autumn, but fiscal policy did not revert to consolidation immediately.

Some may argue for the importance of the replacement of Prime Minister Hashimoto Ryūtarō by Obuchi Keizō following the LDP's resounding loss in the July 1998 Upper House election. Certainly, Obuchi was more willing than Hashimoto to stake his political credibility on fiscal expansion rather than consolidation. But in looking at the main policy actions since 1997, it is not actually that easy to make a convincing argument that Obuchi significantly changed the calculus—the stimulus package of February 1998 occurred on Hashimoto's watch, as did the first major bank recapitalization plan. The second major recapitalization plan and even the glimmerings of the November 1998 fiscal stimulus plan had largely been prepared before Obuchi entered office. Whatever Obuchi's personal impact, however, spending since 1998 has reflected the ascendancy of politicians in making the key fiscal decisions. (Few observers ascribe any policy initiative at all to Obuchi's successor, Mori Yoshirō.)

Despite the contraction of the Japanese economy, there appeared to be real resistance to stimulation among the MOF Budget clique. A number of officials began raising the alarm again about the difficulty of paying back massive public debt in a future characterized by rapid aging of society; on a related front they fought to have health insurance and pension premiums raised. Nonetheless, fiscal stimulus plans and expansionary budgets did come into effect, and they were large. At least publicly, the LDP again took credit for the measures. And for perhaps the first time in a budget debate, the Ministry of Finance appeared to be sitting on the sidelines.

The "Managed Inflation" Debate

An equally striking turnaround in Japanese policy after 1997 was the assertion of autonomy by the Bank of Japan. While it had been recognized for years that deflation in the Japanese economy meant that real interest rates were not particularly low, few observers felt that there was much more that monetary policy could do once the discount rate and other short-term rates dropped to 0.5 percent in 1995. With the continuing recession that began in 1997, deflation worsened, and real interest rates effectively rose. This became particularly evident from September 1998, when the extremely weak yen began to appreciate rapidly. In response, in January 1999 the BOJ acted to lower the overnight interbank call rates all the way down to approximately 0.02 percent (the "zero interest rate policy"), where they remained until August 2000, when they were raised to 0.25 percent.

Despite this apparent responsiveness, consensus grew among many American economists from autumn 1998 that BOJ monetary policy was unnecessarily restrictive. The opening salvo of the attack came from Paul Krugman, who argued that Japan needed some "managed inflation" in order to drag it out of a classic credit crunch caused by high real interest rates.[43] After initial skepticism concerning the desirability and controllability of inflation died off, this became the standard interpretation of Japan's economic mess among many U.S. and some Japanese policy makers.[44]

In spite of the severity of Japan's economic situation, BOJ leaders have strongly resisted the managed inflation prescription. Governor Hayami in particular has been vocal in this regard. The initial reaction was that any inflation is dangerous. When this position became untenable in the face of continued deflation in the Japanese economy (and a rising yen), BOJ officials turned to a different argument—that monetary expansion was in fact impossible under current conditions. This argument has had considerable appeal. In the short-term interbank market, interest rates are so low that there is virtually no difference between loans and cash. Thus, open market operations are ineffective in changing money supply.[45] Also, from around mid-1998, banks' reserve ratios had risen well above the required levels, suggesting that new infusions of cash into the banking system were simply being redeposited for extremely low returns with the Bank of Japan rather than lent.[46]

Advocates of managed inflation have suggested three alternative methods. One has been large-scale unsterilized foreign exchange market intervention by the BOJ.[47] (Setting aside the question of whether unsterilized intervention has any meaning under zero interest rate conditions, advocates of this proposal seem not to realize that it is not the Bank of Japan that has responsibility for intervention, but the Ministry of Finance, using Diet-authorized FEFSA funds. MOF has in fact accumulated huge amounts of foreign currency [see Figure 3.3], but it is not clear if there has been any domestic stimulatory effect.) The second alternative is based on the fact that long-term interest rates were considerably higher than overnight rates, and on a real basis were unattractive to borrowers in an uncertain economic situation. Thus, the BOJ could directly purchase long-term government bonds. This was a highly charged suggestion, however, and would require

43. Krugman 1998.
44. Very few Japanese macroeconomic policy makers I interviewed in August and November 1999 and August 2000 seemed convinced by the managed inflation argument, but an anonymous reviewer points out that the MOF deputy vice-minister for international affairs offered moderate support for the idea.
45. Okina and Shiratsuka 2000; personal interview with BOJ Policy Board member Dr. Ueda Kazuo, November 1999.
46. BOJ downloadable statistics <www.boj.or.jp / en / siryo / stat / tumi9908.htm>.
47. Among others, Ben Bernanke of Princeton University made this point at a talk I gave there on October 6, 1999.

abrogating both the letter and spirit of the BOJ Law (and of an article dating back to the Occupation period). Having the central bank finance government deficits could create both moral hazard regarding government finance and potential solvency problems for the BOJ itself, not to mention a bad precedent for the future. A final suggestion was that the BOJ could attach negative interest rates to excess reserve deposits by banks, but this seemed unlikely at a time when banks were in less than healthy condition and were being urged to be more careful in their lending decisions. Thus, even leaving aside the ambiguous economics of managed inflation, the political trade-offs would have been serious.

Regardless of feasibility, however, the Bank of Japan has effectively resisted the managed inflation prescription. Until a concerted effort by G-7 finance ministers to convince Governor Hayami of the dangers of BOJ policies in September 1999,[48] the BOJ steadfastly refused to step up intervention in a broader range of securities—most notably, longer-term debt instruments and foreign currency–denominated instruments. (Even where MOF had directed intervention in the currency markets, the BOJ was sterilizing it.) It also refused to leave more than ¥1 trillion in excess funds in the overnight market, which seemed odd if leaders really believe that additional liquidity would have no effect.

Stepping even further beyond the managed inflation debate, in April 2000 Governor Hayami made statements that suggested the Bank of Japan was planning to *raise* interest rates in hopes of stamping out inflationary expectations most observers were unable to discern.[49] This was seen by market participants as a continuation of signaling that began earlier in the year of a BOJ desire to end its "zero interest rate" policy. The zero interest rate policy finally came to an end in August 2000. While the negative effects of the policy change were negligible, at least in the short term, the BOJ raised interest rates despite considerable political opposition, including more or less explicit threats by some LDP leaders. Whether or not the decision was correct, the bank's ability to carry it out demonstrated clearly its hard-won autonomy.

There has been considerable speculation that the BOJ leadership was simply trying to assert its independence. Whether or not this is true, it is clear that the BOJ has been far more successful in resisting pressure from all quarters—MOF, politicians, the market, foreign finance ministries—than it had ever been before the structural changes of 1997–98. In a perverse way, it has thus validated the process that led to the revision of the BOJ Law and the establishment of the FSA and FRC: even if the new structure has not ac-

48. See, for example, "Bank of Japan Spat with Ministry of Finance Worsens," *Euromoney*, September 30, 1999.

49. "Yen Climbs Sharply on Bank Rate Hint," *FT*, April 13, 2000, 39. See also the BOJ's optimistic April *Monthly Report of Recent Economic and Financial Developments*, April 12, 2000, which states that "The improvement in Japan's economy is becoming distinct."

tually improved policy outputs, it has certainly *changed* them. The irony is
that if the short-term effects of BOJ attempts to assert autonomy are seen to
increase economic hardship, they may actually undermine its long-term autonomy, just as MOF's fiscal conservatism undermined its own autonomy
earlier in the 1990s.

Bank Recapitalization and Receivership

Important as financial sector woes have been to Japan's macroeconomic
problems in the 1990s, for the purposes of analytical consistency I have
avoided concentrating on those policies that focused on financial sector reform or revitalization. Financial sector policy has for the most part not been
debated as macroeconomic policy. Moreover, the ways in which these
policies are made look much more like standard interest group bargaining,
and it is often difficult to disentangle the preferences of official actors or to
judge whether or by what means a given societal or economic actor "won."

Nevertheless, events in financial sector regulation after 1998 are so striking in their break from previous practice that it is important to deal with
them at least briefly. I refer in particular to the aggressive closing of several
banks and to administrative rulings on disclosure and debt quality. The
large cash infusions by the Japanese government to try to bolster banks' capital bases are not as interesting from my standpoint as one might expect, for
two reasons. First, the actions appeared in the midst of actual crises—the
first attempts occurred in the immediate aftermath of the failures of
Hokkaido Takushoku Bank (the nation's nineteenth largest bank) and Yamaichi Securities (the nation's fourth largest securities firm). Another bankruptcy on the order of Hokkaido Takushoku might have shaken the Japanese financial system to its core. Second, the idea of cash infusion was
clearly favored by MOF, the BOJ, and a number of Diet members, although
different individuals and organizations certainly had their own ideas of what
conditions might be appropriate. In this case, the veto power was essentially
held by public opinion, which had reacted very angrily to the *jūsen* "bailout"
in 1996. The 1997 crisis lifted the public's veto power and allowed officials
to do what most agreed was right, especially since MOF had already been severely weakened by the BOJ Law revision and FSA decision.

What has been most striking in terms of regulation has been the willingness of the new financial regulatory bodies to act directly and publicly
against insolvent banks. This became immediately evident in summer 1998,
when the FSA started doing large-scale investigations of major banks' lending patterns. It became more evident in the fall, when FSA declared Nippon
Credit Bank (NCB) and the Long-Term Credit Bank of Japan (LTCBJ) insolvent. Soon after, FSA issued new accounting guidelines that were much
stricter than previous MOF pronouncements on the subject of bad loans,

and that led to a serious deterioration of many banks' balance sheets. For its part, the FRC under its first chairman, Yanagisawa Hakuo, acted almost immediately after its establishment to nationalize both NCB and LTCBJ, and also issued a series of so-called "Prompt Corrective Action" (PCA) orders to banks whose capital-adequacy ratios had fallen below the legal minimums. In conjunction with the PCA orders, it also ordered virtually all of the nationally active banks (with the exception of the Bank of Tokyo-Mitsubishi) to accept government capital infusions in return for improving lending practices and balance sheets. Most strikingly, in September 1999 it awarded the remains of LTCBJ to a largely foreign group of investors led by the U.S. investment bank Ripplewood Holdings. (Another foreign connection is that the FRC's advisor on both bank disposals was Goldman Sachs.)

The resulting large-scale change in the Japanese financial landscape is fascinating in its own right. In terms of macroeconomic issues, the government has shown a willingness to invest large sums of public money in the financial system in order to improve the efficiency of financial intermediation. Perhaps more importantly, the fact that the FSA and FRC appear to have acted almost completely independently of MOF control suggests an overall weakening of the ministry's grasp over economic issues. Despite the FRC's initial boldness, however, Yanagisawa's successor, Ochi Michio, appeared more susceptible to political—rather than MOF—pressure.[50] While Ochi's successor, Tanigaki Sadazaku, appeared more independent, his successors (the disgraced Kuze Kimitaka followed by Aizawa Hideyuki) created some apprehension among market watchers, who suspected them of preferring a slower pace of financial sector reform. Thus, the danger of clientelism remains, at least until the new Financial Services Agency's operations are more fully institutionalized.

Analysis

The changes in the macroeconomic policy-making structure seen in this chapter are truly historic. It would have been nearly unimaginable in 1985, or even 1995, that the Ministry of Finance could lose its preeminence in monetary policy, let alone be dismembered. Yet both of these events occurred. The Bank of Japan is now largely autonomous, with no legal requirement that it "coordinate" policies with the Ministry of Finance. The Ministry of Finance has become largely a treasury ministry, as confirmed by its name change (at least in Japanese) as of January 2001. And the Diet has not only become the official overseer of the BOJ (whose governor now must make semiannual reports to it) and taken back the initiative in budgeting, but was itself the architect of the dismantling and reconstruction of Japan's macroeconomic policy apparatus.

50. "Japanese Official Ousted over Promises to Banks," *WP*, February 26, 2000, E2.

Despite some of the greatest policy debacles in Japan's postwar history, politicians as a group—though not any specific party—have increased both their legitimacy and their capabilities. One of the most striking conclusions of observers of the process that led to BOJ Law revision and FSA establishment is the extent to which the whole process was initiated, shaped, and concluded by party politicians, with the bureaucracies involved as supplicants rather than as writers.[51] The Diet, on its own, finally acted to restructure a policy-making system that had become dysfunctional. (Whether the new system will necessarily lead to better outcomes is a separate issue, to which I return in chapter 8.) Politicians also led both sides of the 1998 debate on bank recapitalization and FRC establishment, which I do not cover at length in this study.

The story is not a simple one of politicians reasserting their authority over prodigal bureaucrats, however, as principal-agent analysis might suggest. Rather, it occurred within the parameters of a specific, and extraordinary, point in time. Moreover, it depended on a successful campaign to pin the blame for both economic stagnation and financial crisis on the Ministry of Finance, rather than on the politicians who were putatively in charge of the government and had signed off on many of the very policy mistakes for which they would punish the ministry. (Only former Prime Minister Hashimoto seemed unable to avoid political responsibility for the macroeconomic policy mistakes made during his tenure.) As I have demonstrated in this book, that was not an unreasonable charge.

Anger among politicians at the ministry was real, perhaps nowhere more so than in the Liberal Democratic Party upon its return to government in 1994. With full knowledge of the bases of MOF power, it and its junior coalition partners unleashed a wide-ranging attack on the ministry, ranging from rhetoric, to challenges to MOF's personnel autonomy, to threats against its ability to place retiring officials in sinecure positions, and finally to unprecedented legal/structural changes. Realizing that MOF was no longer a reliable partner, large portions of the LDP cooperated with other political reformers not simply to shame the ministry and make it a scapegoat for the purpose of temporary electoral advantage, but to weaken it permanently.

The contractionary fiscal bias of Japan's macroeconomic policy-making structure created the impetus needed for its substantial reorganization in 1997–98. Failed policies and a growing consensus that MOF intransigence (or, perhaps, incompetence) lay at the heart of the problems of the Japanese economy led to considerable political pressure on it for policy change. Rightly or wrongly, LDP politicians who had supported fiscal consolidation largely evaded blame, and MOF found itself partially dismembered as a result. MOF scored its 1997 budget "triumph" in the face of the very political

51. Mabuchi 1997, passim; Mieno 2000, 100; Nakakita 1999, chap. 1.

processes that led to BOJ Law revision and MOF dismemberment, but that was to be its last triumph. As last triumphs go, it was of questionable value.

While there had been noticeable changes in macroeconomic policy even before the structural changes described in this chapter (especially fiscal loosening in 1994–96), policy change after that time was far more substantial. This fact strongly supports my structural approach. While it is difficult to make long-range predictions, especially with more changes taking effect in January 2001, it seems clear that for the first time since a brief interlude in the 1970s fiscal policy has become the near-exclusive province of political actors. And for the first time ever, Japanese monetary policy is in the hands of a meaningfully independent central bank.

8

Conclusions: Fighting the Last War?

Today's and tomorrow's choices are shaped by the past. And the past can only be made intelligible as a story of institutional evolution.

Douglass North, *Institutions, Institutional Change and Economic Performance*

Over the previous seven chapters I have shown that the structure of power and information in Japanese macroeconomic policy making has fundamentally influenced the policies actually followed in the world's second largest economy. The formation, bursting, and after-effects of the bubble that have been the central problems in the Japanese economy since 1985 resulted directly from macroeconomic policy failures. Those policy failures were not the result of incompetence or corruption of bureaucrats or politicians, but were shaped by the political structure in which policy decisions were made.

Because of its institutional strength, the Ministry of Finance was consistently able to adhere to a policy of fiscal consolidation, leaving monetary policy as virtually the only avenue for macroeconomic adjustment, at least until 1993. The ministry's institutional strength was shown to be at least partly conditional even under the old structure during the extended economic slump of the 1990s, as elected politicians of various stripes acted over time to spur fiscal expansiveness. Even then, however, bureaucratic resistance was often more effective than the government and press reports represented them to be. This pattern contributed to both the formation of the bubble in the late 1980s and the inability of the economy to move forward in the aftermath of its bursting. With the structural changes of 1997–98, Japan's policy pattern changed drastically, in the direction of fiscal responsiveness and monetary stubbornness.

The story is one not only of conflict, but also of cooperation and learning. Cooperation existed between organizations as well as within them. Although it often bullied the Bank of Japan, the Ministry of Finance also shielded the bank from political meddling. Meanwhile, in its relations with the ruling party or coalition, the ministry always acted in concert with at least some of the key political actors, even as it used delaying or misinformation tactics generally.

Learning was an important part of the story as well. MOF and BOJ officials attempted to convince each other, politicians, and the media of the
correctness of their own policy preferences. Over time, politicians sometimes learned the opposite lessons, through experience—it took some time
before Cabinets were willing to simply dismiss MOF assessments of the economic environment and the impact of potential policies, but by 1997 they
were. MOF bureaucrats, in turn, learned in 1995 and 1997 that the price of
the resistance on which they had long prided themselves could be close
scrutiny of individual bureaucrats, interference in personnel matters, and
ultimately dismemberment. These attacks on key MOF prerogatives themselves took time to develop, finally arising out of politicians' growing exas-
peration with the ministry's intransigence.

Reality was messy, as it always is. What I offer here is a relatively concise
explanation of the dynamics of that reality, within a framework of institutional competition. This study has clearly demonstrated the usefulness of
that framework in understanding an otherwise dauntingly confusing set of
events and policies in the actual historical record. Thus, I make no apolo-
gies for simplification.

The policy-making structure does not explain everything, of course.
Structure—no matter how important—is in the end only a translator between environment and action. We must always consider the idiosyncrasies
of a given situation before trying to compare it to one or another model. To
expect institutional structure to lead to a uniform policy response in the
face of a variety of different and challenging situations is to ask too much of
the explanation, and too little of the intelligence and abilities of the individuals involved. And while it would be convenient to have a series of totally
comparable situations, the world is not a laboratory, and we must work with
what we have. In this case, what we have is a series of situations with varying
degrees of uniformity across different variables, but with enough similari-
ties that a "structured-focused comparison" makes sense. That comparison
strongly supports the structural argument I offer in this book.

The usefulness of my model is demonstrated by the fact that it helps to
explain macroeconomic policy behavior in so many different circumstances. These include crises with origins that were at various times either
domestic or international, financial or "real." Among the international issues addressed were a yen that was alternately too strong and too weak, bilateral trade imbalances, and fears of insufficient demand at a global level.
The domestic issues ranged from fiscal deficit, to asset price inflation and
deflation, to financial crisis, to recession. My explanation thus provides
broader insights than could be gained by concentrating solely on international explanations for international situations, or on domestic politics for
domestic situations.

Implications for the Study of Japanese Political Economy

In writing this book, I have inevitably entered a series of debates on the nature of the Japanese state, economy, and policy making, which were introduced briefly in chapter 1. I now revisit those debates, to show where this study fits into the field as a whole.

Beyond Agency Slack

Since the publication of Ramseyer and Rosenbluth's *Japan's Political Marketplace* in 1993, principal-agent analyses of Japan's political economy have gained considerable visibility. Works in the principal-agent vein argue that politicians have effective control over the actions of bureaucrats through their constitutional prerogatives, and that they are effectively able to monitor bureaucracies via the complaints of their constituents ("fire-alarm" oversight). These analysts recognize that control is not perfect in any principal-agent situation, but they argue that when an issue is of sufficient interest to a preponderance of ruling party politicians, then the politicians will act to compel the bureaucrats to do their bidding. Thus, bureaucrats will choose to carry out actions that are relatively close to the preferences of their political superiors. The gap between politicians' preferences and bureaucrats' actions is called "agency slack."

True believers might argue that I have described a classic principal-agent situation, and that what I have interpreted as considerable MOF independence was either an illusion (plausible deniability for the ruling party or coalition) or agency slack. The crucial evidence in favor of such a proposition is that in most cases when political intervention was clear and unified, politicians' preferences won out over bureaucratic resistance.

That is a misreading of the evidence. Politicians did not always succeed in getting their way in macroeconomic policy. This is particularly true of the various fiscal stimulus plans, which (with the exceptions of those in 1995 and 1998–99) invariably proved to be of only minor stimulatory effect. Moreover, it is not at all clear that the impacts of the plans were closely monitored—certainly, politicians' public discourse (even that of opposition politicians) refers regularly to the large amounts of stimulus that have been pumped into the economy through those plans. Similarly, in looking at the mismatch between fiscal and monetary policy responses, it is difficult to find cases in which politicians seemed very involved in trying to change the balance, other than then–finance minister Miyazawa's sincere but unsuccessful efforts in 1986. Only when overwhelming political sentiment and economic policy failure led to a change in policy-making structure were political leaders able to retake the reins of fiscal policy.

This is more than just "agency slack," at least as American political scientists have used that term. If the term is to be no more than a receptacle for all observations that do not fit the predictions of principal-agent models, then we are dealing with a tautology—a fundamentally uninteresting exercise. In our case, although over time it is clear that there was significant political involvement in a variety of MOF policies even before 1997, it is equally clear that from 1985 to 1997 leadership was often taken by the Ministry of Finance, with politicians' roles usually at the margins, and only occasionally at the center. Such leadership is not the stuff of an agency discreetly exploiting its "slack" in order to expand its jurisdiction.

Similarly, to argue that MOF leadership on macroeconomic policy was nothing more than a temporary "delegation" that politicians could rescind at will also requires a malleability of belief with which I, at least, feel uncomfortable. At no point in Japan's postwar history have political parties had the capability independently to analyze and predict the impacts of changes in tax or spending policies; only in the last year or two has that begun to change in meaningful ways. Even when they have been deeply involved, such as in tax or welfare policy, they have relied on the central bureaucracies (primarily MOF and the EPA) for analysis of policy effects and the resulting trade-offs. While alternative analyses have become more available and credible, the process has indeed taken time.

Principal-agent analyses in political science often slight the importance of information and the *costs* of obtaining it. Networks that have atrophied or that never existed cannot simply be generated or regenerated overnight, regardless of who ratifies the budget. Until the extent of failure in macroeconomic policy became excruciatingly evident in the latter 1990s, politicians had largely forgone developing the sorts of networks that would allow them not only effective oversight, but also the ability take over the reins of policy drafting. The situation hardly bespeaks conditional delegation.

Bureaucracies Less than Dominant

While I reject the assumptions (sometimes offered as conclusions) of principal-agent analysis in examining macroeconomic policy making since 1985, I do not belong in the "bureaucratic dominance" camp. My analysis makes clear that MOF was not the sort of omnipotent puppet-master of the Japanese political economy that some authors have portrayed it to be.[1]

Even in areas of considerable bureaucratic autonomy, the officials of the Japanese Ministry of Finance always faced constraints—from politicians, from markets, from rival agencies, and from foreign governments (especially the United States). Not only did politicians force a degree of fiscal stimulus on a number of occasions prior to 1997, but MOF's ability to resist those calls generally decreased as the interest and expertise of political and

1. Fingleton 1995a, 1995b; Hartcher 1998.

market opposition gained strength. Démarches by various U.S. administrations in a variety of fora also put pressure on the ministry and appeared in some cases to force at least marginal changes in policy. Domestically, the 1987 agreement on postal savings interest rates required real concessions to MOF's MPT rivals. Even the leadership of the Bank of Japan often had a mind of its own, changing at least the timing and perhaps the magnitude of a number of MOF-preferred policies. And obviously, the BOJ Law revision and partial dismemberment of MOF in 1997–98 showed as never before the long-term limits on the ministry's power in a democratic system.

Nonetheless, bureaucracies are political actors in their own right, not just more or less obedient servants of elected politicians. The bases of bureaucratic power can be found in personnel patterns and information management as well as in legal jurisdiction. My description of the three major institutional actors deductively analyzed their capabilities in the macroeconomic policy-making game. Those capabilities were clearly evident in the extent to which actors shaped policy. The only really successful challenges to MOF dominance in macroeconomic policy making involved concerted attacks on the very sources of MOF power on which I base my analysis, including threats to bureaucratic personnel management and *amakudari,* accusations against and arrests of officials, and the removal of important areas of legal jurisdiction.

Thus, while bureaucracies compete with politicians as political actors, their advantage is not foreordained. Rather, the abilities they do have are based on real, *institutional* factors that define the constraints of both bureaucracies and political parties. Inevitably, that means considerable variance in the power balance among competing actors, depending on the issue area. While MOF's power was considerable in terms of macroeconomic policy over most of the period studied, in a distributive issue area such as construction we can clearly find the principal-agent dynamic at work. This observation conforms with Lowi's typology of state-society relations, and suggests further the comparative utility of this type of analysis.[2]

Foreign Economic Policy

Although this study has ranged widely over both international and domestic issues, it has concentrated for the most part on domestic factors for explaining important policy decisions. Essentially, I have treated international influences as external shocks to which Japan was forced to respond. In so doing, I have placed myself in the middle of the debate on the nature of the Japanese state in the international sphere—that is, is Japan a strategic or a "reactive" state?[3]

2. Lowi 1985. See Woodall (1996) on the construction industry. See Rosenbluth (1989) and Vogel (1996) for different views on the configuration of power in financial liberalization.
3. Views of Japan as a strategic state focus on its international economic policies, and include Johnson (1982) and Prestowitz (1988). The logic of the "reactive state" is most explicitly spelled out by Calder (1988b), Schoppa (1993, 1997), and Hosoya (1977).

Actually, despite the labels, both views are essentially reactive—the question is *how* the state reacts. The strategic view claims that Japan has rationally adapted its policies in order to work efficiently within the international economy. Similarly, in cases of international shocks, the state has generally acted forcefully to push Japan's long-term interests. The "reactive state" view sees the Japanese state as essentially immobilist and fragmented, with a tendency toward ad hoc responses to crises. International shocks thus force the stalemated actors to come to a new policy equilibrium.

My account of international macroeconomic and exchange rate policy coordination clearly falls into the "reactive state" camp. Despite a good deal of in-depth thinking within MOF as to the proper role of the yen in international finance,[4] Japan's path through the Plaza-Louvre period could hardly be described as strategic. Rather, when national interest seemed to clash with organizational objectives, actors did their best to redefine the national interest—to the detriment of the Japanese economy, as it turned out. In later episodes, including the SII negotiations in 1989–90, pressure from the United States in 1993 and 1995 to reflate, and G-7 calls for monetary loosening in September 1999, international economic matters were acted on only when the issue was forced by a pugnacious U.S. government or a rapidly appreciating yen. And again, the responses themselves were fundamentally conditioned by the policy-making structure.

One interesting aspect of the reactive state that was particularly apparent in the Plaza-Louvre period is the advantage that specific actors gained through acting as gatekeepers to the outside world. In macroeconomic and exchange rate coordination, both the Ministry of Finance and the Bank of Japan had highly developed and institutionalized ties to foreign actors that LDP and other politicians simply did not have. This disadvantaged the politicians in understanding exactly what responses would be acceptable to Japan's G-7 partners and left them dependent on their putative agents in the ministry and the bank. Recently, politicians' access to independent information and analysis appears to be broadening considerably, thanks in part to the Internet. The U.S. government has also been making efforts to provide its own analysis directly to politicians, bypassing Japan's bureaucratic gatekeepers.

Institutionalism

From a broader perspective, this study fits most comfortably with works that emphasize the role of institutions in shaping policy.[5] States and economies

---

4. See, for example, Gyohten 1986.
5. In Japanese politics, these include Calder 1993; Kato 1994; and Vogel 1996; among others. A number of theoretical and comparative works outside of Japanese politics are equally relevant (e.g., North 1990; Harsanyi 1986; Pfeffer and Salancik 1978; Keohane and Milner, eds. 1996; Zysman 1983; Mayer, ed. 1990; and many others).

are fantastically complex systems, and policy making for them requires consistent information and analysis that draws on past experience and the accumulation of knowledge—in other words, organizations. And yet an organization's behavior is dependent on the individuals that make it up and the patterns of their internal and external interactions. Crozier calls this "dependence on the indispensable human means."[6]

I have argued that in order to understand policy outcomes, we must understand organizations' behavior, and that in order to understand organizations' behavior, we must understand the ways in which specific organizations reward or punish different types of individual behavior. In that sense, I have followed a rational choice perspective, even as I have rejected principal-agent analysis. The core of this perspective is that rational actors, facing a strategic environment, will do their best to advance their own interests, given their constraints and the expected actions of competitors.

Where institutions as such are important is in the realization that information and personnel management are key factors in determining the shape of a game that is played within an environment of incomplete and asymmetrical information. How organizations gain access to information, and their perceptions of the accuracy of their information and analysis, fundamentally influence their capabilities beyond whatever jurisdictions or responsibilities they are granted by law. My work provides a means of judging the capabilities and constraints of various institutional actors in a given policy area. I look at the variables of legal jurisdiction, personnel patterns, and information management and offer criteria for understanding how each shapes the interaction with other actors. Thus, my analysis avoids the kind of tautological arguments that gauge strength from outcomes while using strength to explain outcomes. These are important points in furthering studies of institutional conflict not only in Japanese politics, but comparatively as well.

Structural Change

A related theme, which has tended not to be emphasized in the Japanese political economy literature, concerns change in policy-making structure. With the exception of a few works on the introduction of whole new categories of public programs, most writers in Japanese politics have described even important power shifts as occurring within the bounds of a structure that has changed in only evolutionary fashion.[7] This tendency is understandable, since in large measure the shape of Japan's policy-making structure has been

6. Crozier 1964, 6.
7. Two exceptions I have in mind are Calder (1988) and Campbell (1992), both of whom address the introduction of major new social welfare programs. However, even they do not focus on changes in the kind of structure I have emphasized. Pempel's (1998) discussion of "regime shifts" addresses a different level of structure.

remarkably stable in the postwar period, despite periodic efforts toward administrative reform. Only with the recent changes concerning MOF and the BOJ have scholars really begun to take these questions seriously.[8]

In regard to the Ministry of Finance and Bank of Japan, several earlier attempts to strip functions or fundamentally change institutional autonomy were unsuccessful. Now we can begin to consider the questions of both *how* structural changes come about and *what effects* they have on policy. In this case, the answer to the "how" question clearly involves the loss of public trust in MOF's competence and integrity in the face of massive economic policy failure. However, change also required both ideas about how to organize macroeconomic and financial policy making to make it more efficient, and deep analysis of the bases of MOF power. If public outrage created the force for change, such ideas and analysis were what gave direction to that force. The causes and patterns of the specific changes in the structure of macroeconomic politics, as well structural change in general, will be important areas of research in coming years.

In addressing structural change, it is also important to specify what "structure" is. Legal change alone does not necessarily equate to structural change, no matter how clear the law may be. Political and bureaucratic forces have often vitiated reorganizations in Japan in the past, through such mechanisms as bureaucratic imperialism and administrative guidance. The 1997–98 reforms specifically excluded such mechanisms, and thus gave added significance to legal reforms, even as the legal reforms buttressed what might otherwise have been short-term political equilibria. Action based on this sort of clear analysis of informal as well as formal structure is essential to making institutional reform meaningful in any context.

Structural Fatigue

Politicians also acted on an understanding that existing institutions were not meeting the needs of the Japanese economy. This fits into the broader "structural fatigue" argument—that the developmentally oriented institutions of Japan's postwar catch-up phase have been unable to adapt to the country's changed circumstances. (Indeed, the April 1998 stimulus plan preamble refers specifically to structural fatigue.)[9] As Japan's economy developed, industrial policy and regulatory bureaucracies lost the ability to look to more advanced economies for direction and also lost any knowledge advantage they had had over leading firms. Meanwhile, the increasing overabundance of capital and foreign exchange took away the bureaucracies'

---

8. Mabuchi 1997 and Nakakita 1999, for example.
9. The phrase is *"Nihonteki na keizai shisutemu no seido hirō."* From *"Sōgō keizai taisaku"* (Comprehensive Economic Measures), April 24, 1998, <www.epa.go.jp/98/b/19980424taisaku .htm>.

most effective market-oriented "sticks," but left in place developmental "carrots" such as weak antitrust rules on cartels and direct subsidies, which became more and more the target of spirited political competition among inefficient sectors.[10]

While overregulation and political compensation have undoubtedly hurt the Japanese economy over the last couple of decades and have probably made recovery from the bursting of the bubble much harder, they did not actually cause or puncture the bubble. But structural fatigue of another sort can be clearly seen in Japan's macroeconomic politics. It is hardly surprising that a 1942 central bank law intended to provide financing for a government at war was not up to the domestic and international challenges of the 1980s and 1990s. Also, the entrenched organizational supremacy of MOF's Budget Bureau gave the ministry as a whole an excessive focus on fiscal stability as the sole component of macroeconomic stability. Over much of Japan's postwar history, this system worked. But from 1985 to 1997, the combination of MOF's exclusively fiscal conservatism and its effective control over monetary policy proved disastrous.

Established patterns of MOF intransigence and use of power politics gave both logical and political force to the argument that meaningful policy change required new structures. It is somewhat ironic, but by no means unintended by political leaders, that one of the greatest changes in policy outcome has been decreased MOF control over fiscal policy—the one major function it did not actually lose.

Broader Implications

While I have not made universalist claims, I believe that my framework of analysis could profitably be extended to other areas of policy making and to other states. Indeed, Kato's account of Japanese domestic tax reform is built on a very similar framework.[11] One important modification for most issue areas would be the inclusion of the organized interest groups that tend to form around most policy making—macroeconomic policy making in Japan is admittedly unusual in the degree to which we can legitimately concentrate on official actors to the near exclusion of interest groups. Nonetheless, the same basic organizational factors I have used in analyzing the capabilities of official actors should also be useful for understanding those of interest groups.

My analytical framework is useful for understanding states' responses to both domestic and international concerns.[12] In order to test its usefulness

10. Katz 1998; Carlile and Tilton, eds. 1998.
11. Kato 1994.
12. Henning (1994) follows a similar approach in his study of U.S., German, and Japanese international economic policy. That analysis is particularly focused on relations between the

in international analysis, one could look at a number of cases where domestic policy-making structures collide with international pressure. There are many instances both in Japan and elsewhere in which a sector with well-established interest structures has suddenly had to confront the outside world. In Japan, these include both sectors that have been the target of strategic planning, such as semiconductors and automobiles, and less studied sectors such as pharmaceuticals, forest products, and legal services.

Central Bank Independence

The story of Japanese macroeconomic politics also holds meaning for the broader debate on central bank independence. As noted in chapter 1, Japan has long been considered an anomaly in that literature, due to its combination of very high price stability and very low central bank independence. A variety of explanations have been offered, including an anti-inflationary bias within the Ministry of Finance, the steepness of Japan's Phillips curve, and the configuration of socioeconomic and political interests.[13] I will not dispute any of these characterizations, all of which are plausible.

What I would like to highlight is that the growth and bursting of Japan's bubble suggest new rationales for central bank independence. It is impossible to fault Japan's performance on traditional price indexes even during the height of the bubble. The bubble was an extraordinary time, however, a time when an independent BOJ would have acted much more preemptively than the actual BOJ did. And an independent BOJ might well have been both more cautious in its monetary tightening in 1989–90 and less stingy in its loosening in 1990–91, confident that future stabilization decisions would not be subject to political veto. Greater independence for Japan's central bank would have been justified not because of the need to hold down inflation, but because of the need to respond objectively to emerging crises. This may add extra force to the existing arguments in favor of central bank independence.

Speculation

Political events tend to fall into two categories: those that are very easy to predict with considerable certainty (e.g., if polling hours are extended then voter turnout should rise, all things being equal) and those that are very dif-

---

central banks and the financial sector in each economy, as well as between the central bank and the central government. Thus, it includes an institutional analysis of the strengths and preferences of a key interest group in each country.
13. McKinnon and Ohno (1997), in contrast, argue that Japan's inflation rates have been *too* low, as a result of U.S. pressures.

ficult to predict with any certainty at all (e.g., the demise of the Soviet Union). Sensible political scientists avoid both types of prediction, since one is likely either to sound trite or to be embarrassingly wrong. Nonetheless, I have put forward a model of political behavior, and I feel I have a responsibility at least to discuss the implications of recent developments on future Japanese macroeconomic policy making.

There are at least two developments that have potentially profound implications for that structure. The first is the electoral reform of 1993–94. While it will probably take several elections to move toward a stable equilibrium, and there still appears to be no consensus at all on how the reform will reconfigure the Japanese political system, politicians and parties should have to compete more and more on the basis of competing policies. As I have argued, in single-member districts, candidates will have to appeal to a majority of constituents rather than cultivate a hard-core minority; in proportional districts, voters have no choice but to vote for parties, who must in turn define themselves. Even if a genuine alternation of power never comes about, this increased focus on policy should over time lead to increased involvement. Thus, we should expect more vigorous activity on the part of politicians when their preferences collide with those of bureaucracies in general.

In the case of macroeconomic policy, politicians (and political parties) should continue to eat into the informational advantages held by MOF and the BOJ, bringing about policies that are more attuned to the desires of the public. I would expect this to mean as a general rule more expansive policies, although there may be one major party or coalition that reflects more conservative, business-oriented preferences. At the least, however, fiscal policy should be much more sensitive to real crises than it was over most of the period in this study.

A second major development has been the continuing move toward financial deregulation and administrative reform. Both amount to attacks on the factors that support the autonomy to which Japanese bureaucracies had become accustomed. With regard to macroeconomic policy making, the revision of the Bank of Japan Law and the establishment of the Financial Supervisory Agency (and its successor, the Financial Services Agency) have real implications for the power balance among the three official actors in macroeconomic policy. Much of MOF's power was based on the breadth of its jurisdiction, its monopoly on financial information, the ability to grant and deny permission for even rather picayune matters, and the political benefit it gained from maintaining politically favored but economically nonviable financial institutions. All of these were harmed or eliminated by the reforms of the late 1990s, even as BOJ autonomy was legally affirmed for the first time. Since 1997, the Ministry of Finance has been much less able to resist political pressures for fiscal stimulation or to shift the focus to monetary policy. The results are recent expansiveness of fiscal policy, and the willingness of top BOJ officials to speak openly about interest rate hikes even in the midst of recession. The structural reforms that occurred suggest that these new patterns are not just some passing fad.

Turning to economic conditions, macroeconomic politics since 1985 have left at least three serious legacies for Japan—widespread weakness among financial institutions, stagnation at the macroeconomic level, and worrisomely high fiscal deficits and debts. While the first of these is gradually but effectively being handled through recapitalization and regulatory change, the latter two are more problematic from a macroeconomic perspective. The deficit and debt problem will only be aggravated by the aging of Japan's population, an issue I have not touched on in this book. That is a long-term problem, although the "long term" is getting closer with every year that growth does not get back on track.

Unfortunately, for the moment, getting growth back on track seems to depend at least partly on continuing the current path of deficit spending. (Of course, overall economic structural adjustment and reform are equally important for long-term growth, as the "structural fatigue" authors argue.) In that sense, the dismemberment of the Ministry of Finance makes it easier to address Japan's most urgent economic needs. But the trade-off between short-term growth and long-term fiscal crisis is growing more and more ambiguous, and it is by no means clear that a political structure that makes fiscal expansion easier and takes monetary policy off the table will be beneficial for Japan in the long term.

In the absence of a powerful and fiscally conservative Ministry of Finance, at some point in the near future Japan will need a political consensus in favor of fiscal austerity. In Japan as in any country, such a consensus is hard to come by. Although some politicians have begun to stake their claim on fiscal consolidation again as others did in the early 1980s, the record of the 1997 fiscal reform effort will likely haunt Japanese politics for a number of years to come. Unfortunately, although we can safely say that the structural changes in the macroeconomic policy-making game will give rise to different policy patterns, it is not clear at this point whether they will make for "better" policies.

References

Note on Statistical Sources: Some basic fiscal and financial statistics are surprisingly hard to obtain in Japan, and in some cases different ministries actually provide different numbers. In the case of FILP statistics, which are all issued by the Ministry of Finance, there are at least two different data series (three, if one includes the series on financing sources), which news reports sometimes use interchangeably. To complicate matters, a number of MOF data series are not actually published as series, so one must occasionally go through decades' worth of annual reports. In some cases, I have been able to find such series in ministry press releases or in internal (but unclassified) guides, which are often provided to researchers by MOF officials.

A welcome development has been the widespread publication of official data on the Internet. The Bank of Japan is particularly helpful in this regard, but more recently the Economic Planning Agency, the Ministry of Finance, and other agencies have also made their statistics accessible via the Internet. In this book, I have made particular efforts to ensure consistency in data series, although in some cases I have had to use multiple sources. I am grateful to Seki Obata for his help in that regard. All data sources are cited either in footnotes or as addenda to figures and tables.

Adachi, Tetsuo. 1997. *Nonbanku: Sono jitsuzō to yakuwari* (Non-Banks: Realities and Roles). Tokyo: Tōyō Keizai Shimbunsha.

Allison, Graham. 1971. *Essence of Decision: Explaining the Cuban Missile Crisis*. Boston: Little, Brown.

Aoki, Masahiko. 1988. *Information, Incentives, and Bargaining in the Japanese Economy*. Cambridge: Cambridge University Press.

Armacost, Michael. 1996. *Friends or Rivals? The Insider's Account of U.S.–Japan Relations*. New York: Columbia University Press.

Asahi Shimbun Economic Bureau. 1997. *Ōkura shihai: Yuganda kenryoku* (MOF Dominance: Distorted Power). Tokyo: Asahi Shimbunsha.

Baerwald, Hans. 1986. *Party Politics in Japan*. Boston: Allen & Unwin.

Bendor, Jonathan, and Thomas Hammond. 1992. "Rethinking Allison's Models." *American Journal of Political Science* 86, no. 2: 301–22.

Bendor, Jonathan, and Terry Moe. 1985. "An Adaptive Model of Bureaucratic Politics." *American Political Science Review* 79, no. 3: 755–774.

Bergsten, C. Fred, and Marcus Noland. 1993. *Reconcilable Differences? United States–Japan Economic Conflict*. Washington, D.C.: Institute for International Economics.

Blinder, Alan. 1998. *Central Banking in Theory and Practice*. Cambridge, Mass.: MIT Press.

——. 1999. "Central Bank Credibility: Why Do We Care? How Do We Build It?" *NBER Working Paper*, no. 7161.

Calder, Kent. 1988a. *Crisis and Compensation: Public Policy and Political Stability in Japan, 1946–1986*. Princeton, N.J.: Princeton University Press

——. 1988b. "Japanese Foreign Economic Policy Formation: Explaining the Reactive State." *World Politics* 40, no. 4: 517–541.

——. 1989. "Elites in an Equalizing Role: Ex-Bureaucrats as Coordinators and Intermediaries in the Japanese Government-Business Relationship." *Comparative Politics* 21, no. 4: 379–403.

——. 1990a. "Linking Welfare and the Developmental State: Postal Savings in Japan." *Journal of Japanese Studies* 16, no. 1: 31–59.

——. 1990b. "Public Corporations and Privatization in Modern Japan." In *Political Economy of Public Sector Reform and Privatization*, ed. Ezra Suleiman and John Waterbury, 163–183. Boulder, Colo.: Westview Press.

——. 1993. *Strategic Capitalism: Private Business and Public Purpose in Japanese Industrial Finance*. Princeton, N.J.: Princeton University Press.

Calvert, Randall, Mark Moran, and Barry Weingast. 1987. "Congressional Influence over Policy Making: The Case of the FTC." In *Congress: Structure and Politics*, ed. Mathew McCubbins and Terry Sullivan, 493–522. Cambridge: Cambridge University Press.

Campbell, John. 1977. *Contemporary Japanese Budget Politics*. Berkeley: University of California Press.

——. 1992. *How Policies Change: The Japanese Government and the Aging Society*. Princeton, N.J.: Princeton University Press.

Cargill, Thomas. 1986. "Japanese Monetary Policy, Flow of Funds, and Domestic Liberalization." *Federal Reserve Bank of San Francisco Economic Review*, summer.

——. 1989. "Central Bank Independence and Regulatory Responsibilities: The Bank of Japan and the Federal Reserve." New York: Salomon Brothers Center for the Study of Financial Institutions, *Monograph Series in Finance and Economics*, no. 1989-2.

———. 1992. "The Bank of Japan and Federal Reserve: An Essay on Central Bank Independence." Presentation at the Bank of Japan (mimeo).

Cargill, Thomas, and Michael Hutchison. 1990. "Monetary Policy and Political Economy: The Federal Reserve and the Bank of Japan." In *The Political Economy of American Monetary Policy*, ed. Thomas Mayer, 165–180. Cambridge: Cambridge University Press.

Cargill, Thomas, Michael Hutchison, and Takatoshi Ito. 1997. *The Political Economy of Japanese Monetary Policy*. Cambridge, Mass.: MIT Press.

Cargill, Thomas, and Shoichi Royama. 1988. *The Transition of Finance in Japan and the United States: A Comparative Perspective*. Stanford, Calif.: Hoover Institution Press.

Carlile, Lonny, and Mark Tilton, eds. 1998. *Is Japan Really Changing Its Ways? Regulatory Reform and the Japanese Economy*. Washington, D.C.: Brookings Institution.

Cohen, Raymond. 1991. *Negotiating across Cultures: Communication Obstacles in International Diplomacy*. Washington, D.C.: United States Institute of Peace.

Cowhey, Peter, and Mathew McCubbins, eds. 1995. *Structure and Policy in Japan and the United States*. New York: Cambridge University Press.

Crozier, Michel. 1964. *The Bureaucratic Phenomenon*. Chicago: University of Chicago Press.

Cukierman, Alex. 1992. *Central Banking Strategy, Credibility and Independence: Theory and Evidence*. Cambridge, Mass.: MIT Press.

Cukierman, Alex, Steven Webb, and Bilin Neyapti. 1993. "Measuring Central Bank Independence and Its Effect on Policy Outcomes." San Francisco: International Center for Economic Growth, *Occasional Papers*, no. 58.

Curtis, Gerald. 1988. *The Japanese Way of Politics*. New York: Columbia University Press.

———. 1999. *The Logic of Japanese Politics: Leaders, Institutions, and the Limits of Change*. New York: Columbia University Press.

Destler, I. M., and C. Randall Henning. 1989. *Dollar Politics: Exchange Rate Policymaking in the United States*. Washington, D.C.: Institute for International Economics.

Dobson, Wendy. 1991. *Economic Policy Coordination: Requiem or Prologue?* Washington, D.C.: Institute for International Economics.

Dominguez, Kathryn. 1989. "Market Responses to Coordinated Central Bank Intervention." *Carnegie-Rochester Conference Papers*, April.

———. 1999. "The Market Microstructure of Central Bank Intervention." *NBER Working Paper*, no. 7337.

Dominguez, Kathryn, and Jeffrey Frankel. 1993. "Does Foreign Exchange Intervention Matter? The Portfolio Effect." *American Economic Review* 83, no. 5: 1356–69.

Drazen, Allan. 2000. *Political Economy in Macroeconomics*. Princeton, N.J.: Princeton University Press.

Eckstein, Harry. 1975. "Case Study and Theory in Political Science." In *Handbook of Political Science, Vol. 7: Strategies of Inquiry*, ed. Fred Greenstein and Nelson Polsby, 79–137. Reading, Mass.: Addison-Wesley.

Economic Planning Agency. 1997. *Sengo Nihon keizai no kiseki: Keizai kikakuchō 50 nenshi* (The Path of the Postwar Japanese Economy: EPA 50-Year History). Tokyo: Ministry of Finance Printing Bureau.

Efron, Sonni. 1999. "Right-to-Know Law Changing Shape of Japan." *Los Angeles Times,* May 11, A1.

Eichengreen, Barry. 1992. "'It' Can Happen Again." *Challenge,* November/December.

Eijffinger, Sylvester, and Jakob de Haan. 1996. "The Political Economy of Central Bank Independence." Princeton University International Finance Section, *Special Papers in International Economics,* no. 19.

Eijffinger, S., and A. van Rixtel. 1992. "The Japanese Financial System and Monetary Policy: A Descriptive Review." *Japan and the World Economy* 4, no. 4: 291–309.

Elster, Jon, ed. 1986. *Rational Choice.* New York: New York University Press.

Evans, Peter, Dietrich Rueschemeyer, and Theda Skocpol. 1985. "On the Road toward a More Adequate Understanding of the State." In *Bringing the State Back In,* ed. Peter Evans, Dietrich Rueschemeyer, and Theda Skocpol, 347–366. Cambridge: Cambridge University Press.

Farley, Maggie. 1996. "Japan's Press and the Politics of Scandal." In *Media and Politics in Japan,* ed. Susan Pharr and Ellis Krauss, 133–163. Honolulu: University of Hawaii Press.

Feldman, Robert. 1992. *Japanese Economic/Market Analysis: Macroeconomic Forecast.* Tokyo: Salomon Brothers, December 28.

——. 1993. *Japanese Economic/Market Analysis: Macroeconomic Forecast.* Tokyo: Salomon Brothers, May 6.

FILP Report. Annual. Tokyo: Ministry of Finance.

Fingelton, Eamonn. 1995a. "Japan's Invisible Leviathan." *Foreign Affairs* 74, no. 2 (March/April): 69–85.

——. 1995b. *Blindside: Why Japan Is Still on Track to Overtake the U.S. by the Year 2000.* Boston: Houghton Mifflin.

Foreign Exchange Council. 1999. *Internationalization of the Yen for the 21st Century: Japan's Response to Changes in Global Economic and Financial Environments.* MOF mimeo, April 20.

Frankel, Jeffrey A. 1984. *The Yen/Dollar Agreement: Liberalizing Japanese Capital Markets.* Washington, D.C.: Institute for International Economics.

Frankel, Jeffrey, and Katherine Rockett. 1986. "International Monetary Coordination when Policy-Makers Disagree on the Model." *NBER Working Paper,* no. 2059.

Fujiwara, Sakuya. 1991. *Sugao no Nichigin sōsaitachi* (BOJ Governors Revealed). Tokyo: Nihon Keizai Shimbunsha.

Funabashi, Yoichi. 1989. *Managing the Dollar: From the Plaza to the Louvre.* Washington, D.C.: Institute for International Economics.

George, Alexander. 1979. "Case Studies and Theory Development: The Method of Structured, Focused Comparison." In *Diplomacy: New Approaches in History, Theory, and Policy,* ed. Paul Lauren, 43–68. New York: Free Press.

Ghosh, Atish. 1990. "Is It Signalling? Exchange Market Intervention and the Dollar-DM Rate." *Ohlin Discussion Paper* 48.

——. 1992. "Central Bank Secrecy in the Foreign Exchange Market." Princeton University International Finance Section, *Working Papers in International Economics* G-92-02.

Gilpin, Robert. 1987. *The Political Economy of International Relations.* Princeton, N.J.: Princeton University Press.

Goodman, John. 1991. "The Politics of Central Bank Independence." *Comparative Politics* 23, no. 3: 329–349.

——. 1992. *Monetary Sovereignty: The Politics of Central Banking in Western Europe.* Ithaca, N.Y.: Cornell University Press.

Gourevitch, Peter. 1978. "The Second Image Reversed: The International Sources of Domestic Politics." *International Organization* 32, no. 4: 881–912.

Green, Donald, and Ian Shapiro. 1994. *Pathologies of Rational Choice: A Critique of Applications in Political Science.* New Haven, Conn.: Yale University Press.

Grimes, William. 1995. "From the Plaza to the Bubble: Japan's Response to International Macroeconomic Policy Coordination, 1985–88." Ph.D. dissertation, Princeton University.

Gyohten, Toyoo. 1986. "En no kokusaika—Sono Nichibei kankei ni ataeru eikyō" (The Internationalization of the Yen—Its Effects on Japan-U.S. Relations). *Finansharu Rebyū* 2, 1–5.

"Gyōsei tetsuzuki hō no seitei to kongo no kadai" (Enactment of the Administrative Procedures Law and Future Issues). 1994. *Jūrisuto* 1039, 8–29.

Haley, John. 1991. *Authority without Power: Law and the Japanese Paradox.* New York: Oxford University Press.

Hall, Peter. 1986. *Governing the Economy: The Politics of State Intervention in Britain and France.* Cambridge: Polity Press.

Halperin, Morton. 1974. *Bureaucratic Politics and Foreign Policy.* Washington, D.C.: Brookings Institution.

Hanson, Richard. 1996. *Ōkura erīto: Hokori to gukō* (MOF Elite: Pride and Folly). Tokyo: TBS Britannica.

Harsanyi, John. 1986. "Advances in Understanding Rational Behavior." In *Rational Choice,* ed. Jon Elster, 82–107. New York: New York University Press.

Hartcher, Peter. 1998. *The Ministry: How Japan's Most Powerful Institution Endangers World Markets.* Boston: Harvard Business School Press.

Henning, C. Randall. 1987. *Macroeconomic Diplomacy in the 1980s.* London: Croom Helm.

——. 1994. *Currencies and Politics in the United States, Germany, and Japan.* Washington, D.C.: Institute for International Economics.

Hetzel, Robert. 1990. "The Political Economy of Monetary Policy." In *The Political Economy of American Monetary Policy,* ed. Thomas Mayer, 99–114. Cambridge: Cambridge University Press.

Horiuchi, Akiyoshi. 1998. *Kin'yū shisutemu no mirai: Furyō saiken mondai to biggu ban* (The Future of the Financial System: Bad Loan Problems and the Big Bang). Tokyo: Iwanami Shinsho.

——. 1999. *Nihon keizai to kin'yū kiki* (The Japanese Economy and Financial Crisis). Tokyo: Iwanami Shoten.

Horne, James. 1985. *Japan's Financial Markets: Conflict and Consensus in Policymaking.* London: Allen & Unwin.

——. 1988. "Politics and the Japanese Financial System." In *Dynamic and Immobilist Politics in Japan,* ed. J.A.A. Stockwin, 171–204. Honolulu: University of Hawaii Press.

Horvat, Andrew. 1998. "MOF Fries in 'No Pan Shabu Shabu.'" *Euromoney,* March.

Hoshi, Takeo. 1995. "Evolution of the Main Bank System in Japan." In *The Structure of the Japanese Economy,* ed. Mitsuaki Okabe, 287–322. New York: St. Martin's Press.

Hosoya, Chihiro. 1977. "Taigai seisaku kettei katei ni okeru Nihon no tokushitsu" (Characteristics of Japan's Foreign Policy Making Process). In *Taigai seisaku kettei katei no Nichibei hikaku* (A Comparison of Japanese and U.S. Foreign Policy Making Processes), ed. Hosoya Chihiro and Watanuki Joji, 1–20. Tokyo: Tokyo University Press.

Hutchison, Michael. 1986. "Japan's 'Money Focused' Monetary Policy." *Federal Reserve Bank of San Francisco Economic Review,* summer.

IFMP. Annual. *Financial Statistics of Japan.* Tokyo: Ministry of Finance, Institute of Fiscal and Monetary Policy.

Iida, Keisuke. 1990. "The Theory and Practice of International Economic Policy Coordination." Ph.D. dissertation, Harvard University.

Iida, Tatsuo. 1987. "Nihon keizai to Amerika keizai: 'Naiju kakudai' to 'rēganomikkusu'" (Japan's Economy and the U.S. Economy: "Demand Expansion" and "Reaganomics"). *Finansharu Rebyū* 6, 1–10.

Ikenberry, G. John, David Lake, and Michael Mastanduno. 1988. "Introduction: Approaches to Explaining American Foreign Economic Policy." *International Organization* 42, no. 1 (Special Issue: The State and American Foreign Policy Making): 1–14.

Ikenberry, G. John, David Lake, and Michael Mastanduno, eds. 1988. *International Organization* 42, no. 1 (Special Issue: The State and American Foreign Policy Making).

Ikuta, Tadahide. 1996. *Dokyumento kanryō no shinsō* (Inner World of Bureaucrats). Tokyo: Dayamondosha.

IMF. Annual. *International Financial Statistics Yearbook.* Washington, D.C.: International Monetary Fund.

Imidas. Annual. *Jōhō chishiki Imidas* (Imidas Yearbook). Tokyo: Shueisha.

Inoguchi, Takashi. 1983. *Gendai Nihon seiji keizai no kōzu* (The Structure of Modern Japanese Political Economy). Tokyo: Tōyō Keizai Shimbunsha.

Inoguchi, Takashi, and Iwai Tomoaki. 1987. *"Zoku giin" no kenkyū: Jimintō seiken gyūji shuyaku toshite* (Research on "Zoku" Politicians: The Lead Actors Dominating LDP Government). Tokyo: Nihon Keizai Shimbunsha.

Ishii, Naoko. 1990. *Seisaku kyōchō no keizaigaku* (The Economics of Policy Coordination). Tokyo: Nihon Keizai Shimbunsha.

Ishii, Naoko, Warwick McKibbin, and Jeffrey Sachs. 1985. "The Economic Policy Mix, Policy Cooperation and Protectionism: Some Aspects of Macroeconomic Interdependence among the United States, Japan and Other OECD Countries." *Journal of Policy Modelling* 7: 533–572.

Ishiwatari, Ei. 1989. *Ōkurashō no ura no ura ga wakaru hon* (Understanding MOF's Inside Story). Tokyo: Piipurusha.

Ishizawa, Yasuharu. 1995. *Za MOF: Ōkurashō kenryoku to demokurashī* (The MOF: Ministry of Finance Power and Democracy). Tokyo: Chūō Kōronsha.

Ito, Takatoshi. 1992. *The Japanese Economy.* Cambridge, Mass.: MIT Press.

Japanese Budget in Brief. Annual. Tokyo: Ministry of Finance.

Johnson, Chalmers. 1982. *MITI and the Japanese Miracle.* Stanford, Calif.: Stanford University Press.

———. 1989. "MITI, MPT, and the Telecom Wars: How Japan Makes Policy for High Technology." In *Politics and Productivity,* ed. Chalmers Johnson, Laura Tyson, and John Zysman, 177–240. Cambridge: Ballinger.

Johnson, Chalmers, and E. B. Keehn. 1994. "A Disaster in the Making: Rational Choice and Asian Studies." *National Interest* 36: 14–22.

Kane, Edward. 1990. "Bureaucratic Self-Interest as an Obstacle to Monetary Reform." In *The Political Economy of American Monetary Policy,* ed. Thomas Mayer, 283–298. Cambridge: Cambridge University Press.

Kanryō kyokuhi jinjiroku (Bureaucrats' Top-Secret Personnel Records). 1996. Tokyo: Takarashimasha.

Kaplan, David, and Andrew Marshall. 1996. *The Cult at the End of the World.* New York: Crown Publishers, Inc.

Kapstein, Ethan. 1991. "Supervising International Banks: Origins and Implications of the Basle Accord." *Princeton University Essays in International Finance,* no. 185.

Kato, Junko. 1994. *The Problem of Bureaucratic Rationality: Tax Politics in Japan.* Princeton, N.J.: Princeton University Press.

Katō, Kan. 1997. *Kanryō shudō kokka no shippai* (The Failures of the Bureaucratic Dominant State). Tokyo: Tōyō Keizai.

Katz, Richard. 1998. *Japan: The System that Soured.* Armonk, N.Y.: M. E. Sharpe.

Katzenstein, Peter. 1978a. "Conclusion: Domestic Structures and Strategies of Foreign Economic Policy." In *Between Power and Plenty: Foreign Economic Policies of Advanced Industrial States,* ed. Peter Katzenstein, 295–336. Ithaca, N.Y.: Cornell University Press.

———. 1978b. "Introduction: Domestic and International Forces and Strategies of Foreign Economic Policy." In *Between Power and Plenty: Foreign Economic Policies of Advanced Industrial States,* ed. Peter Katzenstein, 3–22. Ithaca, N.Y.: Cornell University Press.

Katzenstein, Peter, ed. 1978. *Between Power and Plenty: Foreign Economic Policies of Advanced Industrial States*. Ithaca, N.Y.: Cornell University Press.

Kawakita, Takao. 1989. *Ōkurashō: Kanryō kikō no chōten* (The Ministry of Finance: Apex of the Bureaucratic Structure). Tokyo: Kōdansha Gendai Shinsho.

Kawasaki, Tsuyoshi. 1993a. "Managing Macroeconomic Adjustments: Japanese Fiscal Policy in the Era of Global Capitalism." Ph.D. dissertation, Princeton University.

——. 1993b. "Pressing Japan for Fiscal Expansion: Lessons from the Late 1970s." *Pacific Review* 6, no. 4: 365–374.

Keohane, Robert. 1984. *After Hegemony: Cooperation and Discord in the World Economy*. Princeton, N.J.: Princeton University Press.

Keohane, Robert, and Helen Milner, eds. 1996. *Internationalization and Domestic Politics*. Cambridge: Cambridge University Press.

Kernell, Samuel. 1991. "The Primacy of Politics in Economic Policy." In *Parallel Politics: Economic Policymaking in Japan and the United States*, ed. Samuel Kernell, 325–378. Washington, D.C.: Brookings Institution.

Kernell, Samuel, ed. 1991. *Parallel Politics: Economic Policymaking in Japan and the United States*. Washington, D.C.: Brookings Institution

Kiewiet, D. Roderick, and Mathew McCubbins. 1991. *The Logic of Delegation: Congressional Parties and the Appropriations Process*. Chicago: University of Chicago Press.

King, Gary, Robert Keohane, and Sidney Verba. 1994. *Designing Social Inquiry: Scientific Inference in Qualitative Research*. Princeton, N.J.: Princeton University Press.

Kin'yū Tōkei Geppō. Monthly. Tokyo: Bank of Japan.

Kin'yū Tōkei Nenpō. Annual. Tokyo: Bank of Japan.

Kirshner, Jonathan. 1995. *Currency and Coercion: The Political Economy of International Monetary Power*. Princeton, N.J.: Princeton University Press.

Kishi, Nobuhito. 1996. *Ōkurashō no hōkai: Kenryoku no kyotō o osotta zettai zetsumei no kiki* (The Collapse of the Ministry of Finance: The Overwhelming Crisis that Assaulted the Tower of Power). Tokyo: Tōyō Keizai Shinpōsha.

Kobayashi, Yumi. 1999. "Kin'yū kinō saisei kinkyū sochi hō oyobi kin'yū kinō sōki kenzenka kinkyū sochi hō no gaiyō" (Summary of the Urgent Measures Law for the Revitalization of Financial Functions and of the Urgent Measures Law for the Rapid Recovery of Financial Functions). *Jūrisuto* 1151: 37–46.

Koh, B. C. 1989. *Japan's Administrative Elite*. Berkeley: University of California Press.

Kohno, Masaru. 1992. "Rational Foundations for the Organization of the Liberal Democratic Party in Japan." *World Politics* 44, no. 3: 369–397.

——. 1997. *Japan's Postwar Party Politics*. Princeton, N.J.: Princeton University Press.

Kojo, Yoshiko. 1993. "Domestic Sources of International Payments Adjustment: Japan's Policy Choices in the Postwar Period." Ph.D. dissertation, Princeton University.

Komiya, Ryutaro, and Miyako Suda. 1991. *Japan's Foreign Exchange Policy 1971–82*. Sydney: Allen & Unwin.

Kōsai, Yutaka. 1987. "Naigai fukintō to naiju kakudai" (External Imbalances and Domestic Demand Expansion). *Finansharu Rebyū* 5: 1–7.

Krasner, Stephen. 1978. *Defending the National Interest: Raw Materials Investments and U.S. Foreign Policy.* Princeton, N.J.: Princeton University Press.

———. 1983a. "Structural Causes and Regime Consequences: Regimes as Intervening Variables." In *International Regimes,* ed. Stephen Krasner, 1–22. Ithaca, N.Y.: Cornell University Press.

———. 1983b. "Regimes and the Limits of Realism: Regimes as Autonomous Variables." In *International Regimes,* ed. Stephen Krasner, 355–368. Ithaca, N.Y.: Cornell University Press.

Krasner, Stephen, ed. 1983. *International Regimes.* Ithaca, N.Y.: Cornell University Press.

Krauss, Ellis. 1984. "Conflict in the Diet: Toward Conflict Management in Parliamentary Politics." In *Conflict in Japan,* ed. Ellis Krauss, Thomas Rohlen, and Patricia Steinhoff, 243–293. Honolulu: University of Hawaii.

———. 1989. "Politics and the Policymaking Process." In *Democracy in Japan,* ed. Takeshi Ishida and Ellis Krauss, 39–64. Pittsburgh, Pa.: University of Pittsburgh Press.

———. 1993. "U.S.–Japan Negotiations in Construction and Semiconductors, 1985–1988." In *Double-Edged Diplomacy: International Bargaining and Domestic Politics,* ed. Peter Evans, Harold Jacobson, and Robert Putnam, 265–299. Berkeley: University of California Press.

Krehbiel, Keith. 1991. *Information and Legislative Organization.* Ann Arbor: University of Michigan Press.

Krugman, Paul. 1985. "Is the Strong Dollar Sustainable?" In *The U.S. Dollar: Prospects and Policy Options.* Kansas City: Federal Reserve Bank of Kansas City.

Krugman, Paul. 1998. "Japan's Trap." First published on Internet in May 1998, <web.mit.edu/krugman/www.japtrap.html>. Accessed October 22, 1999.

Kuroda, Haruhiko. 1987. "Keizai seisaku kyōchō no kanō ni tsuite" (Regarding the Prospects for Economic Policy Coordination). *Finansharu Rebyū,* March, 40–50.

Laurence, Henry. 1999. "The Big Bang and the Sokaiya." *JPRI Critique* 6, no. 8 (August).

Lijphart, Arend. 1975. "The Comparable-Cases Strategy in Comparative Research." *Comparative Political Studies* 8, no. 2 (July): 158–177.

Lincoln, Edward. 1988. *Japan: Facing Economic Maturity.* Washington, D.C.: Brookings Institution.

Lowi, Theodore. 1985. "The State in Politics: The Relation between Policy and Administration." In *Regulatory Policy and the Social Sciences,* ed. Roger G. Noll, 67–96. Berkeley: University of California Press.

Mabuchi, Masaru. 1994. *Ōkurashō tōsei no seiji keizaigaku* (The Political Economy of Ministry of Finance Control). Tokyo: Chūō Kōronsha.

———. 1997. *Ōkurashō wa naze oitsumerareta no ka?* (Why Is the Ministry of Finance on the Run?). Tokyo: Chūō Kōronsha.

March, James. 1986. "Bounded Rationality, Ambiguity, and the Engineering of Choice." In *Rational Choice,* ed. Jon Elster, 142–170. New York: New York University Press.

March, James, and Johan Olsen. 1984. "The New Institutionalism: Organizational Factors in Political Life." *American Political Science Review* 78, no. 3: 734–749.

Marris, Stephen. 1985. *Deficits and the Dollar: The World Economy at Risk.* Washington, D.C.: Institute for International Economics.

Mayer, Thomas, ed.. 1990. *The Political Economy of American Monetary Policy.* Cambridge: Cambridge University Press.

McCubbins, Mathew, and Gregory Noble. 1995. "The Appearance of Power: Legislators, Bureaucrats, and the Budget Process in the United States and Japan." In *Structure and Policy in Japan and the United States,* ed. Peter Cowhey and Mathew McCubbins, 56–80. Cambridge: Cambridge University Press.

McCubbins, Mathew, and Thomas Schwartz. 1987. "Congressional Oversight Overlooked: Police Patrols versus Fire Alarms." In *Congress: Structure and Politics,* ed. Mathew McCubbins and Terry Sullivan, 426–440. Cambridge: Cambridge University Press.

McKibbin, Warwick, and Jeffrey Sachs. 1991. *Global Linkages: Macroeconomic Interdependence and Cooperation in the World Economy.* Washington, D.C.: The Brookings Institution.

McKinnon, Ronald, and Kenichi Ohno. 1997. *Dollar and Yen: Resolving Economic Conflict between the United States and Japan.* Cambridge: MIT Press.

Mieno, Yasushi. 2000. *Ri o mite, gi o omou* (Pursuing Gain, Remembering Duty). Tokyo: Chūō Kōronsha.

Milhaupt, Curtis, and Geoffrey Miller. 1998. "Nihon no kin'yū ni okeru jūsen mondai (2): Hōteki bunseki to keizaiteki bunseki" (The Jūsen Problem in Japanese Finance, Part 2: Legal and Economic Analysis). *Jūrisuto,* June 1, 86–92.

Miyawaki, Atsushi. 1993. "The Fiscal Investment and Loan System towards the 21st Century." *Japan Research Quarterly* 2, no. 2: 15–66.

Mizuno, Masayoshi. 1997. *Nichigin: Himerareta "hanran"* (BOJ: Hidden Revolt). Tokyo: Jiji Tsūshinsha.

Moe, Terry. 1984. "The New Economics of Organization." *American Journal of Political Science* 28, no. 4: 739–77.

Muramatsu, Michio, and Ellis Krauss. 1984. "Bureaucrats and Politicians in Policymaking: The Case of Japan." *American Political Science Review* 78, no. 1: 126–147.

——. 1987. "The Conservative Party Line and the Development of Patterned Pluralism." In *The Political Economy of Japan, vol. 1: The Domestic Transformation,* ed. Kozo Yamamura and Yasukichi Yasuba, 516–554. Stanford, Calif.: Stanford University Press.

Muramatsu, Michio, and Masaru Mabuchi. 1991. "Introducing a New Tax in Japan." In *Parallel Politics: Economic Policymaking in Japan and the United States,* ed. Samuel Kernell, 184–207. Washington, D.C.: Brookings Institution.

Murphy, R. Taggart. 1996. *The Weight of the Yen: How Denial Imperils America's Future and Ruins an Alliance.* New York : W. W. Norton.

Mutō, Eiji, and Shirakawa Kataaki, eds. 1993. *Zusetsu: Nihon ginkō* (Introduction to the Bank of Japan). Tokyo: Zaikeishōhōsha.

Nakakita, Tōru. 1999. *Nihon ginkō: Shijōka jidai no sentaku* (Bank of Japan: Choices in the Era of Marketization). Tokyo: PHP Shinsho.

Nakano, Koichi. 1998a. "Becoming a 'Policy' Ministry: The Organization and *Amakudari* of the Ministry of Posts and Telecommunications." *Journal of Japanese Studies* 24, no. 1: 95–117.

——. 1998b. "The Politics of Administrative Reform in Japan, 1993–1998: Toward a More Accountable Government?" *Asian Survey* 38, no. 3: 291–309.

Nakao, Masaaki, and Horii Akinari. 1990. "The Process of Decision-Making and Implementation of Monetary Policy in Japan." Paper presented at the Central Bank Economists' Meeting, Basle, November.

NHK. 1996. *Sono toki Nihon wa, Dai-rokken: Puraza gōi—endaka e no ketsudan* (Japan at that Time, Episode 6: The Plaza Agreement—The Decision that Led to the High Yen). Tokyo: NHK.

Nihon Keizai Shimbunsha. 1989. *Nihon ginkō no kenkyū* (Bank of Japan Studies). Tokyo: Nihon Keizai Shimbunsha.

——. 1992. *Ōkurashō no yūutsu* (MOF's Melancholy). Tokyo: Nihon Keizai Shimbunsha.

——. 1994. *Kanryō: Kishimu kyodai kenryoku* (Bureaucrats: Creaking, Massive Power). Tokyo: Nihon Keizai Shimbunsha.

Nihon Tōkei Geppō (Japan Statistical Monthly). Monthly. Tokyo: Management and Coordination Agency.

Nihon Tōkei Nenpō (Japan Statistical Yearbook). Annual. Tokyo: Management and Coordination Agency.

Niskanen, William A. 1971. *Bureaucracy and Representative Government*. New York: Aldine-Atherton.

Noguchi, Hitoshi. 1995. *Nichibei tsūka kōshō 2000 nichi: Ōkura zaimukan tachi no tatakai* (2000 Days of U.S.–Japan Monetary Negotiations: The Struggle of the Vice-Ministers of Finance). Tokyo: Nihon Keizai Shimbunsha.

——. 1996. "Saitō Jirō wa Nichigin sōsai ni nareruka?" (Can Saitō Jirō Become BOJ Governor?). In *Kanryō kyokuhi jinjiroku* (Bureaucrats' Top-Secret Personnel Records), 6–17. Tokyo: Takarashimasha.

Noguchi, Yukio. 1991. "Budget Policymaking in Japan." In *Parallel Politics: Economic Policymaking in Japan and the United States,* ed. Samuel Kernell, 119–143. Washington, D.C.: Brookings Institution.

——. 1992. *Baburu no keizaigaku* (The Economics of the Bubble). Tokyo: Nihon Keizai Shimbunsha.

——. 1993. "The Development and the Present State of Public Finance." In *Japan's Public Sector,* ed. Tokue Shibata, 35–48. Tokyo: University of Tokyo Press.

North, Douglass. 1990. *Institutions, Institutional Change and Economic Performance.* Cambridge: Cambridge University Press.

Norville, Elizabeth. 1998. "The 'Illiberal' Roots of Japanese Financial Regulatory Reform." In *Is Japan Really Changing Its Ways? Regulatory Reform and the Japanese Economy,* ed. Lonny Carlile and Mark Tilton, 111–141. Washington, D.C.: Brookings Institution.

Ogata, Shijūrō. 1996. *En to Nichigin: Sentoraru bankā no kaisō* (Yen and BOJ: Memoirs of a Central Banker). Tokyo: Chūō Kōronsha.

Ohkawa, Masazo, and Kōtarō Ikeda. 1993. "Government Bonds." In *Japan's Public Sector: How the Government Is Financed,* ed. Tokue Shibata, 131–140. Tokyo: University of Tokyo Press.

Ohta, Takeshi. 1991. *Kokusai kin'yū: Genba kara no shōgen* (International Finance: Testimony from the Scene). Tokyo: Chūō Kōronsha.

Oka, Masao. 1996. *En ga kijiku tsūka ni naru hi* (When the Yen Becomes a Key Currency). Tokyo: Kadokawa Shobō.

Okimoto, Daniel. 1989. *Between MITI and the Market: Japanese Industrial Policy for High Technology.* Stanford, Calif.: Stanford University Press.

Okina, Kunio, and Shigenori Shiratsuka. 2000. "The Illusion of Unsterilized Intervention." Translated from *Shūkan Tōyō Keizai,* January 15, from the BOJ webpage <www.imes.boj.or.jp/Japanese/kouen/kiooo1en.html>.

Okue, Kunji. 1996. "Fiscal Reform or Crisis: Reform of the Fiscal Investment and Loan Programme." Tokyo: Kleinwort-Benson Research, December 16.

Ōkurashō Meikan (Ministry of Finance Directory). Annual. Tokyo: Jihyōsha.

Organization for Economic Cooperation and Development. Annual. *Economic Surveys.*

Oshio, Takashi, and Kishimoto Tatsushi. 1996. *Nichigin wōtchingu* (BOJ Watching). Tokyo: Nihon Keizai Shimbunsha.

Ōtake, Hideo. 1996. *Gendai Nihon no seiji kenryoku keizai kenryoku* (Contemporary Japanese Political Power, Economic Power, expanded edition). Tokyo: San-Ichi Shobō.

Ozawa, Ichiro. 1994. *Blueprint for a New Japan.* New York: Kodansha.

Park, Yung H. 1986. *Bureaucrats and Ministers in Contemporary Japanese Government.* Berkeley: Institute of East Asian Studies.

Pempel, T. J. 1978. "Japanese Foreign Economic Policy: The Domestic Bases for International Behavior." In *Between Power and Plenty: Foreign Economic Policies of Advanced Industrial States,* ed. Peter Katzenstein, 139–190. Ithaca, N.Y.: Cornell University Press.

——. 1984. "Organizing for Efficiency: The Higher Civil Service in Japan." In *Bureaucrats and Policymaking,* ed. Ezra Suleiman, 72–105. New York: Holmes & Meier.

——. 1987. "The Unbundling of 'Japan, Inc.': The Changing Dynamics of Japanese Policy Formation." In *The Trade Crisis: How Will Japan Respond?* ed. Kenneth Pyle, 117–152. Seattle, Wash.: Society for Japanese Studies.

——. 1998. *Regime Shift: Comparative Dynamics of the Japanese Political Economy.* Ithaca, N.Y.: Cornell University Press.

Pempel, T. J., ed. 1990. *Uncommon Democracies: The One-Party Dominant Regimes.* Ithaca, N.Y.: Cornell University Press.

Pfeffer, Jeffrey, and Gerald Salancik. 1978. *The External Control of Organizations: A Resource Dependence Perspective.* New York: Harper and Row.

Pierce, James. 1990. "The Federal Reserve as a Political Power." In *The Political Economy of American Monetary Policy,* ed. Thomas Mayer, 151–164. Cambridge: Cambridge University Press.

Poole, William. 1992. "Exchange-Rate Management and Monetary-Policy Mismanagement: A Study of Germany, Japan, United Kingdom, and United States after Plaza." *Carnegie-Rochester Conference Series on Public Policy,* no. 30, 57–92.

Posen, Adam. 1998. *Restoring Japan's Economic Growth.* Washington, D.C.: Institute for International Economics.

Prestowitz, Clyde. 1988. *Trading Places: How We Allowed Japan to Take the Lead.* New York: Basic Books.

Putnam, Robert. 1988. "Diplomacy and Domestic Politics: The Logic of Two-Level Games." *International Organization* 42, no. 3: 427–460.

Putnam, Robert, and Nicholas Bayne. 1987. *Hanging Together: Cooperation and Conflict in the Seven-Power Summits,* revised edition. Cambridge: Harvard University Press.

Ramseyer, J. Mark, and Minoru Nakazato. 1999. *Japanese Law: An Economic Approach.* Chicago: University of Chicago Press.

Ramseyer, J. Mark, and Frances McCall Rosenbluth. 1993. *Japan's Political Marketplace.* Cambridge: Harvard University Press.

Report of the Advisory Group on Economic Structural Adjustment (Maekawa Report). 1986. Tokyo.

Rosenbluth, Frances McCall. 1989. *Financial Politics in Contemporary Japan.* Ithaca, N.Y.: Cornell University Press.

Saitō, Tetsurō, et al. 1992. *Zusetsu: Zaiseitōyūshi* (Introduction to the Fiscal Investment and Loan Program). Tokyo: Tōyō Keizai Shimpōsha.

Sakakibara, Eisuke. 1991. "The Japanese Politico-Economic System and the Public Sector." In *Parallel Politics: Economic Policymaking in Japan and the United States,* ed. Samuel Kernell, 50–79. Washington, D.C.: Brookings Institution.

Sakatō, Kyōichi. 1996. "Kasumigaseki ni mikudarihan?! Senkyō ni deta kanryō tachi" (Divorce Papers for Kasumigaseki?! Bureaucrats Who Stood for Election). In *Kanryō kyokuhi jinjiroku* (Bureaucrats' Top-Secret Personnel Records), 122–132. Tokyo: Takarashimasha.

Sasaki, Takeshi. 1994. "Agenda for the Post-LDP Era." *Japan Review of International Affairs,* fall, 281–296.

Sasaki-Smith, Mineko. 1999. *Japan's Financial Crisis: The Malaise of Incrementalism.* Harvard University Program on U.S.–Japan Relations *Occasional Paper,* no. 99–12.

Satō, Seizaburō, and Matsuzaki Tetsuhisa. 1986. *Jimintō seiken* (LDP Rule). Tokyo: Chūō Kōronsha.

Schaede, Ulrike. 1995. "The 'Old Boy' Network and Government-Business Relationships in Japan." *Journal of Japanese Studies* 21, no. 2.

Schlesinger, Jacob. 1997. *Shadow Shoguns: The Rise and Fall of Japan's Postwar Political Machine.* New York: Simon & Schuster.

Schoppa, Leonard. 1993. "Gaiatsu and Economic Bargaining Outcomes." *International Organization* 47, no. 3: 353–386.

——. 1997. *Bargaining with Japan: What American Pressure Can and Cannot Do.* New York: Columbia University Press.

Schwartz, Frank. 1997. *Advice and Consent: The Politics of Consultation in Japan*. New York: Cambridge University Press.

Seikai Jinjiroku (Government Personnel). Annual. Tokyo: Tōyō Keizai Shinpōsha.

Seikan Yōran (Legislative and Bureaucratic Manual). Annual. Tokyo: Seisaku Jihōsha.

Shale, Tony. 1990. "The Plot that Triggered Tokyo's Plunge." *Euromoney*, May.

Shibata, Tokue, ed. 1993. *Japan's Public Sector: How the Government Is Financed*. Tokyo: University of Tokyo Press.

Shimada, Haruo. 1991. "Structural Policies in Japan." In *Parallel Politics: Economic Policymaking in Japan and the United States*, ed. Samuel Kernell, 281–321. Washington, D.C.: Brookings Institution.

Shimoda, Hirotsugu. 1989. *Rikurūto: Shin shūdanshugi no kenkyū* (Recruit: A Study of the New Pluralism). Tokyo: Mainichi Shimbunsha.

Shindō, Muneyuki. 1992. *Gyōsei shidō: Kanchō to gyōkai no aida* (Administrative Guidance: Between Agencies and Industries). Tokyo: Iwanami Shinsho.

———. 1997. *Shin no gyōsei kaikaku to wa nani ka* (What Is True Administrative Reform?). Tokyo: Iwanami Pamphlet, no. 422.

Shingikai Sōran (Overview of Advisory Councils). Annual. Tokyo: Management and Coordination Agency.

"Shinsetsu kin'yū kantokuchō no towareru dokuritsusei" (The New Financial Supervisory Agency's Dubious Autonomy). 1997. *Kankai*, June, 212–219.

Shiota, Ushio. 1995. *Ōkura jimujikan no tatakai: Saitō jidai—meisō no 701 nichi* (The Struggle of the Administrative Vice-Minister of Finance: The Saitō Era—701 Days of Confusion). Tokyo: Tōyō Keizai Shimbunsha.

Skocpol, Theda. 1985. "Bringing the State Back In: Strategies of Analysis in Current Research." In *Bringing the State Back In*, ed. Peter Evans, Dietrich Rueschemeyer, and Theda Skocpol, 3–37. Cambridge: Cambridge University Press.

Skocpol, Theda, and Margaret Somers. 1980. "The Uses of Comparative History in Macrosocial Inquiry." *Comparative Studies in Society and History* 22, no. 27: 174–197.

Sumita, Satoshi. 1992. *Wasuregataki hibi: Nana jū go nen* (Unforgettable Days: Seventy-Five Years). Tokyo: Kin'yū Keizai Jijō Kenkyūkai.

Suzuki, Masatoshi. 1992. *Dare ga "Nichigin" o koroshitaka? Kin'yū no seitaigaku* (Who Killed the "BOJ?" The Ecology of Finance). Tokyo: Kōdansha.

Suzuki, Takaaki. 2000. *Japan's Budget Politics: Balancing Domestic and International Interests*. Boulder, Colo.: Lynne Reinner Publishers.

Suzuki, Yoshio. 1990. *Nihon keizai: Hi wa mada takai* (Japan's Economy: The Sun Is Still High). Tokyo: Tōyō Keizai Shimpōsha.

———. 1993. *Nihon no kin'yū seisaku* (Japan's Monetary Policy). Tokyo: Iwanami Shoten.

Tachi, Ryuichiro, et al. 1993. *Shisan kakaku hendō no mekanizumu to sono keizai kōka* (The Asset Price Fluctuation Mechanism and Its Economic Impacts), April. Tokyo: Ministry of Finance.

Tahara, Sōichirō. 1990. *Heisei Nihon no kanryō* (The Bureaucrats of Heisei Japan). Tokyo: Bungei Shunjū.

Takahashi, Fumitoshi. 1999. "Manipulations behind the Consumption Tax Increase: The Ministry of Finance Prolongs Japan's Recession." *Journal of Japanese Studies* 25, no. 1: 91–106.

Takano, Yoshiro. 1992. *Nippon Telegraph and Telephone Privatization Study: Experience of Japan and Lessons for Developing Countries.* Washington, D.C.: World Bank.

Takenaka, Heizo, 1991. *Contemporary Japanese Economy and Economic Policy.* Ann Arbor: University of Michigan Press.

Takenaka, Heizō, et al. 1986. "Nichibei seisaku kyōchō to kan-Taiheiyō keizai: Sakkusu-kei sekai moderu ni yoru shimyurēshon bunseki (Japan-U.S. Policy Coordination and the Economy of the Pacific Basin: A Simulation Analysis Based on a Sachs-Type World Model). *Finansharu Rebyū* 3:70–93.

Takeshita, Noboru. 1991. *Shōgen: Hoshu seiken* (Testimony: Conservative Governance). Tokyo: Yomiuri Shimbunsha.

Tamura, Yoshio. 1997. *Zusetsu: Nihon no zaisei.* (Introduction to Japan's Public Finance). Tokyo: Tōyō Keizai Shimpōsha.

Tango, Yasutake. 1986. "Shōwa roku-jū-ni-nendo hosei yosan no gaiyō" (An Overview of the FY 1986 Supplemental Budget). *Fainansu* 22, no. 9: 22–29.

Taniguchi, Tomohiko. 1993. *Japan's Banks and the "Bubble Economy" of the Late 1980s.* Princeton University Program on U.S.-Japan Relations *Monograph Series,* no. 4.

Tomita, Toshiki. 1993. "Zaisei tai minkan shūshi to Nihon keizai" (Fiscal Absorption and the Japanese Economy). *Finansharu Rebyū* 28 (June): 127–141.

Tsutsumi, Kazuma. 1997. *Amakudari hakusho* (White Paper on Amakudari). Iwanami Booklet, no. 425. Tokyo: Iwanami Shoten.

van Rixtel, Adrian. 1994. "Informal Aspects of Japanese Economic Policy." *Research Memorandum,* no. 1994–15, Free University of Amsterdam.

Vogel, Steven, 1996. *Freer Markets, More Rules: Regulatory Reform in Advanced Industrial Countries.* Ithaca, N.Y.: Cornell University Press.

Volcker, Paul, and Toyoo Gyohten. 1992. *Changing Fortunes: The World's Money and the Threat to American Leadership.* New York: Times Books.

Wada, Junichiro. 1996. *The Japanese Election System: Three Analytical Perspectives.* New York: Routledge.

Watanabe, Tsutomu. 1992. "Gaitame kainyū no shigunaru kōka: Nihon ni kan suru jisshō bunseki" (The Signaling Effect of Foreign Exchange Intervention: Empirical Analysis of Japan). *Kin'yū Kenkyū* 11, no. 4: 27–49.

Wilson, James Q. 1989. *Bureaucracy: What Government Agencies Do and Why They Do It.* New York: Basic Books.

Woodall, Brian. 1996. *Japan under Construction: Corruption, Politics, and Public Works.* Berkeley: University of California Press.

Woolley, John T. 1984. *Monetary Politics: The Federal Reserve and the Politics of Monetary Policy.* Cambridge: Cambridge University Press.

Working Group on Exchange Market Intervention. 1983. *Report of the Working Group on Exchange Market Intervention* (The Jurgensen Report). Washington, D.C.: International Monetary Fund.

Yakushiji, Taizō. 1987. *Seijika vs. kanryō: Sapuraisaido seijigaku no teishō* (Politicians vs. Bureaucrats: In Support of Supply-Side Political Science). Tokyo: Tōyō Keizai Shimpōsha.

Yamaguchi, Jirō. 1987. *Ōkura kanryō shihai no shūen* (The End of the Dominance of Finance Ministry Bureaucrats). Tokyo: Iwanami Shoten.

Yayama, Tarō. 1994. "New Coalition's Lack of Stability Reported, Prospects for Coalition Viewed: Future of 'Illegitimate' Coalition Government." *Seiron*, September, 122–131 [FBIS translation].

Yonehara, Junshichiro. 1993. "Financial Relations between National and Local Governments." In *Japan's Public Sector*, ed. Tokue Shibata, 167–178. Tokyo: University of Tokyo Press.

Yoshitomi, Masaru. 1986. "Growth Gaps, Exchange Rates and Asymmetry: Is It Possible to Unwind Current-Account Imbalances without Fiscal Expansion in Japan?" In *Japan and the United States Today: Exchange Rates, Macroeconomic Policies, and Financial Market Innovations*, ed. Hugh T. Patrick and Ryuichiro Tachi. New York: Center on Japanese Economy and Business.

Zysman, John. 1983. *Governments, Markets, and Growth: Financial Systems and the Politics of Industrial Change*. Ithaca, N.Y.: Cornell University Press.

Index